ARTIFICIAL NEURAL NETWORKS

FOR

(All Indian Universities, Engineering and Technical Colleges and Institutions)

Rachhpal Singh
Head,
PG Deptt of Computer Sc. & Applications,
Khalsa College,
Amritsar.

Ikvinderpal Singh
Lecturer,
PG Deptt of Computer Sc. & Applications,
Khalsa. College,
Amritsar.

ARTIFICIAL NEURAL NETWORKS

RACHHPAL SINGH AND IKVINDERPAL SINGH

Published by ***KHANNA BOOK PUBLISHING CO. (P) LTD.***
Regd. Office : 1694-95 Nai Sarak, Delhi - 110 006
Ph : 011-23256658, 23283211, Fax : 011-23256658
Email contact@khannaedu.com
Website : www.khannaedu.com

ISBN : 978-93-80016-20-7

Laser Typesetted by :
Stride Computers (Delhi)

Printed in India
M.K. Press

Preface

This book is intended for beginners, intermediate level, and all those who want to learn or expand their knowledge in Neural Networks. Since this is a book on the design of neural networks, our choice of topics was guided by two principles. First, we wanted to present the most useful and practical neural network architectures, learning rules and training techniques. Second, we wanted the book to be complete in itself and to flow easily from one chapter to the next.

Indeed, we are strongly believe that Neural Networks are field of both intellectual interest and practical value to all such students and young professionals Artificial neural networks not only provide an understanding into an important computational architecture and methodology, but they also provide an understanding of the mechanism of the biological neural network.

This book presents a wide variety of standard neural networks, with diagrams of the architecture, detailed statements of the training algorithm, and several examples of the application for each net. Derivations, theorems and proofs are included when they serve to illustrate the important features of a particular neural network.

Every effort has been made to present material in a clear and consistent manner so that it can be read and applied with ease.

Best of luck!

RACHHPAL SINGH
rachhpal_kca@yahoo.co.in

IKVINDERPAL SINGH
ips_sikand@yahoo.com

DEDICATION

No project could ever get in progress much less accomplished, without help from a lot of fantastic people. We would like to express gratitude to our reverential parents. We are grateful to Almighty God who has given us strength to take and complete this project.

To my mother Smt. Surinder Kaur and father S. Diwan Singh, biggest embrace and warm thanks to my wife Dr. Satwinderjeet Kaur, Reader, Deptt. of Botanical & Environmental Sciences, GNDU, Amritsar and to my buddies.

RACHHPAL SINGH

To my mother Smt. Sharanjeet Kaur and father S. Jasjit Singh, biggest embrace and warm thanks to my grandmother Narinderjeet Kaur, to my sisters and to my dear students who have encorged me to complete this project.

IKVINDERPAL SINGH

Acknowledgements

We express our deep gratitude to Dr. Karanjit Singh Kahlon, Professor and Head, Department of Computer Science & Engineering, G.N.D.U., Dr. Hardeep Singh, Professor, Department of Computer Science & Engineering, G.N.D.U., Dr. Gurvinder Singh, Reader, DCSE, GNDU, Amritsar, Prof. Amardeep Gupta, Head, Computer Sc, DAV College, Amritsar, Prof. Nishey Behal, Head, DAV College for Boys, Jalandhar city , Mr. Navjeet Singh, Mr. Jagbir Singh, Mr. Avtar Singh Riar, Mr. Lovedeep Singh, Mr. Sukhwant Singh and our colleagues for their valuable co-operation and guidance. We are grateful to the entire team of *Khanna Book Publishing Co. (P) Ltd.* for their encouragement and motivation during this project.

RACHHPAL SINGH **IKVINDERPAL SINGH**

Special Thanks

Our special thanks go to Dr. Daljit Singh, Principal, Khalsa College, Amritsar for their valuable guidance and timely support during the compilation of this book.

RACHHPAL SINGH **IKVINDERPAL SINGH**

ARTIFICIAL NEURAL NETWORKS

CONTENTS

ARTIFICIAL NEURAL NETWORKS

CHAPTER 1

FUNDAMENTALS OF NEURAL NETWORKS

1.1 INTRODUCTION

For many decades, it has been a goal of science and engineering to develop intelligent machines with a large number of simple elements. References to this subject can be found in the scientific literature of the 19th century. During the 1940s, researchers desiring to duplicate the function of the human brain, have developed simple hardware (and later software) models of biological neurons and their interaction systems. McCulloch and Pitts published the first systematic study of the artificial neural network. Four years later, the same authors explored network paradigms for pattern recognition using a single layer perceptron. In the 1950s and 1960s, a group of researchers combined these biological and psychological insights to produce the first artificial neural network (ANN).Initially implemented as electronic circuits, they were later converted into a more flexible medium of computer simulation. However, researchers such as Minsky and Papert later challenged these works. They strongly believed that intelligence systems are essentially symbol processing of the kind readily modeled on the Von Neumann computer. For a variety of reasons, the symbolic–processing approach became the dominant method. Moreover, the perceptron as proposed by Rosenblatt turned out to be more limited than first expected. Although further investigations in ANN continued during the 1970s by several pioneer researchers such as Grossberg, Kohonen, Widrow, and others, their works received relatively less attention. The primary factors for the recent resurgence of interest in the area of neural networks are the extension of Rosenblatt, Widrow and Hoff' s works dealing with learning in a complex, multi-layer network, Hopfield mathematical foundation for understanding the dynamics of an important class of networks as well as much faster computers than those of 50s and 60s.

The interest in neural networks comes from the networks' ability to mimic human brain as well as its ability to learn and respond. As a result, neural networks have been used in a large number of applications and have proven to be effective in performing complex functions in a variety of fields. These include pattern recognition, classification, vision, control systems, and prediction . Adaptation or learning is a major focus of neural net research that provides a degree of robustness to the NN model. In predictive modeling, the goal is to map a set of input patterns onto a set of output patterns. NN accomplishes this task by learning from a series of input/output data sets presented to the network. The trained network is then used to apply what it has learned to approximate or predict the corresponding output.

1.2 HISTORICAL BACKGROUND OF NEURAL NETWORKS

Neural network simulations appear to be a recent development. However, this field was established before the advent of computers, and has survived at least one major setback and several eras.Many importand advances have been boosted by the use of inexpensive computer emulations. Following an initial period of enthusiasm, the field survived a period of frustration and disrepute. During this period when funding and professional support was minimal, important advances were made by relatively few reserchers. These pioneers were able to develop convincing technology which surpassed the limitations identified by Minsky and Papert. Minsky and Papert, published a book (in 1969) in which they summed up a general feeling of frustration (against neural networks) among researchers, and was thus accepted by most without further analysis. Currently, the neural network field enjoys a resurgence of interest and a corresponding increase in funding.

The history of neural networks that was described above can be divided into several periods:

1. First Attempts: There were some initial simulations using formal logic. McCulloch and Pitts (1943) developed models of neural networks based on their understanding of neurology. These models made several assumptions about how neurons worked. Their networks were based on simple neurons which were considered to be binary devices with fixed thresholds. The results of their model were simple logic functions such as "a or b" and "a and b". Another attempt was by using computer simulations. Two groups (Farley and Clark, 1954; Rochester, Holland, Haibit and Duda, 1956). The first group (IBM reserchers) maintained closed contact with neuroscientists at McGill University. So whenever their models did not work, they consulted the neuroscientists. This interaction established a multidiscilinary trend which continues to the present day.

2. Promising & Emerging Technology: Not only was neroscience influential in the development of neural networks, but psychologists and engineers also contributed to the progress of neural network simulations. Rosenblatt (1958) stirred considerable interest and activity in the field when he designed and developed the Perceptron. The Perceptron had three layers with the middle layer known as the association layer.This system could learn to connect or associate a given input to a random output unit.

Another system was the ADALINE (ADAptive LInear Element) which was developed in 1960 by Widrow and Hoff (of Stanford University). The ADALINE was an analogue electronic device made from simple components. The method used for learning was different to that of the Perceptron, it employed the Least-Mean-Squares (LMS) learning rule.

3. Period of Frustration & Disrepute: In 1969 Minsky and Papert wrote a book in which they generalised the limitations of single layer Perceptrons to multilayered systems. In the book they said: "...our intuitive judgment that the extension (to multilayer systems) is sterile". The significant result of their book was to eliminate funding for research with neural network simulations. The conclusions supported the disenhantment of reserchers in the field. As a result, considerable prejudice against this field was activated.

4. Innovation: Although public interest and available funding were minimal, several researchers continued working to develop neuromorphically based computaional methods for problems such as pattern recognition.

During this period several paradigms were generated which modern work continues to enhance.Grossberg's (Steve Grossberg and Gail Carpenter in 1988) influence founded a school of thought which explores resonating algorithms. They developed the ART (Adaptive Resonance Theory) networks based on biologically plausible models. Anderson and Kohonen developed associative techniques independent of each other. Klopf (A. Henry Klopf) in 1972, developed a basis for learning in artificial neurons based on a biological principle for neuronal learning called heterostasis.

Werbos (Paul Werbos 1974) developed and used the back-propagation learning method, however several years passed before this approach was popularized. Back-propagation nets are probably the most well known and widely applied of the neural networks today. In essence, the back-propagation net. is a Perceptron with multiple layers, a different thershold function in the artificial neuron, and a more robust and capable learning rule.

Amari (A. Shun-Ichi 1967) was involved with theoretical developments: he published a paper which established a mathematical theory for a learning basis (error-correction method) dealing with adaptive patern classification. While Fukushima (F. Kunihiko) developed a step wise trained multilayered neural network for interpretation of handwritten characters. The original network was published in 1975 and was called the Cognitron.

5. Re-Emergence: Progress during the late 1970s and early 1980s was important to the re-emergence on interest in the neural network field. Several factors influenced this movement. For example, comprehensive books and conferences provided a forum for people in diverse fields with specialized technical languages, and the response to conferences and publications was quite positive. The news media picked up on the increased activity and tutorials helped disseminate the technology. Academic programs appeared and courses were inroduced at most major Universities (in US and Europe). Attention is now focused on funding levels throughout Europe, Japan and the US and as this funding becomes available, several new commercial with applications in industry and finacial institutions are emerging.

6. Today: Significant progress has been made in the field of neural networks-enough to attract a great deal of attention and fund further research. Advancement beyond current commercial applications appears to be possible, and research is advancing the field on many fronts. Neurally based chips are emerging and applications to complex problems developing. Clearly, today is a period of transition for neural network technology.

1.3 WHAT IS NEURAL NETWORK?

Work on artificial neural networks, commonly referred to as "neural networks" has been motivated right from its inception by the recognition that the human brain computes in an entirely different way from the conventional digital computer. The brain is a highly complex, nonlinear and parallel computer (information-processing system). It has the capability to organize its structural constituents known as neurons so as to perform certain computations (e.g., pattern recognition, perception, and motor control) many times faster than the fastest digital computer in existence today. Consider for example, human vision, which is an information-processing (Marr. 1982: Levine, 1985: Churchland and Sejnowski, 1992). It is the function of the visual system to provide a representation of the environment around us and, more important to supply the information we need to interact with the environment. To be specific the brain routinely accomplishes perceptual recognition tasks (e.g. recognizing a familiar face embedded in an unfamiliar scene) in approximately 100-200 ms, whereas tasks of mush lesser complexity may take days on a conventional computer.

For another example, consider the sonar of a bat. Sonar is an active echo-location system. In addition to providing information about how far away a target e.g. a flying insect) is, a bat sonar conveys information about the relative velocity of the target, the size of the target, the size of various features of the target, and the azimum and evaluation of the target (Suga, 1990a, b). The complex neural computations needed to extract all this information from the target echo occur within a brain the size of a plum. Indeed, an echo-locating bat can pursue and capture its target with a facility and success rate that would be the envy of a radar or sonar engineer.

How, then does a human brain or the brain of a bat do it? At birth a brain has great structure and the ability to build up its own rules through what we usually refer to as "experience." Indeed, experience is built up over time, with the most dramatic development (i.e., hard-wiring) of the human brain taking place during the first two years from birth; but the development continues well beyond that stage.

A "developing" neuron is synonymous with a plastic brain: Plasticity permits the developing nervous system to adapt to its surrounding environment. Just as plasticity appears to be essential to the functioning of neurons as information-processing units in the human brain, so it is with neural networks made up of artificial neurons. In its most general form, a neural network is a machine that is designed to model the way in which the brain performs a particular task or function of interest; the network is usually implemented by using electronic components or is simulated in software on a digital computer. Our interest in this book is confined largely to an important class of neural networks that perform useful computations through a process of learning. To achieve good performance, neural networks employ a massive interconnection of simple computing cells referred to as "neurons" or "processing units." We may thus offer the following definition of a neural network viewed as an adaptive machine:

A neural network is a massively parallel distributed processor made up of simple processing units, which has a natural propensity for storing experiential knowledge and making it available for use. It resembles the brain in two respects:

1. Knowledge is acquired by the network from its environment through a learning process.

2. Interneuron connection strengths, known as synaptic weights, are used to store the acquired knowledge.

The procedure used to perform the learning process is called a learning algorithm, the function of which is to modify the synaptic weights of the network in an orderly fashion to attain a desired design objective. The modification of synaptic weights provides the traditional method for the design of neural networks. Such an approach is the closest to linear adaptive filter theory, which is already well established and successfully applied in many diverse fields (Widrow and Stearns, 1985; Hykin, 1996). However, it is also possible for a neural network to modify its own topology, its own topology, which is motivated by the fact that neurons in the human brain can die and that new synaptic connections can grow.

Neural networks are also referred to in literature as neurocomputers, connectionist networks, parallel distributed processors, etc. Throughout the book we use the term "neural networks"; occasionally the term "neurocomputer" or "connectionist network" is used.

1.4 BENEFITS OF NEURAL NETWORKS

It is apparent that a neural network derives its computing power through, first, its massively parallel distributed structure and, second, its ability to learn and therefore generalize.

Generalization refers to the neural network producing reasonable outputs for inputs not encountered during training (learning). These two information-processing capabilities make it possible for neural networks to solve complex (large-scale) problems that are currently intractable. In practice, however, neural networks cannot provide the solution by working individually. Rather, they need to be integrated into a consistent system engineering approach. Specifically, complex problem of interest is decomposed into a number of relatively simple tasks, and neural networks are assigned a subset of te tasks that match their inherent capabilities. It is important to recognize, however, that we have a long way to go (if ever) before we can build a computer architecture that mimics a human brain.

The use of neural networks offers the following useful properties and capabilities:

1. Nonlinearity: An artificial neuron can be linear or nonlinear. A neural network, made up of an interconnection of nonlinear neurons, is itself nonlinear. Moreover, the nonlinearity is of a special kind in the sense that it is distributed throughout the network. Nonlinearity responsible for generation of the input signal (e.g., speech signal) is inherently nonlinear.

2. Input-Output Mapping: A popular paradigm of learning called learning with a teacher or supervised learning involves modification of the synaptic weights of a neural network by applying a set of labeled training samples or task examples. Each example consists of a unique input signal and a corresponding desired response. The network is presented with an example picked at random from the set, and the synaptic weights (free parameters) of the network are modified to minimize the difference between the desired response and the actual response of the network produced by the input signal in accordance with an appropriate statistical criterion. The training of the network is repeated for many examples in the set until the network reaches a steady state where the are no further significant changes in the synaptic weights. The previously applied training examples may be replied during the training session but in a different order. Thus the network learns from the examples by constructing an input-output mapping for the problem at hand. Such an approach brings to mind the study of nonparametric statistical inference, which is a branch of statistics dealing with model-free estimation, or, from a biological viewpoint, tabula rasa learning (Geman et. al., 1992): the term "nonparametric" is used here to signify the fact that no prior assumptions are made on a statistical model for the input data. Consider, for example, a pattern classification task, where the requirement is to assign an input signal representing a physical object or event to one of several prespecified categories (classes). In a nonparametric approach to this problem, the requirement is to "estimate" arbitrary decision boundaries in the input signal space for the pattern-classification task using a set of example, and to do so without invoking a probabilistic distribution model. A similar point of view is implicit in the supervised learning paradigm, which suggest a close analogy between the input-output mapping performed by a neural network and nonparametric statistical interface.

3. Adaptivity: Neural networks have a built-in capability to adapt their synaptic weights to change sin the surrounding environment. In particular a neural network trained to operate in a specific environment can be easily retained to deal with minor changes in the operating environment conditions. Moreover, when it is operating in a nonstationary environment (i.e., one where statistics change with time), a neural network can be designed to change sits synaptic weights in real time. The natural architecture oa a neural network for pattern classification, adaptive capability of the network, make it a useful tool in adaptive pattern classification, adaptive signal processing, and adaptive control. As a general rule, it may be said that the more adaptive we make a system, all the time ensuring that the system is required to operate in a nonstationary environment. It should be emphasized, however, that adaptivity does not always lead to robustness: indeed, it may do the very opposite. For example, an adaptive short time constants may change reapidly and therefore tend to respond to spurious disturbances, causing a drastic degradation in system performance. To realize the full benefits of adaptivity, the principal time constants of the system should be long enough for the system to ignore spurious disturbances and yet short enough to respond to meaningful changes in the environment: the problem described here is referred to as the stability-plasticity dilemma (Grossberg, 1988b).

4. Evidential Response: In the context of pattern classification, a neural network can be designed to provide information not only about which particular pattern to select, but also about the confidence in the decision made. This latter information may e used to reject ambiguous patterns, should they arise, and thereby improve the classification performance of the network.

5. Contextual Information: Knowledge is represented by the very structure an activation state of the neural network. Every neuron in the network is potentially affected by the global activity of all other neurons in the network. Consequently, contextual information is dealt with naturally by a neural network.

6. Fault Tolerance: A neural network, implemented in hardware from, has the potential to be inherently fault tolerant, of capable of robust computation, in the sense that its performance degrades gracefully under adverse operating conditions. For example, if a neuron or its connecting links are damaged, recall of a stored pattern is impaired in quality. However, due to the distributed nature of information stored in the network, the damage has to be extensive before the overall response of the network is degraded seriously. Thus, in principle, a neural network exhibit exhibits a graceful degradation in performance rather than catastrophic failure. There is some empirical evidence for robust computation, but usually it is uncontrolled. In order to be assured that the neural network is in fact fault tolerant, it may be necessary to take corrective measres in designing the algorithm uses to train the network (Kerlirzin and Vallet, 1993).

7. VLSI Implementability: The massively parallel nature of a neural network makes it potentially fast for the computation of certain tasks. This same feature makes a neural network well suited for implementation using very-large-scale-integrated (VLSI) technology. One particular beneficial virtue of VLSI is that it provides a means of capturing truly complex behavior in a highly hierarchical fashion (Mead, 1989).

8. Uniformity of Analysis and Design: Basically, neural networks enjoy universality as information processors. We say this in the sense that the same notation is used in all domains involving the application of neural networks. This feature manifests itself in different ways:

- Neurons, in one form or another, represent an ingredient common to all neural networks.
- This commonality makes it possible to share theories and learning algorithms in different applications of neural networks.
- Modular networks can be built through a seamless integration of modules.

9. Neurobiological Analogy: The decision of a neural network is motivated by analogy with the brain, which is a living proof that fault tolerant parallel processing is not only physically possible but also fast and powerful. Neurobiologists look to (artificial) neural networks as a research tool for the interpretation of neurobiological phenomena. On the other hand, engineers look to neurobiology for new ideas to solve problems more complex that those based on conventional hard-wired design techniques. These two viewpoints are illustrated by the following respective examples:

- In Anastasio (1993), linear system models of the vestibulo-ocular reflex are compared to neural network models based on recurrent networks that are described in Section 1.6 and discusses in detail in Chapter 15. The vestibulo-ocular reflex (VOR) is part of the oculomotor system. The function of VOR is to maintain visual (i.e., retinal) image stability by making eye rotations that are opposite to head rotations. The VOR is mediated by premotor neurons in the vestibular nuclei that process head rotation signals from vestibular sensory neurons and send the results to the eye muscle motor neurons. The VOR is well suited for modeling because its input (head rotation) and its output (eye rotation) can be precisely specified. It is also a relatively simple reflex and the neuro-physiological properties of its constituent neurons have been well described. Among the three neural types, the premotor neurons (reflex interneurons) in the vestibular nuclei are the most complex and therefore most interesting. The VOR has previously been modeled using lumped, linear system descriptors and control theory. These models were useful in explaining some of the overall properties of the VOR, but gave little insight into the properties of its constituent neurons. This situation has been greatly improved through neural network modeling. Recurrent network models of VOR (programmed using an algorithm called real-time recurrent learning that is described in Chapter 15) can reproduce and help explain many of the static, dynamic, nonlinear, and distributed aspects of signal processing by the neurons that mediate the VOR, especially the vestibular nuclei neurons (Anastasio, 1993).
- The retina, more than any other part of the brain is where we begin to put together the relationships between the outside worked represented by a visual sense, its physical image projected onto an array of receptors, and the first neural images. The retina is a thin sheet of neural tissue that lines the posterior hemihphere of the eyeball. The retina's task is to convert an optical image into a neural image for transmission down the optic nerve to a multitude of centers for further analysis. This is a complex task, as evidenced by the synaptic organization of the retina. In all vertebrate retinas the transformation from optical to neural image involves three stages (Sterling, 1990):

(i) Photo transduation by a layer of receptor neurons.

(ii) Transmission of the resulting signals (produced in response to light) by chemical synapses to a layer of bipolar cells

(iii) Transmission of these signals, also by chemical synapses, to output neurons that are called ganglion cells.

At both synaptic stages (i.e., from receptor to bipolar cells, and from bipolar to ganglion cells) there are specialized laterally connected neurons called horizontal cells and amacrine cells, respectively. The task of these neurons is to modify the transmission across the synaptic layers. There are also centrifugal elements called inter-plexiform cells; their task is to convey signal from the inner synaptic layer back to the outer one. A few researchers have built electronics chips that mimic the structure of the retina (maahowald and Mead, 1989: Boahen and Ardreou, 1992; Boahen, 1996). These electronic chips are called neromorphic integrated circuits,a term coined by Mead (1989). A neuromophic imaging sensor consist of an arrya of photoreceptors combined with analog circuitry at each picture element (pixel). It emulates the retina in that it can adapt locally to changes in brightness, detect edges, and detect motion. The neurobiological integrated circuits is useful in another important way: It provide a hope and belief, and to a certain extent an existence of proof, that physical understanding of neurobiological structures could have a productive influence on the art of electronics and VLSI technology.

With inspiration from neurobiology in mind, it seems appropriate that we take a brief look at the human brain and its structural levels of organization.

1.5 HUMAN BRAIN

The human nervous system may be viewed as a three-stage system, as depicted in the block diagram of Fig. 1.1. Central to the system is the brain, represented by the neural (nerve) net, which continually receives information, perceives it, and makes appropriate decisions. Two sets of arrows are shown in the figure. Those pointing from left to right indicate the forward transmission of information-bearing signals through the system. The arrows pointing from right to left signify the presence of feed-back in the system. The receptors convert stimuli from the human body or the external environment into electrical impulses that convey information to the neural net (brain). The effectors convert electrical impulses generated by the neural net into discernible responses as system outputs.

The struggle to understand the brain has been made easier because of the pioneering work of Random y Cajal (1911), who introduced the idea of neurons as structural constituents of the brain. Typically, neuron are five to six orders of magnitude slower than silicon logic gates; events in a silicon chip happen in the nanosecond (10^{-3}s) range. However, the brain makes up for the relatively slow rate of operation of a neuron by having a truly staggering number of neurons (nerve cells) with massive interconnections between them. It is estimated that there are approximately 10 billion neurons in the human cortex, and 60 trillion synapses or connections (Shepherd and Koch, 1990). The net result is that the brain is an enormously efficient structure. Specifically, the energetic efficiency of the brain is approximately 10^{-16} joules (J) per operation per second, whereas the corresponding value for the best computers in use today is about 10^{-6} joules per operation per second (Faggin, 1991).

Synapses are elementary structural and function units that mediate the interactions between neurons. The most common kind of synapse is a chemical synapse, which operates as follows. A presynaptic process liberates a transmitter substance that diffuses across the synaptic junction between neurons and then acts on a postsnaptic process. Thus a synapse converts a presynaptic electrical signal into a chemical signal and then

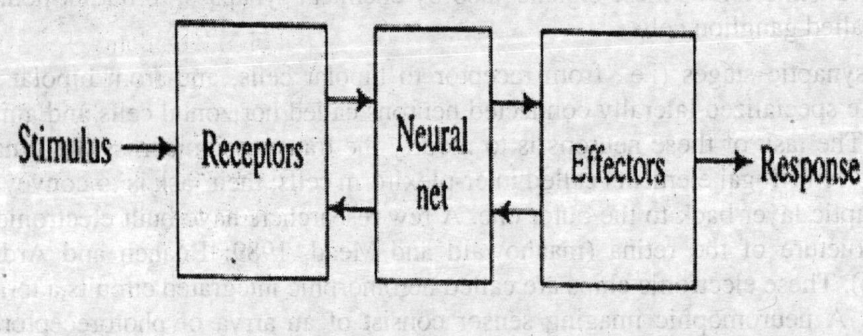

Figure 1.1 Block diagram representation of nervous system.

back into a postsynaptic electrical signal (Spherd and Koch 1990). In electrical terminology, such an element is said to be a nonreciprocal two-part device. In traditional descriptions of neural organization, it is assumed that a synapse is a simple connection that can impose excitation or inhibition, but not both on the receptive neuron.

Earlier we mentioned that plasticity permits the developing nervous system to adapt to its surrounding environment (Eggermont, 1990; Churchland and Sejnowski, 1992). In an adult brain, plasticity may be accounted fro by two mechanism: the creation of new synaptic connections between neurons, and the modification of existing synapses. Axons, the transmission lines, and dendrites, the receptive zones, constitute two types of cell filaments that are distinguished on morphological grounds: an axon has a smoother surface, fewer branches, and greater length, whereas a dendrite (so called because of its resemblance to a tree) has an irregular surface and more branches (Freeman, 1975). Neurons come in a wide variety of shapes and sizes in different parts of the brain. Figure 1.2 illustrates the shape of a pyramidal cell, which is one of the most common types of cortical neurons. Like many other types of neurons, it receives most of its inputs through denritic spines; see the segment of dendrite in the insert in Fig. 1.2 for detail. The pyramidal cell can receive 10,000 or more synaptic contacts and it can project onto thousands of target cells.

The majority of neurons encode their outputs as a series of brief voltage pulses. These pulses, commonly known as action potentials or spikes, originate are or close to the cell body of neurons and then propagate across the individual neurons at constant velocity and amplitude. The reasons for the use of action potentials for communication among neurons are based on the physics of axons. The axon of a neuron is very long and thin and is characterized by high electrical resistance and very large capacitance. Both of these elements are distributed across the axon. The axon may therefore be modeled as an RC transmission line, hence the common use of "cable equation" as the terminology for describing signal propagation along an axon. Analysis of this propagation mechanism reveals that when a voltage is applied at one end of the axon it decays exponentially with distance, dropping to an insignificant level by the time it reaches the other end. The action potentials provide a way to circumvent this transmission problem (Anderson, 1995).

In the brain there are both small-scale and large-scale anatomical organizations, and different functions take place at lower and higher levels. Figure 1.3 shows a hierarchy of interwoven levels of organization that has emerged from the extensive work done on the analysis of local regions in the brain (Shepherd and Koch, 1990; Churchland and Sejnowski, 1992). The synapses represent the most fundamental level, depending on molecules and ions for their action. At the next levels we have neural microcircits, dendritic trees, and then neurons. A neural microcircuit refers to an assembly of synapses organized into patters of connectivity to produce a functional operation of interest.

A neural microcircuit may be likened to a silicon chip made up of an assembly of transistors. The smallest size of microcircuits is measured in milliseconds. The neural micrometers (μm), and their fastest speed of operation is measured in milliseconds. The neural microcircuits are grouped to form dendritic subunits within the dendritic trees of individual neurons. The whole neuron, about 100 μm in size, contains several dendritic subunits. At the next level of complexity we have local circuits (about 1 mm in size) made up of neurons with similar or different properties; these neural assemblies perform

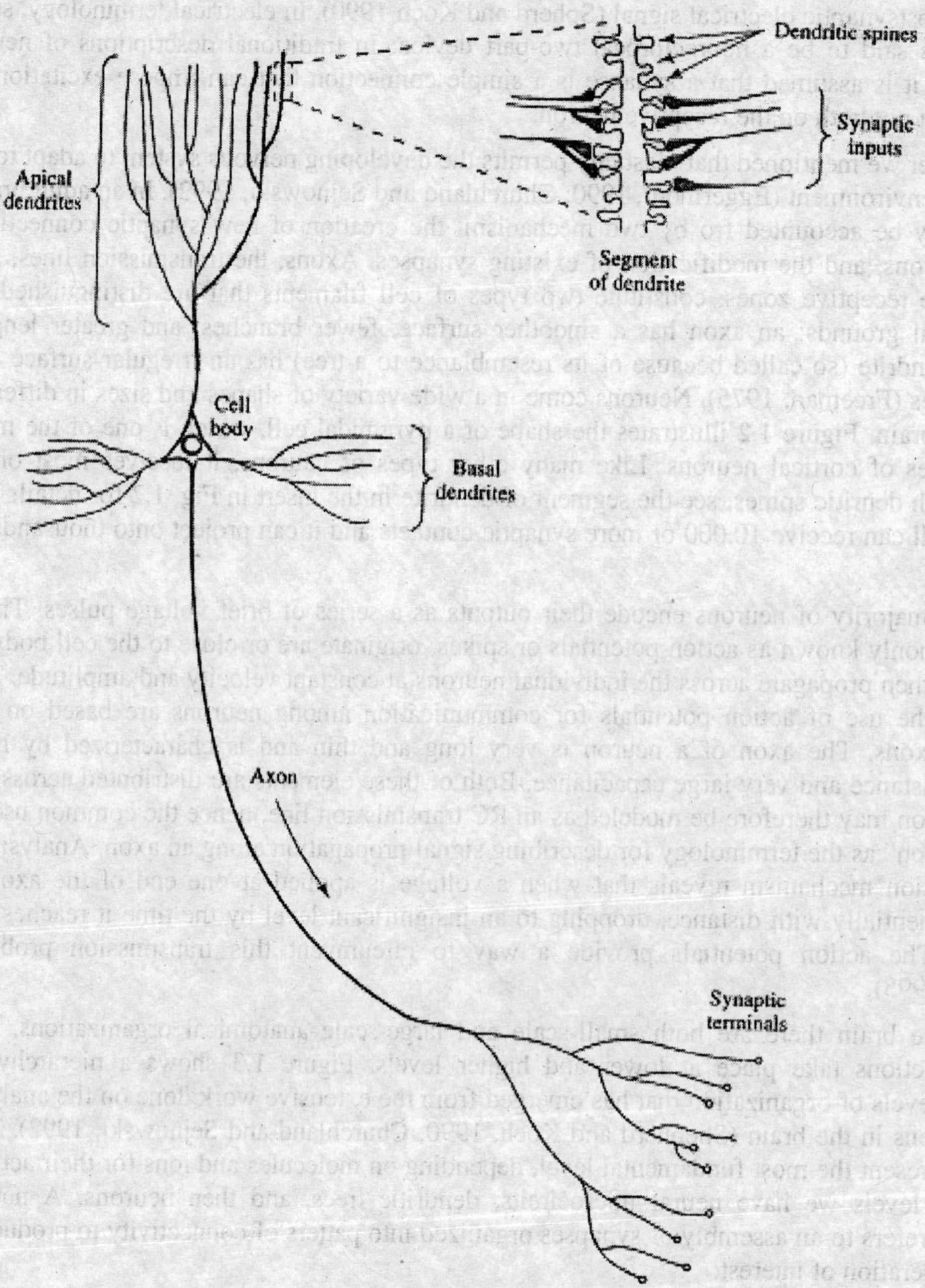

Figure 1.2 The pyramidal cell.

operations characteristic of a localized region in the brain. This is followed by interregional circuits made up of pathways, columns, and topographic maps, which involve multiple region located in different parts of the brain.

Topographic maps are organized to respond to incoming sensory information. These maps are often arranged in sheets, as in the superior colliculus, where the visual,

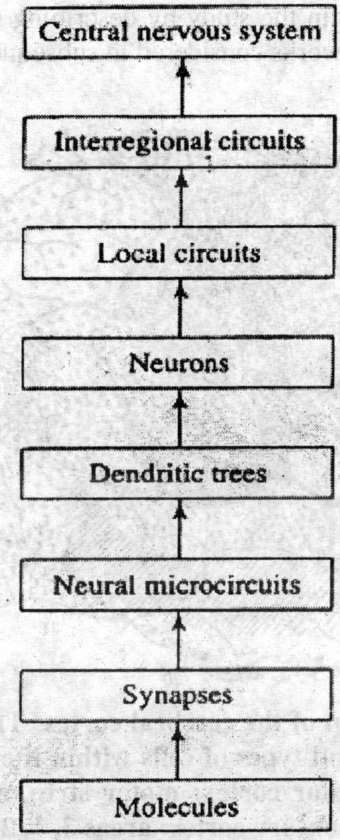

Figure 1.3 Structural organization of levels in the brain.

audiotory, and somatosensory maps are stacked in adjacent layers in such a way that stimuli from corresponding points in space lie above or below each other. Figure 1.4 presents a cytoarchitectural map of the cerebral cortex as worked out by Brodmann (Brodal, 1981). This figure shows clearly that different sensory inputs (motor, somatosensory, visual, auditory, etc.) are mapped onto corresponding areas of the cerebral cortex in an orderly fashion. At the final level of complexity, the topographic maps and other interregional circuits mediate specific types of behavior in the central nervous system.

It is important to recognize that the structural levels of organization described herein are a unique characteristic of the brain. They are nowhere to be found in a digital compute, and we are nowhere close to re-creating them with artificial neural networks. Nevertheless, we are inching our way toward a hierarchy of computational levels similar to that described in Fig. 1.3. The artificial neurons we use to build our neural networks are truly primitive in comparison to those found in the brain. The neural networks we are presently able to design are just as primitive compared to the local circuits and the interregional circuits in the brain. What is really satisfying, however, is the remarkable progress that we have made on so many fronts during the past two decades. With neurobiological analogy as the source of inspiration, and the wealth of theoretical and technological tools that we are bringing together, it is certain that in another decade our understanding of artificial neural networks will be much more sophisticated it is today.

Our primary interest in this book is confined to the study of official neural networks from an engineering perpective.[2] We begin the study by describing the models of (artificial) neurons that form the basis of the neural networks considered in subsequent chapters of the book.

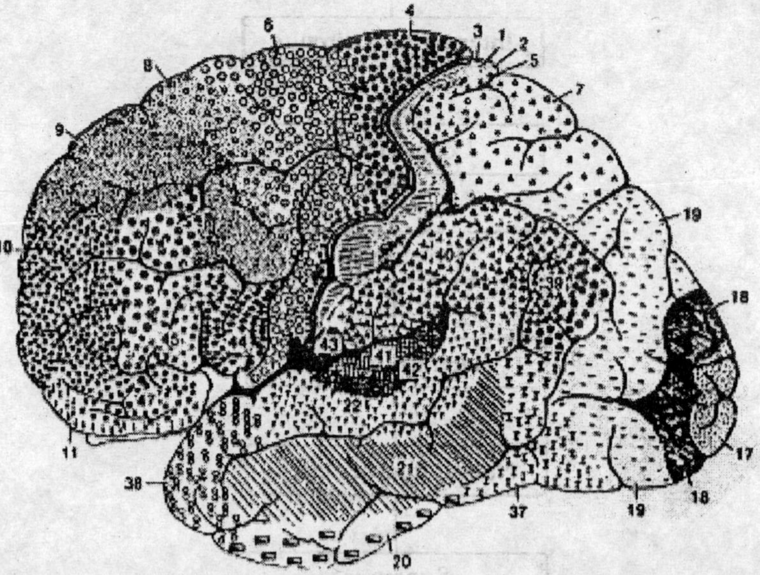

Figure 1.4 Cytoarchitectural map of the cerebral cortex. The different areas are identified by the thickness of their layers and types of cells within them. Some of the most important specific areas are as follows. Motor cortex: motor strip, area 4; premotor area, area 6; frontal eye fields, area 8. Somatosensory cortex: areas 3, 1, 2. Visual cortex: areas 17, 18, 19. Audiotory cortex: area 41 and 2.

1.6 BASIC STRUCTURE OF A NEURON

1.6.1 MODEL OF BIOLOGICAL NEURONS

In general, the human nervous system is a very complex neural network. The brain is the central element of the human nervous system, consisting of near 10^{10} biological neurons that are connected to each other through sub-networks. Each neuron in the brain is composed of a body, one axon and multitude of dendrites. The neuron model shown in Figure 1.5 serves as the basis for the artificial neuron. The dendrites receive signals from other neurons. The axon can be considered as a long tube, which divides into branches terminating in little endbulbs. The small gap between an endbulb and a dendrite is called a synapse. The axon of a single neuron forms synaptic connections with many other neurons. Depending upon the type of neuron, the number of synapses connections from other neurons may range from a few hundreds to 104.

The cell body of a neuron sums the incoming signals from dendrites as well as the signals from numerous synapses on its surface. A particular neuron will send an impulse to its axon if sufficient input signals are received to stimulate the neuron to its threshold level. However, if the inputs do not reach the required threshold, the input will quickly decay and will not generate any action. The biological neuron model is the foundation of an artificial neuron as will be described in detail in the next section.

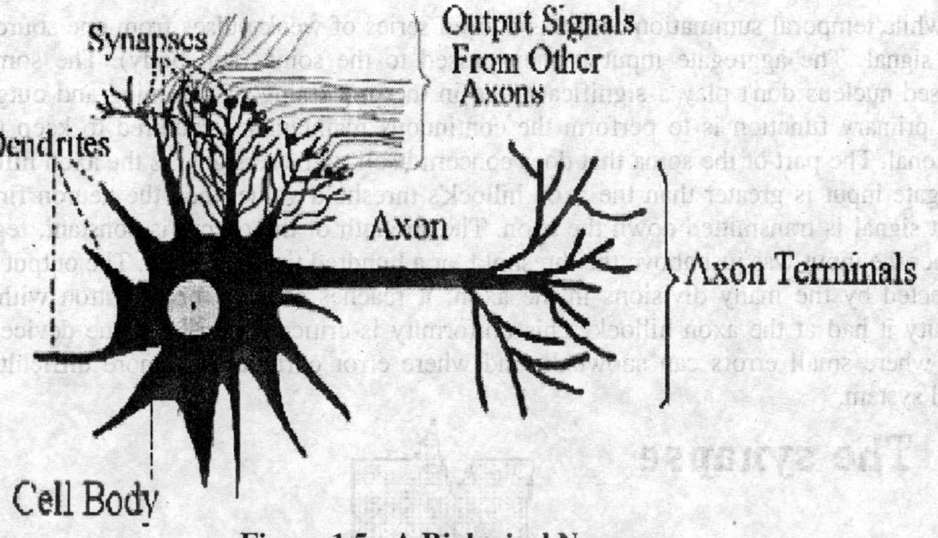

Figure 1.5 : A Biological Neuron.

1.6.2 THE BIOLOGICAL NEURON

The brain is a collection of about 10 billion interconnected neurons. Each neuron is a cell [right] that uses biochemical reactions to receive, process and transmit information.

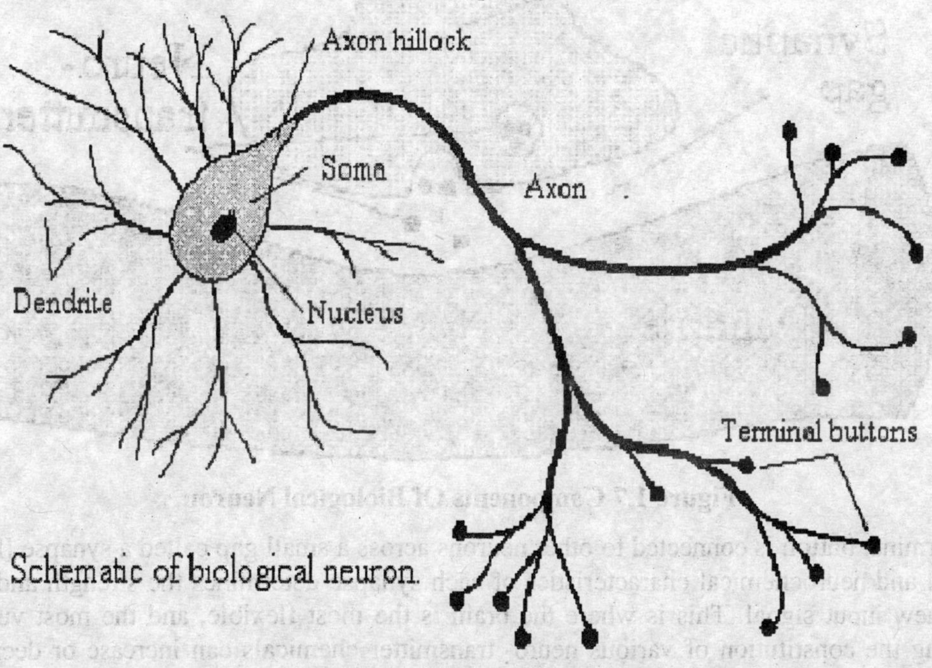

Figure 1.6 Biological Neuron

A neuron's dendritic tree is connected to a thousand neighbouring neurons. When one of those neurons fire, a positive or negative charge is received by one of the dendrites. The strengths of all the received charges are added together through the processes of spatial and temporal summation. Spatial summation occurs when several weak signals are converted into a single large one, while temporal summation converts a rapid series of weak pulses from one source into one large signal. The aggregate input is then passed to the soma (cell body). The soma and the enclosed nucleus don't play a significant role in the processing of incoming and outgoing data. Their primary function is to perform the continuous maintenance required to keep the neuron functional. The part of the soma that does concern itself with the signal is the axon hillock. If the aggregate input is greater than the axon hillock's threshold value, then the neuron fires, and an output signal is transmitted down the axon. The strength of the output is constant, regardless of whether the input was just above the threshold, or a hundred times as great. The output strength is unaffected by the many divisions in the axon; it reaches each terminal button with the same intensity it had at the axon hillock. This uniformity is critical in an analogue device such as a brain where small errors can snowball, and where error correction is more difficult than in a digital system.

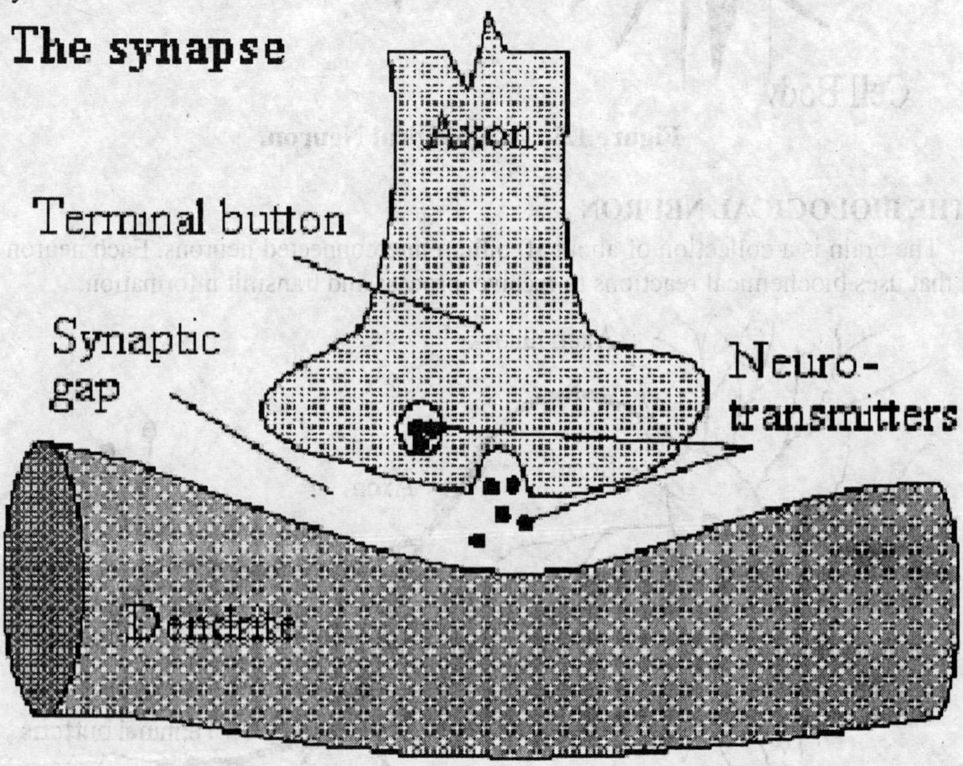

Figure 1.7 Components Of Biological Neuron

Each terminal button is connected to other neurons across a small gap called a synapse [left]. The physical and neurochemical characteristics of each synapse determines the strength and polarity of the new input signal. This is where the brain is the most flexible, and the most vulnerable. Changing the constitution of various neuro- transmitter chemicals can increase or decrease the amount of stimulation that the firing axon imparts on the neighbouring dendrite. Altering the neurotransmitters can also change whether the stimulation is excitatory or inhibitory. Many drugs such as alcohol and LSD have dramatic effects on the production or destruction of these critical chemicals. The infamous nerve gas sarin can kill because it neutralizes a chemical (acetylcholinesterase) that is normally responsible for the destruction of a neurotransmitter (acetylcholine). This means that once a neuron fires, it keeps on triggering all the neurons in the vicinity. One no longer has control over muscles, and suffocation ensues.

1.7 WHAT IS AN ARTIFICIAL NEURAL NETWORK?

An artificial neural network is a system based on the operation of biological neural networks, in other words, is an emulation of biological neural system. Why would be necessary the implementation of artificial neural networks? Although computing these days is truly advanced, there are certain tasks that a program made for a common microprocessor is unable to perform; even so a software implementation of a neural network can be made with their advantages and disadvantages.

1.7.1 ADVANTAGES

1. A neural network can perform tasks that a linear program can not.

2. When an element of the neural network fails, it can continue without any problem by their parallel nature.

3. A neural network learns and does not need to be reprogrammed.

4. It can be implemented in any application.

5. It can be implemented without any problem.

1.7.2 DISADVANTAGES

1. The neural network needs training to operate.

2. The architecture of a neural network is different from the architecture of microprocessors therefore needs to be emulated.

3. Requires high processing time for large neural networks.

4. Another aspect of the artificial neural networks is that there are different architectures, which consequently requires different types of algorithms, but despite to be an apparently complex system, a neural network is relatively simple.

Artificial neural networks (ANN) are among the newest signal-processing technologies in the engineer's toolbox. The field is highly interdisciplinary, but our approach will restrict the view to the engineering perspective. In engineering, neural networks serve two important functions: as pattern classifiers and as nonlinear adaptive filters. We will provide a brief overview of the theory, learning rules, and applications of the most important neural network models. Definitions and Style of Computation An Artificial Neural Network is an adaptive, most often nonlinear system that learns to perform a function (an input/output map) from data. Adaptive means that the system parameters are changed during operation, normally called the training phase . After the training phase the Artificial Neural Network parameters are fixed and the system is deployed to solve the problem at hand (the testing phase).

The Artificial Neural Network is built with a systematic step-by-step procedure to optimize a performance criterion or to follow some implicit internal constraint, which is commonly referred to as the learning rule . The input/output training data are fundamental in neural network technology, because they convey the necessary information to "discover" the optimal operating point. The nonlinear nature of the neural network processing elements (PEs) provides the system with lots of flexibility to achieve practically any desired input/output map, i.e., some Artificial Neural Networks are universal mappers . There is a style in neural computation that is worth describing.

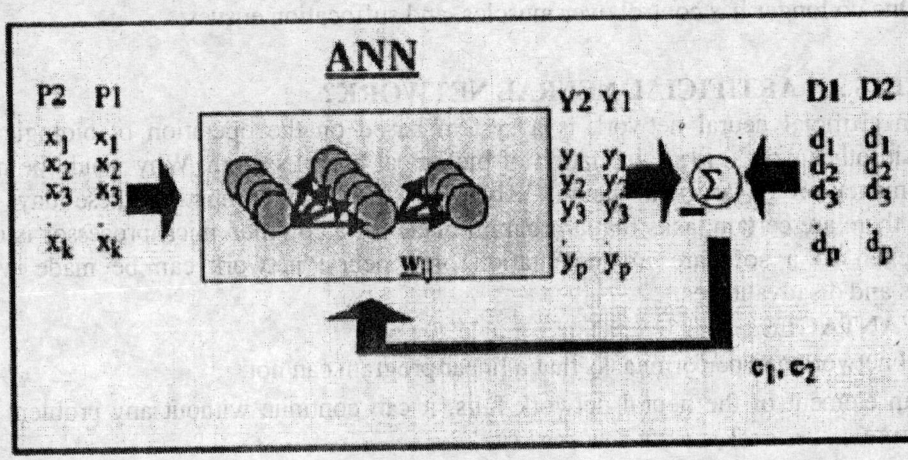

Figure 1.8 Working Of Artificial Neuron

An input is presented to the neural network and a corresponding desired or target response set at the output (when this is the case the training is called supervised). An error is composed from the difference between the desired response and the system output. This error information is fed back to the system and adjusts the system parameters in a systematic fashion (the learning rule). The process is repeated until the performance is acceptable. It is clear from this description that the performance hinges heavily on the data. If one does not have data that cover a significant portion of the operating conditions or if they are noisy, then neural network technology is probably not the right solution. On the other hand, if there is plenty of data and the problem is poorly understood to derive an approximate model, then neural network technology is a good choice. This operating procedure should be contrasted with the traditional engineering design, made of exhaustive subsystem specifications and intercommunication protocols. In artificial neural networks, the designer chooses the network topology, the performance function, the learning rule, and the criterion to stop the training phase, but the system automatically adjusts the parameters. So, it is difficult to bring a priori information into the design, and when the system does not work properly it is also hard to incrementally refine the solution. But ANN-based solutions are extremely efficient in terms of development time and resources, and in many difficult problems artificial neural networks provide performance that is difficult to match with other technologies. Denker 10 years ago said that "artificial neural networks are the second best way to implement a solution" motivated by the simplicity of their design and because of their universality, only shadowed by the traditional design obtained by studying the physics of the problem. At present, artificial neural networks are emerging as the technology of choice for many applications, such as pattern recognition, prediction, system identification, and control.

1.8 SOME OTHER DEFINITIONS OF A NEURAL NETWORK INCLUDE:

... a neural network is a system composed of many simple processing elements operating in parallel whose function is determined by network structure, connection strengths, and the processing performed at computing elements or nodes.

A neural network is a massively parallel distributed processor that has a natural propensity for storing experiential knowledge and making it available for use. It resembles the brain in two respects:

1.Knowledge is acquired by the network through a learning process.

2.Interneuron connection strengths known as synaptic weights are used to store the knowledge.

ANNs have been applied to an increasing number of real-world problems of considerable complexity. Their most important advantage is in solving problems that are too complex for conventional technologies -- problems that do not have an algorithmic solution or for which an algorithmic solution is too complex to be found. In general, because of their abstraction from the biological brain, ANNs are well suited to problems that people are good at solving, but for which computers are not. These problems includes pattern recognition and forecasting (which requires the recognition of trends in data).

1.9 VARIOUS TYPES OF ARTIFICIAL NEURAL NETWORKS:

Network	Application	Description
ADALINE Adaline Network	**Pattern Recognition** Classification of Digits 0-9	The Adaline is essentially a single-layer backpropagation network. It is trained on a pattern recognition task, where the aim is to classify a bitmap representation of the digits 0-9 into the corresponding classes. Due to the limited capabilities of the Adaline, the network only recognizes the exact training patterns. When the application is ported into the multi-layer backpropagation network, a remarkable degree of fault-tolerance can be achieved.
BPN Backpropagation Network	**Time-Series Forecasting** Prediction of the Annual Number of Sunspots	This program implements the now classic multi-layer backpropagation network with bias terms and momentum. It is used to detect structure in time-series, which is presented to the network using a simple tapped delay-line memory. The program learns to predict future sunspot activity from historical data collected over the past three centuries. To avoid overfitting, the termination of the learning procedure is controlled by the so-called stopped training method.
HOPFIELD Hopfield Model	**Autoassociative Memory** Associative Recall of Images	The Hopfield model is used as an autoassociative memory to store and recall a set of bitmap images. Images are stored by calculating a corresponding weight matrix. Thereafter, starting from an arbitrary configuration, the memory will settle on exactly that stored image, which is nearest to the starting configuration in terms of Hamming distance. Thus given an incomplete or corrupted version of a stored image, the network is able to recall the

		corresponding original image.
BAM Bidirectional Associative Memory	**Heteroassociative Memory** Association of Names and Phone Numbers	The bidirectional associative memory can be viewed as a generalization of the Hopfield model, to allow for a heteroassociative memory to be implemented. In this case, the association is between names and corresponding phone numbers. After coding the set of exemplars, the network, when presented with a name, is able to recall the corresponding phone number and vice versa. The memory even shows a limited degree of fault-tolerance in case of corrupted input patterns.
BOLTZMAN Boltzmann Machine	**Optimization** Traveling Salesman Problem	The Boltzmann machine is a stochastic version of the Hopfield model, whose network dynamics incorporate a random component in correspondence with a given finite temperature. Starting with a high temperature and gradually cooling down, allowing the network to reach equilibrium at any step, chances are good, that the network will settle in a global minimum of the corresponding energy function. This process is called simulated annealing. The network is then used to solve a well-known optimization problem: The weight matrix is chosen such that the global minimum of the energy function corresponds to a solution of a particular instance of the traveling salesman problem.
CPN Counterpropagation Network	**Vision** Determination of the Angle of Rotation	The counterpropagation network is a competitive network, designed to function as a self-programming lookup table with the additional ability to interpolate between entries. The application is to determine the angular rotation of a rocket-shaped object, images of which are presented to the network as a bitmap pattern. The performance of the network is a little limited due to the low resolution of the bitmap.
SOM Self-Organizing Map	**Control** Pole Balancing Problem	The self-organizing map is a competitive network with the ability to form topology-preserving mappings between its input and output spaces. In this program the network learns to balance a pole by applying forces at the base of the pole. The behavior of the pole is simulated by numerically integrating the differential equations for its law of motion using Euler's method. The task of the network is to establish a mapping between the state variables of

		the pole and the optimal force to keep it balanced. This is done using a reinforcement learning approach: For any given state of the pole, the network tries a slight variation of the mapped force. If the new force results in better control, the map is modified, using the pole's current state variables and the new force as a training vector.
ART1 Adaptive Resonance Theory	**Brain Modeling** Stability-Plasticity Demonstration	This program is mainly a demonstration of the basic features of the adaptive resonance theory network, namely the ability to plastically adapt when presented with new input patterns while remaining stable at previously seen input patterns.

1.10 WHY USE A NEURAL NETWORK?

Neural networks, with their remarkable ability to derive meaning from complicated or imprecise data, can be used to extract patterns and detect trends that are too complex to be noticed by either humans or other computer techniques. A trained neural network can be thought of as an "expert" in the category of information it has been given to analyze. This expert can then be used to provide projections given new situations of interest and answer "what if" questions.

1. Adaptive learning: An ability to learn how to do tasks based on the data given for training or initial experience.

2. Self-Organisation: An ANN can create its own organisation or representation of the information it receives during learning time.

3. Real Time Operation: ANN computations may be carried out in parallel, and special hardware devices are being designed and manifactured which take advantage of this capability.

4. Fault Tolerance via Redundant Information Coding: Partial destruction of a network leads to the corresponding degradation of performance. However, some network capabilites may be retained even with major network damage.

1.11 HOW NEURAL NETWORKS DIFFER FROM TRADITIONAL COMPUTING

Neural networks offer a different way to analyze data, and to recognize patterns within that data, than traditional computing methods. However, they are not a solution for all computing problems. Traditional computing methods work well for problems that can be well characterized. Balancing checkbooks, keeping ledgers, and keeping tabs of inventory are well defined and do not require the special characteristics of neural networks. Table 1.1 identifies the basic differences between the two computing approaches. Traditional computers are ideal for many applications. They can process data, track inventories, network results, and protect equipment. These applications do not need the special characteristics of neural networks. Expert systems are an extension of traditional computing and are sometimes called the fifth generation of computing. (First generation computing used switches and wires. The second generation occurred because of the development of the transistor. The third generation involved solid-state technology, the use of integrated circuits, and higher level languages like COBOL, Fortran, and "C". End user tools, "code generators," are known as the fourth generation.) The fifth generation involves artificial intelligence.

CHARACTERISTICS	TRADITIONAL COMPUTING (including Expert Systems)	ARTIFICIAL NEURAL NETWORKS
Processing style Functions	Sequential Logically (left brained) via Rules Concepts Calculations	Parallel Gestault (right brained) via Images Pictures Controls
Learning Method Applications	by rules (didactically) Accounting word processing math inventory digital communications	by example (Socratically) Sensor processing speech recognition pattern recognition text recognition

Table 1.1 Comparison of Computing Approaches

Typically, an expert system consists of two parts, an inference engine and a knowledge base. The inference engine is generic. It handles the user interface, external files, program access, and scheduling. The knowledge base contains the information that is specific to a particular problem. This knowledge base allows an expert to define the rules which govern a process. This expert does not have to understand traditional programming. That person simply has to understand both what he wants a computer to do and how the mechanism of the expert system shell works. It is this shell, part of the inference engine, that actually tells the computer how to implement the expert's desires. This implementation occurs by the expert system generating the computer's programming itself, it does that through "programming" of its own. This programming is needed to establish the rules for a particular application. This method of establishing rules is also complex and does require a detail oriented person. Efforts to make expert systems general have run into a number of problems. As the complexity of the system increases, the system simply demands too much computing resources and becomes too slow. Expert systems have been found to be feasible only when narrowly confined. Artificial neural networks offer a completely different approach to problem solving and they are sometimes called the sixth generation of computing. They try to provide a tool that both programs itself and learns on its own. Neural networks are structured to provide the capability to solve problems without the benefits of an expert and without the need of programming. They can seek patterns in data that no one knows are there. A comparison of artificial intelligence's expert systems and neural networks is contained in Table 1.2.

Characteristics	Von Neumann Architecture Used for Expert Systems	Artificial Neural Networks
Processors	VLSI (traditional processors)	Artificial Neural Networks; variety of technologies; hardware development is on going
Processing Approach	Separate	The same
Processing Approach	Processes problem rule at a one time; sequential	Multiple, simultaneously
Connections	Externally programmable	Dynamically self programming
Self learning	Only algorithmic parameters modified	Continuously adaptable
Fault tolerance	None without special processors	Significant in the very nature of the interconnected neurons
Neurobiology in design	None	Moderate
Programming	Through a rule based complicated	Self-programming; but network must be set up properly
Ability to be fast	Requires big processors	Requires multiple custom-built chips

Table 1.2 Comparisons of Expert Systems and Neural Networks

Expert systems have enjoyed significant successes. However, artificial intelligence has encountered problems in areas such as vision, continuous speech recognition and synthesis, and machine learning. Artificial intelligence also is hostage to the speed of the processor that it runs on. Ultimately, it is restricted to the theoretical limit of a single processor. Artificial intelligence is also burdened by the fact that experts don't always speak in rules. Yet, despite the advantages of neural networks over both expert systems and more traditional computing in these specific areas, neural nets are not complete solutions. They offer a capability that is not ironclad, such as a debugged accounting system. They learn, and as such, they do continue to make "mistakes." Furthermore, even when a network has been developed, there is no way to ensure that the network is the optimal network. Neural systems do exact their own demands. They do require their implementor to meet a number of conditions. These conditions include:

- a data set which includes the information which can characterize the problem.
- an adequately sized data set to both train and test the network.
- an understanding of the basic nature of the problem to be solved so that basic first-cut decision on creating the network can be made. These decisions include the activization and transfer functions, and the learning methods.
- an understanding of the development tools.
- adequate processing power (some applications demand real-time processing that exceeds what is available in the standard, sequential processing hardware. The development of hardware is the key to the future of neural networks).

Once these conditions are met, neural networks offer the opportunity of solving problems in an arena where traditional processors lack both the processing power and a step-by-step methodology. A number of very complicated problems cannot be solved in the traditional computing environments. For example, speech is something that all people can easily parse and understand. A person can understand a southern drawl, a Bronx accent, and the slurred words of a baby. Without the massively paralleled processing power of a neural network, this process is virtually impossible for a computer. Image recognition is another task that a human can easily do but which stymies even the biggest of computers. A person can recognize a plane as it turns, flies overhead, and disappears into a dot. A traditional computer might try to compare the changing images to a number of very different stored patterns.

This new way of computing requires skills beyond traditional computing. It is a natural evolution. Initially, computing was only hardware and engineers made it work. Then, there were software specialists - programmers, systems engineers, data base specialists, and designers. Now, there are also neural architects. This new professional needs to be skilled different than his predecessors of the past. For instance, he will need to know statistics in order to choose and evaluate training and testing situations. This skill of making neural networks work is one that will stress the logical thinking of current software engineers.

In summary, neural networks offer a unique way to solve some problems while making their own demands. The biggest demand is that the process is not simply logic. It involves an empirical skill, an intuitive feel as to how a network might be created.

1.12 NEURAL NETWORKS IN PRACTICE

Given this description of neural networks and how they work, what real world applications are they suited for? Neural networks have broad applicability to real world business problems. In fact, they have already been successfully applied in many industries.

Since neural networks are best at identifying patterns or trends in data, they are well suited for prediction or forecasting needs including:

1. Sales forecasting
2. Industrial process control
3. Customer research
4. Data validation

5. Risk management
6. Target marketing

But to give you some more specific examples; ANN are also used in the following specific paradigms: recognition of speakers in communications; diagnosis of hepatitis; recovery of telecommunications from faulty software; interpretation of multimeaning Chinese words; undersea mine detection; texture analysis; three-dimensional object recognition; handwritten word recognition; and facial recognition.

1.13 APPLICATIONS OF NEURAL NETWORKS

The *1988 DARPA Neural Network Study* [DARP88] lists various neural network applications, beginning in about 1984 with the adaptive channel equalizer. This device, which is an outstanding commercial success, is a single- neuron network used in long-distance telephone systems to stabilize voice signals. The DARPA report goes on to list other commercial applications, including a small word recognizer, a process monitor, a sonar classifier, and a risk analysis system.

Neural networks have been applied in many other fields since the DARPA report was written, as described in the next table.

Industry	Business Applications
Aerospace	High-performance aircraft autopilot, flight path simulation, aircraft control systems, autopilot enhancements, aircraft component simulation, and aircraft component fault detection
Automotive	Automobile automatic guidance system, and warranty activity analysis
Banking	Check and other document reading and credit application evaluation
Industry	Business Applications
Defense	Weapon steering, target tracking, object discrimination, facial recognition, new kinds of sensors, sonar, radar and image signal processing including data compression, feature extraction and noise suppression, and signal/image identification
Electronics	Code sequence prediction, integrated circuit chip layout, process control, chip failure analysis, machine vision, voice synthesis, and nonlinear modeling
Entertainment	Animation, special effects, and market forecasting

Financial	Real estate appraisal, loan advising, mortgage screening, corporate bond rating, credit-line use analysis, credit card activity tracking, portfolio trading program, corporate financial analysis, and currency price prediction
Industrial	Prediction of industrial processes, such as the output gases of furnaces, replacing complex and costly equipment used for this purpose in the past
Insurance	Policy application evaluation and product optimization
Manufacturing	Manufacturing process control, product design and analysis, process and machine diagnosis, real-time particle identification, visual quality inspection systems, beer testing, welding quality analysis, paper quality prediction, computer-chip quality analysis, analysis of grinding operations, chemical product design analysis, machine maintenance analysis, project bidding, planning and management, and dynamic modeling of chemical process system

Industry	Business Applications
Medical	Breast cancer cell analysis, EEG and ECG analysis, prosthesis design, optimization of transplant times, hospital expense reduction, hospital quality improvement, and emergency-room test advisement
Oil and gas	Exploration
Robotics	Trajectory control, forklift robot, manipulator controllers, and vision systems
Speech	Speech recognition, speech compression, vowel classification, and text-to-speech synthesis
Securities	Market analysis, automatic bond rating, and stock trading advisory systems
Telecommunications	Image and data compression, automated information services, real-time translation of spoken language, and customer payment processing systems
Transportation	Truck brake diagnosis systems, vehicle scheduling, and routing systems

1.13.1. PATTERN RECOGNITION

The act of recognition can be divided into two broad categories: recognizing concrete items and recognizing abstract items. The recognition of concrete items involves the recognition of spatial and temporal items. Examples of spatial items are fingerprints, weather maps, pictures and physical objects. Examples of temporal items are waveforms and signatures. Recognition of abstract items involves the recognition of a solution to a problem, an old conversation or argument, etc. In other words, recognizing items that do not exist physically.

In this article, I am concerned with recognition of concrete items. Applications include finger print identification, voice recognition, face recognition, character recognition, signature recognition and classification of objects in scientific/research areas such as astronomy, engineering, statistics, medical, machine learning and neural networks. Recognition of an item involves three levels of processing: input filtering, feature extraction and classification

- **Filtering** is removing unwanted information or data from input. Depending on the application, the filter algorithm or method will change. For example, consider finger print identification. Each time we scan our fingerprints through a (non-ink) fingerprint device, the scanned output may be different. The difference may be due to a change in contrast or brightness or in the background of the image. There could be some distortion. In order to process the input, we may need only lines in the fingerprints and we may not need the other parts or background of the fingerprint. In order to filter out the unwanted portion of the image and replace it with a white background, we need a filter mechanism. Once the image is filtered through the filter mechanism, we will get standard clean finger prints only with lines, which in turn helps with the process of feature extraction.
- **Feature extraction** is a process of studying and deriving useful information from the filtered input patterns. The derived information may be general features, which are evaluated to ease further processing. For example, in image recognition, the extracted features will contain information about gray shade, texture, shape or context of the image. This is the main information used in image processing. The methods of feature extraction and the extracted features are application dependent.
- **Classification** is the final stage of the pattern recognition. This is the stage where an automated system declares that the inputted object belongs to a particular category. There are many classification methods in the field. Classification method designs are based on the following concepts.

1.13.2 MORE USEFUL APPLICATIONS:

- **Member-roster concept:** Under this template-matching concept, a set of patterns belonging to a same pattern is stored in a classification system. When an unknown pattern is given as input, it is compared with existing patterns and placed under the matching pattern class.
- **Common property concept:** In this concept, the common properties of patterns are stored in a classification system. When an unknown pattern comes inside, the system checks its extracted common property against the common properties of existing classes and places the pattern/object under a class, which has similar, common properties.
- **Clustering concept:** Here, the patterns of the targeted classes are represented in vectors whose components are real numbers. So, using its clustering properties, we can easily classify the unknown pattern. If the target vectors are far apart in geometrical arrangement, it is easy to classify the unknown patterns. If they are nearby or if there is any overlap in the cluster arrangement, we need more complex algorithms to classify the unknown patterns. One simple algorithm based on the clustering concept is Minimum

Distance Classification. This method computes the distance between the unknown pattern and the desired set of known patterns and determines which known pattern is closest to the unknown and, finally, the unknown pattern is placed under the known pattern to which it has minimum distance. This algorithm works well when the target patterns are far apart.

- **Detection of medical phenomena:** A variety of health-related indices (e.g., a combination of heart rate, levels of various substances in the blood, respiration rate) can be monitored. The onset of a particular medical condition could be associated with a very complex (e.g., nonlinear and interactive) combination of changes on a subset of the variables being monitored. Neural networks have been used to recognize this predictive pattern so that the appropriate treatment can be prescribed.
- **Stock market prediction:** Fluctuations of stock prices and stock indices are another example of a complex, multidimensional, but in some circumstances at least partially-deterministic phenomenon. Neural networks are being used by many technical analysts to make predictions about stock prices based upon a large number of factors such as past performance of other stocks and various economic indicators.
- **Credit assignment:** A variety of pieces of information are usually known about an applicant for a loan. For instance, the applicant's age, education, occupation, and many other facts may be available. After training a neural network on historical data, neural network analysis can identify the most relevant characteristics and use those to classify applicants as good or bad credit risks.
- **Monitoring the condition of machinery:** Neural networks can be instrumental in cutting costs by bringing additional expertise to scheduling the preventive maintenance of machines. A neural network can be trained to distinguish between the sounds a machine makes when it is running normally ("false alarms") versus when it is on the verge of a problem. After this training period, the expertise of the network can be used to warn a technician of an upcoming breakdown, before it occurs and causes costly unforeseen "downtime."
- **Engine management:** Neural networks have been used to analyze the input of sensors from an engine. The neural network controls the various parameters within which the engine functions, in order to achieve a particular goal, such as minimizing fuel consumption.
- **Character Recognition:** The idea of character recognition has become very important as handheld devices like the Palm Pilot are becoming increasingly popular. Neural networks can be used to recognize handwritten characters.
- **Image Compression:** Neural networks can receive and process vast amounts of information at once, making them useful in image compression. With the Internet explosion and more sites using more images on their sites, using neural networks for image compression is worth a look.
- **Traveling Saleman's Problem:** Interestingly enough, neural networks can solve the traveling salesman problem, but only to a certain degree of approximation.
- **Neural Networks in Medicine:** Neural networks are being used increasingly in the field

of medicine. They are particularly well suited to problems with a high degree of complexity for which there is no algorithmic solution or the solution is too complex for traditional techniques to determine. Medical areas that have seen the successful implementation of this technology include drug development, patient diagnosis, and image analysis. Two major cornerstones are the detection of coronary artery disease and the processing of EEG signals.

- **NeuroXL Predictor and Classifier:** NeuroXL Predictor and Classifier are both add-ins to Microsoft Excel that harness the power of artificial intelligence for forecasting and classification tasks. They both have easy-to-use interfaces that hide the underlying complexity of the networks, so the time between installing the product and performing useful classifications and predictions is short.
- **Advanced Technology for Forecasting and Classification:** Neural networks are a well-established technology for solving prediction and classification problems, using training and testing data to build a model. The data involves historical data sets containing input variables, or data fields, which correspond to an output. The network uses the training data to "learn" the solution to the problem by example. Since the network learns in this way, no complex models need to be created. Also, it is not necessary for your data to be complete or show a clear trend - neural networks can still converge to a solution under these conditions. Because they are modeled after the human brain, these networks are well suited to problems that people are good at solving but computers are not. These problems include pattern recognition and forecasting (which requires the recognition of trends in data). However, unlike humans, these networks are not affected by factors such as fatigue, emotional state, and working conditions.

1.14 THE FIRST ARTIFICIAL NEURON

Much of this section is taken from (Fausett, 1994). As mentioned in the research history McCulloch and Pitts (1943) produced the first neural network, which was based on their artificial neuron. Although this work was developed in the early forties, many of the principles can still be seen in the neural networks of today.

We can make the following statements about a McCulloch-Pitts network

- The activation of a neuron is binary. That is, the neuron either fires (activation of one) or does not fire (activation of zero).
  For the network shown below the activation function for unit Y is

  $f(y\_in) = 1$, if $y\_in >= t$ else 0

where *y_in* is the total input signal received *t* is the threshold for Y.

- Neurons is a McCulloch-Pitts network are connected by directed, weighted paths.
- If the weight on a path is positive the path is excitatory, otherwise it is inhibitory.
- All excitatory connections into a particular neuron have the same weight, although different weighted connections can be input to different neurons.
- Each neuron has a fixed threshold. If the net input into the neuron is greater than the threshold, the neuron fires.

- The threshold is set such that any non-zero inhibitory input will prevent the neuron from firing.
- It takes one time step for a signal to pass over one connection.

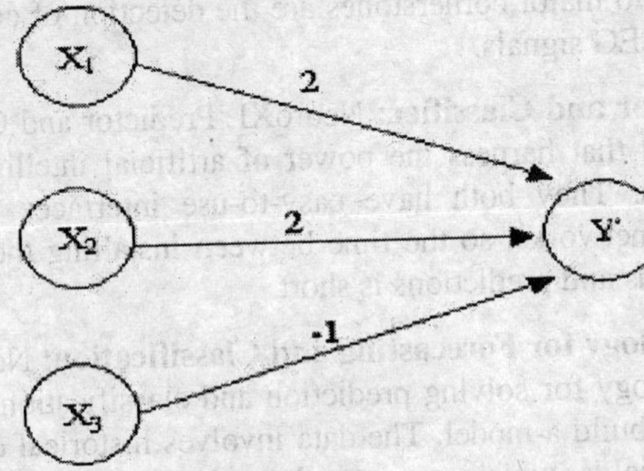

Figure 1.9 Mcculloch And Pitts Model

A sample McCulloch-Pitts network is shown above and some of the statements can be observed. In particular, note that the threshold for Y has equal 4 as this is the only value that allows it to fire, taking into account that a neuron cannot fire if it receives a nonzero inhibitory input. Using the McCulloch-Pitts model we can model logic functions. Below we show and describe the architecture for four logic functions (the truth tables for each function is also shown)

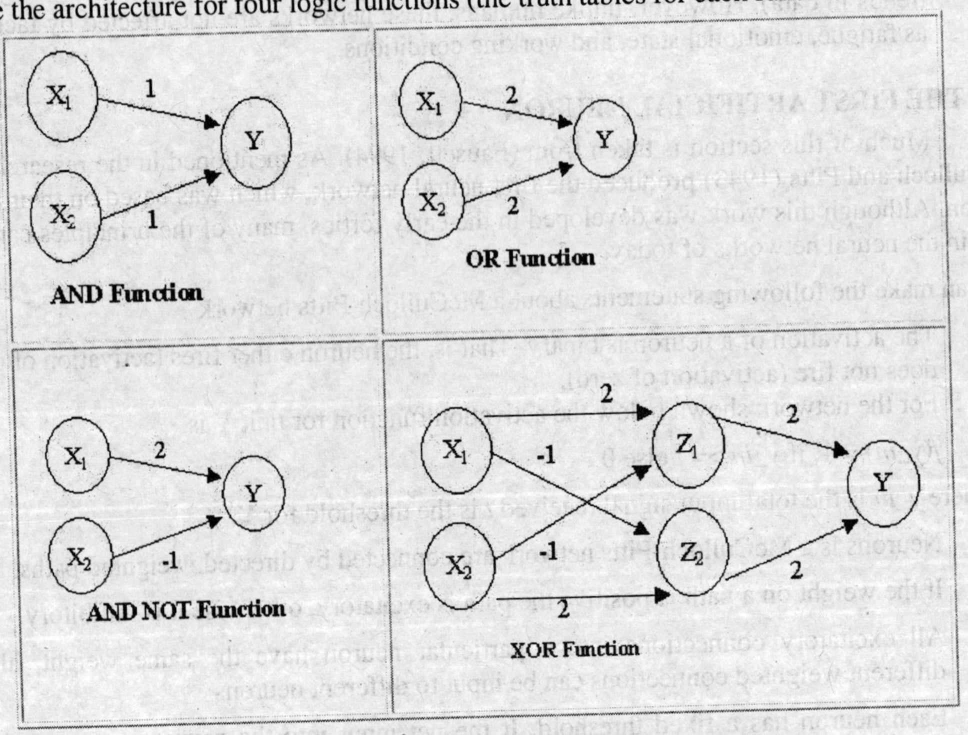

Figure 1.10 Architecture For Four Logic Functions

AND		
X_1	X_2	Y
1	1	1
1	0	0
0	1	0
0	0	0

OR		
X_1	X_2	Y
1	1	1
1	0	1
0	1	1
0	0	0

AND NOT		
X_1	X_2	Y
1	1	0
1	0	1
0	1	0
0	0	0

XOR		
X_1	X_2	Y
1	1	0
1	0	1
0	1	1
0	0	0

Figure 1.11 The Truth Tables For Each Function

1.14.1 AND FUNCTION

As both inputs (X_1 and X_2) are connected to the same neuron the connections must be the same, in this case 1. To model the AND function the threshold on Y is set to 2.

1.14.2 OR FUNCTION

This is almost identical to the AND function except the connections are set to 2 and the threshold on Y is also set to 2.

1.14.3 AND NOT FUNCTION

Although the truth table for the AND NOT function is shown above it deserves just a small explanation as it is not often seen in the textbooks. The function is not symmetric in that an input of 1,0 is treated differently to an input of 0,1. As you can see from the truth table the only time true (value of one) is returned is when the first input is true and the second input is false. Again, the threshold on Y is set to 2 and if you apply each of the inputs to the AND NOT network you will find that we have modeled X_1 AND NOT X_2.

1.14.4 XOR FUNCTION

XOR can be modeled using AND NOT and OR;

X_1 XOR X_2 = (X_1 AND NOT X_2) OR (X_2 AND NOT X_1)

(To prove it draw the truth table)

This explains the network shown above. The first layer performs the two AND NOT's and the second layer performs the OR. Both Z neurons and the Y neuron have a threshold of 2.As a final example of a McCulloch-Pitts network we will consider how to model the phenomenon that if you touch something very cold you initially perceive heat. Only after you have left your hand on the cold source for a while do you perceive cold. This example (from Fausett, 1994) is an elaboration of one originally presented by (McCulloch and Pitts, 1943). To model this we will assume that time is discrete. If cold is applied for one time step then heat will be perceived. If a cold stimulus is applied for two time steps then cold will be perceived. If heat is applied then we should perceive heat.

Take a look at this figure. Each neuron has a threshold of 2. This, as we shall see, allows us to model this phenomenon.

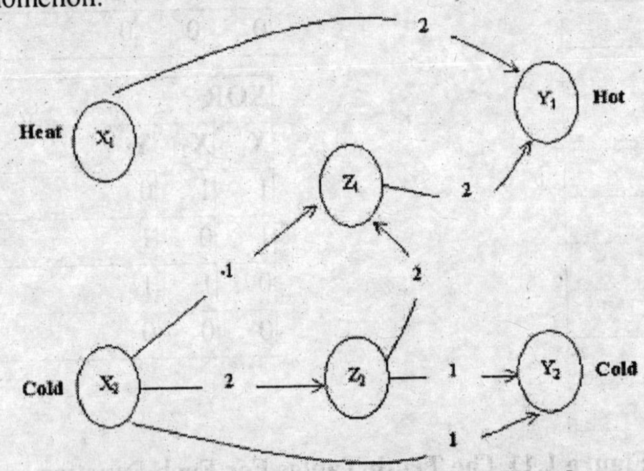

Figure 1.12 Neuron Model Having Weights

First though, remember that time is discrete, so it takes time for the stimulus (applied at X_1 and X_2) to make its way to Y_1 and Y_2 where we perceive either heat or cold.
Therefore, at t(0), we apply a stimulus to X_1 and X_2.
At t(1) we can update Z_1, Z_2 and Y_1.
At t(2) we can perceive a stimulus at Y_2.
At t(2+n) the network is fully functional.

Before we see if the network performs as we hope let's consider what we are trying to do. Input to the system will be (1,0) or (0,1), which represents hot and cold respectively. We want the system to perceive cold if a cold stimulus is applied for two time steps. That is

$Y_2(t) = X_2(t - 2)$ **AND** $X_2(t - 1)$ (formula 1)

This truth table (i.e. the truth table for AND) shows that this model is correct

$X_2(t - 2)$	$X_2(t - 1)$	$Y_2(t)$
1	1	1
1	0	0
0	1	0
0	0	0

Figure 1.13 Truth Table For AND

We want the system to perceive heat if either a hot stimulus is applied or a cold stimulus is applied (for one time step) and then removed. We can express this as follows

$Y_1(t) = [\ X_1(t - 1)\ ]$ **OR** $[\ X_2(t - 3)$ **AND NOT** $X_2(t - 2)\ ]$ (formula 2)

This truth table shows that it gives us the required result

X2(t-3)	X2(t-2)	AND NOT	X1(t-1)	OR
1	1	0	1	1
1	0	1	1	1
0	1	0	1	1
0	0	0	1	1
1	1	0	0	0
1	0	1	0	1
0	1	0	0	0
0	0	0	0	0

Figure 1.14 Truth Table For AND NOT and OR

The way to read this table is to firstly consider the first three columns. This gives the result (in the AND NOT column) of the AND NOT expression in the formula. This result is then OR'ed with the $X_1(t-1)$ to give the final column in the table, which is the result of the entire expression. You can see that if we apply heat (i.e. $X_1(t-1)$) then we always perceive heat as the output. If we apply cold for one time step (i.e. the row in red) we also perceive heat as the output.

So, if we are convinced that we have the correct logical statements to represent the hot/cold problem, we now need to convince ourselves that the network above represents the logical statements.

The figure of the network shows that

$Y_1(t) = X_1(t - 1)$ **OR** $Z_1(t - 1)$ (formula 3)

(compare this to the OR network we developed earlier).

Now consider the Z_1 neuron. This is how it is formed

$Z_1(t - 1) = Z_2(t - 2)$ **AND NOT** $X_2(t - 2)$ (formula 4)

(again, compare this to the AND NOT network above).

Now Z_2, this is simply

$Z_2(t - 2) = X_2(t - 3)$ (formula 5)

If we take formula 3, and substitute in formula 4 and 5 we end up with

$Y_1(t) = [X_1(t - 1)]$ **OR** $[X_2(t - 3)$ **AND NOT** $X_2(t - 2)]$ (formula 6)

which is the same as formula 2, showing that our network (*Y1* anyway) works correctly (as we have proved formula 2 works using a full analysis by using the truth table). We can perform a similar analysis for Y_2, and show that Y_2 in the network acts in the way we developed above (formula 1). You should do this to convince yourself that this is correct.

1.14.5 MODELLING A NEURON

To model the brain we need to model a neuron. Each neuron performs a simple computation. It receives signals from its input links and it uses these values to compute the activation level (or output) for the neuron. This value is passed to other neurons via its output links. The input value received of a neuron is calculated by summing the weighted input values from its input links. That is

$$in_i = \sum_j W_{j,i} a_j$$

An activation function takes the neuron input value and produces a value which becomes the output value of the neuron. This value is passed to other neurons in the network. This is summarised in this diagram and the notes below.

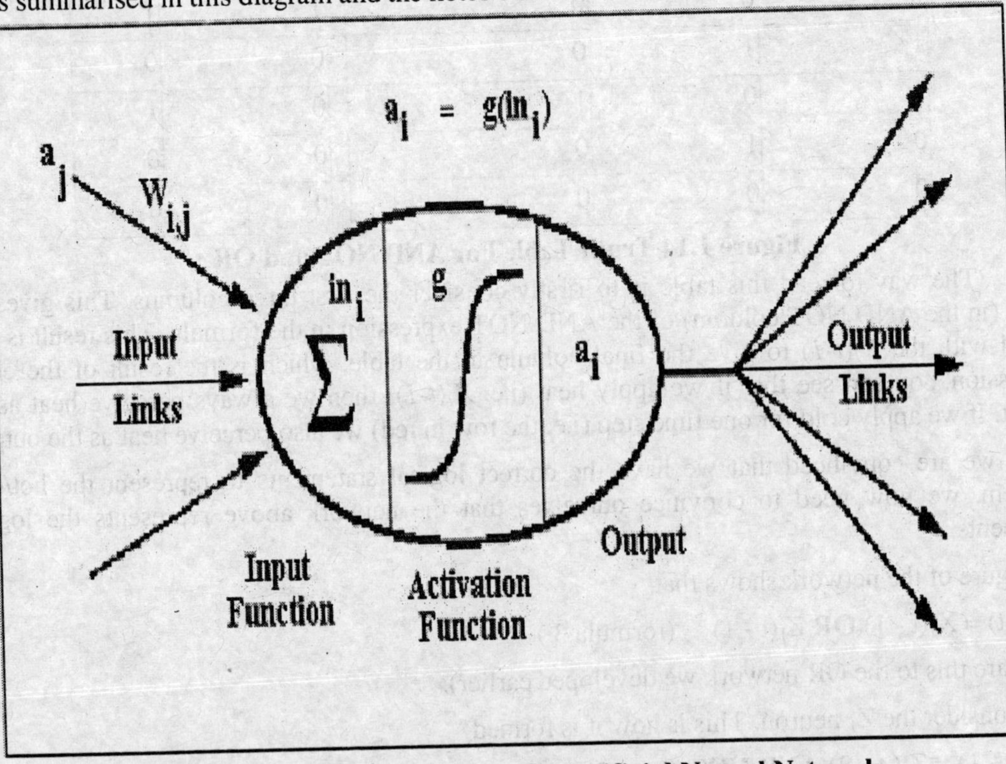

Figure 1.15 Labelled Diagram Of Artificial Neural Network

a_j : Activation value of unit j

$w_{j,i}$: Weight on the link from unit j to unit i

in_i : Weighted sum of inputs to unit i

a_i : Activation value of unit i (also known as the output value)

g : Activation function

A neuron is connected to other neurons via its input and output links. Each incoming neuron has an activation value and each connection has a weight associated with it. The neuron sums the incoming weighted values and this value is input to an activation function. The output of the activation function is the output from the neuron. Some common activation functions are shown below.

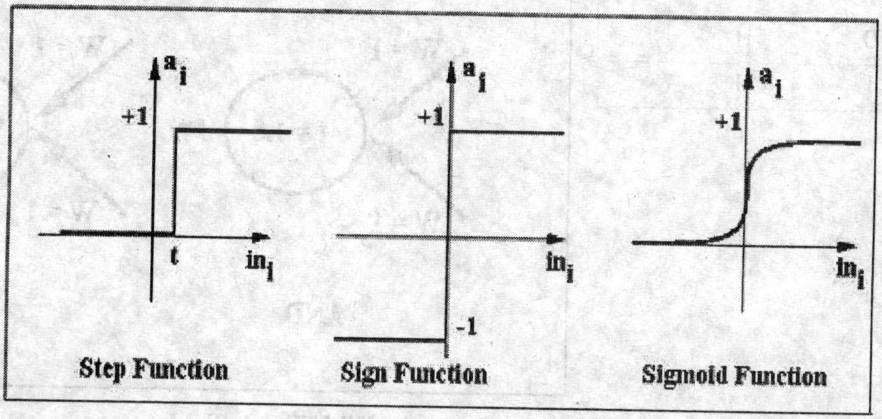

Figure 1.16 Activation Functions

These functions can be defined as follows.

$Step_t(x)$ = 1 if x >= t, else 0
Sign(x) = +1 if x >= 0, else -1
Sigmoid(x) = $1/(1+e^{-x})$

On occasions an identify function is also used (i.e. where the input to the neuron becomes the output). This function is normally used in the input layer where the inputs to the neural network are passed into the network unchanged.

1.14.6 SOME SIMPLE NETWORKS

We can use what we have learnt above to demonstrate a simple neural network which acts as a logic gate. The diagram below is modelling the following truth tables

AND		
$Input_1$	**$Input_2$**	**Output**
0	0	0
0	1	0
1	0	0
1	1	1

NOT		
Input		**Output**
0		1
1		0

OR		
$Input_1$	**$Input_2$**	**Output**
0	0	0
0	1	1
1	0	1
1	1	1

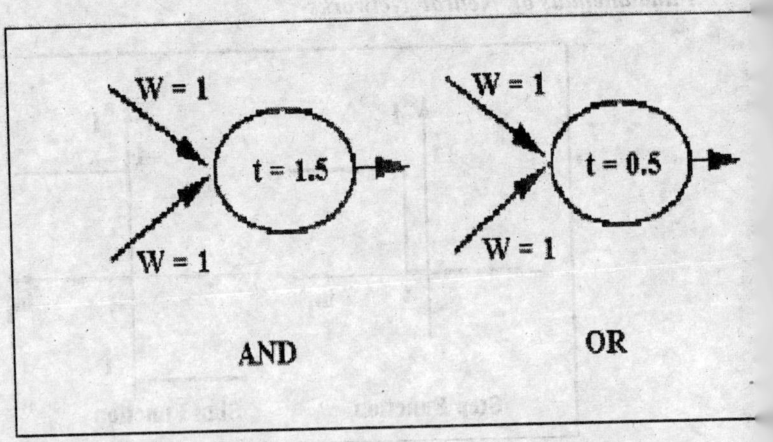

Figure 1.17 Simple Networks With Truth Tables

In these networks we are using the step activation function.

You should convince yourself that these networks produce the correct output for all the allowed inputs. You will notice that each neuron has a different threshold. From a computational viewpoint it would be easier if all the neurons had the same threshold value and the actual threshold was somehow modelled by the weights.

In fact, it is possible to do exactly this. Consider this network

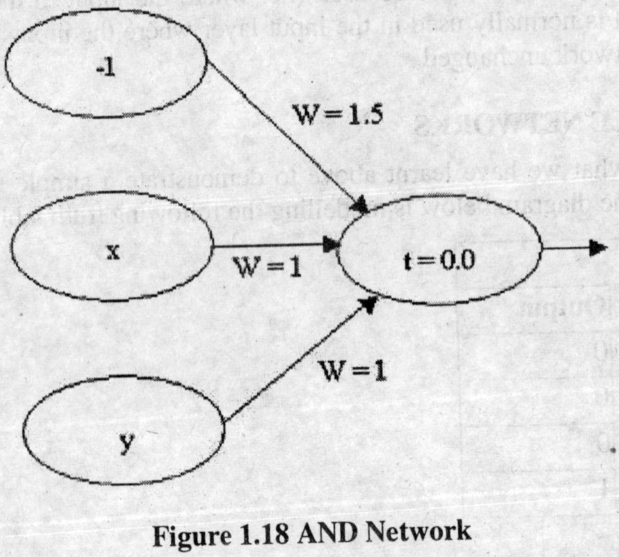

Figure 1.18 AND Network

It is the same as the AND network in the diagram above except that there is an extra input neuron whose activation is always set to -1. The threshold of the neuron is represented by the weight that links this extra neuron to the output neuron.This means the threshold of the neuron can be set to zero. You might like to work through this network using the four possible combinations of x and y and convince yourself that the network operates correctly.This advantage of this method is that we can always set the threshold for every neuron to zero and from a computational point of view, when "training" the network, we only have to update weights and not both thresholds and weights.

1.15 ELEMENTS OF ARTIFICIAL NEURAL NETWORKS

An artificial neuron as shown in Figure 1.19, is the basic element of a neural network.It consists of three basic components that include weights, thresholds, and a single activation function .

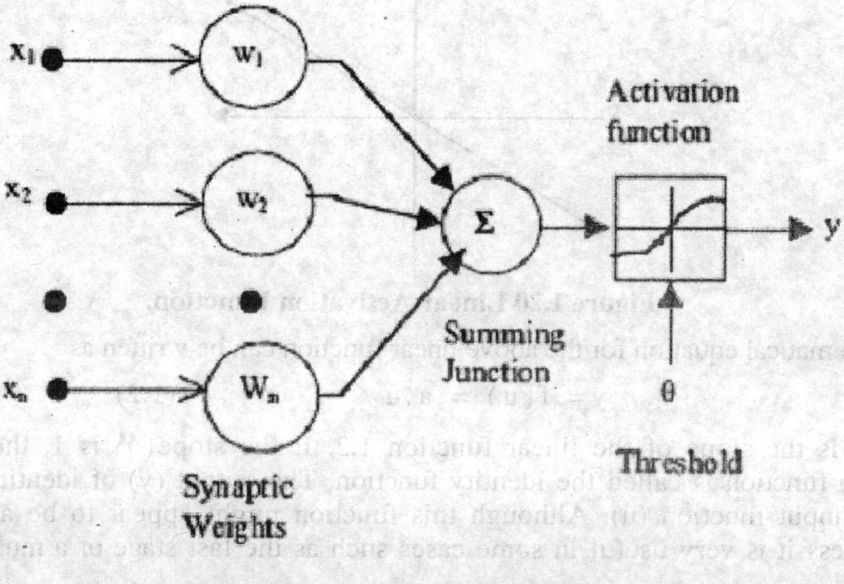

Figure 1.19 Basic Elements of an Artificial Neuron .

1.15.1 WEIGHTING FACTORS

The values W1 ,W2 ,W3 ,.....,W_n are weight factors associated with each node to determine the strength of input row vector $X = [x1\ x2\ x3.....,x_n]^T$. Each input is multiplied by the associated weight of the neuron connection X^TW. Depending upon the activation function, if the weight is positive, X^TW commonly excites the node output; whereas, for negative weights, X^TW tends to inhibit the node output.

1.15.2 THRESHOLD

The node's internal threshold θ is the magnitude offset that affects the activation of the node output y as follows:

$$y = \sum_{i=1}^{n} (X_i W_i) - \theta \qquad (1.1)$$

1.15.3 ACTIVATION FUNCTION

In this subsection, five of the most common activation functions are presented. An activation function performs a mathematical operation on the signal output. More sophisticated activation functions can also be utilized depending upon the type of problem to be solved by the network.

1.15.3.1 LINEAR FUNCTION

As is known, a linear function satisfies the superposition concept. The function is shown in Figure 1.20.

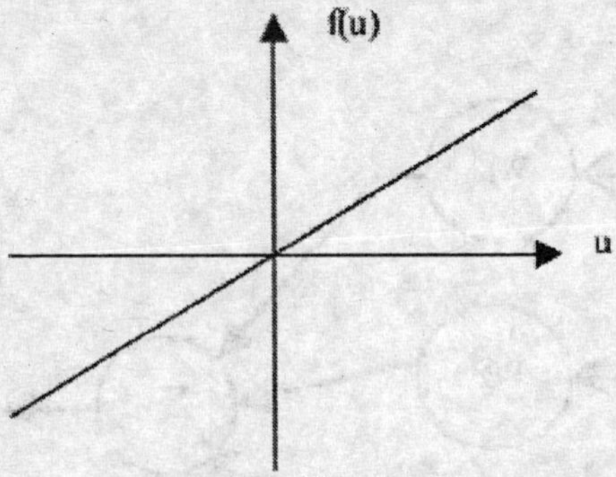

Figure 1.20 Linear Activation Function.

The mathematical equation for the above linear function can be written as

$$y = f(u) = a.u \tag{1.2}$$

where α is the slope of the linear function 1.2. If the slope α is 1, then the linear activation function is called the identity function. The output (y) of identity function is equal to input function (u). Although this function might appear to be a trivial case, nevertheless it is very useful in some cases such as the last stage of a multilayer neural network.

1.15.3.2 THRESHOLD FUNCTION

A threshold (hard-limiter) activation function is either a *binary* type or a *bipolar* type as shown in Figures 1.21 and 1.22, respectively. The output of a *binary* threshold function can be written as:

$$y = f(u) = \begin{cases} 0 \text{ if } u < 0 \\ 1 \text{ if } u \geq 0 \end{cases}$$

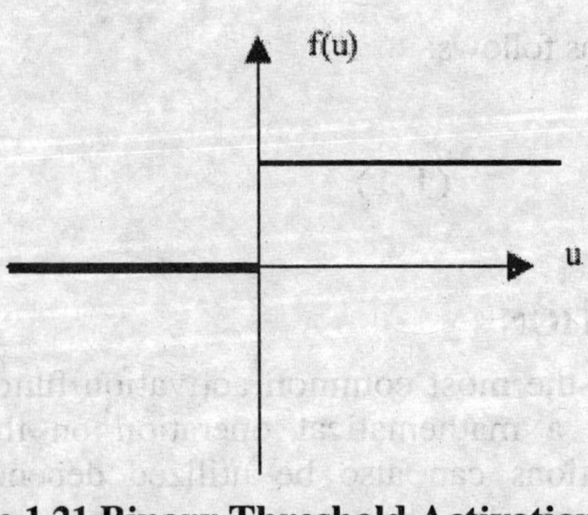

Figure 1.21 Binary Threshold Activation Function

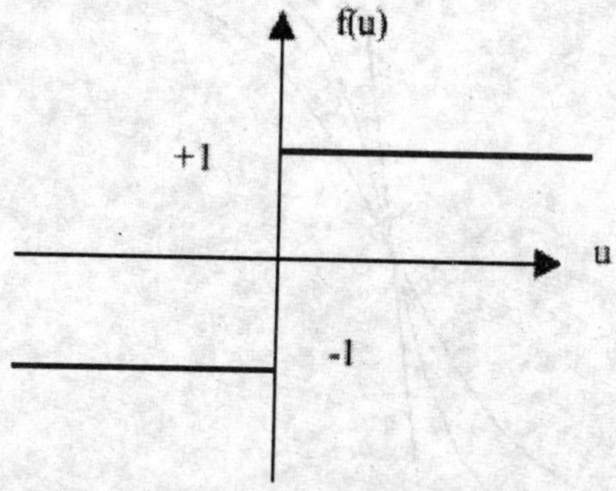

Figure 1.22 Bipolar Threshold Activation Function.

The neuron with the hard limiter activation function is referred to as the McCulloch-Pitts model.

1.15.3.3 PIECEWISE LINEAR FUNCTION

This type of activation function is also referred to as saturating linear function and can have either a binary or bipolar range for the saturation limits of the output. The mathematical model for a symmetric saturation function (Figure 1.23) is described as follows:

$$y = f(u) = \begin{cases} -1 & \text{if } u < -1 \\ u & \text{if } -1 \geq u \geq 1 \\ 1 & \text{if } u \geq 1 \end{cases}$$

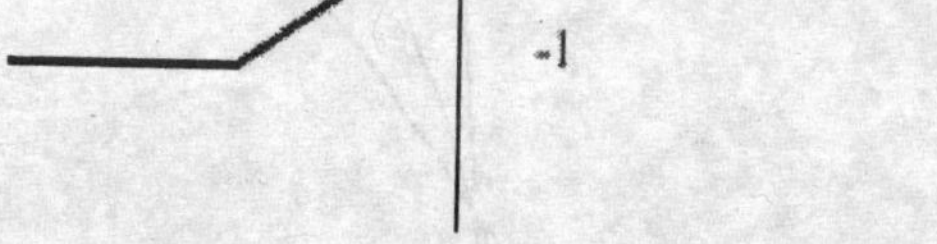

Figure 1.23 Piecewise Linear Activation Function.

1.15.3.4 SIGMOIDAL (S SHAPED) FUNCTION

This nonlinear function is the most common type of the activation used to construct the neural networks. It is mathematically well behaved, differentiable and strictly increasing function. A sigmoidal transfer function can be written in the following form:

$$f(x) = \frac{1}{1 + e^{-ax}}, \quad 0 \leq f(x) \leq 1$$

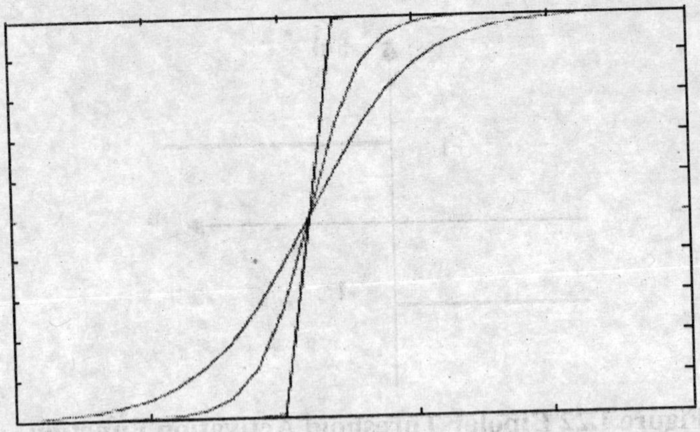

Figure 1.24 A Sigmoid Activation Function.

where α is the shape parameter of the sigmoid function. By varying this parameter, different shapes of the function can be obtained as illustrated in Figure 1.24. This function is continuous and differentiable.

1.15.3.5 TANGENT HYPERBOLIC FUNCTION

This transfer function is described by the following mathematical form:

$$f(x) = \frac{e^{\alpha x} - e^{-\alpha x}}{e^{\alpha x} + e^{-\alpha x}} \qquad -1 \le f(x) \le 1$$

It is interesting to note that the derivatives of Equations 2.5 and 2.6 can be expressed in terms of the individual function itself (please see problems appendix). This is important for the learning development rules to train the networks as shown in the next chapter.

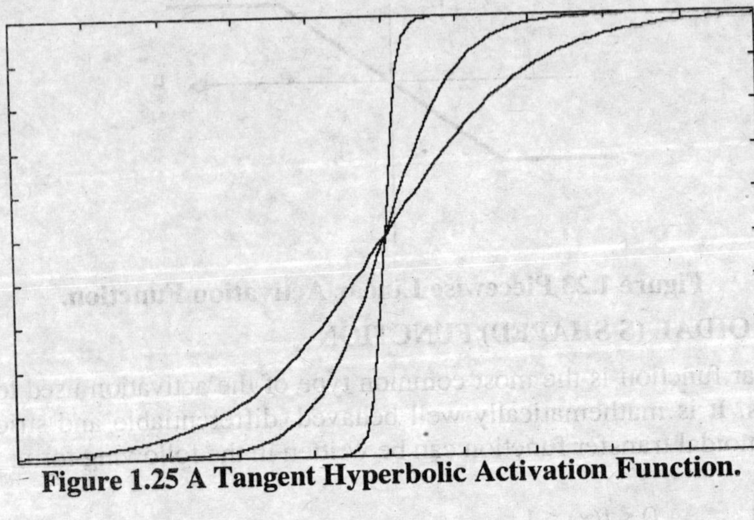

Figure 1.25 A Tangent Hyperbolic Activation Function.

Example 1.1:

Consider the following network consists of four inputs with the weights as shown

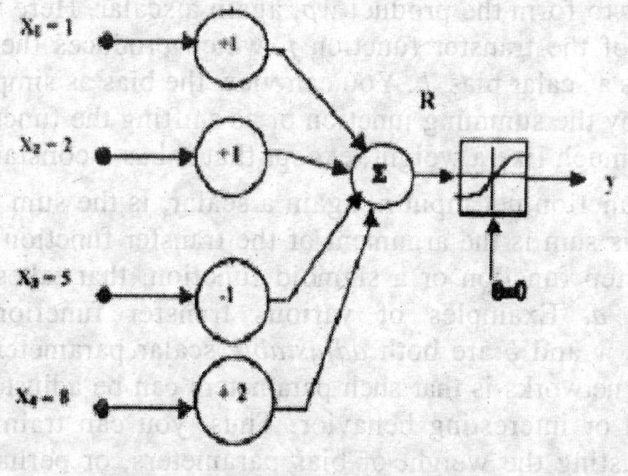

Figure 1.26 Neuron Structure

The output R of the network, prior to the activation function stage, is calculated as follows:

$$R = W^T.X = \begin{bmatrix} 1 & 1 & -1 & 2 \end{bmatrix} \begin{bmatrix} 1 \\ 2 \\ 5 \\ 8 \end{bmatrix} = 14$$

With a binary activation function, and a sigmoid function, the outputs of the neuron are respectively as follow:

y(*Threshold*) = 1;

y(*Sigmoid*) = $1.5*2^{-8}$

1.16 ARCHITECTURE OF ARTIFICIAL NEURAL NETWORK

1.16.1 SIMPLE NEURON

A neuron with a single scalar input and no bias appears on the left below.

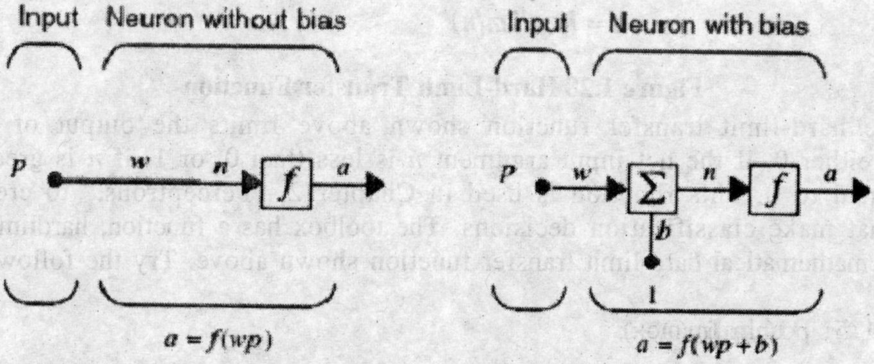

Figure 1.27 Simple Neuron

The scalar input *p* is transmitted through a connection that multiplies its strength by the scalar weight *w* to form the product *wp*, again a scalar. Here the weighted input *wp* is the only argument of the transfer function *f*, which produces the scalar output *a*. The neuron on the right has a scalar bias, *b*. You can view the bias as simply being added to the product *wp* as shown by the summing junction or as shifting the function *f* to the left by an amount *b*. The bias is much like a weight, except that it has a constant input of 1.

The transfer function net input *n*, again a scalar, is the sum of the weighted input *wp* and the bias *b*. This sum is the argument of the transfer function *f*. Here *f* is a transfer function, typically a step function or a sigmoid function, that takes the argument *n* and produces the output *a*. Examples of various transfer functions are in "Transfer Functions". Note that *w* and *b* are both *adjustable* scalar parameters of the neuron. The central idea of neural networks is that such parameters can be adjusted so that the network exhibits some desired or interesting behavior. Thus, you can train the network to do a particular job by adjusting the weight or bias parameters, or perhaps the network itself will adjust these parameters to achieve some desired end.

All the neurons in the Neural Network ToolboxTM software have provision for a bias, and a bias is used in many of the examples and is assumed in most of this toolbox. However, you can omit a bias in a neuron if you want. As previously noted, the bias *b* is an adjustable (scalar) parameter of the neuron. It is *not* an input. However, the constant *1* that drives the bias is an input and must be treated as such when you consider the linear dependence of input vectors in Chapter 4, "Linear Filters."

1.16.2 TRANSFER FUNCTIONS

Many transfer functions are included the Neural Network Toolbox software. A complete list of them can be found in the reference pages. Three of the most commonly used functions are shown below.

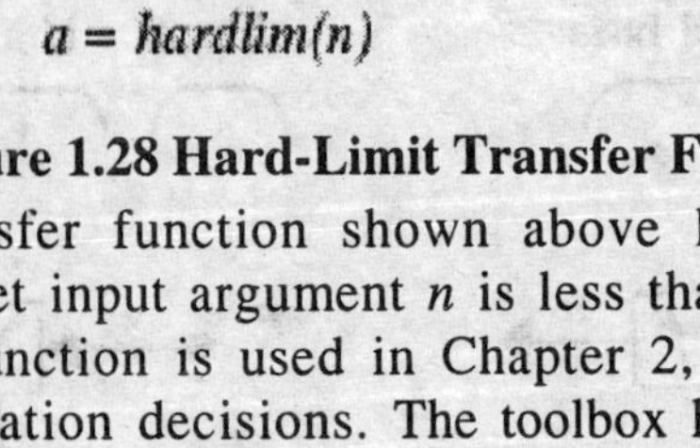

Figure 1.28 Hard-Limit Transfer Function

The hard-limit transfer function shown above limits the output of the neuron to either 0, if the net input argument *n* is less than 0, or 1, if *n* is greater than or equal to 0. This function is used in Chapter 2, "Perceptrons," to create neurons that make classification decisions. The toolbox has a function, hardlim, to realize the mathematical hard-limit transfer function shown above. Try the following code:

```
n = -5:0.1:5; plot(n,hardlim(n),'c+:');
```

It produces a plot of the function hardlim over the range -5 to +5.

All the mathematical transfer functions in the toolbox can be realized with a function having the same name.

The following figure illustrates the linear transfer function.

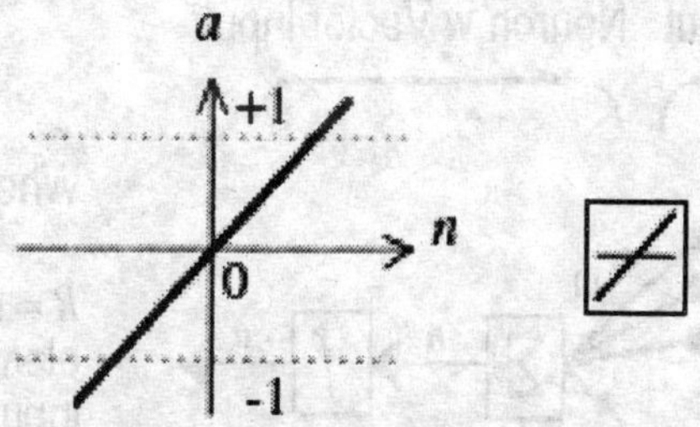

a = purelin(n)

Figure 1.29 Linear Transfer Function

Neurons of this type are used as linear approximators in Chapter 4, "Linear Filters."

The sigmoid transfer function shown below takes the input, which can have any value between plus and minus infinity, and squashes the output into the range 0 to 1.

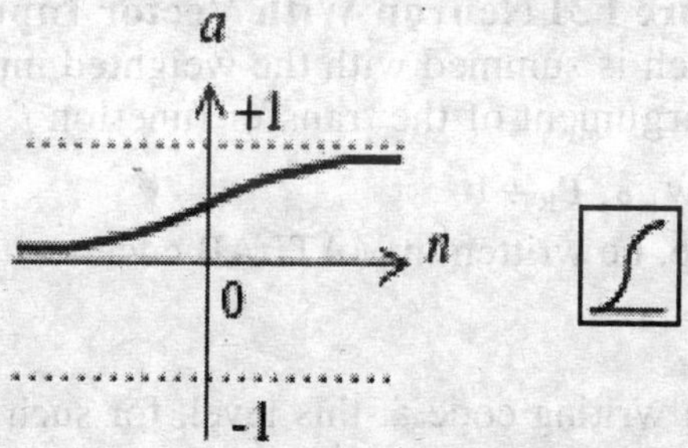

a = logsig(n)

Figure 1.30 Log-Sigmoid Transfer Function

This transfer function is commonly used in backpropagation networks, in part because it is differentiable.The symbol in the square to the right of each transfer function graph shown above represents the associated transfer function. These icons replace the general *f* in the boxes of network diagrams to show the particular transfer function being used.

For a complete listing of transfer functions and their icons, see the reference pages. You can also specify your own transfer functions.

You can experiment with a simple neuron and various transfer functions by running the demonstration program.

1.16.3 NEURON WITH VECTOR INPUT

A neuron with a single R-element input vector is shown below. Here the individual element inputs

$P_1, P_2, \ldots, P_R$

are multiplied by weights

$w_{1,1}, w_{1,2} \ldots\ldots\ldots w_{1,R}$

and the weighted values are fed to the summing junction. Their sum is simply **Wp**, the dot product of the (single row) matrix **W** and the vector **p**.

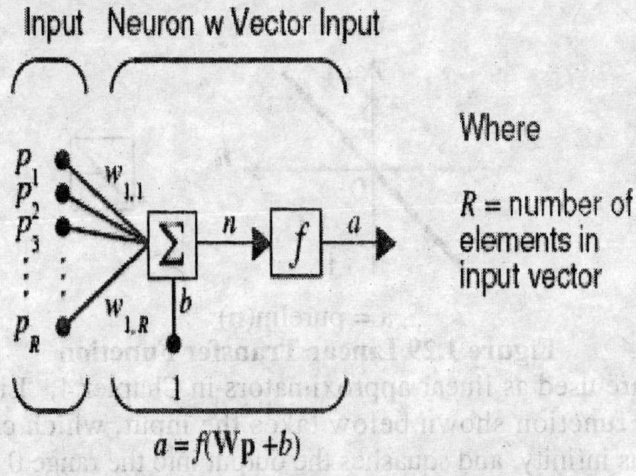

Figure 1.31 Neuron With Vector Input

The neuron has a bias *b*, which is summed with the weighted inputs to form the net input *n*. This sum, *n*, is the argument of the transfer function *f*.

$n = w_{1,1}, P_1 + w_{1,2}, P_2 \ldots\ldots\ldots w_{1,R}, P_R + b$

This expression can, of course, be written in MATLAB code as

```
n=W*p+b
```

However, you will seldom be writing code at this level, for such code is already built into functions to define and simulate entire networks.

1.16.4 ABBREVIATED NOTATION

The figure of a single neuron shown above contains a lot of detail. When you consider networks with many neurons, and perhaps layers of many neurons, there is so much detail that the main thoughts tend to be lost. Thus, the authors have devised an abbreviated notation for an individual neuron. This notation, which is used later in circuits of multiple neurons, is shown.

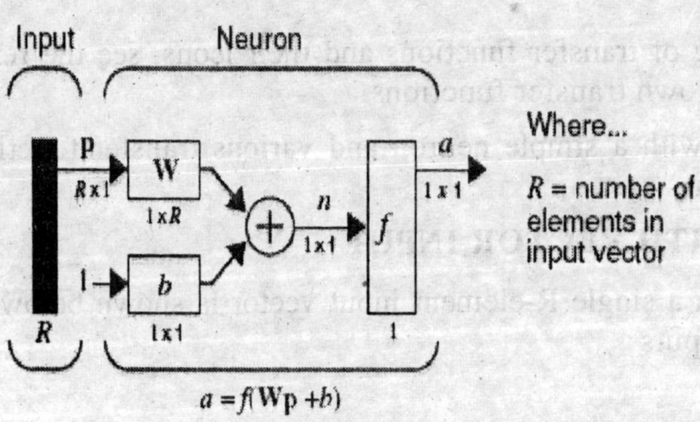

Figure 1.32 Abbreviated Notation Of Neural Network

Here the input vector **p** is represented by the solid dark vertical bar at the left. The dimensions of **p** are shown below the symbol **p** in the figure as *R*x1. (Note that a capital letter, such as *R* in the previous sentence, is used when referring to the *size* of a vector.) Thus, **p** is a vector of *R* input elements. These inputs postmultiply the single-row, *R*-column matrix **W**. As before, a constant 1 enters the neuron as an input and is multiplied by a scalar bias *b*. The net input to the transfer function *f* is *n*, the sum of the bias *b* and the product **Wp**. This sum is passed to the transfer function *f* to get the neuron's output *a*, which in this case is a scalar. Note that if there were more than one neuron, the network output would be a vector.

A *layer* of a network is defined in the previous figure. A layer includes the combination of the weights, the multiplication and summing operation (here realized as a vector product **Wp**), the bias *b*, and the transfer function *f*. The array of inputs, vector **p**, is not included in or called a layer.

Each time this abbreviated network notation is used, the sizes of the matrices are shown just below their matrix variable names. This notation will allow you to understand the architectures and follow the matrix mathematics associated with them.

As discussed in "Transfer Functions", when a specific transfer function is to be used in a figure, the symbol for that transfer function replaces the *f* shown above. Here are some examples.

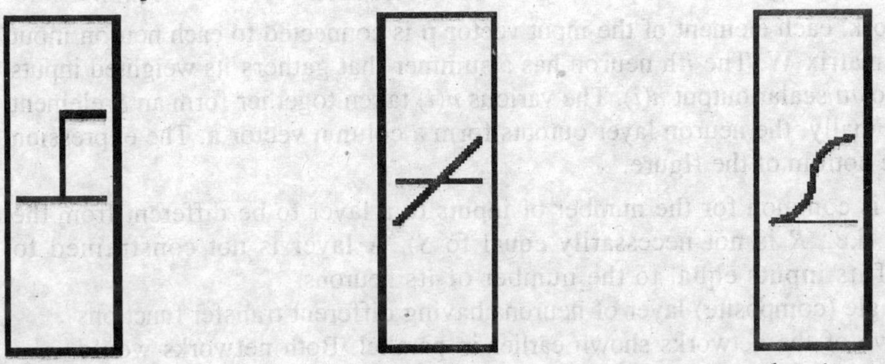

Hardlim *purelin* *logsig*

Figure 1.33 Transfer Functions

You can experiment with a two-element neuron by running the demonstration program.

1.17 NETWORK ARCHITECTURES

Two or more of the neurons shown earlier can be combined in a layer, and a particular network could contain one or more such layers. First consider a single layer of neurons.

1.17.1 A LAYER OF NEURONS

A one-layer network with *R* input elements and *S* neurons follows. Inputs Layer

of Neurons

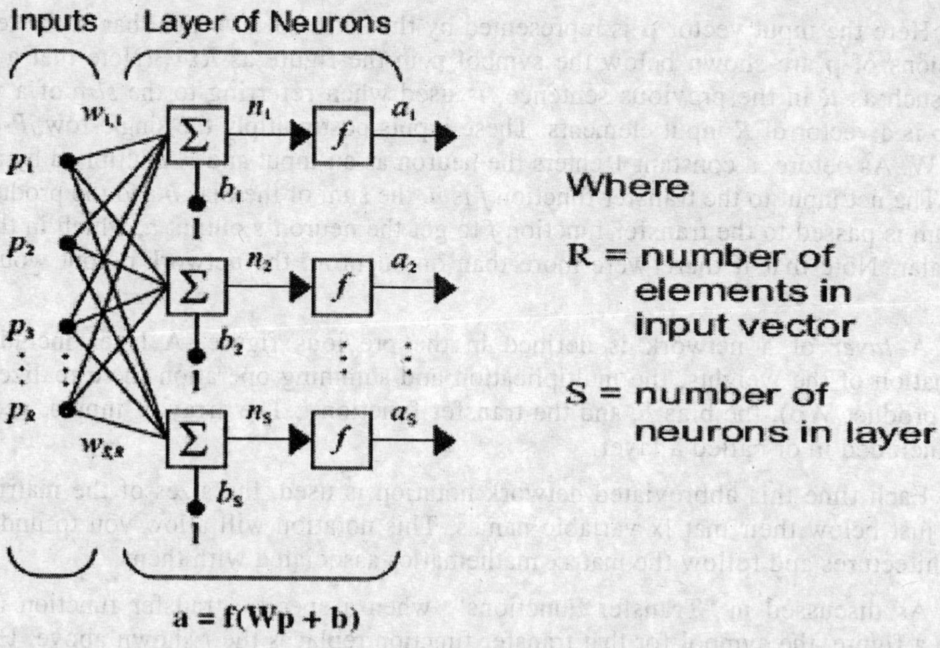

Figure 1.34 Input-Layer Neural Network

In this network, each element of the input vector **p** is connected to each neuron input through the weight matrix **W**. The *i*th neuron has a summer that gathers its weighted inputs and bias to form its own scalar output $n(i)$. The various $n(i)$ taken together form an *S*-element net input vector **n**. Finally, the neuron layer outputs form a column vector **a**. The expression for **a** is shown at the bottom of the figure.

Note that it is common for the number of inputs to a layer to be different from the number of neurons (i.e., *R* is not necessarily equal to *S*). A layer is not constrained to have the number of its inputs equal to the number of its neurons.
You can create a single (composite) layer of neurons having different transfer functions simply by putting two of the networks shown earlier in parallel. Both networks would have the same inputs, and each network would create some of the outputs.

The input vector elements enter the network through the weight matrix **W**.

$$\mathbf{W} = \begin{bmatrix} w_{1,1} & w_{1,2} & \cdots & w_{1,R} \\ w_{2,1} & w_{2,2} & \cdots & w_{2,R} \\ w_{S,1} & w_{S,2} & \cdots & w_{S,R} \end{bmatrix}$$

Note that the row indices on the elements of matrix **W** indicate the destination neuron of the weight, and the column indices indicate which source is the input for that weight. Thus, the indices in $w_{1,2}$ say that the strength of the signal *from* the second input element *to* the first (and only) neuron is $w1,2$.

The *S* neuron R input one-layer network also can be drawn in abbreviated notation.

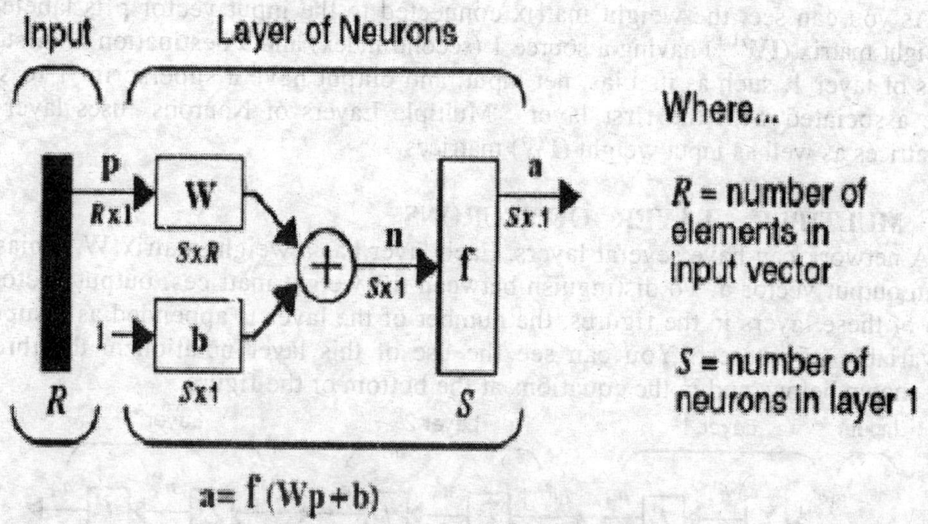

Figure 1.35 Abbreviated Notation

Here **p** is an *R* length input vector, **W** is an *S*x*R* matrix, and **a** and **b** are *S* length vectors. As defined previously, the neuron layer includes the weight matrix, the multiplication operations, the bias vector **b**, the summer, and the transfer function boxes.

1.17.2 INPUTS AND LAYERS

To describe networks having multiple layers, the notation must be extended. Specifically, it needs to make a distinction between weight matrices that are connected to inputs and weight matrices that are connected between layers. It also needs to identify the source and destination for the weight matrices.

We will call weight matrices connected to inputs *input weights;* we will call weight matrices coming from layer outputs *layer weights.* Further, superscripts are used to identify the source (second index) and the destination (first index) for the various weights and other elements of the network. To illustrate, the one-layer multiple input network shown earlier is redrawn in abbreviated form below.

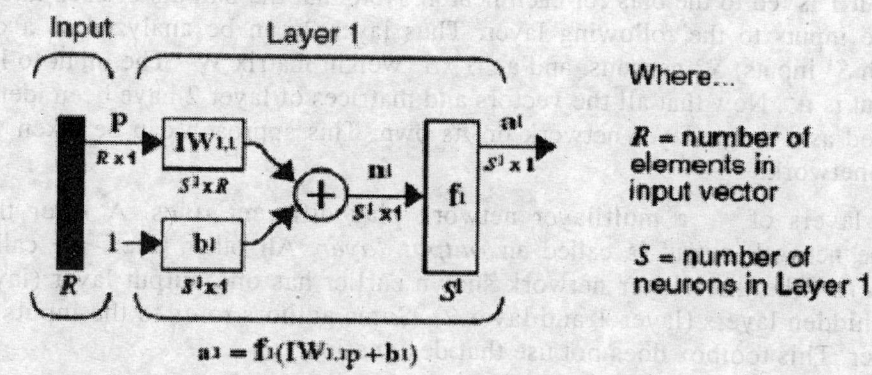

Figure 1.36 Inputs And Layers

As you can see, the weight matrix connected to the input vector **p** is labeled as an input weight matrix ($\mathbf{IW}^{1,1}$) having a source 1 (second index) and a destination 1 (first index). Elements of layer 1, such as its bias, net input, and output have a superscript 1 to say that they are associated with the first layer. "Multiple Layers of Neurons" uses layer weight (**LW**) matrices as well as input weight (**IW**) matrices.

1.17.3 MULTIPLE LAYER OF NEURONS

A network can have several layers. Each layer has a weight matrix **W**, a bias vector **b**, and an output vector **a**. To distinguish between the weight matrices, output vectors, etc., for each of these layers in the figures, the number of the layer is appended as a superscript to the variable of interest. You can see the use of this layer notation in the three-layer network shown below, and in the equations at the bottom of the figure.

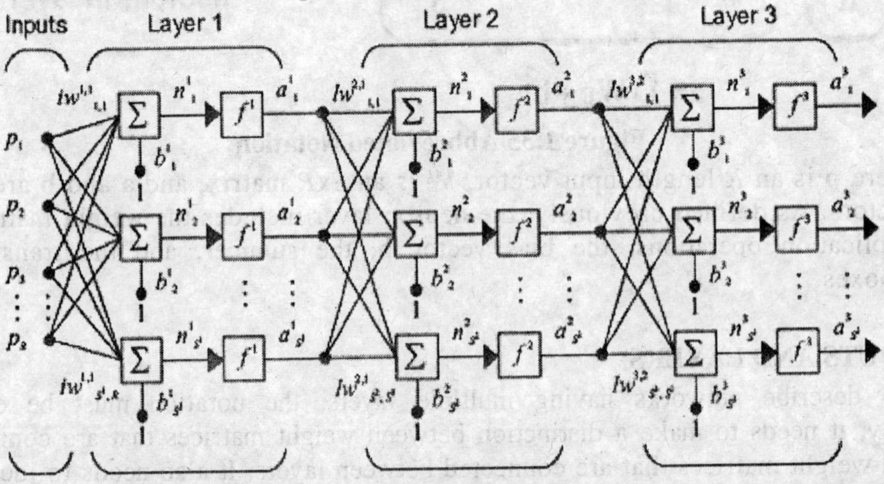

$$\mathbf{a}^1 = \mathbf{f}^1(\mathbf{IW}^{1,1}\mathbf{p}+\mathbf{b}^1) \quad \mathbf{a}^2 = \mathbf{f}^2(\mathbf{LW}^{2,1}\mathbf{a}^1+\mathbf{b}^2) \quad \mathbf{a}^3 = \mathbf{f}^3(\mathbf{LW}^{3,2}\mathbf{a}^2+\mathbf{b}^3)$$

$$\mathbf{a}^3 = \mathbf{f}^3(\mathbf{LW}^{3,2}\mathbf{f}^2(\mathbf{LW}^{2,1}\mathbf{f}^1(\mathbf{IW}^{1,1}\mathbf{p}+\mathbf{b}^1)+\mathbf{b}^2)+\mathbf{b}^3)$$

Figure 1.37 Multiple Layers Of Neurons

The network shown above has R^1 inputs, S^1 neurons in the first layer, $S2$ neurons in the second layer, etc. It is common for different layers to have different numbers of neurons. A constant input 1 is fed to the bias for each neuron. Note that the outputs of each intermediate layer are the inputs to the following layer. Thus layer 2 can be analyzed as a one-layer network with S^1 inputs, $S2$ neurons, and an $S^2 x S^1$ weight matrix W^2. The input to layer 2 is $\mathbf{a}^1$; the output is $\mathbf{a}^2$. Now that all the vectors and matrices of layer 2 have been identified, it can be treated as a single-layer network on its own. This approach can be taken with any layer of the network.

The layers of a multilayer network play different roles. A layer that produces the network output is called an *output layer*. All other layers are called *hidden layers*. The three-layer network shown earlier has one output layer (layer 3) and two hidden layers (layer 1 and layer 2). Some authors refer to the inputs as a fourth layer. This toolbox does not use that designation.

The same three-layer network can also be drawn using abbreviated notation.

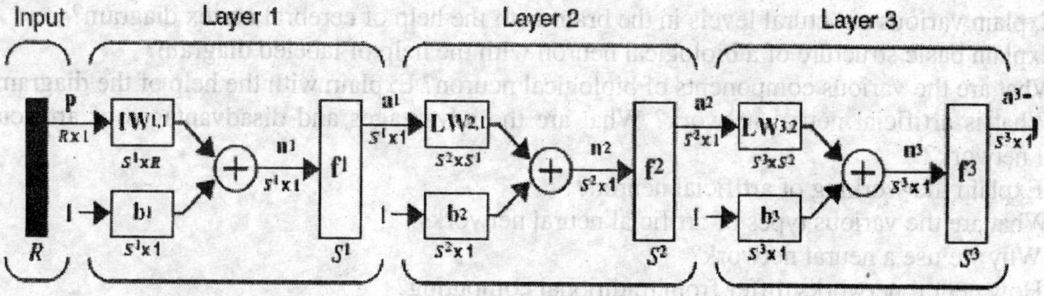

$$a^1 = f^1(IW^{1,1}p + b^1) \qquad a^2 = f^2(LW^{2,1}a^1 + b^2) \qquad a^3 = f^3(LW^{3,2}a^2 + b^3)$$

$$a^3 = f^3(LW^{3,2} f^2(LW^{2,1} f^1(IW^{1,1}p + b^1) + b^2) + b^3 = y$$

Figure 1.38 Abbreviated Notation Of Multiple Layers Neural Network

Multiple-layer networks are quite powerful. For instance, a network of two layers, where the first layer is sigmoid and the second layer is linear, can be trained to approximate any function (with a finite number of discontinuities) arbitrarily well. This kind of two-layer network is used extensively in Chapter 3, "Backpropagation."

Here it is assumed that the output of the third layer, $\mathbf{a}^3$, is the network output of interest, and this output is labeled as **y**. This notation is used to specify the output of multilayer networks.

1.17.4 INPUT AND OUTPUT PROCESSING FUNCTIONS

Network inputs might have associated processing functions. Processing functions transform user input data to a form that is easier or more efficient for a network.For instance, map min max transforms input data so that all values fall into the interval [-1, 1]. This can speed up learning for many networks. Remove constant rows removes the values for input elements that always have the same value because these input elements are not providing any useful information to the network. The third common processing function is fix unknowns, which recodes unknown data (represented in the user's data with Null values) into a numerical form for the network. fix unknowns preserves information about which values are known and which are unknown. Similarly, network outputs can also have associated processing functions. Output processing functions are used to transform user-provided target vectors for network use. Then, network outputs are reverse-processed using the same functions to produce output data with the same characteristics as the original user-provided targets.

QUESTION BANK

Q1. What do you mean by Neural network?
Q2. Discuss historical background of the neural network?
Q3. What are the various benefits of neural network?
Q4. Explain the working of human brain with the block diagram?
Q5. What is biological neural network? Explain all the components of pyramidal cells?

Q6. Explain various structural levels in the brain with the help of cerebral cortex diagram?
Q7. Explain basic structure of a biological neuron with the help of labeled diagram?
Q8. What are the various components of biological neuron? Explain with the help of the diagram?
Q9. What is artificial neural network? What are the advantages and disadvantages of artificial neural network?
Q10. Explain the working of artificial neuron?
Q11 What are the various types of artificial neural networks?
Q12. Why we use a neural network?
Q13. How neural networks differ from traditional computing?
Q14. Give comparison of computing approaches?
Q15. Give comparison of expert system and neural network?
Q16. What are the various practical application of artificial neural network?
Q17. What are the various application of neural network? Explain all in detail?
Q18. What is pattern recognition? Explain the processing levels of pattern recognition?
Q19. Explain the McCulloch and pitts model?
Q20. Explain the architecture of AND, OR, AND NOT, XOR functions with the help of truth tables?
Q21. Explain the modeling of a neuron with the help of labeled diagram of artificial neural network?
Q22. Explain various simple networks with the diagrams?
Q23. What are the various elements of neural networks?
Q23. Explain the various types of activation functions?
Q24. Explain the architecture of single neuron and explain various transfers functions?
Q25. Explain the concept of neuron with vector input using diagrammatic approach?
Q26. Explain the abbreviated notation of artificial neuron network with the help of labeled diagram?
Q27. What are the various networks architecture of neural network?
Q28. Explain the working of input layer neural network with the help of diagram?
Q29. Explain the abbreviated notations input layer of neurons?
Q29. Explain the working of multiple layer of neurons with the help of diagram?
Q30. Draw the abbreviated notations of multiple layer of neurons?

CHAPTER 2

PERCEPTRONS

2.1 INTRODUCTION

This chapter has a number of objectives. First, it introduces you to learning rules, methods of deriving the next changes that might be made in a network, and training, a procedure whereby a network is actually adjusted to do a particular job. Along the way, this chapter describes a toolbox function to create a simple perceptron network and functions to initialize and simulate such networks. The perceptron is used as a vehicle for tying these concepts together. Rosenblatt [Rose61] created many variations of the perceptron.

One of the simplest was a single-layer network whose weights and biases could be trained to produce a correct target vector when presented with the corresponding input vector. The training technique used is called the perceptron learning rule. The perceptron generated great interest due to its ability to generalize from its training vectors and learn from initially randomly distributed connections. Perceptrons are especially suited for simple problems in pattern classification. They are fast and reliable networks for the problems they can solve. In addition, an understanding of the operations of the perceptron provides a good basis for understanding more complex networks.This chapter defines what is meant by a learning rule, explains the perceptron network and its learning rule, and tells you how to initialize and simulate perceptron networks.

2.2 NEURON MODEL

A perceptron neuron, which uses the hard-limit transfer function hardlim, is shown below.

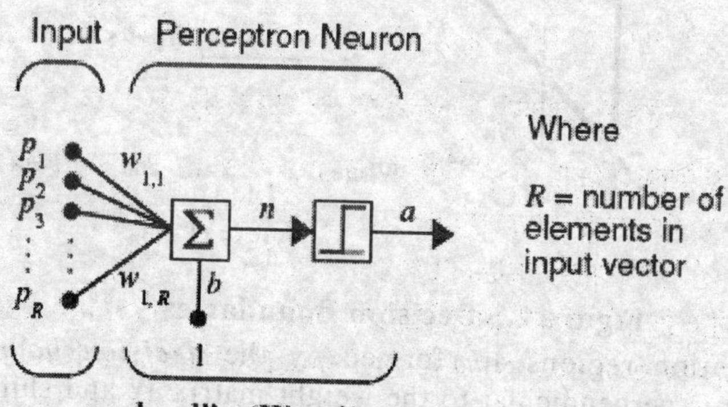

Figure 2.1. Perceptron Neuron Model

Each external input is weighted with an appropriate weight $w1j$, and the sum of the weighted inputs is sent to the hard-limit transfer function, which also has an input of 1 transmitted to it through the bias. The hard-limit transfer function, which returns a 0 or a 1, is shown below.

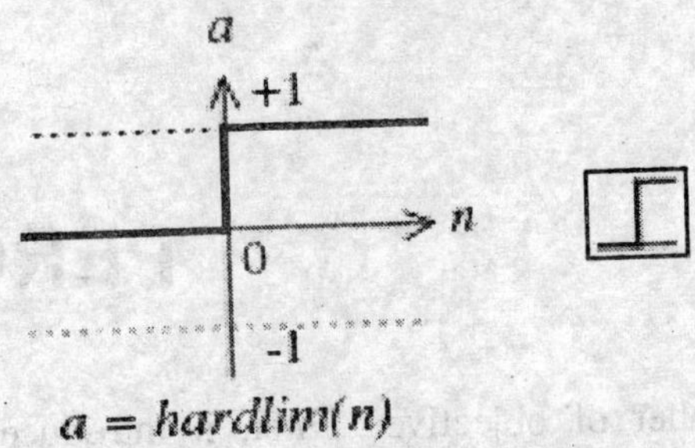

Figure 2.2 Transfer Function

The perceptron neuron produces a 1 if the net input into the transfer function is equal to or greater than 0; otherwise it produces a 0.

The hard-limit transfer function gives a perceptron the ability to classify input vectors by dividing the input space into two regions. Specifically, outputs will be 0 if the net input n is less than 0, or 1 if the net input n is 0 or greater. The following figure show the input space of a two-input hard limit neuron with the weights $w_{1,1} = -1$, $w_{1,2} = 1$ and a bias $b = 1$.

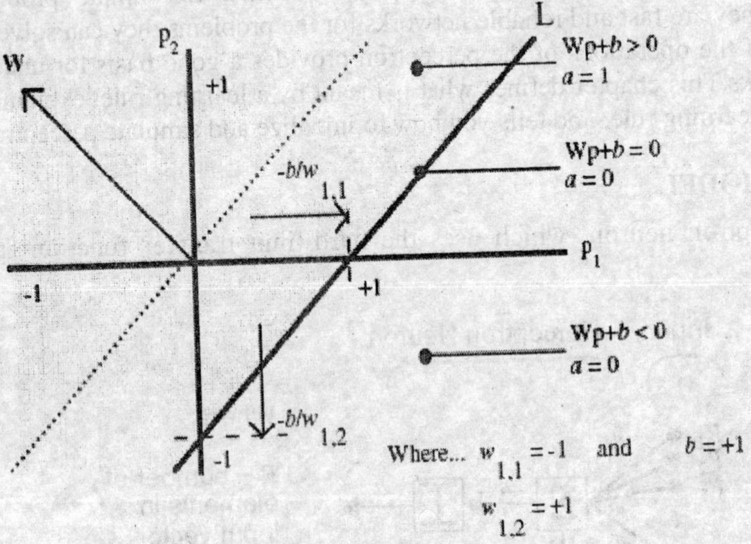

Figure 2.3 Decision Boundaries

Two classification regions are formed by the *decision boundary* line L at $\mathbf{W}\mathbf{p}+b = 0$. This line is perpendicular to the weight matrix **W** and shifted according to the bias b. Input vectors above and to the left of the line L will result in a net input greater than 0 and, therefore, cause the hard-limit neuron to output a 1. Input vectors below and to the right of the line L cause the neuron to output 0. You can pick weight and bias values to orient and move the dividing line so as to classify the input space as desired. Hard-limit neurons without a bias will always have a classification line going through the origin. Adding a bias allows the neuron to solve problems where the two sets of input vectors are not located on different sides of the origin. The bias allows the decision boundary to be shifted away from the origin, as shown in the plot above.

2.3 PERCEPTRON ARCHITECTURE

The perceptron network consists of a single layer of S perceptron neurons connected to *R* inputs through a set of weights $w_{i,j}$, as shown below in two forms. As before, the network indices *i* and *j* indicate that $w_{i,j}$ is the strength of the connection from the *j*th input to the *i*th neuron.

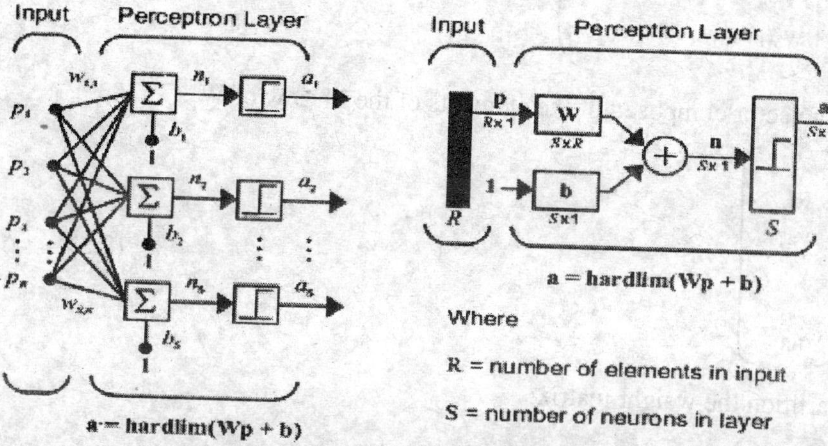

Figure 2.4 Perceptron Architecture

The perceptron learning rule described shortly is capable of training only a single layer. Thus only one-layer networks are considered here. This restriction places limitations on the computation a perceptron can perform. The types of problems that perceptrons are capable of solving are discussed in "Limitations and Cautions".

Before we present the perceptron learning rule, let's explain and out investigation of the perceptron network, which we began in 2.3. The general perceptron network is shown in Figure 2.5.

The output of the network is given by

$$a = \text{hardlim}\,(Wp + b) \qquad (2.1)$$

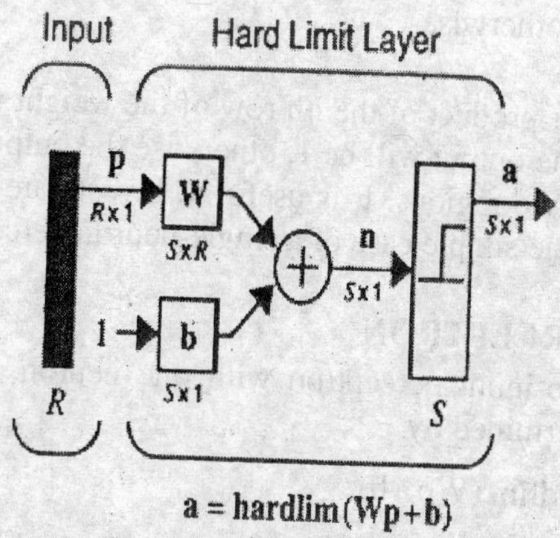

Figure 2.5 Perceptron Network

It will be useful in out development of the perceptron learning rule to be able to conveniently reference individual elements of the network output. Let's see how this can be done. First, consider the network weight matrix:

$$W = \begin{pmatrix} w_{1,1} & w_{1,2} \dots & w_{1,R} \\ w_{2,1} & w_{2,2} \dots & w_{2,R} \\ \vdots & \vdots & \vdots \\ w_{S,1} & w_{S,2} \dots & w_{S,R} \end{pmatrix} \quad (2.2)$$

We will define a vector composed of the elements of the ith row of W:

$$w = \begin{pmatrix} w_{i,1} \\ w_{i,1} \\ \vdots \\ w_{i,R} \end{pmatrix} \quad (2.3)$$

Now we can partition the weight matrix:

$$W = \begin{pmatrix} {}_1w^T \\ {}_2w^T \\ \vdots \\ {}_Sw^f \end{pmatrix} \quad (2.4)$$

This allows us to write the ith element of the network output vactor as

$$a_i = \text{hardlim}\ (n_i) = \text{hardlim}\ ({}_iw^T\ p + b). \quad (2.5)$$

Recall that the hardlim transfer function (shown at left) is defined as:

$$a = \text{hardlim}\ (n) = \begin{cases} 1 & \text{if } n \geq 0 \\ 0 & \text{otherwise} \end{cases} \quad (2.6)$$

Therefore, if the inner product of the ith row of the weight matrix with the input vector is greater than or equal to $-b_i$, the output will be 1, otherwise the output will be 0. Thus each neuron divides the input space into two regions. It is useful to investigate the boundaries between these regions. We will begin with the simple case of a single-neuron perceptron with two inputs.

2.4 SINGLE-NEURON PERCEPTRON

Let's consider a two-input perceptron with one neuron, as shown in Figure 2.6. The output of this network is determined by

$$a - \text{hardlim}\ (n) = \text{hardlim}\ (Wp + b)$$
$$= \text{hardlim}\ ({}_1w^T\ p + b) = \text{hardlim}\ (w_{1,1}p_1 + w_{2,2}p_2 + b) \quad (2.7)$$

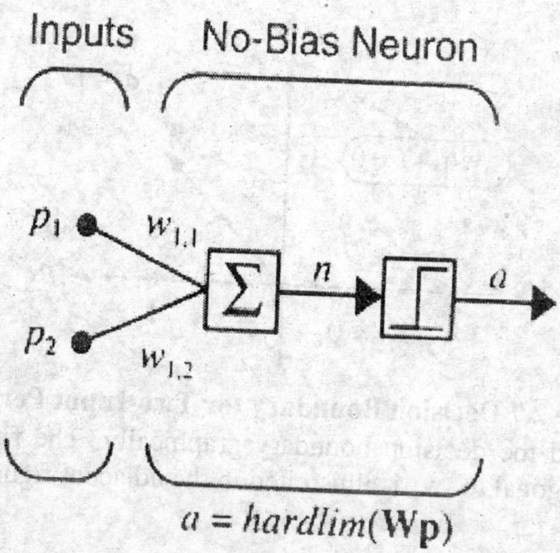

Figure 2.6 Two-Input/Output Perceptron

The decision boundary is determined by the input vectors for which the net input n is zero:

$$n = {}_1w^T p + b = \text{hardlim } w_{1,1}p_1 + w_{2,2}p_2 + b = 0 \quad (2.8)$$

To make the example more concrete, let's assign the following values for the weights and bias:

$$w_{1,1} = 1,\ w_{1,2} = 1,\ b = -1. \quad (2.9)$$

The decision boundary is then

$$n = {}_1w^T p + b = \text{hardlim } w_{1,1}p_1 + w_{2,2}p_2 + b = p_1 + p_2 - 1 = 0. \quad (2.10)$$

This defines a line in the input space. On one side of the line the network output will be 0; on the line and on the other side of the line the output will be 1. To draw the line, we can find the points where it intersects the p_1 and p_2 axes. To find the p_2 intercept set $p_1 = 0$:

$$P_2 = -\frac{b}{w_{1,2}} = \frac{-1}{1} = 1 \quad \text{if } p_1 = 0 \quad (2.11)$$

To find the p_1 intercept, set $p_2 = 0$:

$$P_2 = -\frac{b}{w_{1,1}} = \frac{-1}{1} = 1 \quad \text{if } p_2 = 0 \quad (2.12)$$

The resulting decision boundary is illustrated in Figure 4.3.

To find out which side of the boundary corresponds to an output of 1, we just need to test one point. For the input p $[2\ 0]^T$, the network output will be

$$a \text{ hardlim } ({}_1w^T p + b) = \text{hardlim } \left([1\ 1] \begin{bmatrix} 2 \\ 0 \end{bmatrix} -1 = 1 \right) \quad (2.13)$$

Therefore, the network output will be 1 for the region above and to the right of the decision boundary. This region is indicated by the shared area in Figure 2.7.

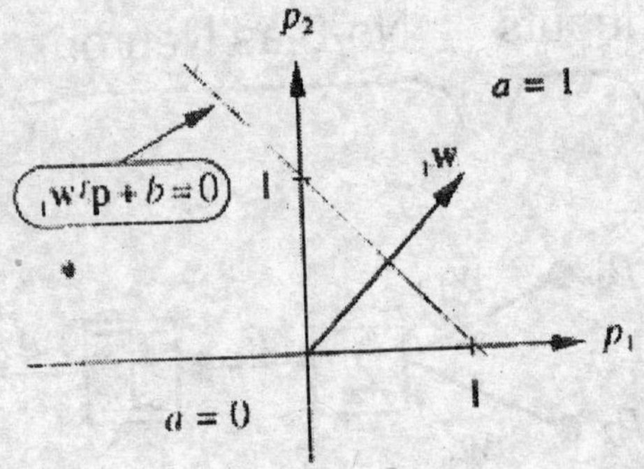

Figure 2.7 Decision Boundary for Two-Input Perceptron

We can also find the decision boundary graphically. The first step is to note that the boundary is always orthogonal to $_1w$, as illustrated in the adjacent figure. The boundary is defined by

$$_1w^T p + b = 0 \tag{2.14}$$

For all points on the boundary, the inner product of the input vector with the weight vector is the same. This implies that these input vectors will all have the same projection onto the weight vector, so they must lie on a line orthogonal to the weight vector. In addition, any vector in the shaded region of Figure 2.7 will have an inner product greater that –b, and vectors in the unshared region will have inner products less than –b. Therefore the weight vector $_1w$ will always point toward the region where the neuron output is 1.

After we have selected a weight vector with the correct angular orientation, the bias value can be computed by selecting a point on the boundary and satisfying Eq. (2.14).

Let's apply some of these concepts to the design of a perception network to implement a simple logic function: the AND gate. The input/target pairs for the AND gate are

$$\left\{P_1 = \begin{bmatrix}0\\0\end{bmatrix}, t_1 = 0\right\} \left\{P_2 = \begin{bmatrix}0\\0\end{bmatrix}, t_2 = 0\right\} \left\{P_3 = \begin{bmatrix}1\\0\end{bmatrix}. t_3 = 0\right\} \left\{P_4 = \begin{bmatrix}1\\1\end{bmatrix}, t_4 = 1\right\}$$

The figure to the left illustrates the problem graphically. It displays the input space, with each input vector labeled according to its target. The dark circles • indicate that the target is 1, and the light circles O indicate that the target is 0.

The first step of the design is to select a decision boundary. We want to have a lime that separates the dark circles and the light circles. There are an infinite number of solution to this problem. It seems reasonable to choose the line that falls "halfway" between the categories of inputs, as shown in the adjacent figure.

Next we want to choose a weight vector that is orthogonal to the decision boundary. The weight vector can be any length, so there are infinite possibilities. One choice is

$$_1w = \begin{bmatrix}2\\2\end{bmatrix} \tag{2.15}$$

as displayed in the figure to the left.

Finally, we need to find the bias b. We can do this picking a point on the decision boundary and satisfying Eq. (2.14). If we use p = [1.5 0] we find

$$ {}_1w^T p + b = [2\ 2] \begin{bmatrix} 1.5 \\ 0 \end{bmatrix} + b = 3 + b = 0 \rightarrow b = -3, \quad (2.16)$$

We can now test the network on one of the input/target pairs. If we apply p_2 to the network, the output will be

$$a = \text{hardlim}\,({}_1w^T p + b) = \text{hardlim}\left([2\ 2] \begin{bmatrix} 0 \\ 1 \end{bmatrix} -3 \right) \quad (2.17)$$

$$a = \text{hardlim}\,(-1) = 0$$

which is equal to the target output t_2. Verify for your that all inputs are correctly classified.

To experiment with decision boundaries, use the Neural Network Design Demonstration Decision Boundaries.

2.5 MULTIPLE-NEURON PERCEPTRON

Note that for perceptron with multiple neurons, as in figure 2.5 , there will be one decision boundary for each neuron. The decision boundary for neuron i will be defined by

$$ {}_iw^T p + b_i = 0 \quad (2.18)$$

A single-neuron perception can classify input vectors into two categories, since its output can be either 0 or 1. A multiple-neuron perceptron can classify inputs into may categories. Each category is represented by a different output vector. Since each element of the output vector can be either 0 or 1, there are a total of 2^S possible categories, where S is the number of neurons. Explaination is given in 2.14, 2.15.

2.6 LEARNING RULES

A *learning rule* is defined as a procedure for modifying the weights and biases of a network. (This procedure can also be referred to as a training algorithm.) The learning rule is applied to train the network to perform some particular task. Learning rules in this toolbox fall into two broad categories: supervised learning, and unsupervised learning.

In *supervised learning*, the learning rule is provided with a set of examples (the *training set*) of proper network behavior

$\{p_1, t_1\}, \{p_2, t_2\}, \ldots. \{p_Q, t_Q\}$

Where P_q is an input to the network, and T_q is the corresponding correct (*target*) output. As the inputs are applied to the network, the network outputs are compared to the targets. The learning rule is then used to adjust the weights and biases of the network in order to move the network outputs closer to the targets. The perceptron learning rule falls in this supervised learning category.

In *unsupervised learning*, the weights and biases are modified in response to network inputs only. There are no target outputs available. Most of these algorithms perform clustering operations. They categorize the input patterns into a finite number of classes. This is especially useful in such applications as vector quantization.

2.6.1 PERCEPTRON LEARNING RULE

Now that we have examined the performance of perceptron networks, we are in a position to introduce the perceptron learning rule. This learning rule is an example of supervised training, in which the learning rule is provided with a set of examples of proper network behavior:

$$\{p_1,t_1,\}, \{p_2,t_2\} \ \ldots\ldots \{p_q, t_q\} \tag{2.19}$$

where p_q is an input to the network and t_q is the corresponding target output. As each input is applied to the network, the network output is compared to the target. The learning rule then adjusts the weights and biases of the network in order to move the network output closer to the target.

2.6.2 TEST PROBLEM

In our presentation of the perceptron learning rule we will begin with a simple test problem and will experiment with possible rules to develop some intuition about how the rule should work. The input/target pairs for our test problem are

$$\left\{P_1 = \begin{bmatrix}1\\2\end{bmatrix}, t_1 = 1\right\} \left\{P_2 = \begin{bmatrix}-1\\2\end{bmatrix}, t_2 = 0\right\} \left\{P_3 = \begin{bmatrix}0\\-1\end{bmatrix}, t_3 = 0\right\}$$

The problem is displayed graphically in the adjacent figure, where the two input vectors whose target is 0 are represented with a light circle O, and the vector whose target is 1 is represented with a dark circle •. This is a very simple problem, and we could almost obtain a solution by inspection. This simplicity will help us gain some intuitive understanding of the basic concepts of the perceptron learning rule.

The network for this problem should have two-inputs and one output. To simplify out development of the learning rule, we will begin with a network without a bias. The network will then have just two parameters, $w_{1,1}$ and $w_{1,2}$ as shown in Figure 2.8

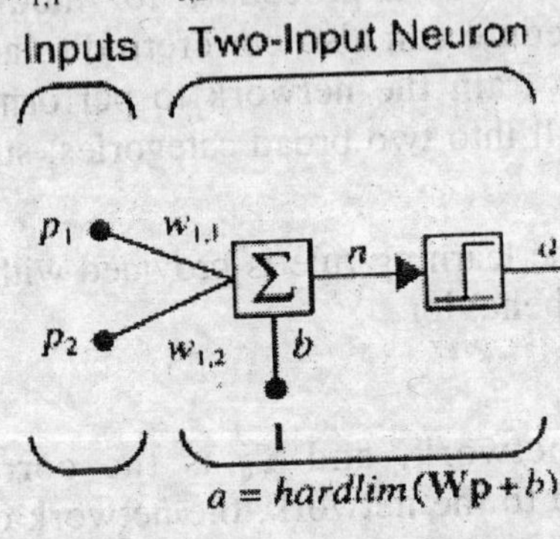

Figure 2.8 Test Problem Network

By removing the bias we are left with a network whose decision boundary must pass through the origin. We need to be sure that this network is still able to solve the test problem. There must be an allowable decision boundary that can separate the vectors p_2 and p_3 from the vector p_1. The figure to the left illustrates that there are indeed an infinite number of such boundaries.

The adjacent figure shown the weight vectors that correspond to the allowable decision boundaries. (Recall that the weight vector is orthogonal to the decision boundary.) We would like a learning rule that will find a weight vector that points in one of these directions. Remember that the length of the weight vector does not matter; only its direction is important.

2.6.3 CONSTRUCTING LEARNING RULES

Training begins by assigning some initial values for the network parameters. In this case we are training a two-input/single-output network without a bias, so we only have to initialize its two weights. Here we set the elements of the weight vector, ${}_1w$, to the following randomly generated values:

$$ {}_1w^T = [1.0\ -0.8] \tag{2.20}$$

We will now begin presenting the input vectors to the network. We begin with p_1:

$$a = \text{hardlim}\ ({}_1w^T p_1) = \text{hardlim}\left([1.0\ -0.8]\begin{bmatrix}1\\2\end{bmatrix}\right)$$

$$a = \text{hardlim}\ (-0.6) = 0 \tag{2.21}$$

The network has not returned the correct value. The network output is 0, while the target response, t_i is 1.

One approach would be to set ${}_1w$ equal to p_1. The initial weight vector results in a decision boundary that incorrectly classifies the vector p_1. We need to alter the weight vector so that it points more toward p_1 so that in the future it has a better chance of classifying it correctly.

One approach would be to set ${}_1w$ equal to p_1. This is simple and would ensure that p_1 was classified properly in the future. Unfortunately, it is easy to construct a problem for which this rule cannot find a solution. The diagram to the lower left shown a problem that cannot be solved with the weight vector pointing directly at either of the two class 1 vectors. If we apply the rule ${}_1w = p$ every time one of these vectors is misclassified, the network's weights will simply oscillate back and forth and will never find a solution.

Another possibility would be to add $p_1$to ${}_1w$. Adding p_1 would make ${}_1w$ point more in the direction of p_1. repeated presentations of p_1 would cause the direction of ${}_1w$ to asymptotically approach the direction of p_1. This rule can be stated:

$$\text{If } t = 1 \text{ and } a = o, \text{ then } {}_1w^{new} = {}_1w^{old} + p \tag{2.22}$$

Applying this rule our test problem results in new values for ${}_1w$:

$$ {}_1w^{new} = {}_1w^{old} + p_1 = \begin{bmatrix}1.0\\-0.8\end{bmatrix} + \begin{bmatrix}1\\2\end{bmatrix} = \begin{bmatrix}2.0\\1.2\end{bmatrix} \tag{2.23}$$

This operation is illustrated in the adjacent figure.

We now move on to the next input vector and will continue making changes to the weights and cycling through the inputs until they are all classified correctly.

The next input vector is p_2. When it is presented to the network we find:

$$a = \text{hardlim}\ ({}_1w^T p_2) = \text{hardlim} = \left([2.0\ -1.2]\begin{bmatrix}-1\\2\end{bmatrix}\right)$$

$$a = \text{hardlim}\ (0.4) = 1 \tag{2.24}$$

The target t_2 associated with p_2 is 0 and the output a is 1. A class 0 vector was misclassified as a 1.Since we would now like to move the weight vector ${}_1w$ away from the input, we can simply change the addition in Eq. (2.22) to subtraction:

If t = 0 and a = 1, then ${}_1w^{new} = {}_1w^{old} - p$. (2.25)

If we apply this to the test problem we find

$$ {}_1w^{new} = {}_1w^{old} - p_2 = \begin{pmatrix} 2.0 \\ 1.2 \end{pmatrix} + \begin{bmatrix} -1 \\ 2 \end{bmatrix} = \begin{pmatrix} 3.0 \\ -0.8 \end{pmatrix} \quad (2.26)$$

Which is illustrated in the adjacent figure.

Now we present the third vector p_3:

$$a = \text{hardlim}\,({}_1w^T p_3) = \text{hardlim} = \left([3.0\ -0.8] \begin{bmatrix} 0 \\ -1 \end{bmatrix} \right)$$

$$a = \text{hardlim}\,(0.8) = 1 \quad (2.27)$$

The current ${}_1w$ results in a decision boundary that misclassifies p_3. This is a situation for which we already have a rule, so ${}_1w$ will be updated again, according to Eq. (2.25):

$$ {}_1w^{new} = {}_1w^{old} + p_3 = \begin{pmatrix} 3.0 \\ -0.8 \end{pmatrix} + \begin{bmatrix} 0 \\ -1 \end{bmatrix} = \begin{pmatrix} 3.0 \\ 0.2 \end{pmatrix} \quad (2.28)$$

The diagram to the left shows that the perceptron has finally learned to classify the three vectors properly. If we present any of the input vectors to the neuron, it will output te correct class for that input vector.

This bring us to our third and final rule: if it works, don't fix it.

If t = a, then ${}_1w^{new} = {}_1w^{old}$ (2.29)

Here are the three rules, which cover all possible combinations of output and target values:

If t=1 and a=0 then ${}_1w^{new} = {}_1w^{old} + p$.

If t=1 and a=1, then ${}_1w^{new} = {}_1w^{old} - p$.

If t=a, then ${}_1w^{new} = {}_1w^{old}$ (2.30)

2.7 PERCEPTRON LEARNING RULE (LEARNP)

Perceptrons are trained on examples of desired behavior. The desired behavior can be summarized by a set of input, output pairs

$p_1t_1, p_2t_1, \ldots, p_qt_q$

where **p** is an input to the network and **t** is the corresponding correct (target) output. The objective is to reduce the error **e**, which is the difference **t** - **a** between the neuron response **a** and the target vector **t**. The perceptron learning rule learnp calculates desired changes to the perceptron's weights and biases, given an input vector **p** and the associated error **e**. The target vector **t** must contain values of either 0 or 1, because perceptrons (with hardlim transfer functions) can only output these values.

Each time learnp is executed, the perceptron has a better chance of producing the correct outputs. The perceptron rule is proven to converge on a solution in a finite number of iterations if a solution exists.If a bias is not used, learnp works to find a solution by altering only the weight vector **w** to point toward input vectors to be classified as 1 and away from vectors to be classified as 0. This results in a decision boundary that is perpendicular to **w** and that properly classifies the input vectors.

There are three conditions that can occur for a single neuron once an input vector **p** is presented and the network's response **a** is calculated:

CASE 1. If an input vector is presented and the output of the neuron is correct (**a** = **t** and **e** = **t** – **a** = 0), then the weight vector **w** is not altered.

CASE 2. If the neuron output is 0 and should have been 1 (**a** = 0 and **t** = 1, and **e** = **t** – **a** = 1), the input vector **p** is added to the weight vector **w**. This makes the weight vector point closer to the input vector, increasing the chance that the input vector will be classified as a 1 in the future.

CASE 3. If the neuron output is 1 and should have been 0 (**a** = 1 and **t** = 0, and **e** = **t** – **a** = –1), the input vector **p** is subtracted from the weight vector **w**. This makes the weight vector point farther away from the input vector, increasing the chance that the input vector will be classified as a 0 in the future.

2.8 EXAMPLE FOR LEARNING RULE

The perceptron learning rule can be written more succinctly in terms of the error **e** = **t** – **a** and the change to be made to the weight vector Δw:

CASE 1. If **e** = 0, then make a change Δw equal to 0.

CASE 2. If **e** = 1, then make a change Δw equal to p^T.

CASE 3. If **e** = –1, then make a change Δw equal to $-p^T$.

All three cases can then be written with a single expression:

$$\Delta w = (t - \alpha)p^T = ep^T$$

You can get the expression for changes in a neuron's bias by noting that the bias is simply a weight that always has an input of 1:

$$\Delta b = (t - \alpha))\ (1) = e$$

For the case of a layer of neurons you have

$$\Delta W = (t - a)(p)^T = e(p)^T$$

and

$$\Delta b = (t - \alpha) = e$$

The perceptron learning rule can be summarized as follows: $W^{new} = W^{old} + ep^T$
and

$$b^{new} = b^{old} + e$$

where

$$\mathbf{e = t - a}$$

Now try a simple example. Start with a single neuron having an input vector with just two elements. Here are input vectors with the values -2 and 2, and outputs with values 0 and 1.

```
net = newp([-2 2;-2 2],[0 1]);
```

To simplify matters, set the bias equal to 0 and the weights to 1 and -0.8:

```
net.b{1} =[0];
w = [1 -0.8];
```

net.IW{1,1} = w;

The input target pair is given by

p = [1; 2]; t = [1];

You can compute the output and error with

```
a = sim(net,p)
a =0
e = t-a
e =1
```

and use the function learnp to find the change in the weights.

```
dw = learnp(w,p,[],[],[],[],e,[],[],[])
dw =1.2
```

The new weights, then, are obtained as

```
w = w + dw
w =2.0000 + 1.2000
```

The process of finding new weights (and biases) can be repeated until there are no errors. Recall that the perceptron learning rule is guaranteed to converge in a finite number of steps for all problems that can be solved by a perceptron. These include all classification problems that are linearly separable. The objects to be classified in such cases can be separated by a single line.

2.8.1 TRAINING (TRAIN)

If sim and learnp are used repeatedly to present inputs to a perceptron, and to change the perceptron weights and biases according to the error, the perceptron will eventually find weight and bias values that solve the problem, given that the perceptron *can* solve it. Each traversal through all the training input and target vectors is called a *pass*. The function train carries out such a loop of calculation. In each pass the function train proceeds through the specified sequence of inputs, calculating the output, error, and network adjustment for each input vector in the sequence as the inputs are presented.

Note that train does not guarantee that the resulting network does its job. You must check the new values of **W** and **b** by computing the network output for each input vector to see if all targets are reached. If a network does not perform successfully you can train it further by calling train again with the new weights and biases for more training passes, or you can analyze the problem to see if it is a suitable problem for the perceptron. Problems that cannot be solved by the perceptron network are discussed in Limitations and Cautions.

To illustrate the training procedure, work through a simple problem. Consider a one-neuron perceptron with a single vector input having two elements. This network, and the problem you are about to consider, are simple enough that you can follow through what is done with hand calculations if you want. Suppose you have the following classification problem and would like to solve it with a single vector input, two-element perceptron network.

$$\left\{P_1 = \begin{bmatrix} 2 \\ 2 \end{bmatrix}, t_1 = 0\right\} \left\{P_2 = \begin{bmatrix} 1 \\ -2 \end{bmatrix}, t_2 = 1\right\} \left\{P_3 = \begin{bmatrix} -2 \\ 2 \end{bmatrix}, t_3 = 0\right\} \left\{P_4 = \begin{bmatrix} -1 \\ 1 \end{bmatrix}, t_4 = 1\right\}$$

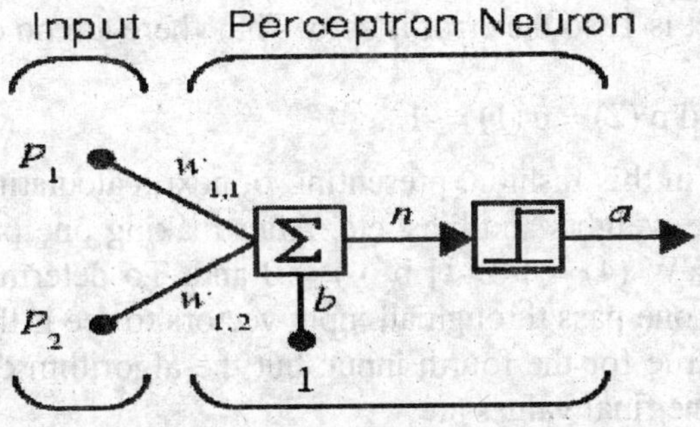

= hardlim (Wp + b)

Figure 2.9 Perceptron Training

Use the initial weights and bias. Denote the variables at each step of this calculation by using a number in parentheses after the variable. Thus, above, the initial values are **W**(0) and *b*(0).

$$\mathbf{W}(0) = \begin{bmatrix} 0 & 0 \end{bmatrix} \qquad b(0) = 0$$

Start by calculating the perceptron's output *a* for the first input vector $\mathbf{p}_1$, using the initial weights and bias.

$$a = hardlim(\mathbf{W}(0)\mathbf{p}_1 + b(0))$$

$$= hardlim\left(\begin{bmatrix} 0 & 0 \end{bmatrix}\begin{bmatrix} 2 \\ 2 \end{bmatrix} + 0\right) = hardlim(0) = 1$$

The output *a* does not equal the target value t_1, so use the perceptron rule to find the incremental changes to the weights and biases based on the error.

$$e = t_1 - a = 0 - 1 = -1$$

$$\Delta\mathbf{W} = e\mathbf{p}_1^T = (-1)\begin{bmatrix} 2 & 2 \end{bmatrix} = \begin{bmatrix} -2 & -2 \end{bmatrix}$$

$$\Delta b = e = (-1) = -1$$

You can calculate the new weights and bias using the perceptron update rules.

$$\mathbf{W}^{new} = \mathbf{W}^{old} + e\mathbf{p}^T = \begin{bmatrix} 0 & 0 \end{bmatrix} + \begin{bmatrix} -2 & -2 \end{bmatrix} = \begin{bmatrix} -2 & -2 \end{bmatrix} = \mathbf{W}(1)$$

$$b^{new} = b^{old} + e = 0 + (-1) = -1 = b(1)$$

Now present the next input vector, $\mathbf{p}_2$. The output is calculated below.

$$a = hardlim(\mathbf{W}(1)\mathbf{p}_2 + b(1))$$

$$= hardlim\left(\begin{bmatrix} -2 & -2 \end{bmatrix}\begin{bmatrix} -2 \\ -2 \end{bmatrix} - 1\right) = hardlim(1) = 1$$

On this occasion, the target is 1, so the error is zero. Thus there are no changes in weights or bias, so
W (2) = W (1) = [-2 -2] and p (2) = p (1) = -1.

You can continue in this fashion, presenting $\mathbf{p}_3$ next, calculating an output and the error, and making changes in the weights and bias, etc. After making one pass through all of the four inputs, you get the values W (4) = [-3 -1] b (4) = 0 and. To determine whether a satisfactory solution is obtained, make one pass through all input vectors to see if they all produce the desired target values. This is not true for the fourth input, but the algorithm does converge on the sixth presentation of an input. The final values are

W (6) = [-2 -3] and b(6) = 1

This concludes the hand calculation. Now, how can you do this using the train function?

The following code defines a perceptron like that shown in the previous figure, with initial weights and bias values of 0.

```
net = newp([-2 2;-2 2],[0 1]);
```

Consider the application of a single input.

```
p = [2; 2];
```

having the target

```
t = [0];
```

Set epochs to 1, so that train goes through the input vectors (only one here) just one time.

```
net.trainParam.epochs = 1;
net = train(net,p,t);
```

The new weights and bias are

```
w = net.iw{1,1}, b = net.b{1}
w =  -2  -2
b =  -1
```

Thus, the initial weights and bias are 0, and after training on only the first vector, they have the values [-2 -2] and -1, just as you hand calculated.

Now apply the second input vector P_2. The output is 1, as it will be until the weights and bias are changed, but now the target is 1, the error will be 0, and the change will be zero. You could proceed in this way, starting from the previous result and applying a new input vector time after time. But you can do this job automatically with train.

Apply train for one epoch, a single pass through the sequence of all four input vectors. Start with the network definition.

```
net = newp([-2 2;-2 2],[0 1]);
net.trainParam.epochs = 1;
```

The input vectors and targets are

```
p = [[2;2] [1;-2] [-2;2] [-1;1]]
```

```
t = [0 1 0 1]
```

Now train the network with

```
net = train(net,p,t);
```

The new weights and bias are

```
w =net.iw{1,1}, b = net.b{1}
w =   -3   -1
b =    0
```

This is the same result as you got previously by hand.

Finally, simulate the trained network for each of the inputs.

```
a = sim(net,p)
a =     0   0   1   1
```

The outputs do not yet equal the targets, so you need to train the network for more than one pass. Try more epochs. This run gives a mean absolute error performance of 0 after two epochs:

```
net.trainParam.epochs = 1000;
net = train(net,p,t);
```

Thus, the network was trained by the time the inputs were presented on the third epoch. (As you know from hand calculation, the network converges on the presentation of the sixth input vector. This occurs in the middle of the second epoch, but it takes the third epoch to detect the network convergence.) The final weights and bias are

```
w =w = net.iw{1,1}, b = net.b{1}
w =   -2  -3
b =   1
```

The simulated output and errors for the various inputs are

```
a = sim(net,p)
a =         0         1         0         1
error = a-t
error =     0         0         0         0
```

You confirm that the training procedure is successful. The network converges and produces the correct target outputs for the four input vectors.The default training function for networks created with newp is trainc. (You can find this by executing net.trainFcn.)

This training function applies the perceptron learning rule in its pure form, in that individual input vectors are applied individually, in sequence, and corrections to the weights and bias are made after each presentation of an input vector. Thus, perceptron training with train will converge in a finite number of steps unless the problem presented cannot be solved with a simple perceptron.The function train can be used in various ways by other networks as well. Type help train to read more about this basic function.

You might want to try various demonstration programs. For instance, demop1 illustrates classification and training of a simple perceptron.

2.9 LIMITATIONS AND CAUTIONS

Perceptron networks should be trained with adapt, which presents the input vectors to the network one at a time and makes corrections to the network based on the results of each presentation. Use of adapt in this way guarantees that any linearly separable problem is solved in a finite number of training presentations.

As noted in the previous pages, perceptrons can also be trained with the function train, which is discussed in detail in the next chapter. Commonly when train is used for perceptrons, it presents the inputs to the network in batches, and makes corrections to the network based on the sum of all the individual corrections. Unfortunately, there is no proof that such a training algorithm converges for perceptrons. On that account the use of train for perceptrons is not recommended.

Perceptron networks have several limitations. First, the output values of a perceptron can take on only one of two values (0 or 1) because of the hard-limit transfer function. Second, perceptrons can only classify linearly separable sets of vectors. If a straight line or a plane can be drawn to separate the input vectors into their correct categories, the input vectors are linearly separable. If the vectors are not linearly separable, learning will never reach a point where all vectors are classified properly. However, it has been proven that if the vectors are linearly separable, perceptrons trained adaptively will always find a solution in finite time. You might want to try demop6. It shows the difficulty of trying to classify input vectors that are not linearly separable.

It is only fair, however, to point out that networks with more than one perceptron can be used to solve more difficult problems. For instance, suppose that you have a set of four vectors that you would like to classify into distinct groups, and that two lines can be drawn to separate them. A two-neuron network can be found such that its two decision boundaries classify the inputs into four categories. For additional discussion about perceptrons and to examine more complex perceptron problems.

2.10 OUTLIERS AND THE NORMALIZED PERCEPTRON RULE

Long training times can be caused by the presence of an *outlier* input vector whose length is much larger or smaller than the other input vectors. Applying the perceptron learning rule involves adding and subtracting input vectors from the current weights and biases in response to error. Thus, an input vector with large elements can lead to changes in the weights and biases that take a long time for a much smaller input vector to overcome. You might want to try demop4 to see how an outlier affects the training.

By changing the perceptron learning rule slightly, you can make training times insensitive to extremely large or small outlier input vectors.Here is the original rule for updating weights:

$\Delta w = (t - a)\, p^T = ep^T$

As shown above, the larger an input vector **p**, the larger its effect on the weight vector **w**. Thus, if an input vector is much larger than other input vectors, the smaller input vectors must be presented many times to have an effect. The solution is to normalize the rule so that the effect of each input vector on the weights is of the same magnitude:

$$\Delta \mathbf{w} = (t-a)\frac{\mathbf{p}^T}{\|\mathbf{p}\|} = e\frac{\mathbf{p}^T}{\|\mathbf{p}\|}$$

The normalized perceptron rule is implemented with the function learnpn, which is called exactly like learnp. The normalized perceptron rule function learnpn takes slightly more time to execute, but reduces the number of epochs considerably if there are outlier input vectors. You might try demop5 to see how this normalized training rule works.

2.11 PERCEPTRON LEARNING RULE CONVERGENCE THEOREM

PERCEPTRON CONVERGENCE THEOREM: Says that there if there is a weight vector **w*** such that f(**w*p**(q)) = t(q) for all q, then for any starting vector **w**, the perceptron learning rule will converge to a weight vector (not necessarily unique and not necessarily **w***) that gives the correct response for all training patterns, and it will do so in a finite number of steps.

IDEA OF THE PROOF: The idea is to find upper and lower bounds on the length of the weight vector. If the length is finite, then the perceptron has converged, which also implies that the weights have changed a finite number of times.

PROOF:

1) Assume that the inputs to the perceptron originate from two linearly separable classes. **That is, the classes can be distinguished by a perceptron**. Let $X1$ be the subset of training vectors belonging to $C1$. That is, **p**(1), **p**(2),... . Let $X2$ be the set of training vectors belonging to $C2$. That is, **p**(1), **p**(2),... . Then we can say that $X_1 \cup X_2$ is the complete training set X.

2) Given the set of vectors $X1$ and $X2$ to train this perceptron to train this perceptron, the training process (as we have seen) involves the adjustment of the weight vector **w** such that $C1$ and $C2$ are linearly separable. That is, there exists some **w** such that

   $\mathbf{w}^T\mathbf{p} > 0$ for every input vector $\mathbf{p}\ \varepsilon\ C1$ (1)

   $\mathbf{w}^T\mathbf{p} < 0$ for every input vector $\mathbf{p}\ \varepsilon\ C2$

3) What need to do is find some **w** such that the above is satisfied, which is the purpose of the perceptron algorithm.

   One algorithm for adapting the weight vector for the perceptron algorithm can be formulated as follows (there are others):

   a. If the kth member of the training set **p**(k) is correctly classified at the kth iteration no correction is made to **w**. This is done according to the following rule:

   $\mathbf{w}(k+1) = \mathbf{w}(k)$ if $\mathbf{w}^T\mathbf{p}(k) > 0$ and $\mathbf{p}(k) \in C1$

   $\mathbf{w}(k+1) = \mathbf{w}(k)$ if $\mathbf{w}^T\mathbf{p}(k) < 0$ and $\mathbf{p}(k) \in C2$ (2)

b. Otherwise, the weight vector of the perceptron is updated according to the following rule:

$$\mathbf{w}(k+1) = \mathbf{w}(k) + \mathbf{p}(k) \text{ if } \mathbf{w}^T\mathbf{p}(k) < 0 \text{ and } \mathbf{p}(k) \in C1$$

$$\mathbf{w}(k+1) = \mathbf{w}(k) - \mathbf{p}(k) \text{ if } \mathbf{w}^T\mathbf{p}(k) > 0 \text{ and } \mathbf{p}(k) \in C2 \quad (3)$$

4) The proof begins assuming that $\mathbf{w}(1) = \mathbf{0}$ (i.e., the zero vector). Suppose that $\mathbf{w}^T(k)\mathbf{p}(k) < 0$ for k = 1, 2, ..., and all the input vectors $\mathbf{p}(k) \in X1$ (or $C1$).

Here, the perceptron **incorrectly** classifies the vectors $\mathbf{p}(1)$, $\mathbf{p}(2)$,... since the second condition in Equation (1) is violated (i.e., $\mathbf{w}^T(k)\mathbf{p}(k)$ should be greater than 0). Now we can use Equation (3) to write the adjustments to the weight matrix according to the perceptron learning rule

$$\mathbf{w}(k+1) = \mathbf{w}(k) + \mathbf{p}(k) \text{ for } \mathbf{p}(k) \in C1 \quad (4)$$

Recall, what we are doing is modifying the weight vector so that it points in the right direction.

5) Given the initial condition $\mathbf{w}(1) = \mathbf{0}$, we can iteratively solve for $\mathbf{w}(k+1)$ obtaining:

$$\mathbf{w}(k+1) = \mathbf{p}(1) + \mathbf{p}(2) + \ldots + \mathbf{p}(k) \quad (5)$$

CLS EXERCISE: Show $\mathbf{w}(k+1) = \mathbf{p}(1) + \mathbf{p}(2) + \ldots + \mathbf{p}(k)$

ANSWER:

$\mathbf{w}(1) = \mathbf{0}$

$\mathbf{w}(2) = \mathbf{w}(1) + \mathbf{p}(1) = \mathbf{p}(1)$

$\mathbf{w}(3) = \mathbf{w}(2) + \mathbf{p}(2) = \mathbf{w}(1) + \mathbf{p}(1) + \mathbf{p}(2) = \mathbf{p}(1) + \mathbf{p}(2)$

$= \mathbf{p}(1) + \mathbf{p}(2) + \mathbf{p}(3)$

So, in general:

$\mathbf{w}(k+1) = \mathbf{p}(1) + \mathbf{p}(2) + \ldots + \mathbf{p}(k)$

Since $C1$ and $C2$ are assumed to be linearly separable, then there exists a **wo** that can correctly classify all input vectors belonging to $C1$ and $C2$.

In this proof, we have assumed the existence of **wo** for which

$$\mathbf{wo}^T\mathbf{p}(k) > 0 \text{ if } \mathbf{p}(k) \in C1$$

and

$\mathbf{wo}^T\mathbf{p}(k) < 0$ if $\mathbf{p}(k) \in C2$

This is equivalent to the existence of a weight vector **wo** for which

$\mathbf{wo}^T\mathbf{p}(k) > 0$ if $\mathbf{p}(k) \in C1 \cup C2$ or X

The reason is that the training set can be considered to consist of two parts:

$C1 = \{\mathbf{p}$ such that the target value is $1\}$

and

$C2 = \{\mathbf{p}$ such that the target value is $0\}$ So we

can think of the training set X as

$$X = C1 \cup C2$$

Where

$$C2 = \{-\mathbf{p} \text{ such that } \mathbf{p} \in C2\}$$

Now, if the response for the network is incorrect, then this allows the weights to be updated according to:

$$\mathbf{w}(k+1) = \mathbf{w}(k) + \mathbf{p}(k)$$

since $-\mathbf{wo}^T\mathbf{p}(k) < 0 = \mathbf{wo}^T\mathbf{p}(k) > 0$ if $\mathbf{p}(k)\ \varepsilon\ C2$. Now in this case the perceptron is updated by $\mathbf{w}(k+1) = \mathbf{w}(k) - (-\mathbf{p}(k)) = \mathbf{w}(k+1) = \mathbf{w}(k) + \mathbf{p}(k)$ since $\mathbf{w}^T\mathbf{p}(k) > 0$ and $\mathbf{p}(k)\ \varepsilon\ C2$.

For the solution **wo**, we can define some $\alpha > 0$ as

$$\alpha = \min_{p(x)\, \varepsilon X} w^T_o\, p(k) \qquad (6)$$

which is just the minimum (scalar) value of all woTp(k) for all p ε X.

By multiplying each side of Equation (5) by woT, we get

$$\mathbf{wo}^T\mathbf{w}\,(k+1) = \mathbf{wo}^T\mathbf{p}(1) + \mathbf{wo}^T\mathbf{p}(2) + \ldots + \mathbf{wo}^T\mathbf{p}(k)$$

6) And, by applying Equation (6), we get

$$w_o^T w\,(k+1) \geq k\alpha \qquad (7)$$

since $w_o^T w(k+1)$ has to be greater than or equal to $k \times \min_{p(x)\, \varepsilon X} w^T_o p(k)$

7) Next, use the Cauchy-Swartz inequality for $\mathbf{wo}^T$ and $\mathbf{wo}^T(k+1)$, which states for any two vectors **x** and **y**:

$$[x\,y]^2 \leq ||x||^2\ ||y||^2$$

Or

$$||x||^2\ [x\,y]^2\ ||y||^2$$

where $||\mathbf{x}||$ is the Euclidian norm.

Example. Suppose $\mathbf{x} = [-1\ 0\ 4]$.

Then, $||x|| = \sqrt{(-1) + 0^2 + 4^2} = \sqrt{17}$

Thus, we can say:

$$||w_o^T||^2\ ||w(k+1)||^2 \geq [w_o^T w\,(k+1)]^2 \qquad (8)$$

8) From Equation (7), we know by applying Cauchy-Swartz that

$w_o^T w\ (k+1) \geq k\alpha \Rightarrow$

$|| w_o^T ||^2 || w(k+1) ||^2 \geq [k\alpha] \Rightarrow$

$|| w_o^T ||^2 || w(k+1) ||^2 \geq [k^2\alpha^2]$

and we get:

$$|| w(k+1) ||^2 \geq \frac{k^2 \alpha^2}{|| w_o ||^2} \qquad (9)$$

which shows that the squared length of the weight vector ($\|\mathbf{w}(k+1)\|^2$) grows by a factor of k^2, where k is the number of time the weights have changed.

9)So, what we have established from Equation (9) is a **lower-bound** in the terms of the squared Euclidian norm of the weight vector **w** at iteration k + 1.

But there is another aspect we must consider. In order to show that the weights cannot continue to grow indefinitely, we must establish an **upper- bound** for the weight vector **w**.

10) To find an **upper-bound**, we now do the following. Write Equation (4) as the following (where q is the number of patterns in *X*):

$$\mathbf{w}(k+1) = \mathbf{w}(k) + \mathbf{p}(k) \text{ for } k = 1,\ldots,q\ \mathbf{p}(k) \in X$$

11) After taking the square of the Euclidian norm, we get

$$\|\mathbf{w}(k+1)\|^2 = \|\mathbf{w}(k)\|^2 + 2\mathbf{w}^T(k)\,\mathbf{p}(k) + \|\mathbf{p}(k)\|^2 \qquad (10)$$

12) But assuming that the perceptron incorrectly classifies an input vector belonging to *X* (i.e., we have to make the adjustment $\mathbf{w}(k+1) = \mathbf{w}(k) + \mathbf{p}(k)$) since $\mathbf{w}^T(k)\,\mathbf{p}(k) < 0$, then from Equation (10), it follows that:

$$\|\mathbf{w}(k+1)\|^2 \leq \|\mathbf{w}(k)\|^2 + \|\mathbf{p}(k)\|^2$$

CLS EXERCISE: Why can we make this claim?

ANSWER:

Because since the input vector **p**(k) was incorrectly classified, this implies that $\mathbf{w}^T(k)\,\mathbf{p}(k) < 0$. Thus, given that $\|\mathbf{w}(k+1)\|^2 = \|\mathbf{w}(k)\|^2 + 2\mathbf{w}^T(k)\,\mathbf{p}(k) + \|\mathbf{p}(k)\|^2$, then clearly $2\mathbf{w}^T(k)\,\mathbf{p}(k)$ must be < 0 also. Thus, we can claim that:

$$\|\mathbf{w}(k+1)\|^2 \leq \|\mathbf{w}(k)\|^2 + \|\mathbf{p}(k)\|^2 .$$

We can rewrite the above as:

$$\|\mathbf{w}(k+1)\|^2 - \|\mathbf{w}(k)\|^2 \leq \|\mathbf{p}(k)\|^2 \qquad (11)$$

13) Adding these quantities for k = 1,...,q (where q is the number of patterns in *C*1) and using the initial condition that **w**(1) = **0**, it can be shown **(this will be for homework)** that:

$$|| w(K+1) ||^2 \leq \sum_{n=1}^{k} || P(n) ||^2 \leq k\beta \qquad (12)$$

where $\beta > 0$ and is defined by the following:

$$\beta = \max_{p(k)\,\varepsilon X} \| p(k) \|^2 \qquad (13)$$

14) Equation (13) says that the Euclidian norm of the weight vector **w**(k+1), grows at most linearly with the number of iterations, k, given the input patterns. In other words, $\| w(k+1) \|^2 \leq k\beta$. (14)

15) Thus, we have established both upper and lower bounds for a perceptron to classify correctly the input patterns **p**(k) for k = 1 ,...,q for two class *C*1 and *C*2 given they are lineary separable.

16) Observe that $\| w(k+1) \|^2 \leq k\beta$ conflicts with the earlier result of $\| w(k+1) \|^2 \geq \dfrac{k^2\alpha^2}{\| w_0 \|^2}$.

namely, it can be shown that they don't agree for ||w(k+1)|| for large values of k.

So we can state that k cannot be larger than some kmax for which Equations (9) and (14) are **both** satisfied; and they must be equal to determine the maximum number of iterations for the two linearly separable classes to converge. To determine this, set Equations (9) and (14) equal to each other and substitute and solve for kmax. Thus we get

$$\frac{k^2_{max}\alpha^2}{\| w_o \|^2} = k_{max}\,\beta,$$

$$k_{max} = \frac{\| w_o \|^2 \beta}{\alpha^2}$$

which means that changing the weights of the perceptron must terminate after at most kmax iterations, which means that the machine has solved the (linearly separable) problem correctly.

2.12 THE MULTILAYER PERCEPTRON NEURAL NETWORK MODEL

The following diagram illustrates a perceptron network with three layers:

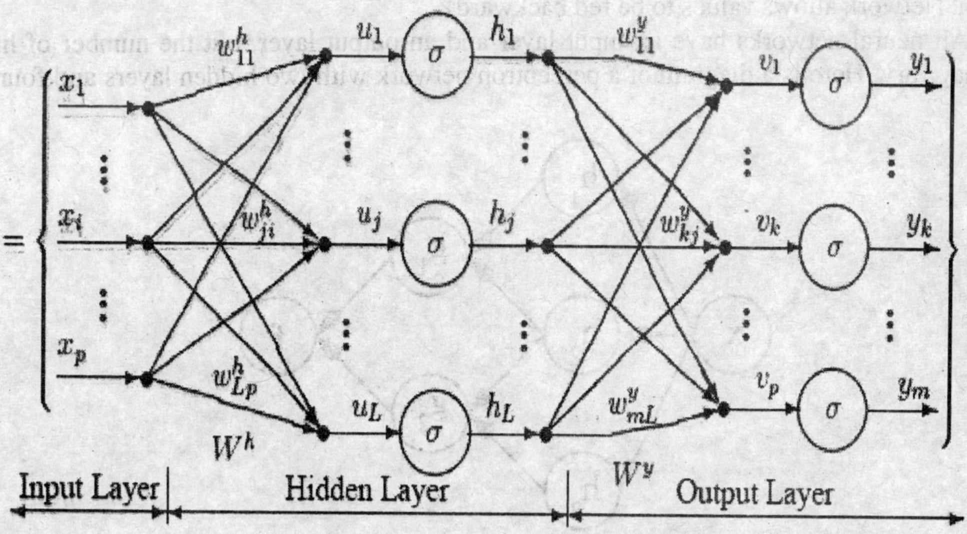

Figure 2.10 The Multilayer Perceptron Neural Network Model

This network has an **input layer** (on the left) with three neurons, one **hidden layer** (in the middle) with three neurons and an **output layer** (on the right) with three neurons. There is one neuron in the input layer for each predictor variable. In the case of categorical variables, *N*-1 neurons are used to represent the *N* categories of the variable.

1. Input Layer — A vector of predictor variable values ($x_1 ... x_p$) is presented to the input layer. The input layer (or processing before the input layer) standardizes these values so that the range of each variable is -1 to 1. The input layer distributes the values to each of the neurons in the hidden layer. In addition to the predictor variables, there is a constant input of 1.0, called the *bias* that is fed to each of the hidden layers; the bias is multiplied by a weight and added to the sum going into the neuron.

2. Hidden Layer — Arriving at a neuron in the hidden layer, the value from each input neuron is multiplied by a weight (w_{ji}), and the resulting weighted values are added together producing a combined value u_j. The weighted sum (u_j) is fed into a transfer function, σ, which outputs a value h_j. The outputs from the hidden layer are distributed to the output layer.

3. Output Layer — Arriving at a neuron in the output layer, the value from each hidden layer neuron is multiplied by a weight (w_{kj}), and the resulting weighted values are added together producing a combined value v_j. The weighted sum (v_j) is fed into a transfer function, σ, which outputs a value y_k. The *y* values are the outputs of the network.

If a regression analysis is being performed with a continuous target variable, then there is a single neuron in the output layer, and it generates a single y value. For classification problems with categorical target variables, there are *N* neurons in the output layer producing *N* values, one for each of the *N* categories of the target variable.

2.12.1 MULTILAYER PERCEPTRON ARCHITECTURE

The network diagram shown above is a full-connected, three layer, feed-forward, perceptron neural network. "Fully connected" means that the output from each input and hidden neuron is distributed to all of the neurons in the following layer. "Feed forward" means that the values only move from input to hidden to output layers; no values are fed back to earlier layers (a Recurrent Network allows values to be fed backward).

All neural networks have an input layer and an output layer, but the number of hidden layers may vary. Here is a diagram of a perceptron network with two hidden layers and four total layers:

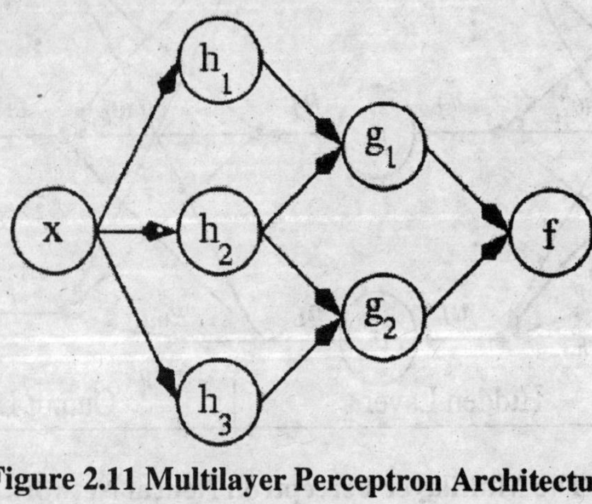

Figure 2.11 Multilayer Perceptron Architecture

When there is more than one hidden layer, the output from one hidden layer is fed into the next hidden layer and separate weights are applied to the sum going into each layer.

2.12.2 TRAINING MULTILAYER PERCEPTRON NETWORKS

The goal of the training process is to find the set of weight values that will cause the output from the neural network to match the actual target values as closely as possible. There are several issues involved in designing and training a multilayer perceptron network:

- Selecting how many hidden layers to use in the network.
- Deciding how many neurons to use in each hidden layer.
- Finding a globally optimal solution that avoids local minima.
- Converging to an optimal solution in a reasonable period of time.
- Validating the neural network to test for overfitting.

2.12.3 SELECTING THE NUMBER OF HIDDEN LAYERS

For nearly all problems, one hidden layer is sufficient. Two hidden layers are required for modeling data with discontinuities such as a saw tooth wave pattern. Using two hidden layers rarely improves the model, and it may introduce a greater risk of converging to a local minima. There is no theoretical reason for using more than two hidden layers. DTREG can build models with one or two hidden layers. Three layer models with one hidden layer are recommended.

2.12.4 DECIDING HOW MANY NEURONS TO USE IN THE HIDDEN LAYERS

One of the most important characteristics of a perceptron network is the number of neurons in the hidden layer(s). If an inadequate number of neurons are used, the network will be unable to model complex data, and the resulting fit will be poor. If too many neurons are used, the training time may become excessively long, and, worse, the network may *over fit* the data. When overfitting occurs, the network will begin to model random noise in the data. The result is that the model fits the training data extremely well, but it generalizes poorly to new, unseen data. Validation must be used to test for this.

DTREG includes an automated feature to find the optimal number of neurons in the hidden layer. You specify the minimum and maximum number of neurons you want it to test, and it will build models using varying numbers of neurons and measure the quality using either cross validation or hold-out data not used for training. This is a highly effective method for finding the optimal number of neurons, but it is computationally expensive, because many models must be built, and each model has to be validated. If you have a multiprocessor computer, you can configure DTREG to use multiple CPU's during the process.

The automated search for the optimal number of neurons only searches the first hidden layer. If you select a model with two hidden layers, you must manually specify the number of neurons in the second hidden layer.

2.12.5 FINDING A GLOBALLY OPTIMAL SOLUTION

A typical neural network might have a couple of hundred weighs whose values must be found to produce an optimal solution. If neural networks were linear models like linear regression, it would be a breeze to find the optimal set of weights. But the output of a neural network as a function of the inputs is often highly nonlinear; this makes the optimization process complex.

If you plotted the error as a function of the weights, you would likely see a rough surface with many local minima such as this:

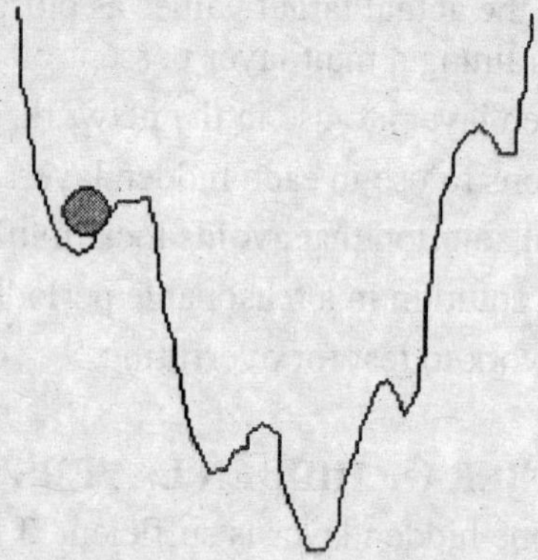

Figure 2.12 Optimal Solution

This picture is highly simplified because it represents only a single weight value (on the horizontal axis). With a typical neural network, you would have a 200-dimension, rough surface with many local valleys.

Optimization methods such as steepest descent and conjugate gradient are highly susceptible to finding local minima if they begin the search in a valley near a local minimum. They have no ability to see the big picture and find the global minimum.

Several methods have been tried to avoid local minima. The simplest is just to try a number of random starting points and use the one with the best value. A more sophisticated technique called *simulated annealing* improves on this by trying widely separated random values and then gradually reducing ("cooling") the random jumps in the hope that the location is getting closer to the global minimum.

DTREG uses the Nguyen-Widrow algorithm to select the initial range of starting weight values. It then uses the conjugate gradient algorithm to optimize the weights. Conjugate gradient usually finds the optimum weights quickly, but there is no guarantee that the weight values it finds are globally optimal. So it is useful to allow DTREG to try the optimization multiple times with different sets of initial random weight values. The number of tries allowed is specified on the Multilayer Perceptron property page.

2.13 LINEAR SEPARABILITY

when two sets of points in a two-dimensional graph can be completely separated by a single line, they are said to be **linearly separable**. In general, two groups are linearly separable in n-dimensional space if they can be separated by an (n – 1)-dimensional <u>hyperplane</u>. For 2-dimensional inputs, if there exists a line (whose equation us $\omega_0 + \omega_1 x_1 + \omega_2 x_2 = 0$) that separates all samples of one class from the other class, then an appropriate perceptron (with weights ω_0, ω_1,

ω_2 for the connections from inputs 1, x_1, x_2, respectively) can be derived from the equation of the separating line. Such classification problems are said to be "linearly separable," i.e., separable by a linear combination of inputs.

The close correspondence between perceptron weights and the coefficients of terms in the equations of lines can be used to arrive at the converse result as well. If there is a simple perceptron (with weight ω_0, ω_1, ω_2 for the connections from inputs 1, x_1, x_2, respectively) that can separate samples of two classes, then we can obtain the equation $(\omega_0 + \omega_1 x_1 + \omega_0, \omega_2 x_2 = 0)$ of a line that separates samples of the two classes.

Therefore, if the samples are NOT linearly separable, i.e., no straight line can possibly separate samples belonging to two classes, then there CANNOT be any simple perceptron that achieves the classification task. This is the fundamental limitation of simple perceptron, considered here for 2-dimensional input samples. Example of linearly nonseparable classes are illustrated in Figure 2.13. Most real-life classification problem are linearly nonseparable, and hence cannot be solved using perceptrons.

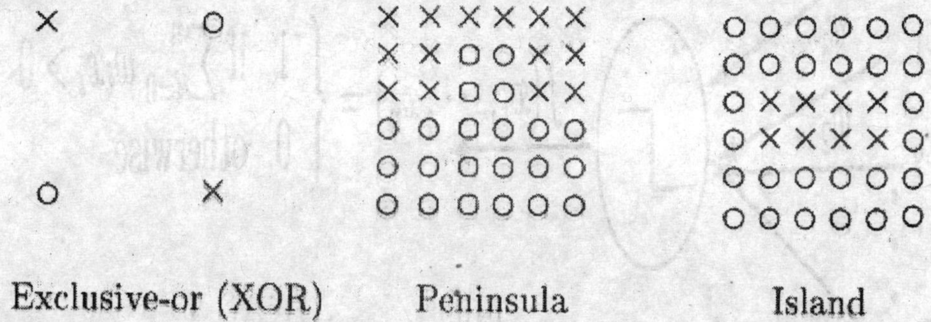

Figure 2.13 Examples of linearly nonseparable classes: Crosses indicate samples of one class, and circles indicate samples of another class.

So far, we have examined with two input dimensions (say x_1, x_2). If there is only one input dimension (say x), then the 2-class problem can be solved using a perceptron if and only if there is some value x_0 of x such that all samples of one class occur for $x > x_0$, and all samples of the other class occur for $x < x_0$. (See Figure 2.14)

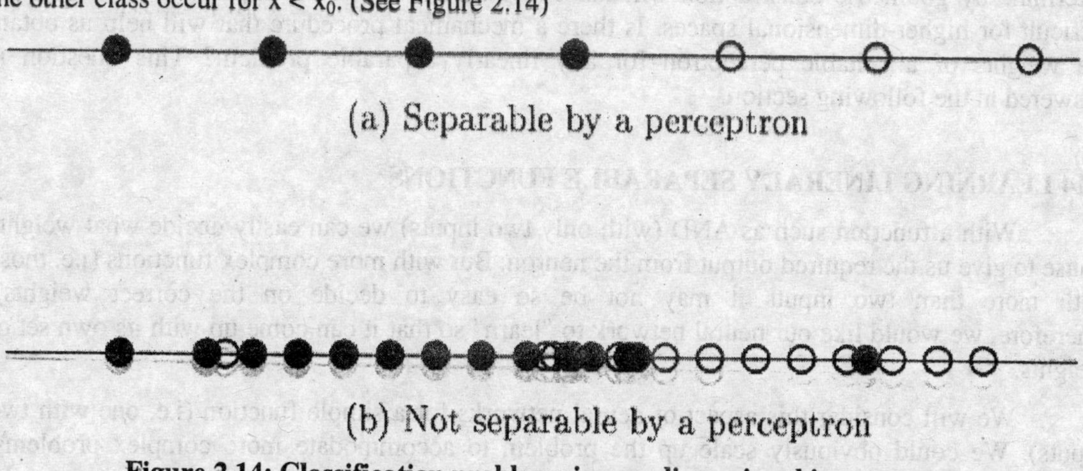

Figure 2.14: Classification problems in one-dimensional input space.

If there are 3 input dimensions, a 2-class problem can be solved using a perceptron if and only if there is a plane that separates samples of different classed. As in the 2-dimensional case, coefficients of terms in the equation of the plane correspond to the weights of the perceptron. For spaces having a higher number of input dimensions, out geometric intuitions need to be suitably extended, imagining "hyperplanes" that can separate samples of different classes. Each hyperplane in n dimensions is defined by the equation

$$\omega_0,\ \omega_1 x_1 + \omega_2\omega_2 + \ldots + \omega_n\ \omega_n = 0$$

dividing the n-dimensional space into two regions, in which $\omega_0 + \omega_1 x_1 + \ \omega_2\omega_2 \ldots + \omega_n x_n > 0$ and $\omega_0 + \omega_1 x_1 + \ \omega_2\omega_2 \ldots + \omega_n x_n < 0$, respectively. This again corresponds exactly with the decision made by the perception whose weights are $\omega_1 + \omega_2, \ldots, \omega_n$ and threshold is ω_0, as shown in Figure 2.15.

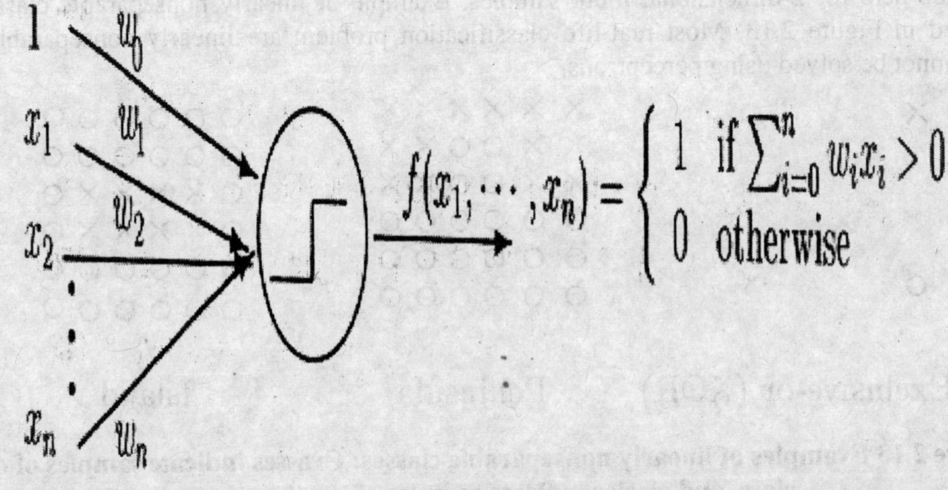

Figure 2.15: Generic perceptron for n-dimensional input space, implementing the hyperplane $\sum^{n}_{i=0} \omega_i x_i = 0$.

For simple examples, and for two-dimensional input spaces, it is relatively easy to determine by geometric construction whether two classes are linearly separable. Become very difficult for higher-dimensional spaces. Is there a mechanical procedure that will help us obtain the weights of a suitable perceptron for any linearly separable problem? This question is answered in the following section.

2.14 LEARNING LINERALY SEPARABLE FUNCTIONS

With a function such as AND (with only two inputs) we can easily decide what weights to use to give us the required output from the neuron. But with more complex functions (i.e. those with more than two inputs it may not be so easy to decide on the correct weights). Therefore, we would like our neural network to "learn" so that it can come up with its own set of weights.

We will consider this aspect of neural networks for a simple function (i.e. one with two inputs). We could obviously scale up the problem to accommodate more complex problems, providing the problems are linearly separable.

Consider this truth table (AND) and the neuron that we **hope** will represent it.

AND		
$Input_1$	$Input_2$	Output
0	0	0
0	1	0
1	0	0
1	1	1

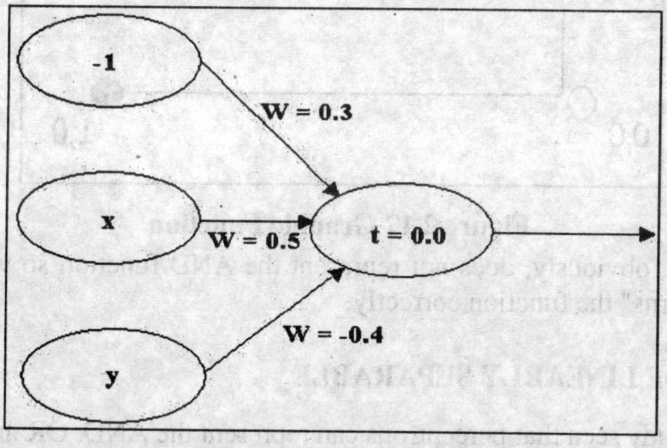

Figure 2.16 AND Map

In fact, all we have done is set the weights to random values between -0.5 and 0.5

By applying the activation function for each of the four possible inputs to this neuron (try it) it actually gives us the following truth table

???		
$Input_1$	$Input_2$	Output
0	0	0
0	1	0
1	0	1
1	1	0

Which can be graphically represented as follows

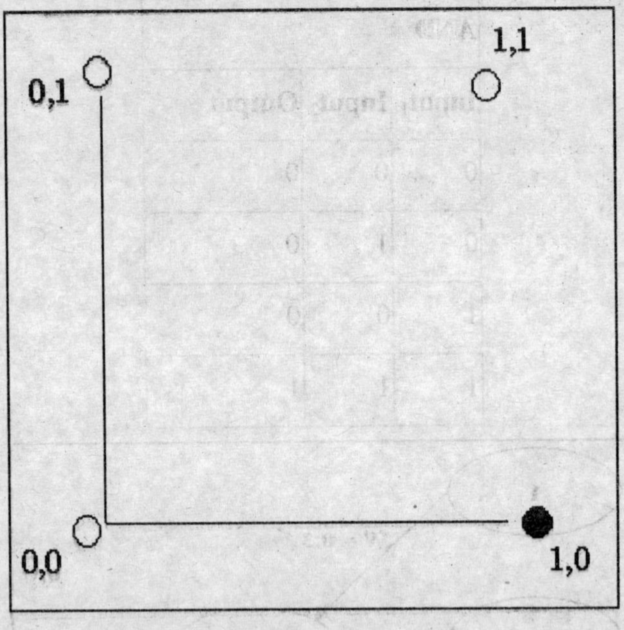

Figure 2.17 Graphic Function

The network, obviously, does not represent the AND function so we need to adjust the weights so that it "learns" the function correctly.

2.14.1 EXAMPLE OF LINEARLY SEPARABLE

We have already seen that perceptrons can represent the AND, OR and NOT logic functions. But does it follow that a perceptron (a single-layer, feed-forward network) can represent any boolean function?
Unfortunately, this is not the case.

To see why, consider these two truth tables

AND		
$Input_1$	**$Input_2$**	**Output**
0	0	0
0	1	0
1	0	0
1	1	1

XOR		
$Input_1$	**$Input_2$**	**Output**
0	0	0
0	1	1
1	0	1
1	1	0

We can represent these two truth tables

graphically. Like this

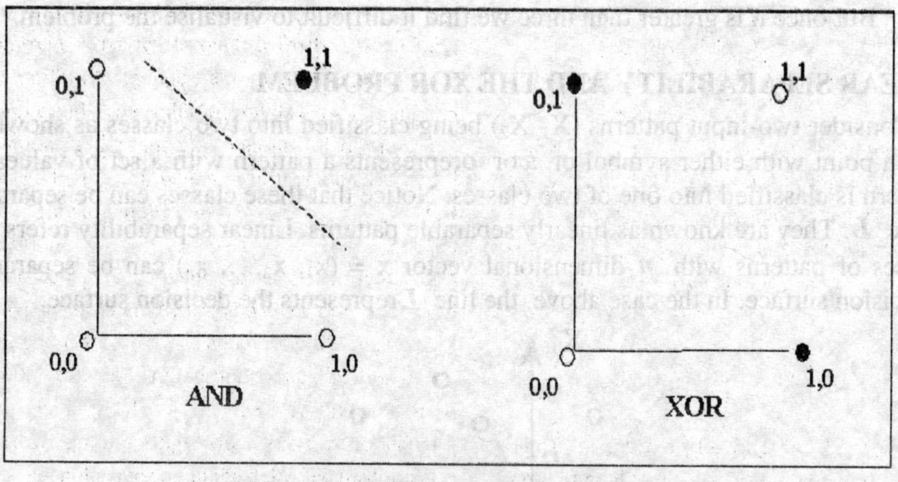

Figure 2.18 AND and XOR Function

(where a filled circle represents an output of one and a hollow circle represents an output of zero).

If you look at the AND graph you will see that we can divide the one's from the zero's with a line. This is not possible with XOR.Functions such as AND are called linearly separable.It was the proof by Minsky & Papert in 1969 that perceptrons could only learn linearly separable functions that led to decline in neural network research until the mid 1980's when it was proved that other network architectures could learn these type of functions.Although, only being able to learn linearly separable functions is a major disadvantage of the perceptron it is still worth studying as it is relatively simple and can help provide a framework for other architectures.It should however, be realised that perceptrons are not only limited to two inputs (e.g. the AND function). We can have n inputs which gives us an n-dimension problem.When n=3 we can still visualise the linear separability of the problem (see diagram below).

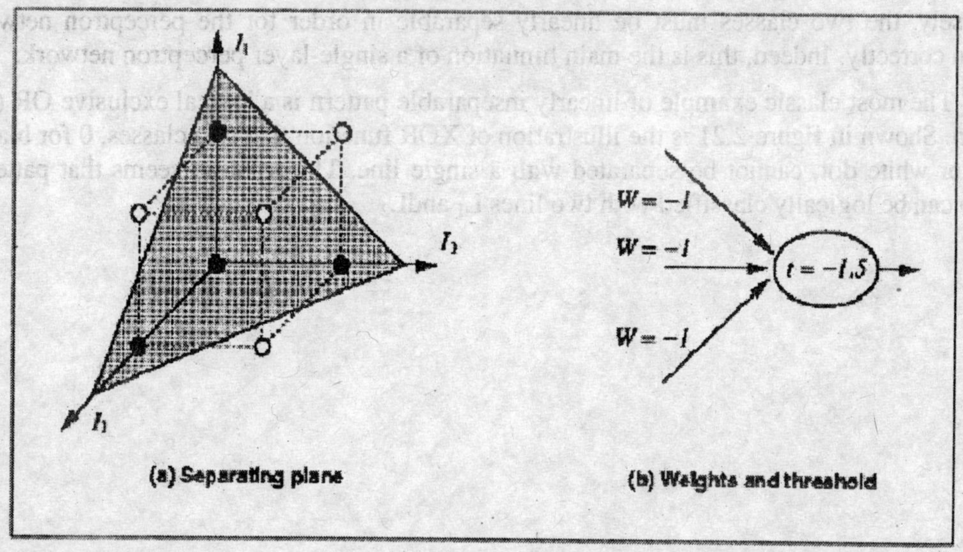

Figure 2.19 Seperating Plane

But once n is greater than three we find it difficult to visualise the problem.

2.15 LINEAR SEPARABILITY AND THE XOR PROBLEM

Consider two-input patterns (X_1, X_2) being classified into two classes as shown in figure 2.20. Each point with either symbol of *x* or *o* represents a pattern with a set of values (X_1, X_2). Each pattern is classified into one of two classes. Notice that these classes can be separated with a single line *L*. They are known as linearly separable patterns. Linear separability refers to the fact that classes of patterns with *n*-dimensional vector x = (x_1, x_2,..., x_n) can be separated with a single decision surface. In the case above, the line *L* represents the decision surface.

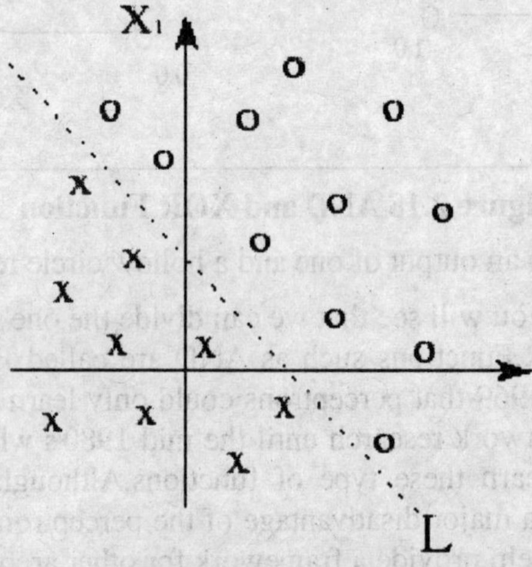

Figure 2.20: Linearly Separable Pattern

The processing unit of a single-layer perceptron network is able to categorize a set of patterns into two classes as the linear threshold function defines their linear separability. Conversely, the two classes must be linearly separable in order for the perceptron network to function correctly. Indeed, this is the main limitation of a single-layer perceptron network.

The most classic example of linearly inseparable pattern is a logical exclusive-OR (XOR) function. Shown in figure 2.21 is the illustration of XOR function that two classes, 0 for black dot and 1 for white dot, cannot be separated with a single line. The solution seems that patterns of (X_1, X_2) can be logically classified with two lines L_1 and L_2.

X_1	X_2	Y
0	0	0
0	1	1
1	0	1
1	1	0

$$Y = X_1 \oplus X_2$$

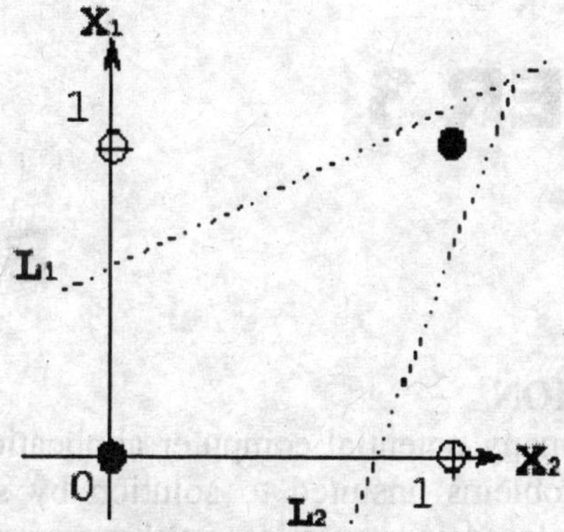

Figure 2.21: Exclusive-OR Function

QUESTION BANK

Q1. What is perceptron?
Q2. Explain the concept of perceptron neuron model with the help of diagram?
Q3. What is decision boundary? Explain with the help of example?
Q4. Discuss architecture of perceptron with the help of diagram?
Q5. Draw the diagram of perceptron network and explain its working?
Q6. What is single neuron perceptron? Explain with the help of two input/output perceptron example?
Q7. Draw the decision boundary diagram for two input perceptron and also explain it?
Q8. What is multi neuron perceptron?
Q9. What is learning rule? Discuss the perceptron learning rule with the help of test problem?
Q10. How we can construct learning rules for perceptron network? Explain one example of learning rule?
Q11. How we can train a network? Explain the perceptron training with the help of example?
Q12. What are the limitations of perceptron network?
Q13. Explain the convergence theorem of perceptron learning rule?
Q14. Explain the model of multi layer perceptron neural network with the help of the labeled diagram?
Q15. Explain the architecture level of multi layer perceptron?
Q16. Write various steps used for training multi layer perceptron network?
Q17. What is linear separability? Explain the linearly separable classes with the help of examples?
Q18. How we can say AND function is linear separable?
Q19. What is separating plane? Explain with the help of the example?
Q20. Explain the XOR problem with the help of linear separability?

CHAPTER 3

BACKPROPAGATION

3.1 INTRODUCTION

There are many potential computer applications that are difficult to implement because there are many problems unsuited to solution by sequential process. Applications that must perform some complex data translation, yet have no predefined mapping function to describe the translation process, or those that must provide a "best guess" as output when presented with noisy input data are but two examples of problems of this type. An ANS that we have found to be useful in addressing problems requiring recognition of complex patterns and performing nontrivial mapping functions is the backpropagation network (BPN), formalized first by Werbos , and later by Parker and by Rummelhart and McClelland. This network, illustrated generically in Figure3.1, is designed to operate as a multilayer, feedforward network, using the supervised mode of learning. The chapter begins with a discussion of an example of a problem mapping character image to ASCII, which appears simple, but can quickly overwhelm traditional approaches. Then, we look at how the backpropagation network operates to solve such a problem. Following that discussion is a detailed derivation of the equations that govern the learning process in the backpropagation network.

3.2 THE BACKPROPAGATION NETWORK

To illustrate some problems that often arise when we are attempting to automate complex pattern-recognition applications, let us consider the design of a computer program that must translate a 5 x 7 matrix of binary numbers representing the bit-mapped pixel image of an alphanumeric character to its equivalent eight-bit ASCII code. This basic problem, pictured in Figure 3.2, appears to be relatively trivial at first glance. Since there is no obvious mathematical function

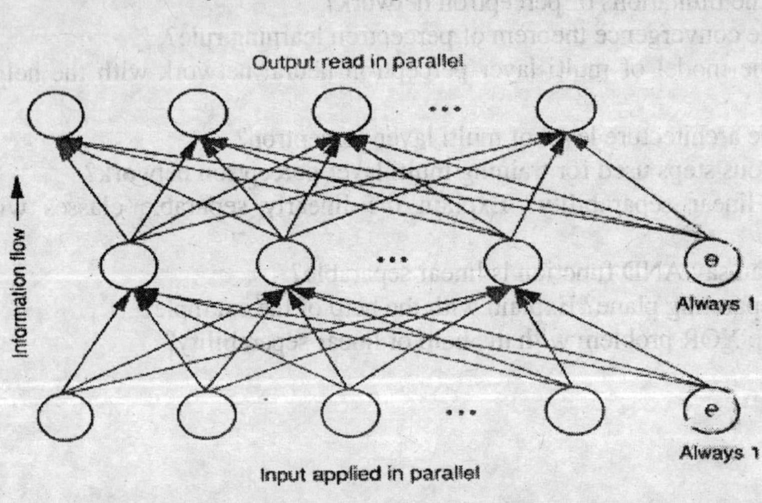

Figure 3.1 The general backpropagation network architecture is shown.

that will perform the desired translation, and because it would undoubtedly take too much time (both human and computer time) to perform a pixel-by-pixel correlation, the best algorithmic solution would be to use a lookup table.

The lookup table needed to solve this problem would be a one-dimensional linear array of ordered pairs, each taking the form:

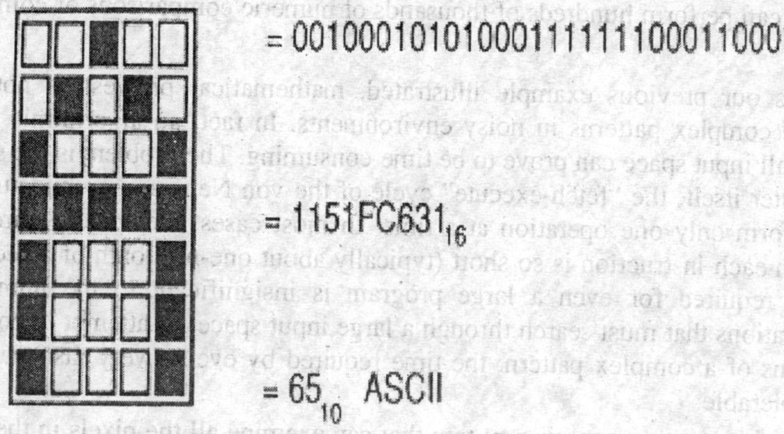

Figure 3.2Each character image is mapped to its corresponding ASCII code.

The first is the numeric equivalent of the bit-pattern code, which we generate by moving the system rows of the matrix to a single row and considering the result to be a 35-bit binary number. The second is the ASCII code associated with the character. The array would contain exactly the same number of ordered-pairs as there were characters to convert. The algorithm needed to perform the conversion process would take the following form.

Although the lookup-table approach is reasonability fast and easy to maintain, there are many situations that occur in real systems that cannot be handled by this method. For example, consider the dame pixel-image-to-ASCII conversion process in a more realistic environment. Let's suppose that our character image scanner alters a random pixel in the input image matrix due to noise when the image was read. This single pixel error would cause the lookup algorithm to return either a null or the wrong ASCII code, since the match between the input pattern and the target pattern must be exact.

Now consider the amount of additional software (and, hence, CPU time) that must be added to the lookup-table algorithm to improve the ability of the computer to "guess" at which character the noisy image should have been. Single-bit errors are fairly easy to find and correct. Multibit errors become increasingly difficult as the number of bit errors grows. To complicate matters even further, how could our software compensate for noise on the image if that noise happened to make an "O" look like a "Q", or an "E" look like an "F"? If our character-conversion system had to produce an accurate output all the time, an inordinate amount of CPU time would be spent eliminating noise form the from the input pattern prior to attempting to translate it to ASCII.

One solution to this dilemma is to take advantage of parallel nature of neural networks to reduce the time required by a sequential processor to perform the mapping. In addition, system-development time can be reduced because the network can learn the proper algorithm without having someone deduce that algorithm in advance.

3.3 THE BACKPROPAGATION APPROACH

Problem such as the noisy image-to-ASCII example are difficult to solve by computer due to the basic incompatibility between the machine and the problem. Most of today's computer systems have been designed to perform mathematical and logic functions at speeds that are incomprehensible to humans. Even the relatively unsophisticated desktop microcomputers commonplace today can perform hundreds of thousands of numeric comparisons or combinations every second.

However, as our previous example illustrated, mathematical prowess is not what is needed to recognize complex patterns in noisy environments. In fact, an algorithmic search of even a relatively small input space can prove to be time-consuming. The problem is the sequential nature of the computer itself; the "fetch-execute" cycle of the von Neumann architecture allows the machine to perform only one operation at a time. In most cases, the time required by the computer to perform each instruction is so short (typically about one-millionth of a second) that the aggregate time required for even a large program is insignificant to the human users. However, for applications that must search through a large input space, or attempt to correlate all possible permutations of a complex pattern, the time required by even a very fast machine can quickly become intolerable.

What we need is a new processing system that can examine all the pixels in the image in parallel. Ideally, such a system would not have to be programmed explicitly; rather, it would adapt itself to "learn" the relationship between a set of example patterns, and would be able to apply the same relationship to new input patterns. This system would be able to focus on the features of an arbitrary input that resemble other patterns seen previously, such as those pixels in the noisy image that "look" like a known character, and to ignore the noise. Fortunately, such a system exists: we call this system the backpropagation network (BPN).

3.4 BPN OPERATION

We will cover the details of the mechanics of backpropagation. A summary description of the network operation is appropriate here, to begin with, the network learns a predefined se of input-output example pairs by using a two-phase propagate-adapt cycle. After an input pattern has been applied as a stimulus to the first later of network units, it is propagated through each upper layer until an output is generated. This output pattern is then compared to the desired output, and an error signal is computed for each output unit.

The error signals are then transmitted backward from the output layer to each node in the intermediate layer that contributes directly to the output. However, each unit in the intermediate layer receives only a portion of the total error signal, based roughly on the relative contribution the unit made to the original output. This process repeats, layer by layer, until each node in the network has received an error signal that describes its relative contribution to the total error. Based on the error signal received, connection weights are then updated by each unit ti cause the network to converge toward a state that allows all the training patterns to be encoded.

The significance of this process is that, as the network trains, the nodes in the intermediate layers organize themselves such that different nodes learn to recognize different features of the total input space. After training, when presented with an arbitrary input pattern that is noisy or incomplete, the units in the hidden layers of the network will respond with an active output if the new input contains a pattern that resembles the feature the individual units learned to recognize during training. Conversely, hidden-layer units have a tendency to inhibit their outputs if the input pattern does not contain the feature that they were trained to recognize.

As the signals propagate through the different layers in the network, the activity pattern present at each upper layer can be thought of as a pattern with features that can be recognized by units in the subsequent layer. The output pattern generated can be thought of as a feature map that presence of many different feature combinations at the input. The total effect of this behavior is that the BPN provides an effective means of allowing a computer system examine data patterns that may be incomplete or noisy, and to recognize subtle patterns from the partial input.

Several researchers have shown that during training, BPNs tend to develop internal relationships between nodes so as to organize the training data into classes of patterns. This tendency can be extrapolated to the hypothesis that all hidden-layer units BPN are somehow associated with specific features of the input pattern as a result of training. Exactly what the association is may or may not be evident to the human observer. What is important is that the network has found an internal representation that enables it to generate the desired outputs when given the training inputs. This same internal representation can be applied to inputs that were not used during training. The BPN will classify these previously unseen inputs according to the features they share with the training examples.

3.5 USING BAKPROPAGATION

The perception learning rule of Frank Rosenblatt and the LMS algorithm of Bernard Windrow and Marcian Hoff were to train single-layer perceptron-like networks. As we have discussed in previous chapters, these single-layer networks suffer from the disadvantage that they are only able to solve linearly separable classification problems. Both Rosenblatt and Widrow were aware of these limitations and proposed multilayer networks that could overcome them, but they were not able to generalize their algorithms to train these more powerful networks.

Apparently the first description of an algorithm to train multilayer networks was contained in the thesis of Paul Verbose in 1974. This thesis presented the algorithm in the context of general networks, with neural networks as a special case, and was not disseminated in the neural network community, It was not until the mid 1980s that the back propagation algorithm was rediscovered and widely publicized. It was rediscovered independently by David Rumelhart, Geoffrey Hinton and Ronald Williams, David Parker , and Yawn Le Cun . The algorithm was popularized by its inclusion in the book parallet Distributed Processing, which described the work of the Parallel Distributed processing Group led by psychologists David Rumelhart and James McClelland. The publication of this book soured a torrent of research in neural networks. The multilayer perception, trained by the back propagation algorithm, is currently the most widely used neural network.

In this chapter we will first investigate the capabilities of multilayer networks and then present the back propagation algorithm.

3.6 MULTILAYER PERCEPTRONS

We first introduced the notation for multilayer networks in Chapter 2. For ease of reference we have reproduced the diagram of the three-layer perception in Figure 3.3. Note that we have simply cascaded three perception networks, The output of the first network is the input to the second network, and the output of the second network is the input to the third network Each layer may have a different number of neurons, and even a different transfer function .Recall from Chapter 2 that we are using Superscripts to identify the layer number, Thus, the weight matrix for the first layer is written as W^1 and the weight matrix for the second layer is written W^2. To identify the structure of a multilayer network, we will sometimes use the following shorthand notation, where the number of input is followed by the number of neurons in each layer:

$$R - S^1 - S^2 - S^3 \qquad (3.1)$$

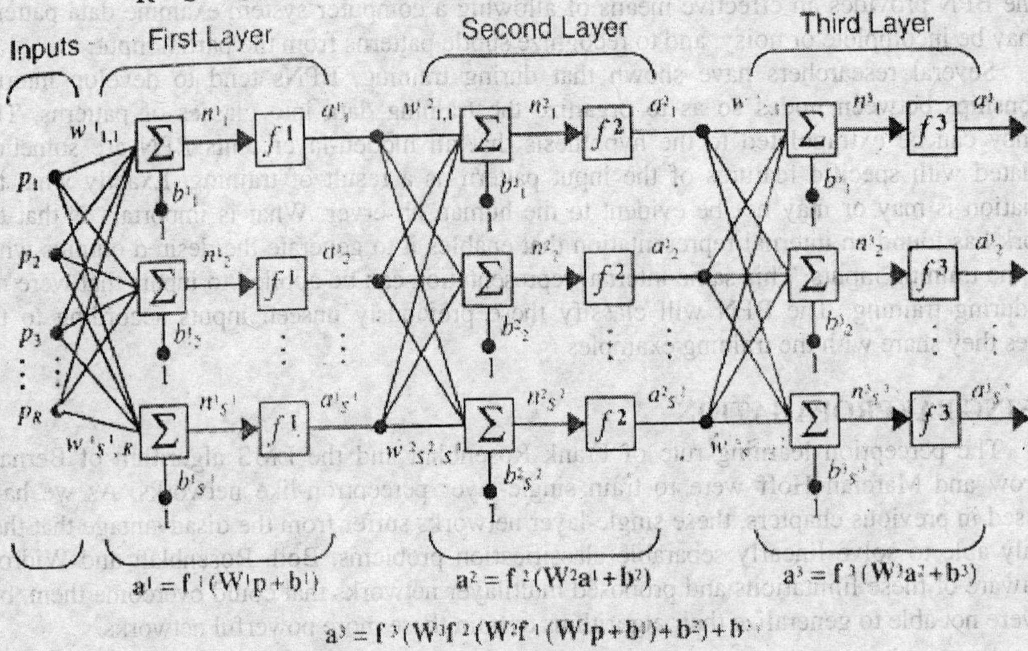

Figure 3.3 Three-layer network

Let's now investigate the capabilities of these multilayer perception networks. First we will look at the use of multilayer networks for pattern classification, and then we will discuss their application to function approximation.

3.6.1 PATTERN CLASSIFICATION

To illustrate the capabilities of the multilayer perceptron for pattern classification, consider the classic exclusive-or (XOR) problem. The input/target pairs for the XOR gate are

$$\left\{ P_1 = \begin{bmatrix} 0 \\ 0 \end{bmatrix}, t_1 = 0 \right\} \left\{ P_2 = \begin{bmatrix} 0 \\ 1 \end{bmatrix}, t_2 = 1 \right\} \left\{ P_3 = \begin{bmatrix} 1 \\ 0 \end{bmatrix}, t_3 = 1 \right\} \left\{ P_4 = \begin{bmatrix} 1 \\ 1 \end{bmatrix}, t_4 = 0 \right\}$$

This problem, which is illustrated graphically in the figure to the left, was used by Minsky and Papert in 1969 to demonstrate the limitations of the single-layer perceptron. Because the two categories are not linearly separable, a single-layer perceptron cannot perform the classification. A two-layer network can solve the XOR problem. In fact, there are many different multilayer solutions. One solution is to use two neurons in the first layer to create two p decision boundaries.

The first boundary separates p_1 from the other patterns, and the second boundary separates p_4. Then the second layer is used to combine the two boundaries together using an AND operation. The decision boundaries for each first-layer neuron are shown in figure 3.4.

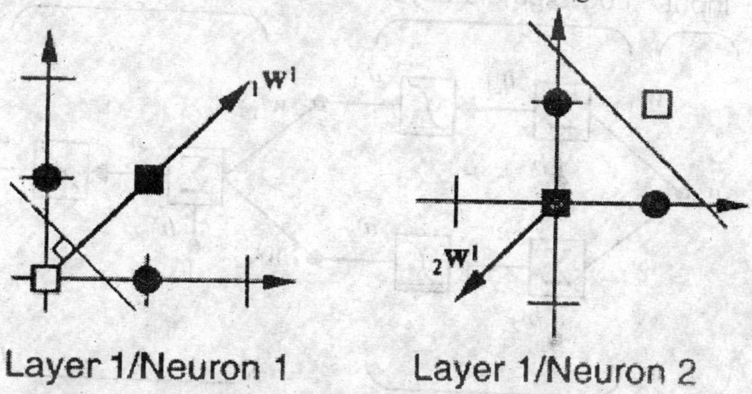

Figure 3.4 Decision Boundaries for XOR Network

The resulting two-layer, 2-2-1 network is shown in Figure 3.5. The overall decision regions for this network are shown in the figure in the left margin. The shaded region indicated those input that will produce a network output of 1.

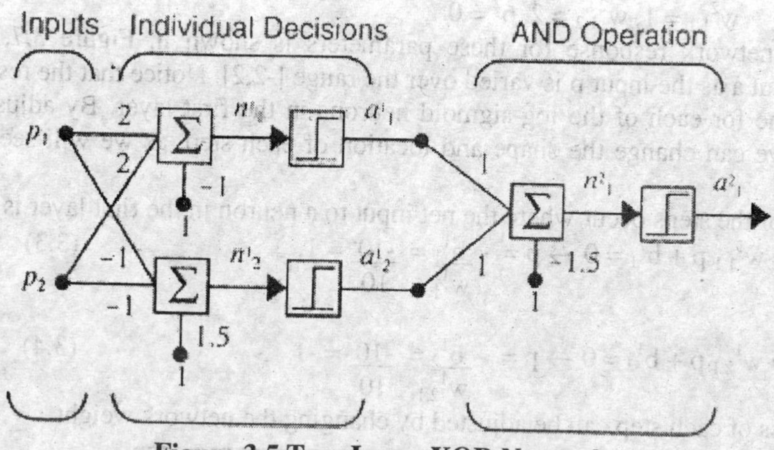

Figure 3.5 Two-Layer XOR Network

See Problems P3.3 and P3.4 for more on the use of multilayer networks for pattern classification.

3.6.2 FUNCTION APPROXIMATION

Up to this point in text we have viewed neural networks mainly in the in the context of pattern classification. It is also instructive to view networks as function approximates. In control systems, for example, the objective is to find an appropriate feedback function that maps from measured outputs to control inputs. In adaptive filtering (Chapter 4) the objective is to find a function that maps from delayed values of an input single to an appropriate output single. The following example will illustrate the flexibility of the multilayer perceptron for implementing functions.Consider the two-layer, 1-2-1 network shown in figure 3.6. For this example the transfer function for the first layer is log-sigmoid and the transfer function for the second layer is linear. In other words.

$$f^1(n) = \frac{1}{1+e^{-n}} \text{ and } f^2(n) = n. \quad (3.2)$$

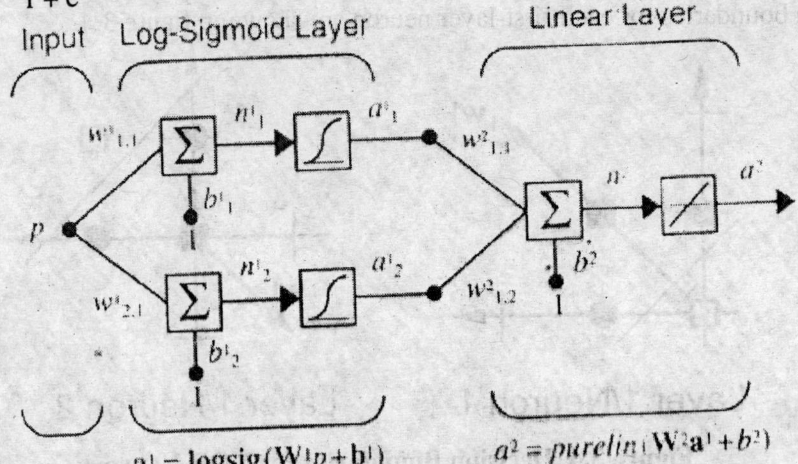

Figure 3.6 Example Function Approximation Network

Suppose that the nominal values of the weight and biases for this network are

$w^1_{1,1} = 10$, $w^1_{2,1} = 10$, $b^1_1 = -10$, $b^1_2 = 10$,

$w^2_{1,1} = 1$, $w^2_{1,2} = 2$, $b^2 = 0$

The network response for these parameters is shown in Figure 3.7, which plots the network output a as the input p is varied over the range [-2,2]. Notice that the response consists of two steps, one for each of the log-sigmoid neurons in the first layer. By adjusting the network parameters we can change the shape and location of each step, as we will see in the following discussion.

The centers of the steps occur where the net input to a neuron in the first layer is zero:

$$n^1_1 = w^1_{1,1}\,p + b^1_1 = 0 \rightarrow p = -\frac{b^1_1}{w^1_{1,1}} = \frac{-10}{10} = 1, \quad (3.3)$$

$$n^1_2 = w^1_{2,1}\,p + b^1_2 = 0 \rightarrow p = -\frac{b^1_2}{w^1_{2,1}} = \frac{-10}{10} = -1, \quad (3.4)$$

The steepness of each step can be adjusted by changing the network weight.

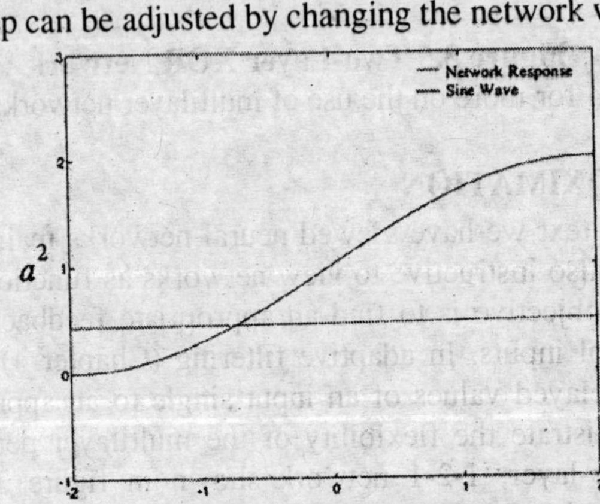

Figure 3.7 Nominal Response of Network of Figure 3.6

Figure 3.7 illustrates the effects of parameters change on the network response. The blue curve is the nominal response. The other curves correspond to the network response when one parameter at a time is varied over the following ranges:

$$-1 \le w^2_{1,1} \le 1,\ -1 \le w^2_{1,2} \le b^1_2 \le 20,\ -1 \le b^2 \le 1. \qquad (3.5)$$

Figure 3.8 (a) shows how the network biases in the first (hidden) layer can be used to locate the position of the steps. Figure 3.8 (b) illustrates how the weights determine the slope of the steps. The bias in the second (output) layer shifts the entire network response u or down, as can be seen in Figure 3.8 (d).

From this example we can see how flexible the multilayer network is. It would appear that we could use such networks to approximate almost any function, if we had a sufficient number of neurons in the hidden layer. In fact, it has been shown that two-layer networks, with sigmoid transfer functions in the hidden layer and linear transfer functions in the output layer, can approximate virtually any function of interest to any degree of accuracy, provided sufficiently many hidden units are available .

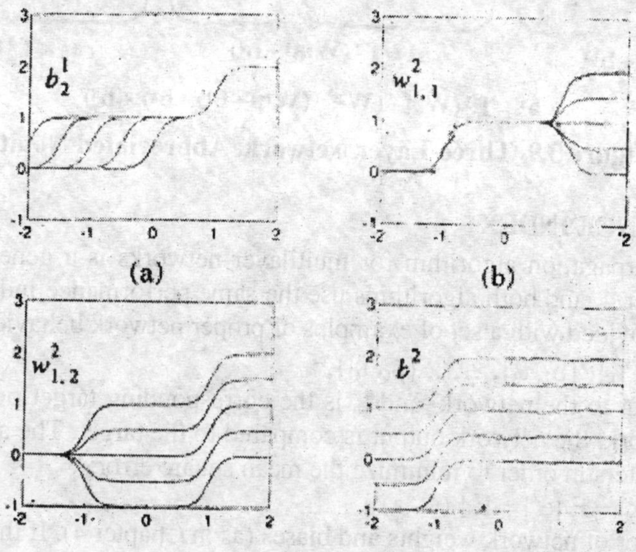

Figure 3.8 Effect of parameter Changes on Network Response

Now that we have some idea of the power of multilayer perceptron networks for pattern recognition and function approximation, then next step is to develop an algorithm to train such networks.

3.7 THE BACKPROPAGATION ALGORITHM

It will simplify our development of the backpropagation algorithm if we use the abbreviated notation for the multilayer network, which we introduced in Chapter 2. The three-layer network in abbreviated notation is shown in Figure 3.9.

As we discussed earlier, for multilayer networks the output of one layer becomes the input to the following layer. The equations that describe this operation are

$$a^{m+1} = f^{m+1}(W^{m+1} a^m + b^{m+1}) \text{ for } m = 0, 1, \ldots, M-1, \qquad (3.6)$$

where M is the number of layers in the network. The neurons in the first layer revive external inputs:

$$a^0 = p, \tag{3.7}$$

which provides the starting point for Eq. (3.6). The outputs of the neurons in the last layer are considered the network outputs:

$$a = a^M \tag{3.8}$$

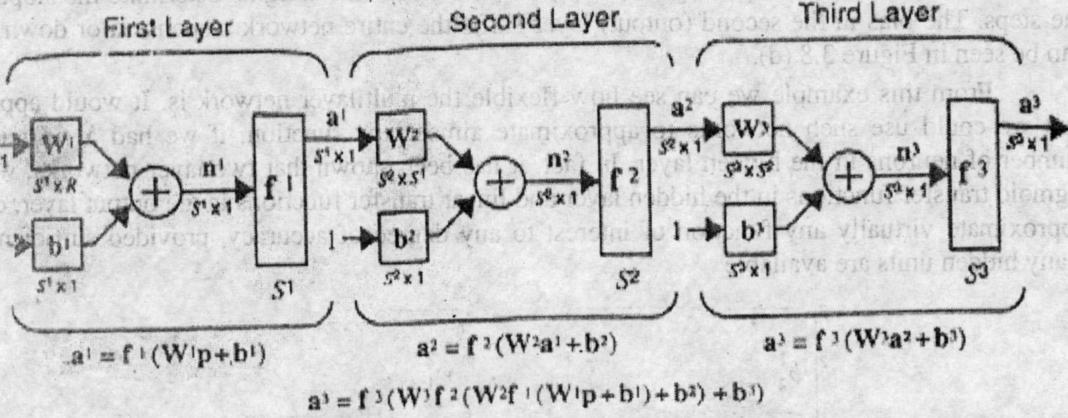

Figure 3.9 Three-Layer Network. Abbreviated Notation

3.7.1 PERFORMANCE INDEX

The backporpagation algorithm for multilayer networks is a generalization of the LMS algorithm of Chapter 4, and both algorithms use the same performance index: mean square error. The algorithm is provided with a set of examples of proper network behavior:

$$\{p_1, t_1\}, \{p_2, t_2\}, \ldots\ldots, \{p_Q, t_Q\}, \tag{3.9}$$

where p_q is an input to the network, and t_q is the corresponding target output. As each input is applied to the network, the network output is compared to the target. The algorithm should adjust the network parameters in order to minimize the mean square error:

$$F(x) = E[e^2] = E[(t - a)^2] \tag{3.10}$$

Where x is the vector of network weights and biases (as in Chapter 4). If the network has multiple outputs this generalizes to

$$F(x) = E[e^T e] = E[(t - a)^T (t - a)] \tag{3.11}$$

As with the LMS algorithm, we will approximate the mean square error by

$$F(x) = (t(k) - a(k))^T (t(k) - a(k)) = e^T(k)\, e(k), \tag{3.12}$$

where the expectation of the squared error has replaced by the squared error at iteration k.

The steepest descent algorithm for the approximate mean square error is

$$w^m_{i,j}(k + 1) = w^m_{i,j}(k) - \alpha \frac{\partial F}{\partial w^m_{i,j}}, \tag{3.13}$$

$$b^m_i(k+1) = b^m_i(k) - \alpha \frac{\partial F}{\partial b^m_i}, \tag{3.14}$$

where α is the learning rate.

So far, this development is identical to that for the LMS algorithm. Now we come to the difficult part – the computation of the partial derivatives.

3.7.2 CHAIN RULE

For a single-layer linear network (the ADALINE) these partial derivatives are conveniently computed using LMS. For the multilayer network the error is not an explicit function of the weights in the hidden layers, therefore these derivatives are not computed so easily.

Because the error is an indirect function of the weights in the hidden layers, we will use the chain rule of calculus to calculate the derivatives. To review the chain rule, suppose that we have a function f that is an explicit function only of the variable n. We want to take the derivative of f with respect to a third variable w. The chain rule is then:

$$\frac{df\,(n\,(w))}{dw} = \frac{df\,(n)}{dw} \times \frac{dn\,(w)}{dw} \qquad (3.15)$$

For example, if

$$f\,(n) = e^n \text{ and } n = 2w, \text{ so that } f\,(n(w)) = e^2 \qquad (3.16)$$

then

$$\frac{df\,(n\,(w))}{dw} = \frac{df\,(n)}{dw} \times \frac{dn\,(w)}{dw} = (e^n)\,(2). \qquad (3.17)$$

We will use this concept to find the derivatives in Eq. (3.13) and Eq. (3.14):

$$\frac{\partial F}{\partial w_{i,j}^m} = \frac{\partial F}{\partial n_i^m} \times \frac{\partial_i^m}{\partial w_{i,j}^m} \qquad (3.18)$$

$$\frac{\partial F}{\partial b_i^m} = \frac{\partial F}{\partial n_i^m} \times \frac{\partial n_i^m}{\partial b_i^m} \qquad (3.19)$$

The second term in each of these equations can be easily computed, since the net input to layer m is an explicit function of the weights and bias in that layer:

$$n_i^m = \sum_{j=1}^{S^{m-1}} w_i^m\, a_j^{m-1} + b_i^m \qquad (3.20)$$

Therefore

$$\frac{\partial n_i^m}{\partial w_{i,j}^m} = a_j^{m-1}, \quad \frac{\partial n_i^m}{\partial b_i^m} = 1. \qquad (3.21)$$

If we now define

$$s_i^m \equiv \frac{\partial F}{\partial n_i^m}, \qquad (3.22)$$

(the sensitivity of F to changes in the ith element of the net input at layer m), then Eq. (3.18) and Eq. (3.19) can be simplified to

$$\frac{\partial F}{\partial w_{ij}^{m}} = s_i^{m-1} a_j^{m-1}, \tag{3.23}$$

$$\frac{\partial F}{\partial b_i^{m}} = s_i^{m} \tag{3.24}$$

We can now express the approximate steepest descent algorithm as

$$w_{i,j}^{m}(k+1) = w_{i,j}^{m}(k) - \alpha s_i^{m} a_j^{m-1} \tag{3.25}$$

$$b_i^{m}(k+1) = b_i^{m}(k) - \alpha s_i^{m}, \tag{3.26}$$

In matrix form this becomes:

$$W^{m}(k+1) = W^{m}(k) - \alpha s^{m}(a^{m-1}) \tag{3.27}$$

$$b^{m}(k+1) = b^{m}(k) - \alpha s^{m}, \tag{3.28}$$

where

$$s^{m} \equiv \partial F = \begin{pmatrix} \frac{\partial F}{\partial n_1^{m}} \\ \frac{\partial F}{\partial n_2^{m}} \\ \vdots \\ \frac{\partial F}{\partial n_{1\,s}^{m\,n}} \end{pmatrix} \tag{3.29}$$

SUMMARY

Let's summarize the backpropagation algorithm. The first step is to propagate the input forward through the network:

$$a^{0} = p, \tag{3.30}$$

$$a^{m+1} = f^{m+1}(W^{m+1}a^{m} + b^{m+1}) \text{ for } m = 0, 1, \ldots, M-1, \tag{3.31}$$

$$a = a^{M}, \tag{3.32}$$

The next step is to propagate the sensitivities backward through the network:

$$s^{M} = -2F^{M}(n^{M})(t-a), \tag{3.33}$$

$$s^{m} = F^{m}(n^{m})(W^{m+1})^{T}s^{m+1}, \text{ for } m = M-1, \ldots, 2, 1. \tag{3.34}$$

Finally, the weights and biases are updated using the approximate steepest descent rule:

$$W^{m}(k+1) = W^{m}(k) - \alpha s^{m}(a^{m-1})^{T}, \tag{3.35}$$

$$b^{m}(k+1) = b^{m}(k) - \alpha s^{m} \tag{3.36}$$

EXAMPLE

To illustrate the backporpagatin algorithm, let's choose a network and apply it to a particular problem. To begin, we will use the 1-2-1 network that we discussed earlier in this chapter. For convenience we have reproduced the network in Figure 3.10.

Next we want to define a problem for the network to solve. Suppose that we want to use the network to approximate the function

$$g(p) = 1 + \sin \frac{\pi}{4} p \quad \text{for } -2 \le p \le 2. \tag{3.37}$$

To obtain our training set we willevaluate this function at several values of p.

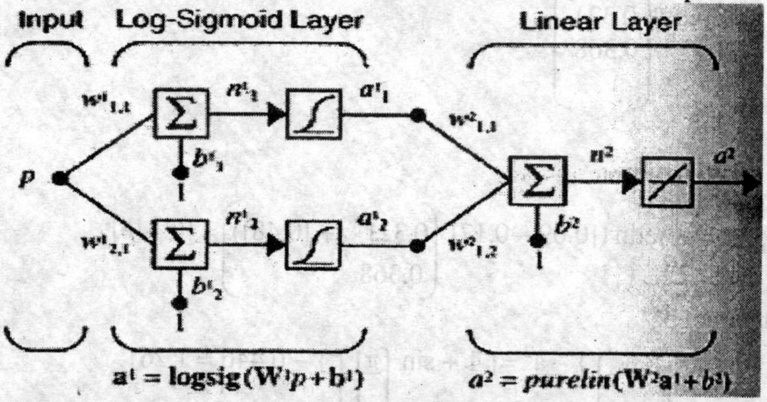

Figure 3.10 Example Function Approximation Network

Before we begin the backpropagation algorithm we need to choose some initial values for the network weights and biases. Generally these are chosen to be small random values. In the next chapter we will discuss some reasons for this. For now let's choose the values.

$$W^1(0) = \begin{pmatrix} -0.27 \\ -0.41 \end{pmatrix},\ b^1(0) = \begin{pmatrix} -0.48 \\ -0.13 \end{pmatrix},\ W^2(0) = [0.09\ -0.17],\ b^2(0) = [0.48].$$

The response of the network for these initial values is illustrated in Figure 3.11, along with the sine function we wish to approximate.

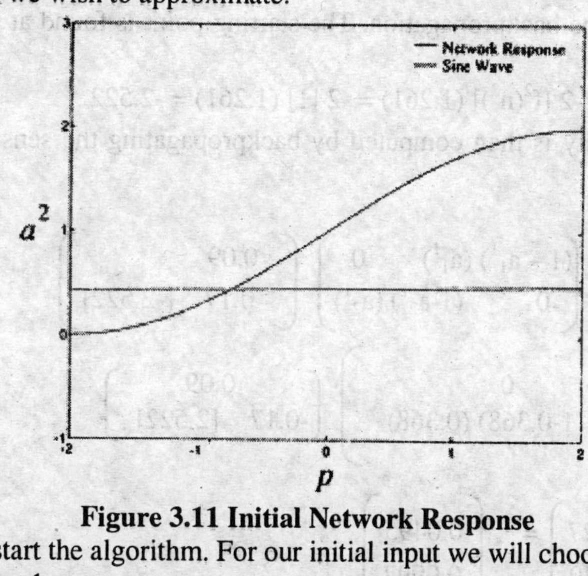

Figure 3.11 Initial Network Response

Now we are ready to start the algorithm. For our initial input we will choose p = 1:

$$a^0 = p = 1$$

The output of the first layer is then

$$a^1 = f^1(W^1a^0 + b^1) = \text{logsig}\left(\begin{pmatrix} -0.27 \\ -0.41 \end{pmatrix}[1] + \begin{pmatrix} -0.48 \\ -0.13 \end{pmatrix}\right) = \text{logsig}\left(\begin{pmatrix} -0.75 \\ -0.54 \end{pmatrix}\right)$$

$$\begin{pmatrix} \dfrac{1}{1+e^{0.75}} \\ \dfrac{1}{1+e^{0.54}} \end{pmatrix} = \begin{pmatrix} 0.321 \\ 0.368 \end{pmatrix}$$

The second layer output is

$$a^2 = f^2 (W^2a^1 + b^2) = \text{purelin}\left([0.09 - 0.17] \begin{pmatrix} 0.321 \\ 0.368 \end{pmatrix} + [0.48]\right) = [0.446]$$

The error would then be

$$e = t - a = \{1 + \sin \left(\frac{\pi p}{4}\right)\} - a^2 = \{1 + \sin\left(\frac{\pi 1}{4}\right)\} - 0.446 = 1.261.$$

The next stage of the algorithm is to backporpagate the sensitivities. Before we begin the backpropagation, recall that we will need the derivatives of the transfer functions, $f^1(n)$ and $f^2(n)$. For the first layer

$$f^1(n) = \frac{d}{dn}\left(\frac{1}{1+e^{-n}}\right) = \left(\frac{e^{-n}}{(1+e^{-n})^2}\right) = 1 - \left(\frac{1}{1+e^{-n}}\right)\left(\frac{1}{1+e^{-n}}\right) = (1-a^1)(a^1)$$

For the second layer we have

$$f^2(n) = \frac{d}{dn}(n) = 1$$

We can now perform the backpropagation. The starting point is found at the second layer, using Eq. (3.33):

$$s^2 = -2F^2(n^2)(t-a) = -2\,[f^2(n^2)]\,(1.261) = -2\,[1]\,(1.261) = -2.522.$$

The first layer sensitivity is then computed by backpropagating the sensitivity from the second layer, using Eq. (3.34):

$$s^1 = F^1(n^1)(W^2)^T s^2 = \begin{pmatrix} (1-a_1^1)(a_1^1) & 0 \\ 0 & (1-a_2^1)(a_2^1) \end{pmatrix} \begin{pmatrix} 0.09 \\ 0.17 \end{pmatrix} [-2.522]$$

$$= \begin{pmatrix} (1-0.321)\,(0.321) & 0 \\ 0 & (1-0.368)\,(0.368) \end{pmatrix} \begin{pmatrix} 0.09 \\ -0.17 \end{pmatrix} [2.522]$$

$$\begin{pmatrix} 0.218 & 0 \\ 0 & 0.233 \end{pmatrix} \begin{pmatrix} -0.227 \\ 0.429 \end{pmatrix} = \begin{pmatrix} -0.0495 \\ 0.0997 \end{pmatrix}$$

The final stage of the algorithm is to update the weights. For simplicity, we will use a learning rate $\alpha = 0.1$. (In Chapter 12 the choice of learning rate will be discussed in more detail.) From Eq. (3.35) and Eq. (3.36) we have

$$W^2(1)\, W^2(0) - \alpha s^2 (a^1)^T = [0.09\ -0.17] - 0.1\,[-2.522]\,[0.321\ 0.368]$$

$$= [0.171 \ -0.0772],$$

$$b^2(1) = b^2(0) - \alpha s^2 = [0.48] - 0.1\,[-2.522] = [0.732],$$

$$W^1(1) = W^1(0) - \alpha s^1 (a^0)^T = \begin{pmatrix} -0.27 \\ -0.41 \end{pmatrix} - 0.1 \begin{pmatrix} 0.0495 \\ 0.0997 \end{pmatrix} [1] = \begin{pmatrix} -0.265 \\ -0.420 \end{pmatrix}$$

$$b^1(1) = b^1(0) - \alpha s^1 = \begin{pmatrix} -0.48 \\ -0.13 \end{pmatrix} - 0.1 \begin{pmatrix} -0.0495 \\ 0.0997 \end{pmatrix} = \begin{pmatrix} -0.475 \\ -0.140 \end{pmatrix}$$

This completes the first iteration of the backpropagation algorithm. we next proceed to choose another input p and perform another iteration of the algorithm. we continue to iterate unitl the difference between the network response and the target function reaches some acceptable level.

3.8 PRINCIPLES OF TRAINING MULTI-LAYER NEURAL NETWORK USING BACKPROPAGATION

The project describes teaching process of multi-layer neural network employing *backpropagation* algorithm. To illustrate this process the three layer neural network with two inputs and one output,which is shown in the picture below, is used:

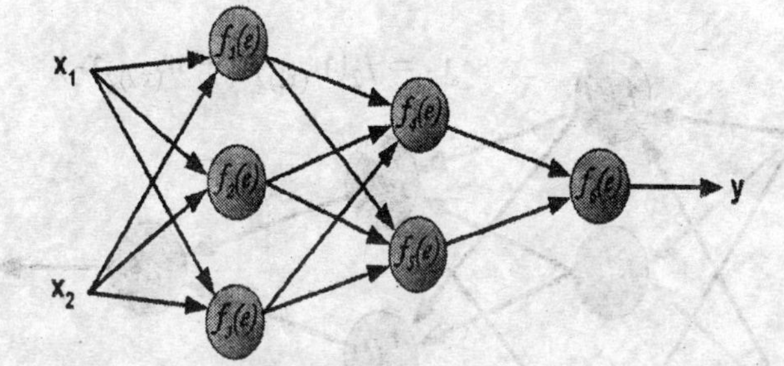

Each neuron is composed of two units. First unit adds products of weights coefficients and input signals. The second unit realise nonlinear function, called neuron activation function. Signal *e* is adder output signal, and *y* = *f(e)* is output signal of nonlinear element. Signal *y* is also output signal of neuron.

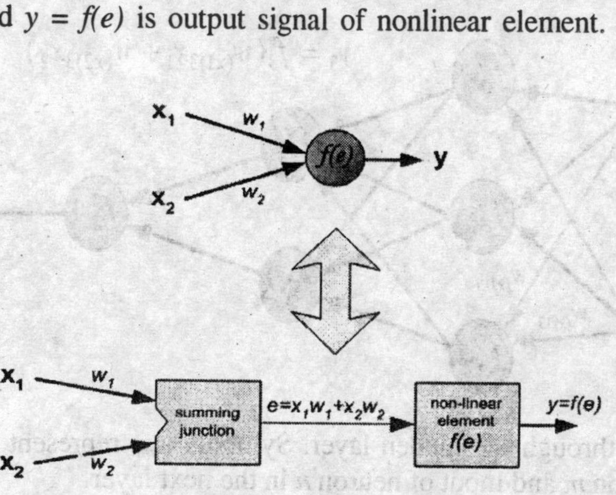

To teach the neural network we need training data set. The training data set consists of input signals (x_1 and x_2) assigned with corresponding target (desired output) z. The network training is an iterative process. In each iteration weights coefficients of nodes are modified using new data from training data set. Modification is calculated using algorithm described below: Each teaching step starts with forcing both input signals from training set. After this stage we can determine output signals values for each neuron in each network layer. Pictures below illustrate how signal is propagating through the network, Symbols $w_{(xm)n}$ represent weights of connections between network input x_m and neuron n in input layer. Symbols y_n represents output signal of neuron n.

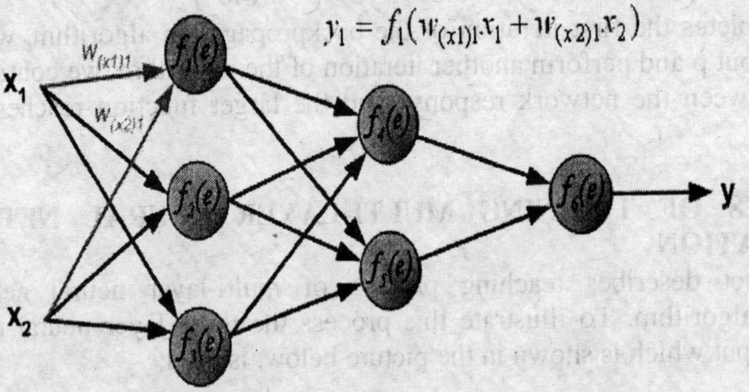

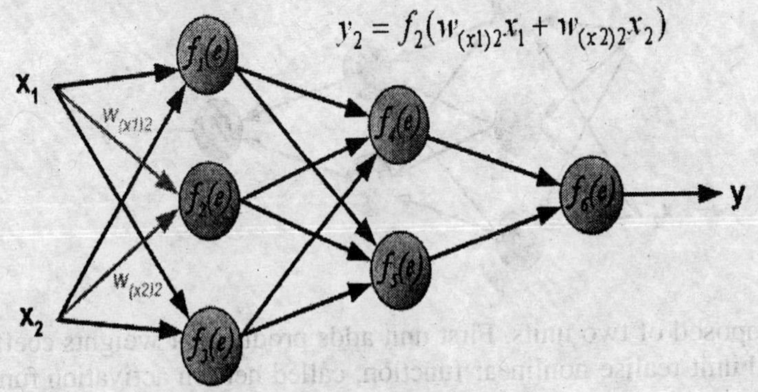

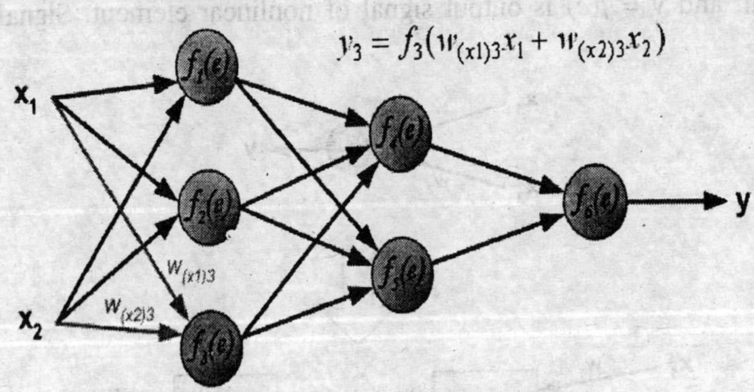

Propagation of signals through the hidden layer. Symbols w_{mn} represent weights of connections between output of neuron m and input of neuron n in the next layer.

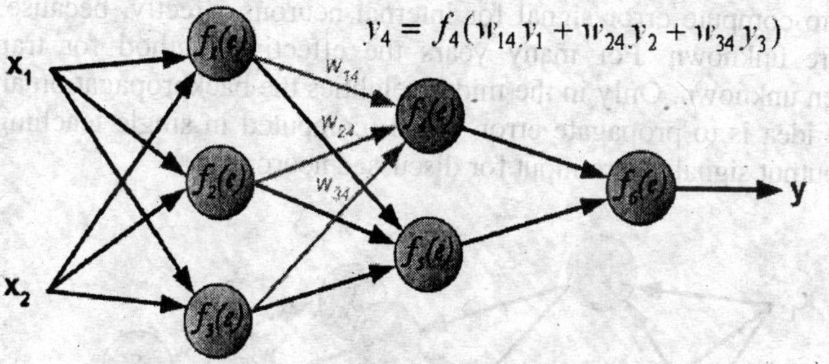

$$y_4 = f_4(w_{14}y_1 + w_{24}y_2 + w_{34}y_3)$$

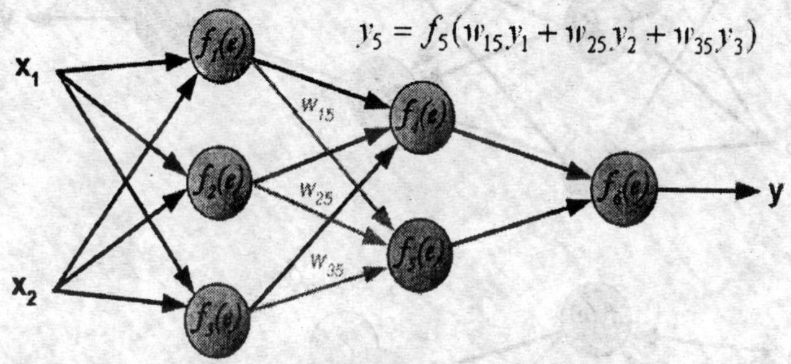

$$y_5 = f_5(w_{15}y_1 + w_{25}y_2 + w_{35}y_3)$$

Propagation of signals through the output layer.

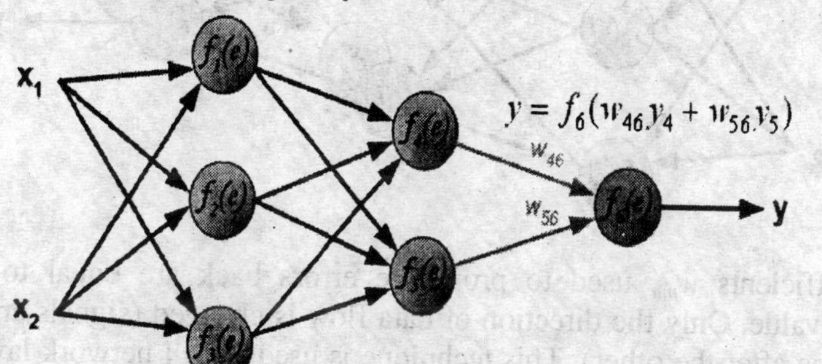

$$y = f_6(w_{46}y_4 + w_{56}y_5)$$

In the next algorithm step the output signal of the network y is compared with the desired output value (the target), which is found in training data set. The difference is called error signal of output layer neuron.

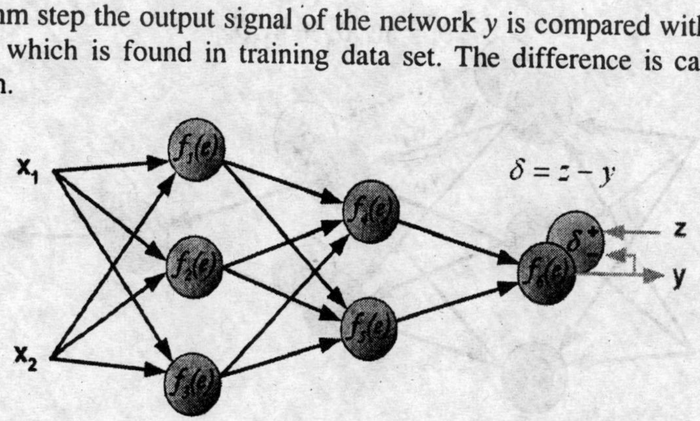

$$\delta = z - y$$

It is impossible to compute error signal for internal neurons directly, because output values of these neurons are unknown. For many years the effective method for training multiplayer networks has been unknown. Only in the middle eighties the backpropagation algorithm has been worked out. The idea is to propagate error signal (computed in single teaching step back to all neurons, which output signals were input for discussed neuron.

$$\delta_4 = w_{46}\delta$$

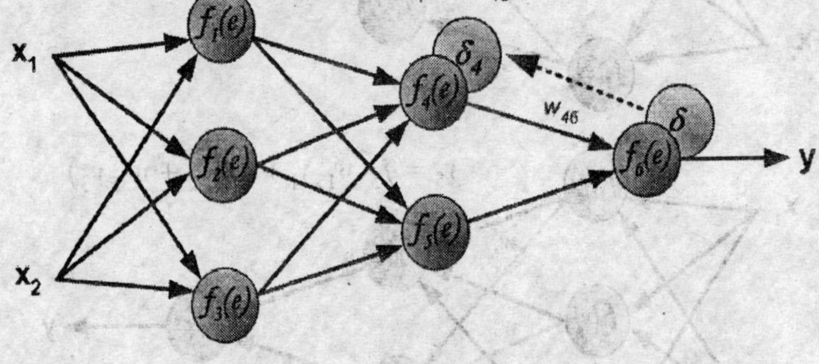

$$\delta_5 = w_{56}\delta$$

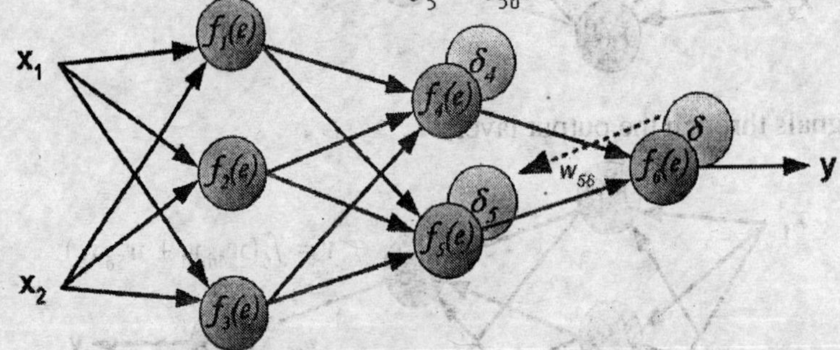

The weights' coefficients w_{mn} used to propagate errors back are equal to this used during computing output value. Only the direction of data flow is changed (signals are propagated from output to inputs one after the other). This technique is used for all network layers. If propagated errors came from few neurons they are added. The illustration is below:

$$\delta_1 = w_{14}\delta_4 + w_{15}\delta_5$$

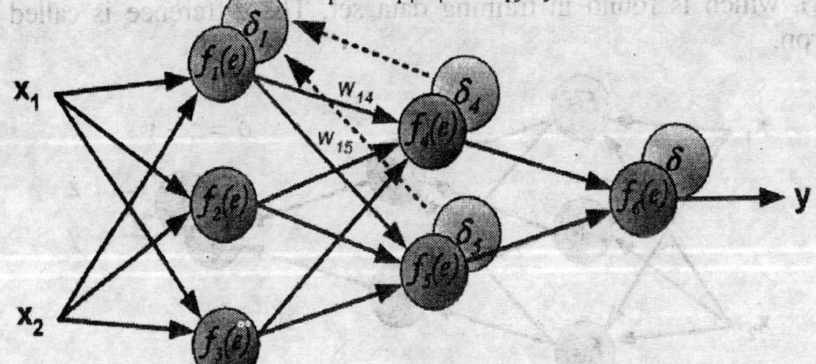

$$\delta_2 = w_{24}\delta_4 + w_{25}\delta_5$$

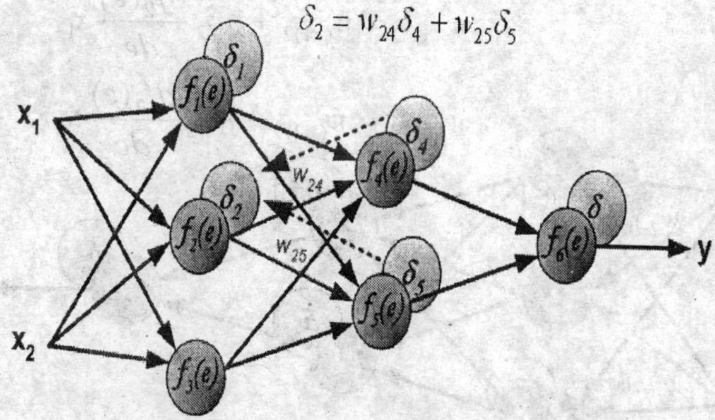

$$\delta_3 = w_{34}\delta_4 + w_{35}\delta_5$$

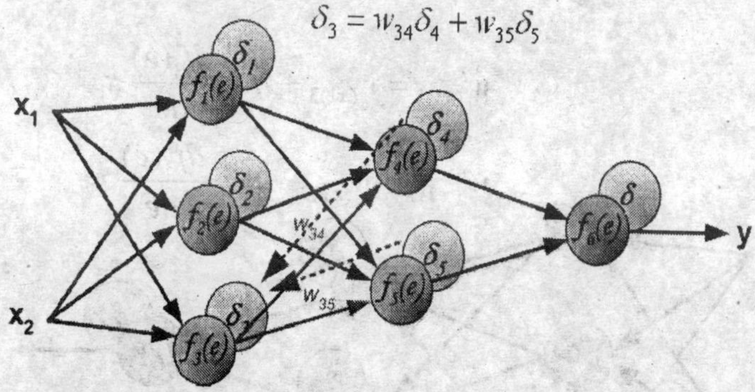

When the error signal for each neuron is computed, the weights coefficients of each neuron input node may be modified. In formulas below *df(e)/de* represents derivative of neuron activation function (which weights are modified).

$$w'_{(x1)1} = w_{(x1)1} + \eta\delta_1 \frac{df_1(e)}{de} x_1$$

$$w'_{(x2)1} = w_{(x2)1} + \eta\delta_1 \frac{df_1(e)}{de} x_2$$

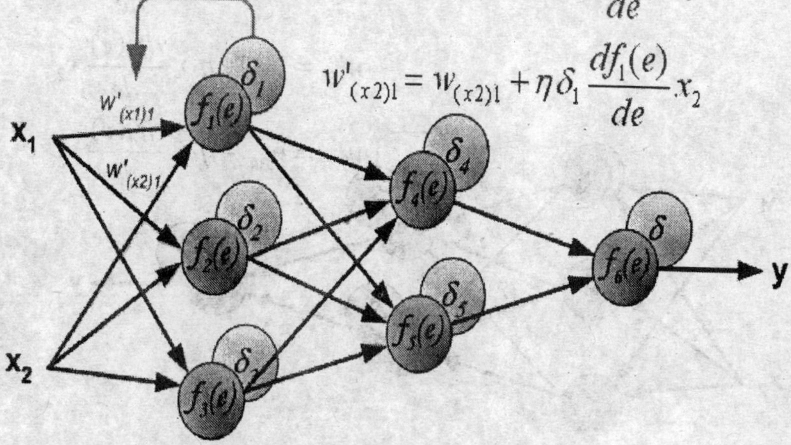

$$w'_{(x1)2} = w_{(x1)2} + \eta\delta_2 \frac{df_2(e)}{de} x_1$$

$$w'_{(x2)2} = w_{(x2)2} + \eta\delta_2 \frac{df_2(e)}{de} x_2$$

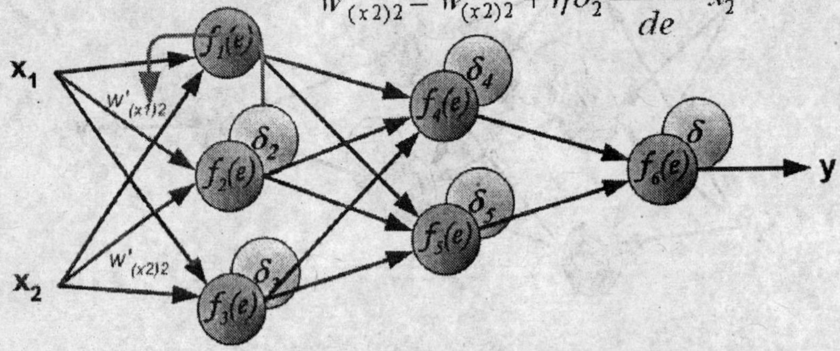

$$w'_{(x1)3} = w_{(x1)3} + \eta\delta_3 \frac{df_3(e)}{de} x_1$$

$$w'_{(x2)3} = w_{(x2)3} + \eta\delta_3 \frac{df_3(e)}{de} x_2$$

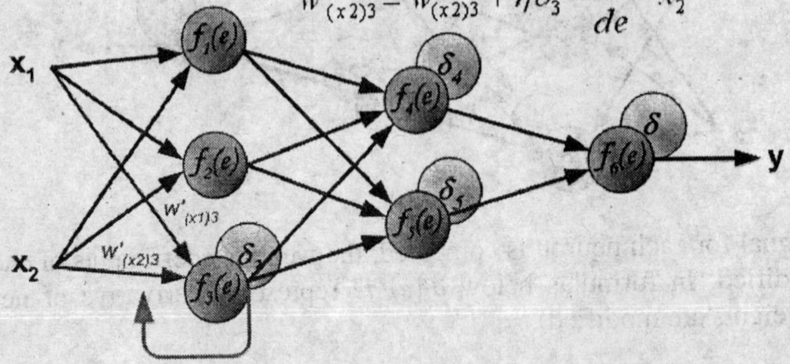

$$w'_{14} = w_{14} + \eta\delta_4 \frac{df_4(e)}{de} y_1$$

$$w'_{24} = w_{24} + \eta\delta_4 \frac{df_4(e)}{de} y_2$$

$$w'_{34} = w_{34} + \eta\delta_4 \frac{df_4(e)}{de} y_3$$

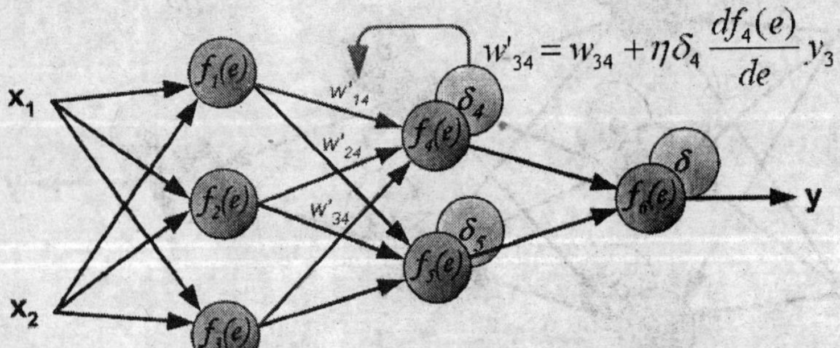

$$w'_{15} = w_{15} + \eta\delta_5 \frac{df_5(e)}{de} y_1$$

$$w'_{25} = w_{25} + \eta\delta_5 \frac{df_5(e)}{de} y_2$$

$$w'_{35} = w_{35} + \eta\delta_5 \frac{df_5(e)}{de} y_3$$

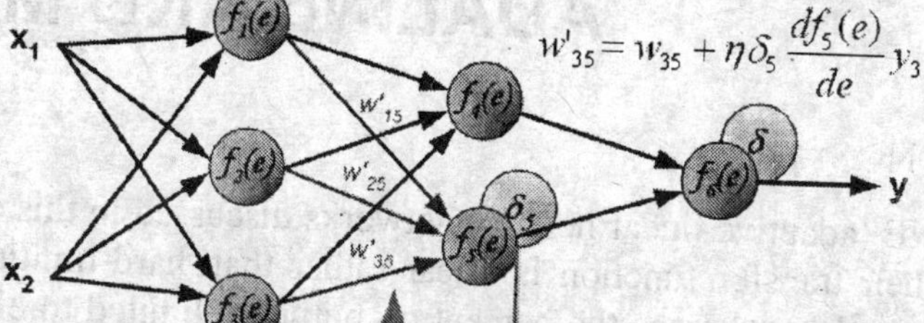

$$w'_{46} = w_{46} + \eta\delta \frac{df_6(e)}{de} y_4$$

$$w'_{56} = w_{56} + \eta\delta \frac{df_6(e)}{de} y_5$$

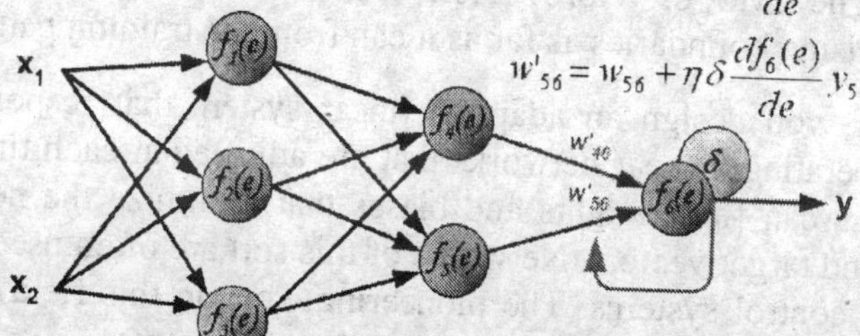

Coefficient affects network teaching speed. There are a few techniques to select this parameter. The first method is to start teaching process with large value of the parameter. While weights coefficients are being established the parameter is being decreased gradually. The second, more complicated, method starts teaching with small parameter value. During the teaching process the parameter is being increased when the teaching is advanced and then decreased again in the final stage. Starting teaching process with low parameter value enables to determine weights coefficients signs.

QUESTION BANK

Q1. What is backpropagation network?
Q2. Explain the general architecture of backprpagation network?
Q3. Explain the character image of ASCII code with the help of backprpagation network?
Q4. Explain the practical approach of BPN network?
Q5. What is operation of BPN network?
Q6. What is three layer network? Explain with the help of labeled diagram?
Q7. Explain pattern classification problem for XOR functions with the help of two layer XOR network?
Q8. Explain function approximation network with the help of example?
Q9. Explain the working of backprpagation algorithm with the help of diagram?
Q10. What are the various principles of training multi layer neural network using backprpagation?

CHAPTER 4

ADALINE AND MADALINE

4.1 INTRODUCTION

The ADALINE (adaptive linear neuron) networks discussed in this chapter are similar to the perceptron, but their transfer function is linear rather than hard-limiting. This allows their outputs to take on any value, whereas the perceptron output is limited to either 0 or 1. Both the ADALINE and the perceptron can only solve linearly separable problems. However, here the LMS (least mean squares) learning rule, which is much more powerful than the perceptron learning rule, is used. The LMS, or Widrow-Hoff, learning rule minimizes the mean square error and thus moves the decision boundaries as far as it can from the training patterns.

In this chapter, you design an adaptive linear system that responds to changes in its environment as it is operating. Linear networks that are adjusted at each time step based on new input and target vectors can find weights and biases that minimize the network's sum-squared error for recent input and target vectors. Networks of this sort are often used in error cancellation, signal processing, and control systems. The pioneering work in this field was done by Widrow and Hoff, who gave the name ADALINE to adaptive linear elements.

Signal processing developed as an engineering discipline with the advent of electronic communication. Initially, analog filters using resistor-inductor-capacitor (RLC) circuits were designed to remove noise from the communication signals. Today, signal processing has evolved into a many-faceted technology, with the emphasis having shifted from turned circuit implementation to digital signal processors (DSPs) that can perform the same types of filtering applications by executing convolution filters implemented in software. The basis for the industry remains the design and implementation of filters to perform noise removal from information-bearing signals.

4.2 REVIEW OF SIGNAL PROCESSING

We begin our discussion of the Adaline and Madaline networks with a review of basic signal-processing theory. An understanding of this material is essential if we are to appreciate the operation and applications of these network. However, this material is also typically covered as part of an undergraduate curriculum in information coding and data communication. Therefore, readers already comfortable with signal-processing concepts may skip this first section without fear of missing material relevant to the Adaline and Madaline topics. For those readers who are not familiar with the techniques commonly used to implement electronic communications and signal processing, we shall begin by describing briefly the data-encoding and modulation schemes used in an amplitude-modulation (AM) radio transmission. As part of this-discussion, we shall illustrate the need for filters in the communications industry. We will then review the concepts of the frequency domain, the four basic filter types, and Fourier analysis. This preliminary section concludes with a brief overview of digital signal processing, because many of the concepts realized in digital fitters are directly applicable to the Adaline and Madaline (and many other) neural networks.

4.2.1 SIGNAL PROCESSING AND FILTERS

Signal processing is an engineering discipline that deals primarily with the implementation of filters to remove or reduce unwanted frequency components from an information-bearing signal. Let's consider, for example, an AM radio broadcast. Electronic communication techniques, whether for audio signals or other data, consist of signal encoding and modulation. Information to be transmitted-in this case, audiblc sounds, such as voice or music-can be encoded electronically by an analog signal that exactly reproduces the frequencies and amplitudes of the original sounds. Since the sounds being encoded represent a continuum from silence through voice to music, the instantaneous frequency of the encoded signal will vary with time, ranging from 0 to approximately 10,000 hertz (Hz).

Rather than attempt to transmit this encoded signal directly, we transform the signal into a form more suitable for radio transmission. We accomplish this transformation by modulating the amplitude of a high-frequency carrier signal with the analog information signal. This process is illustrated in Figure 4.1. Here, the carrier is nothing more than a sine wave with a frequency mush greater than the information signal. For AM radio, the carrier frequency will be in the range of 550 to 1600 kilohertz (KHz). Since the frequency of the carrier is significantly greater than is the maximum frequency of the information signal, little information is lost by this modulation. The modulated signal can then be transmitted to a receiving station (or broadcast to anyone with a radio receiver), where the signal is demodulated and is reproduced as sound.

The most obvious reason for a filter in AM radio is that different people have different preferences in music and entertainment. Therefore, the government and the communication industry have allowed many different radio stations to operate in the same geographical area, so that everyone's tastes in entertainment can be accommodated. With so many different radio stations all broadcasting in close proximity, how is it that we can listen to only one station at a time? The answer is to allow each receiver to be tuned by the user to a selectable frequency. In tuning the radio, we are essentially changing the frequency-response characteristics of a bandpass filter inside the radio. This filter allows only the signals from the station is which we are interested to pass, while eliminating all the other signals being broadcast within the spectrum of the AM radio.

To illustrate how the bandpass filter operates, we will change out reference from the time domain to the frequency domain. We begin by constructing a two-axis graph, where the x axis represents increasing frequencies and the y axis represents decreasing attenuation in a unit called the decibel (dB). Such a graph us illustrated in Figure 4.2(a). For the AM radio example, let us imagine that there are seven AM radio stations, labeled. A through G, operating in the area where we are listening. The frequencies at which these stations transmit are graphed as vertical lines located on the frequency axis at the point corresponding to their transmitting, or carrier, frequency. The amplitude of the lines, as illustrated in Figure 4.2(a), is almost 0 dB, indicating that each station is transmitting at full power, and each can be received equally well.

Now we will tune bandpass filter to select one of the seven stations. The frequency response of a typical bandpass filter is illustrated in Figure 4.2(b). Notice that the frequency-response curve is such that all frequencies that fall outside the inverted notch are attenuated to very little attenuation-hence the name "bandpass filter."

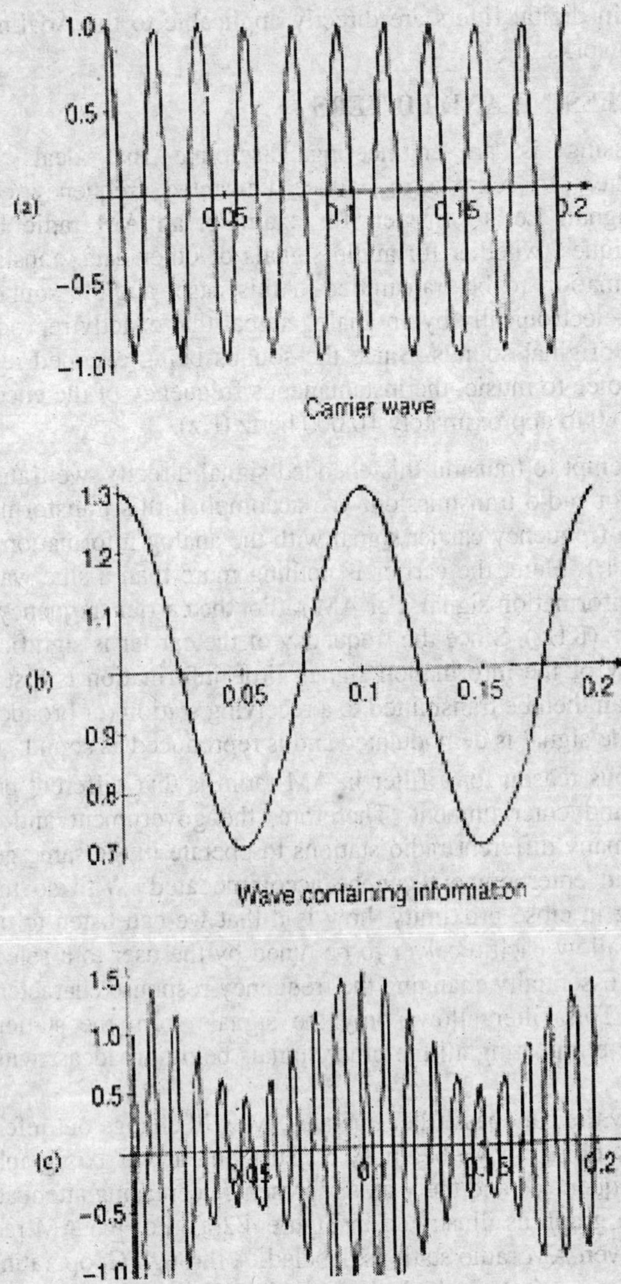

Figure 4.1 Information-encoding and amplitude-modulation techniques for electronic communication are shown. (a) The carrier wave has a frequency much higher than that of (b) The information-bearing signal. (c) The carrier wave is modulated by the information-bearing signal.

To tune our radio receiver to any one of the seven broadcasting stations, we simply adjust the frequency response of the filter such that the carrier frequency of the desired station is within the passband.

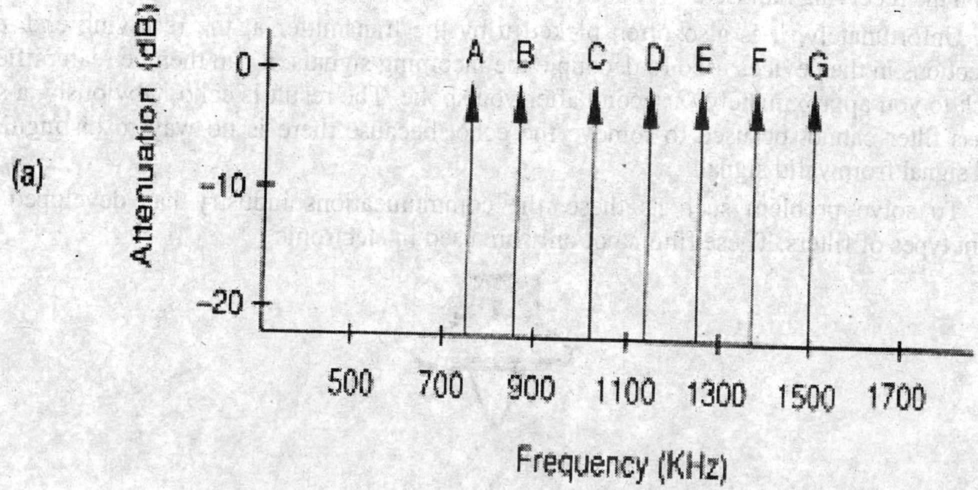

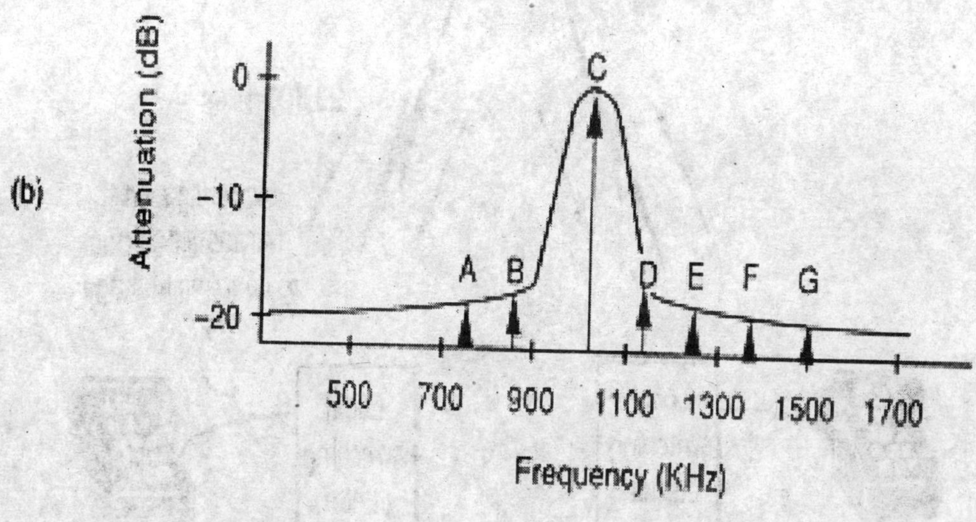

Figure 4.2 These are frequency domain graphs of (a) AM radio reception of seven different stations, (b) the frequency response of the tuning filter and the magnitude of the received signals after filtering.

As another example of the use of filters in the communication industry, consider the problem of echo suppression in long-distance telephone communication. As indicated in Figure 4.3, the problem is caused by the interaction between the amplifiers and series coupling used on both ends of the line, and the delay time required to transmit the voice information between the switching office and the communications satellite in geostationary orbit, 23,000 miles above the earth. Specifically, you hear an echo of your own voice in the telephone when you speak. The signal carrying your voice arrives at the receiving telephone approximately 270 milliseconds after you speak. This delay is the amount of time required by the microwave signal to travel the 46,000 miles between the transmitting station, the satellite, and the receiving station on the ground. Once received and routed to the destination telephone, the signal is again amplified and reproduced as sound on the receiving handset.

Unfortunately, it is also often picked u by the transmitter at the receiving end, due to imperfections in the devices used to decouple the incoming signals. It can then be reamplified and fed back to you approximately /2 second after you spoke. The result is echo. Obviously, a simple bandpass filter cannot be used to remove the echo, because there is no way to distinguish the echoed signal from valid signals.

To solve problem such as these, the communications industry has developed many different types of filters. These filters not only are used in electronic

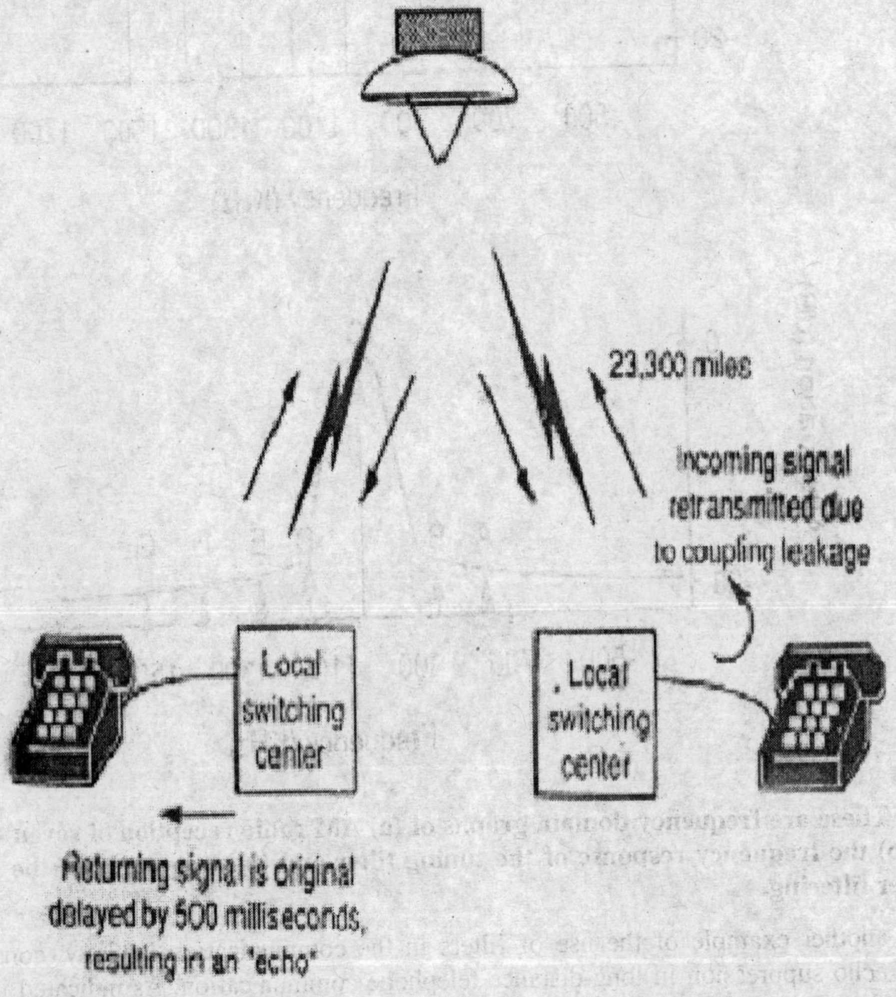

Figure 4.3 Echo can occur in long-distance telecommunications.

communications, but also have an application base that includes radar and sonar imaging, electronic warfare, and medical technology. However, all the application-specific filter implementations can be grouped into four general filter types: lowpass, highpass, bandpass, and bandstop. The characteristic frequency response of these filters is depicted in Figure 4.4. The adaptive filter, which is the subject of the remainder of the chapter, has characteristics unique to the application it serves. It can reproduce the characteristics of any of the four basic filter types, alone or in combination.

As we shall show later, the adaptive filter is ideally suited to the telephone-echo problem just discussed.

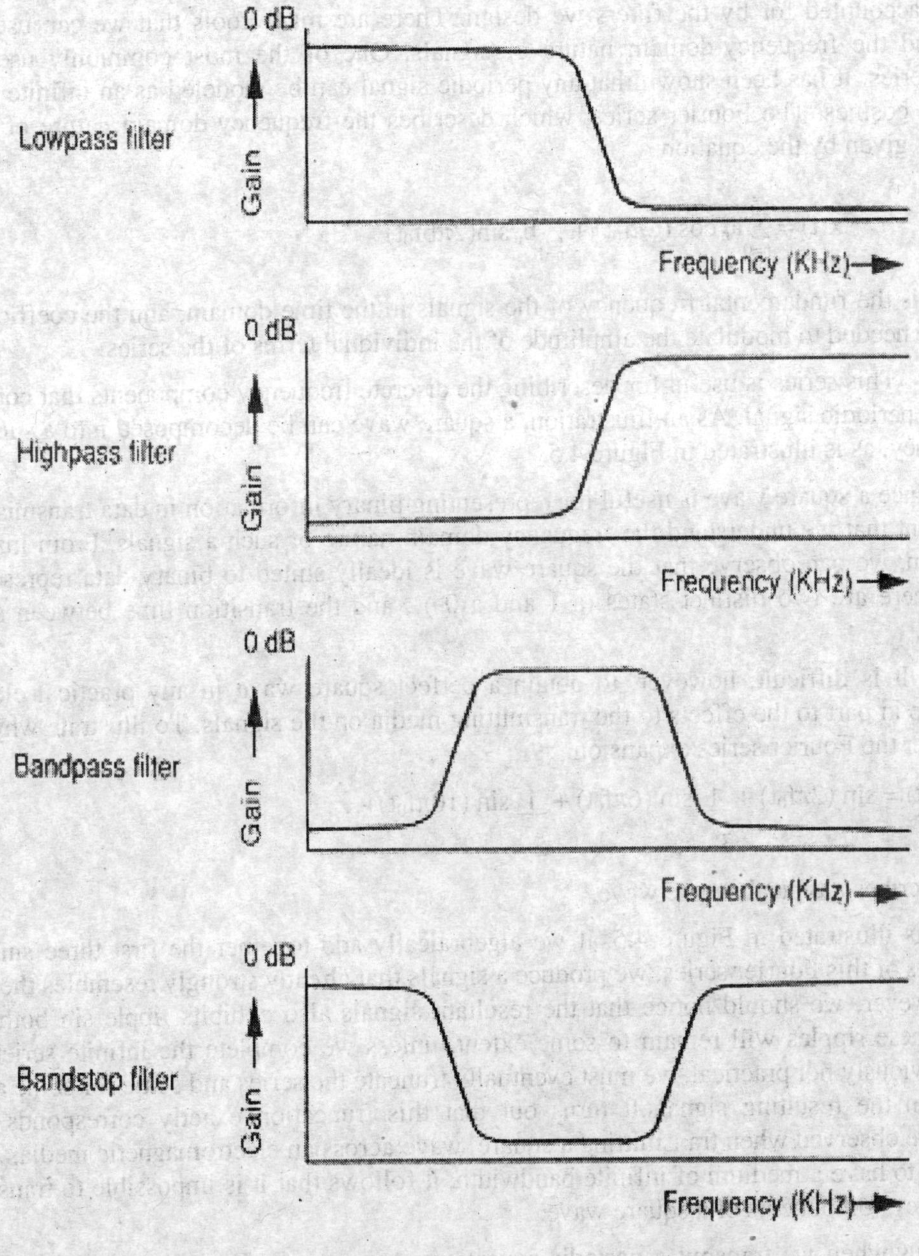

Figure 4.4 Frequency-response characteristics of the four basic filter types are shown.

4.2.2 FOURIER ANALYSIS AND THE FREQUENCY DOMAIN

To analyze a signal-processing problem that requires a filter. we must leave the time domain and find a tool for translating our filter models into the frequency domain. Because most of the signals we will analyze cannot be completely understood in the time domain.

For example, most signals consist not only of a fundamental frequency, but also harmonics that must be considered, or they consist of many discrete frequency components that must be accounted for by the filters we design. There are many tools that we can use to help understand the frequency-domain nature of signals. One of the most commonly used is the Fourier series. It has been shown that any periodic signal can be modeled as an infinite series of sines and cosines. The Fourier series, which describes the frequency-domain nature of periodic signals, is given by the equation.

$$x(t) = \sum_{n=0}^{\infty} a_n \cos(2\pi f_0 t) + \sum_{n=1}^{\infty} b_n \sin(2\pi b f_0 t)$$

Where f_0 is the fundamental frequency of the signals in the time domain, and the coefficients, a_n and b_n, are needed to modulate the amplitude of the individual terms of the series.

This series is useful for describing the discrete frequency components that comprise a nontrivial periodic signal. As an illustration, a square wave can be decomposed into a summation of frequency, as is illustrated in Figure 4.5.

Since a square wave is useful for representing binary information in data transmission , it is important that we understand the frequency-domain nature of such a signals. From Inspection the domain, we can observe that the square wave is ideally suited to binary data representation because there are two distinct states (a 1 and a 0) , and the transition time between states is negligible.

It is difficult, however, to obtain a perfect square wave in any practical electronic circuit, due in part to the effects to the transmitting media on the signals. To illustrate why this is so, consider the Fourier series expansion.

$$x(t) = \sin(2\pi f_0 t) + \frac{1}{3}\sin(6\pi f_0 t) + \frac{1}{5}\sin(10\pi f_0 t) + \ldots$$

Which describes a typical square wave.

As illustrated in Figure 4.5, if we algebraically add together the first three sinusoidal components of this Fourier series, we produce a signals that already strongly resembles the square wave. However, we should notice that the resultant signals also exhibits ripple sin both active regions. These ripples will remain to some extent, unless we complete the infinite series.Since that the obviously not practical, we must eventually truncate the series and settle for some amount of ripple in the resulting signals.It turns out that this truncation exactly corresponds to the behavior we observed when transmitting a square wave across an electromagnetic media. As it is impossible to have a medium of infinite bandwidth, it follows that it is impossible to transmit all the frequency components of a square wave.

Thus when we transmit a periodic square wave, we can observe the frequency-domain effects in the time-domain signals as overshoot, undershoot, and ripple.

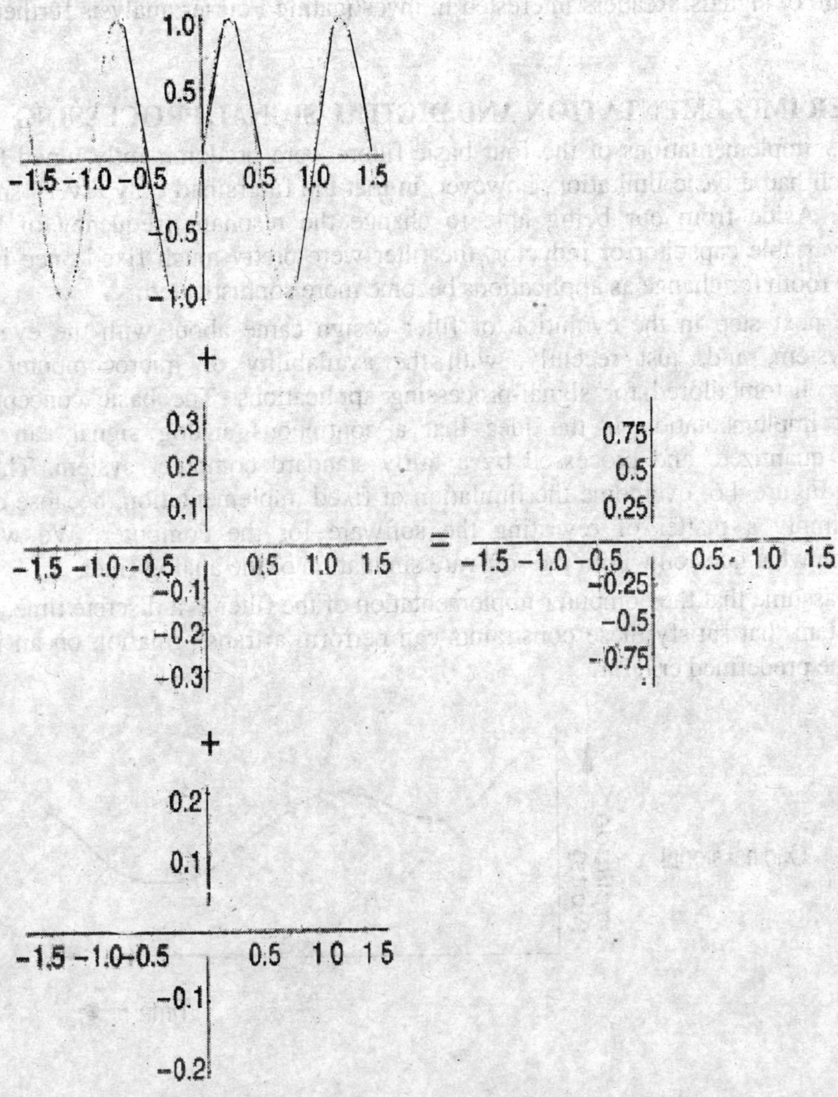

Figure 4.5 The first three frequency-domain components of a square wave are shown. Notice that the sine waves each have different magnitudes, as indicated by the coordinates on the y axis, even though they are graphed to the same height.

This example shows that the Fourier series can be a powerful tool in helping us to understand the frequency domain nature of any periodic signals, and to predict ahead of time what transmission effects we must consider as we design filters for our signals-processing applications.

We can also apply Fourier analysis to a periodic signals, by evaluating the Fourier integral, which is given by

$$X(f) = \int_{-\infty}^{\infty} x(t)e^{-j2\pi ft}dt.$$

We will not, however belabor this point. Our purpose here is merely to understand the frequency-domain nature of signals. Readers interested in investigating Fourier analysis further are referred to Kaplan.

4.2.3 FILTER IMPLEMENTATION AND DIGITAL SIGNAL PROCESSING

Early implementations of the four basic filters were predominantly tuned RLS circuits. This approach had a basic limitation, however, in that the filters had only a very small range of adjustability. Aside from our being able to change the resonant frequency of the filter by adjusting a variable capacitor or inductor, the filter were pretty much fixed once implemented, leaving little room for change as applications become more sophisticated.

The next step in the evolution of filter design came about with the event of digital computer system, and, just recently, with the availability of microcomputer chips with architectures customtailored for signal-processing applications. The basic concept underlying digital filter implementation is the idea that a continuous analog signal can be sampled periodically, quantized, and processed by a fairly standard computer system. This approach, illustrated in Figure 4.6, overcome the limitation of fixed implementation, because changing the filter was simply a matter of rewriting the software for the computer. We will therefore concentrate on what goes on within the software simulation of the analog filter.

We assume that the computer implementation of the filter is a discrete time, linear, time-invariant system that satisfy these constraints can perform a transformation on an input signal, based on some predefined criteria

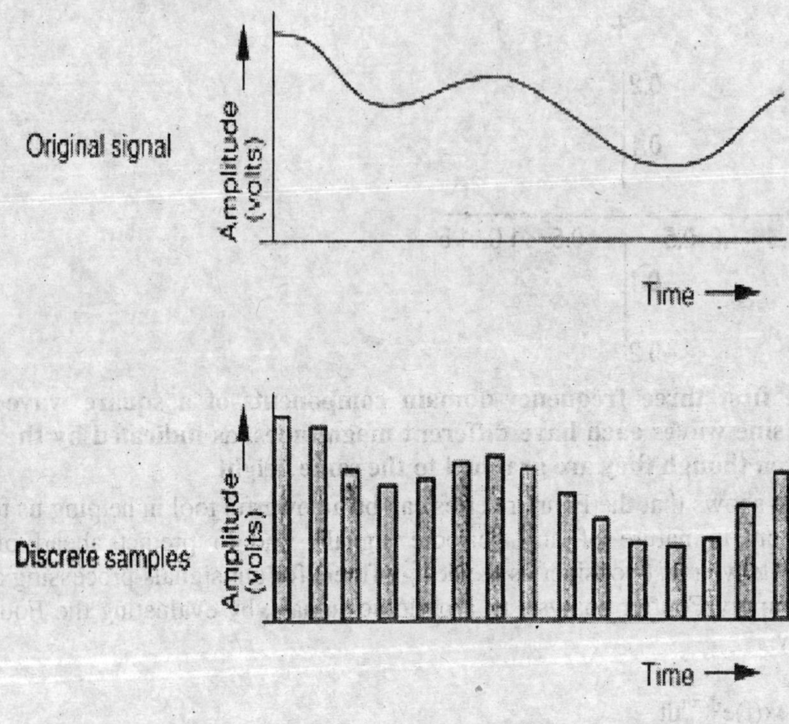

Figure 4.6 Discrete-time sampling of a continuous signal is shown.

to produce an output that corresponds to the input as though it had passed through an analog filter. Thus, a computer, executing a program that applies a given transformation operation, R, to discrete, digitized approximations of a continuous input signal, x(n), can produce an output value y(n) for each input sample, where n is the discrete timestep variable. In its role in performing this transformation, the computer can be thought of as a digital filter. Moreover, any filter can be completely characterized by its response, h(n), to the unit impulse function, represented as b(n) .More precisely.

$$h(n) = R\,[\partial(n)]$$

The benefit of this formulation is that, once the system response to the unit impulse is known, the system output for any input is given by

$$Y(n)\ R[x(n)]$$

$$= \sum_{\infty}^{\infty} h(i)\ x(n-i)$$

where x(n) is the system input

This equation is meaningful to us in that it describes a convolution some between the input signal and the unit inpluse response of the system. The process can be pictured as a window slidingpast a scene of interest. As illustrated in Figure 4.7, for each time step, the system output is produced by transposing and sifting h(n) one position to the right. The summation is then performed over all nonzero values of x(n) for the finite length of the filter.

In this manner, we can realize the filter by repetitively performing floating-point multiplications and additions, coupled with sample time delays and shift operations. Repetitive mathematical operations are what computer to best; therefore, the convolution sum provides us with a mechanism for building the digital signal processing are referred to Oppenheim and Schafer or Hamming.

It is sufficient for our purposes to note that the convolution sum is a sum-of –products operation similar to the type of operation an ANS PE performs when computing its input activation signal. Specifically, the Adaline uses exactly this sum-of-products calculation, without the sample time delays and shift operations., to determine how much input stimulation it receives from an instantaneous input signal. As we shall see in the next section, the Adaline extends the basis filter operation one step further, in that it has implemented within itself a means of adapting the weighting coefficients to allow it to increase or decrease the stimulation it receives the next time it is presented with the same signal.

The ability of the Adaline to adapt us weighting coefficients is extremely useful. When writing a digital filter program on a computer, the programmer must know exactly how to specify the filtering algorithm and what the details of the signal characteristics are.

If modification are desired, or if the signal characteristics change, reprogramming is requires, When the programmer uses an Adaline, the problem shifts to one of being able to specify the desired output signal. given a particular input signal. The Adaline takes the input and the desired output, and adjusts itself so that it can perform the desired transformation. Furthermore, if the signal characteristics, the Adaline can adapt automatically we shall now expend these ideas, and begin our investigation of the adaline

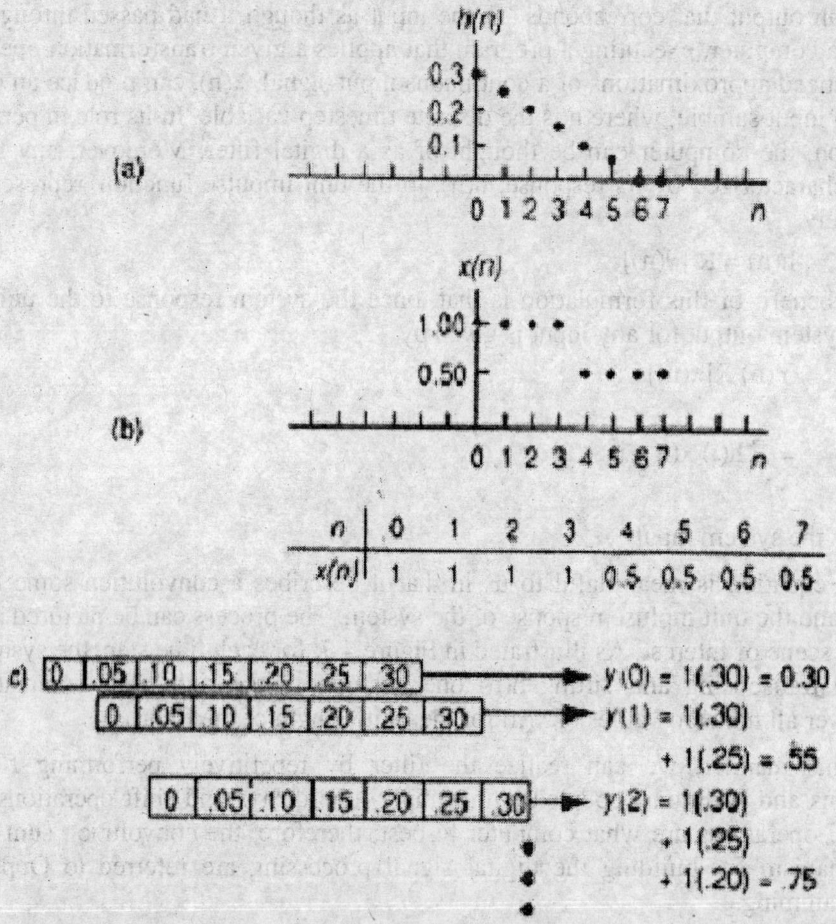

Figure 4.7 Convolution sum calculation is shown (a) The process begins by determining the desired response of the filter to the unit impulse function at eight discrete timesteps. (b) The input signal is sampled and quartized eight times. (c) The output of the filter is produced for each timestep by multiplication of each term in (a) with the corresponding value of (b) for all valid timesteps.

4.3 ADALINE AND THE ADAPTIVE LINER COMBINER

The Adaline is a device consisting of a single processing element; as such , it is not technically a neural network. Nevertheless, it is a very important structure that deserve close study. Moreover, we will show how it can form the basis of a network in a later section.

The term Adaline is an acronym: however, its meanings has changed some-what over the years. Initially called the ADAptive LINear Element, when neural networks fell out of favor in the late 1960s. It is almost identical in structure to the general PE described in Chapter 1. Figure 4.8 shows the Adaline structure. There are two basic modifications required to make the general PE structure into an Adaline. The first modification is the addition of a connection with weight,w_0, which we refer to as the bias term. This term is a weight on a connection that has its input value always equal to 1. The inclusion of such a term is largely a matter of experience. We show it here for completeness, but it will not appear in the discussion of the next sections. We shall resurrect the idea of a bias term in Chapter 3, on the backpropagation network.

The second modification is the addition of a bipolar condition on the output. The dashed box in Figure 4.8 encloses a part of the Adaline called the adaptive linear combiner (ALC). (If the output of the ALC is positive, the Adaline output is +1. If the ALC output is negative; the Adaline output is -1. Because much of the interesting processing takes place in the ALC portion of the Adaline, we shall concentrate on the ALC. Later, we shall add back the binary output condition.

The processing done by the ALC is that of the typical processing element described in the previous chapter. The ALC performs a sum-of-products calculation

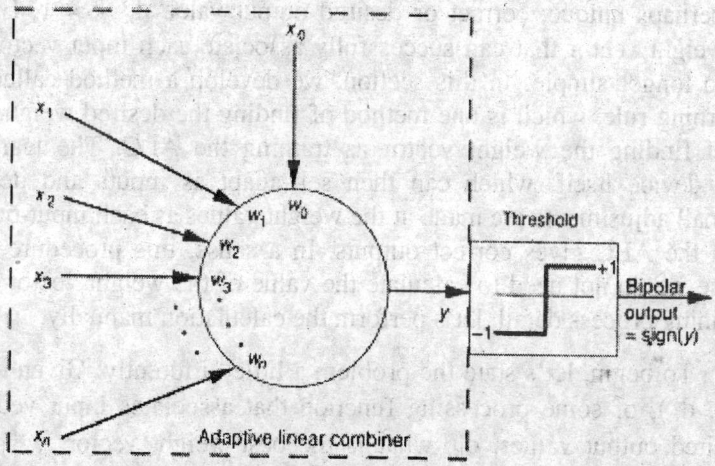

Figure 4.8 The complete Adaline consist of the adaptive linear combiner, in the dashed box, and a bipolar output function. The adaptive linear combiner resembles the general PE described in Chapter 1.

using the input and weight vectors, and applies an output function to get a single output value. Using the notation in figure 4.8.

$$y = u_0 + \sum_{j=1}^{n} w_j x_j$$

Where w_0 is the bias weight. If we make the identification, $x_0 = 1$, we can rewrite the preceding equation as

$$y = \sum_{j=1}^{n} w_j x_j$$

or, in vector notation,

$$y = w^t x \qquad (4.1)$$

The output function in this case is the identity function, as is the activation function. The use of the identity function as both output and activation function means that the output is the same as the activation, which is the same as the net input to the unit.

The Adaline (or the ALC) is is ADAptive in the sense that there exists a well-defined procedure for the given input. What output value is correct depends on the particular processing function being performed by the device. The Adaline (or the ALC) is Linear because the output is a simple linear function of the input values. It is a NEuron only in the very limited sense of the PEs described in the previous chapter. The Adaline could also be said to be a LINear Element, avoiding the NEuron issue altogether. In the next section, look at a method to train the Adaline to perform a given processing function.

4.3.1 THE LMS LEARNING RULE

Given an input vector, x, it is straightforward to determine a set of weights, w, which will result in a particular output value, y. Suppose we have a set of input vectors, $\{x_1, x_2, \ldots, x_L)$, each having its own, perhaps unique, correct or desired output value d_k, k = 1, L. The problem of finding a single weight vector that can successfully associate each input vector with its desired output value is no longer simple. In this section, we develop a method called the least-mean-square (LMS) learning rule, which is one method of finding the desired weight vector. We refer to this process of finding the weight vector as training the ALC. The learning rule can be embedded in the device itself, which can then self-adapt as inputs and desired outputs are presented to it. Small adjustments are made at the weight values as each input-output combination is processed until the ALC gives correct outputs. In a sense, this procedure is a true training procedure, because we do not need to calculate the value of the weight vector explicitly. Before describing the training process detail, let's perform the calculation manually.

Calculation of w*. To begin, let's state the problem a little differently: Given examples, (x_1, d_1), $(x_2, d_2), \ldots, (x_L, d_L)$, of some processing function that associates input vectors, x_k, with (or maps to) the desired output values, d_k, what is the best weight vector, w*, for an ALC that performs this mapping?

To answer this question, we must first define what is is that constitutes the best vector. clearly, once the best weight vector is found, we would like the application of each input vector to result in the precise, corresponding output value. Thus, we want to eliminate, or at least to minimize, the difference between the desired output and the actual output for each input vector. the approach we select her is to minimize the mean squared error for the set of input vectors.

If the actual output value is y_k for the input vector, then the corresponding error term is $\varepsilon_k = d_k - y_k$. The mean squared error, or expectation value of the error, is defined by

$$(\varepsilon_k^2) = \frac{1}{L} \sum_{k=1}^{L} \varepsilon_k^2 \tag{4.2}$$

where L is the number of input vectors in the training set.[1]

Using Eq. (4.1), we can expand the mean squared error as follows:

$$(\varepsilon_k^2) = \{(d_k - w^t x_k)^2 \tag{4.3}$$

$$= \{d^2_k) + w^t (x_k x^t_k\} w - 2 \{d_k x^t_k) w \tag{4.4}$$

In going from Eq. (4.3) to Eq. (4.4), we have made the assumption that the training set is statistically stationary, meaning that any expectation values vary slowly with respect to time. This assumption allows us to factor out the weight vectors from the expectation value terms in Eq. (4.4)

4.4 IMPORTANT ADAPTIVE FUNCTIONS

This chapter introduces the function adapt, which changes the weights and biases of a network incrementally during training. You can type help linnet to see a list of linear and adaptive network functions, demonstrations, and applications.

4.4.1 LINEAR NEURON MODEL

A linear neuron with *R* inputs is shown below.

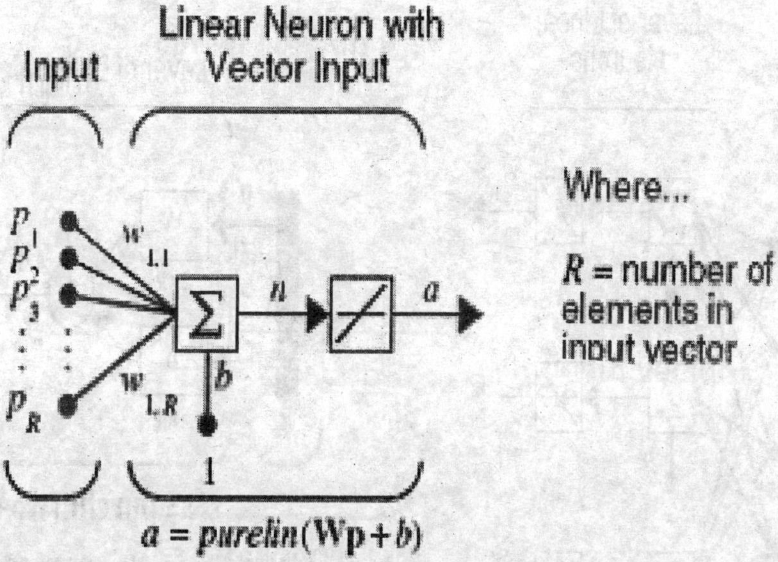

Figure 4.9 Linear Neuron Model

This network has the same basic structure as the perceptron. The only difference is that the linear neuron uses a linear transfer function, named purelin.

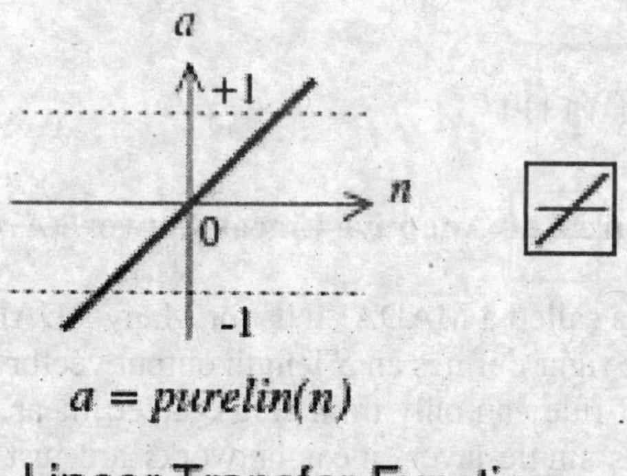

The linear transfer function calculates the neuron's output by simply returning the value passed to it.

a= purelin(n)= purelin(Wp + b)= Wp + b

This neuron can be trained to learn an affine function of its inputs, or to find a linear approximation to a nonlinear function. A linear network cannot, of course, be made to perform a nonlinear computation.

4.5 ADAPTIVE LINEAR NETWORK ARCHITECTURE

The ADALINE network shown below has one layer of S neurons connected to R inputs through a matrix of weights **W**.

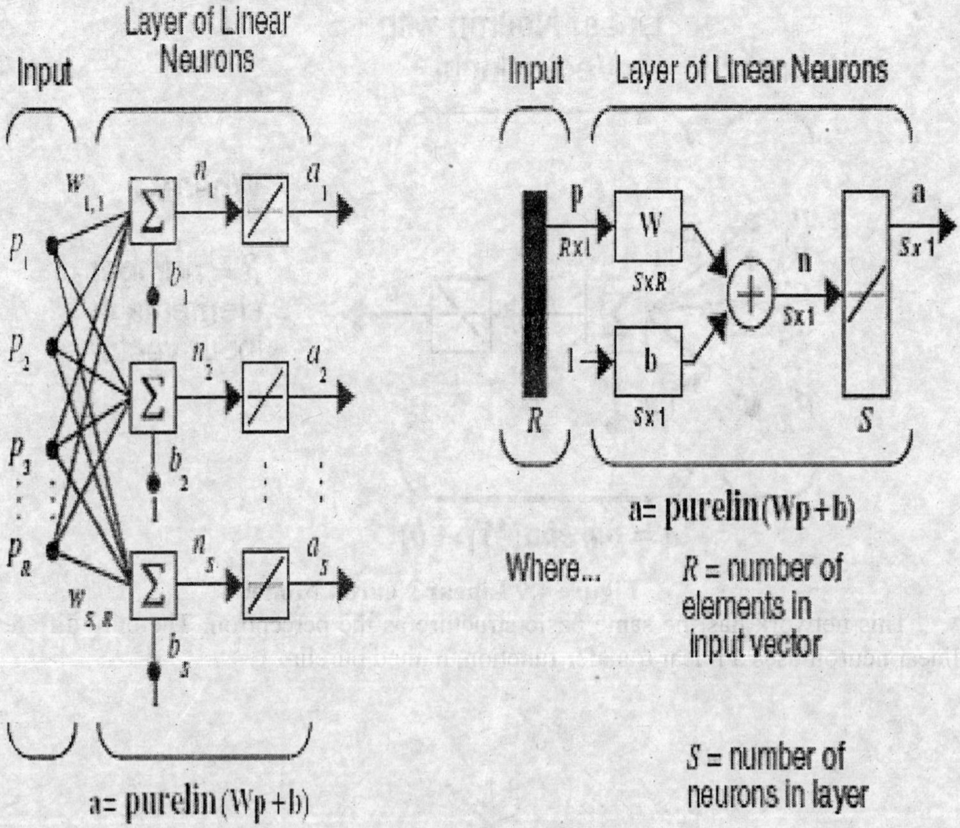

Figure 4.10 Adaptive Linear Network Architecture

This network is sometimes called a MADALINE for Many ADALINEs.
Note that the figure on the right defines an S-length output vector **a**.

The Widrow-Hoff rule can only train single-layer linear networks. This is not much of a disadvantage, however, as single-layer linear networks are just as capable as multilayer linear networks. For every multilayer linear network, there is an equivalent single-layer linear network.

4.5.1 SINGLE ADALINE (NEWLIN)

Consider a single ADALINE with two inputs. The following figure shows the diagram for this network.

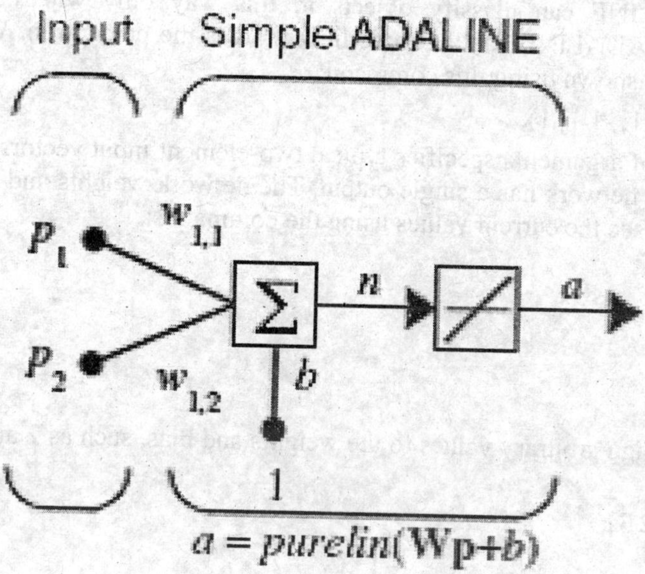

Figure 4.11 Single Adaline

The weight matrix **W** in this case has only one row. The network output is

$$a = purelin(n) = purelin(\mathbf{Wp} + b) = \mathbf{Wp} + b$$

or

$$a = w_{1,1}p_1 + w_{1,2}p_2 + b$$

Like the perceptron, the ADALINE has a *decision boundary* that is determined by the input vectors for which the net input n is zero. For $n = 0$ the equation $\mathbf{Wp} + b = 0$ specifies such a decision boundary, as shown below.

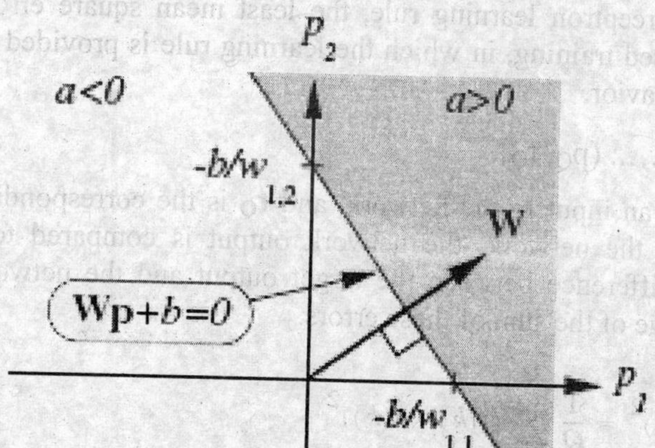

Input vectors in the upper right gray area lead to an output greater than 0. Input vectors in the lower left white area lead to an output less than 0. Thus, the ADALINE can be used to classify objects into two categories.

However, ADALINE can classify objects in this way only when the objects are linearly separable. Thus, ADALINE has the same limitation as the perceptron. We can create a network similar to the one shown using this command:

```
net = newlin ([-1 1; -1 1],1);
```

The first matrix of arguments specifies typical two-element input vectors, and the last argument 1 indicates that the network has a single output. The network weights and biases are set to zero, by default. You can see the current values using the commands:

```
W = net.IW{1,1}
W =0 0
```

and

```
b = net.b{1}
b =0
```

You can also assign arbitrary values to the weights and bias, such as 2 and 3 for the weights and -4 for the bias:

```
net.IW{1,1} = [2 3];
net.b{1} = -4;
```

You can simulate the ADAPLINE for a particular input vector.

```
p = [5; 6];
a = sim(net,p)
a =24
```

To summarize, you can create an ADALINE network with newlin, adjust its elements as you want, and simulate it with sim. You can find more about newlin by typing help newlin.

4.5.2 LEAST MEAN SQUARE ERROR

Like the perceptron learning rule, the least mean square error (LMS) algorithm is an example of supervised training, in which the learning rule is provided with a set of examples of desired network behavior.

$$\{p_1, t_1\}, \{p_2, t_2\}, \ldots (p_Q, t_Q\}$$

Here p_Q is an input to the network, and t_Q is the corresponding target output. As each input is applied to the network, the network output is compared to the target. The error is calculated as the difference between the target output and the network output. The goal is to minimize the average of the sum of these errors.

$$mse = \frac{1}{Q}\sum_{k=1}^{Q} e(k)^2 = \frac{1}{Q}\sum_{k=1}^{Q} (t(k) - a(k))^2$$

The LMS algorithm adjusts the weights and biases of the ADALINE so as to minimize this mean square error. Fortunately, the mean square error performance index for the ADALINE network is a quadratic function. Thus, the performance index will either have one global minimum, a weak minimum, or no minimum, depending on the characteristics of the input vectors. Specifically, the characteristics of the input vectors determine whether or not a unique solution exists.

4.5.3 LMS ALGORITHM (LEARNWH)

Adaptive networks will use the LMS algorithm or Widrow-Hoff learning algorithm based on an approximate steepest descent procedure. Here again, adaptive linear networks are trained on examples of correct behavior.

The LMS algorithm, shown above.

$$\mathbf{W}(k+1) = \mathbf{W}(k) + 2\alpha\mathbf{e}(k)\mathbf{p}^T(k)$$

$$\mathbf{b}(k+1) = \mathbf{b}(k) + 2\alpha\mathbf{e}(k)$$

4.5.4 ADAPTIVE FILTERING (ADAPT)

The ADALINE network, much like the perceptron, can only solve linearly separable problems. It is, however, one of the most widely used neural networks found in practical applications. Adaptive filtering is one of its major application areas.

4.5.5 TAPPED DELAY LINE

You need a new component, the tapped delay line, to make full use of the ADALINE network. Such a delay line is shown in the next figure. The input signal enters from the left and passes through *N*-1 delays. The output of the tapped delay line (TDL) is an *N*-dimensional vector, made up of the input signal at the current time, the previous input signal, etc.

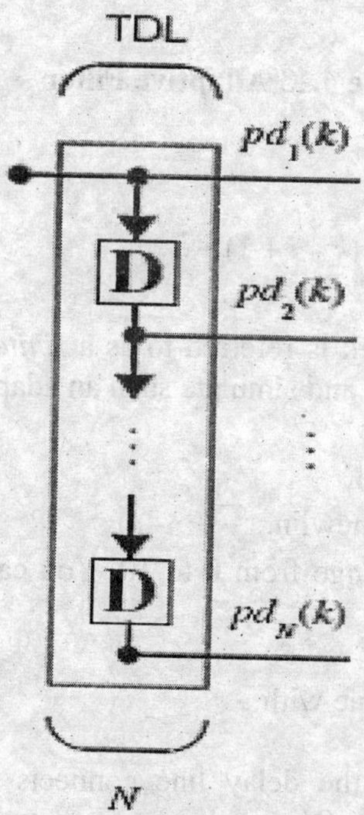

Figure 4.12 Tapped Delay Line

4.5.6 ADAPTIVE FILTER

You can combine a tapped delay line with an ADALINE network to create the *adaptive filter* shown in the next figure.

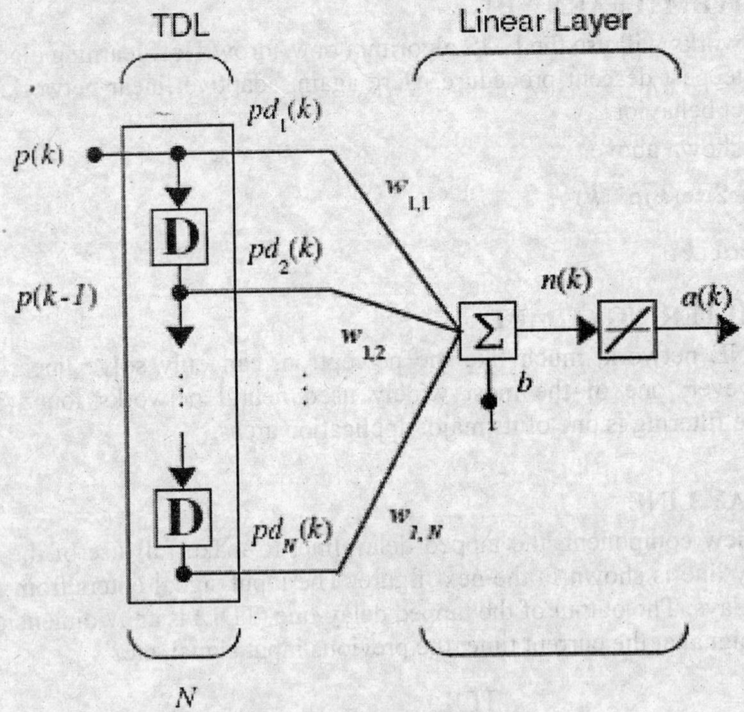

Figure 4.13 Adaptive Filter

The output of the filter is given by

$$a(k) = purelin(\mathbf{W}\mathbf{p} + b) = \sum_{i=1}^{R} w_{1,i}a(k-i+1) + b$$

In digital signal processing, this network is referred to as a *finite impulse response (FIR)* filter. Take a look at the code used to generate and simulate such an adaptive network.

4.5.7 ADAPTIVE FILTER EXAMPLE

First define a new linear network using newlin.

Assume that the input values have a range from 0 to 10. You can now define the single output network.

```
net = newlin([0,10],1);
```

Specify the delays in the tapped delay line with

```
net.inputWeights{1,1}.delays = [0 1 2];
```

This definition indicates that the delay line connects to the network weight matrix through delays of 0, 1, and 2 time units. (You can specify as many delays as you want, and can omit some values if you like. They must be in ascending order.)

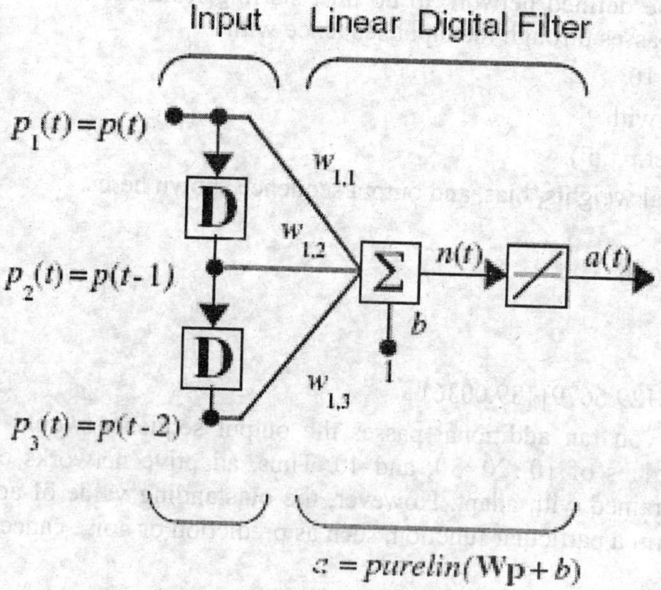

Figure 4.14 Adaptive Filter Example

You can give the various weights and the bias values with

net.IW{1,1} = [7 8 9];

net.b{1} = [0];

Finally, define the initial values of the outputs of the delays as

pi = {1 2};

These are ordered from left to right to correspond to the delays taken from top to bottom in the figure. This concludes the setup of the network. To set up the input, assume that the input scalars arrive in a sequence:

First the value 3, then the value 4, next the value 5, and finally the value 6. You can indicate this sequence by defining the values as elements of a cell array in curly braces.

```
p = {3 4 5 6};
```

Now, you have a network and a sequence of inputs. Simulate the network to see what its output is as a function of time.

[a,pf] = sim(net,p,pi)

This simulation yields an output sequence

a = [46] [70] [94] [118]

and final values for the delay outputs of

pf = [5] [6]

The example is sufficiently simple that you can check it without a calculator to make sure that you understand the inputs, initial values of the delays, etc. The network just defined can be trained with the function adapt to produce a particular output sequence. Suppose, for instance, you want the network to produce the sequence of values 10, 20, 30, 40.

t = {10 20 30 40};

You can train the defined network to do this, starting from the initial delay conditions used above. Specify 10 passes through the input sequence with

net.adaptParam.passes = 10;

Then launch the training with

[net,y,E,pf,af] = adapt(net,p,t,pi);

This code returns the final weights, bias, and output sequence shown here.

wts = net.IW{1,1}

wts = 0.5059 3.1053 5.7046

bias = net.b{1}

bias = -1.5993

y = [11.8558] [20.7735] [29.6679] [39.0036]

Presumably, if you ran additional passes the output sequence would have been even closer to the desired values of 10, 20, 30, and 40. Thus, adaptive networks can be specified, simulated, and finally trained with adapt. However, the outstanding value of adaptive networks lies in their use to perform a particular function, such as prediction or noise cancellation.

4.6 PREDICTION EXAMPLE

Suppose that you want to use an adaptive filter to predict the next value of a stationary random process, *p(t)*. You can use the network shown in the following figure to do this prediction.

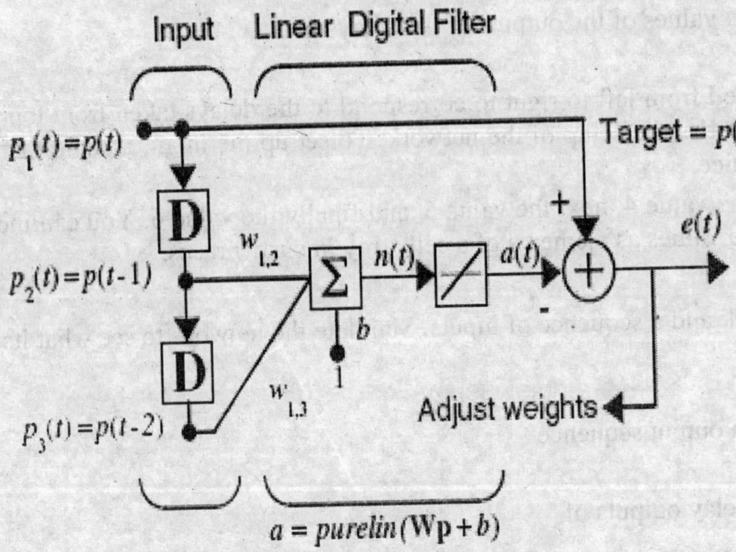

Predictive Filter: *a(t)* is approximation to *p(t)*

Figure 4.15 Prediction Example

The signal to be predicted, *p(t)*, enters from the left into a tapped delay line. The previous two values of *p(t)* are available as outputs from the tapped delay line. The network uses adapt to change the weights on each time step so as to minimize the error *e(t)* on the far right. If this error is 0, the network output *a(t)* is exactly equal to *p(t)*, and the network has done its prediction properly.

Given the autocorrelation function of the stationary random process *p(t)*, you can calculate the error surface, the maximum learning rate, and the optimum values of the weights. Commonly, of course, you do not have detailed information about the random process, so these calculations cannot be performed. This lack does not matter to the network. After it is initialized and operating, the network adapts at each time step to minimize the error and in a relatively short time is able to predict the input *p(t)*.

4.7 NOISE CANCELLATION EXAMPLE

Consider a pilot in an airplane. When the pilot speaks into a microphone, the engine noise in the cockpit combines with the voice signal. This additional noise makes the resultant signal heard by passengers of low quality. The goal is to obtain a signal that contains the pilot's voice, but not the engine noise. You can cancel the noise with an adaptive filter if you obtain a sample of the engine noise and apply it as the input to the adaptive filter.

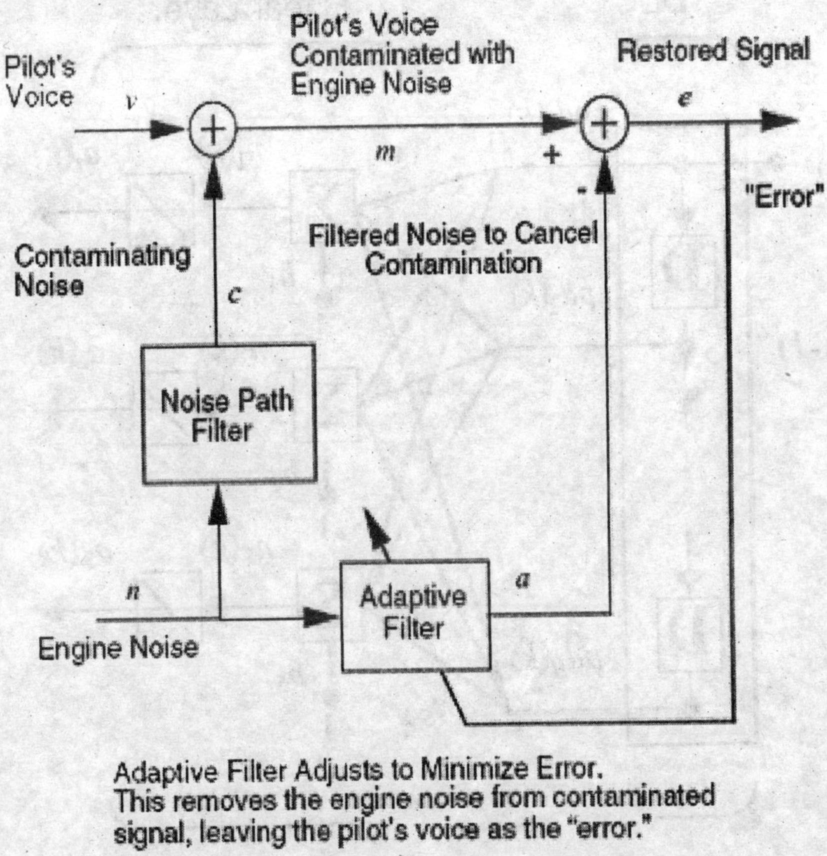

Figure 4.16 Noise Cancellation Example

As the preceding figure shows, you adaptively train the neural linear network to predict the combined pilot/engine signal *m* from an engine signal *n*. The engine signal *n* does not tell the adaptive network anything about the pilot's voice signal contained in *m*. However, the engine signal *n* does give the network information it can use to predict the engine's contribution to the pilot/engine signal *m*.

The network does its best to output *m* adaptively. In this case, the network can only predict the engine interference noise in the pilot/engine signal *m*. The network error *e* is equal to *m*, the pilot/engine signal, minus the predicted contaminating engine noise signal. Thus, *e* contains only the pilot's voice. The linear adaptive network adaptively learns to cancel the engine noise. Such adaptive noise canceling generally does a better job than a classical filter, because it sibtracts from the signal rather than filtering it out the noise of the signal *m*.

4.8 MULTIPLE NEURON ADAPTIVE FILTERS

You might want to use more than one neuron in an adaptive system, so you need some additional notation. You can use a tapped delay line with *S* linear neurons, as shown in the next figure.

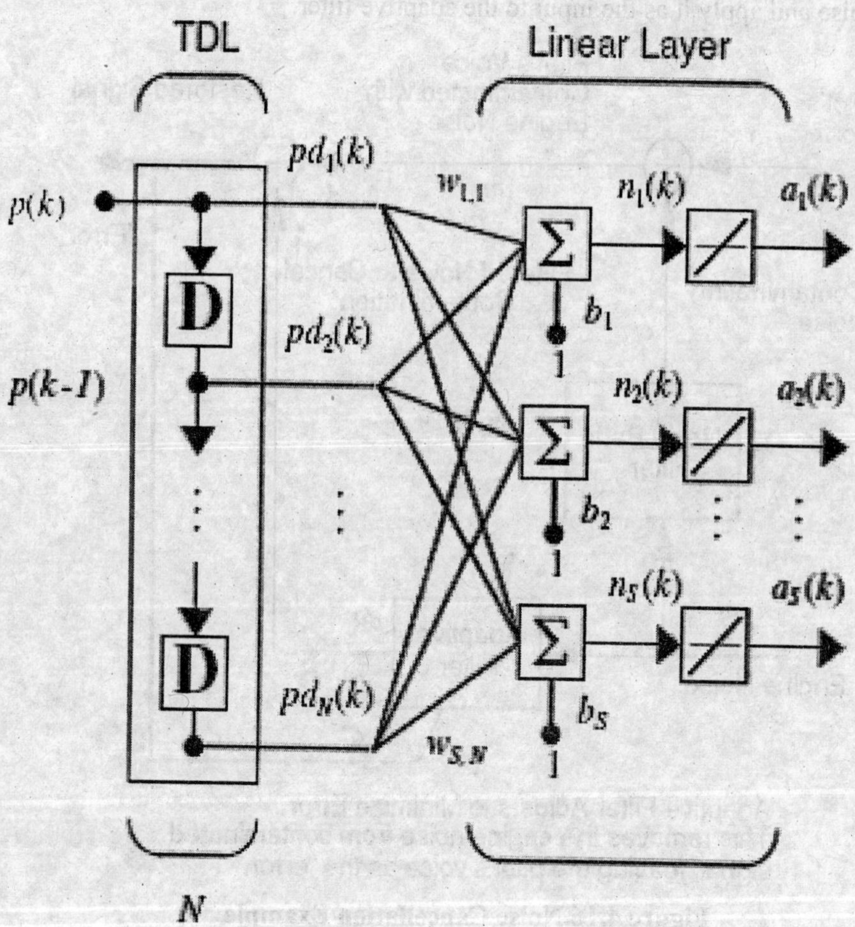

Figure 4.17 Multiple Adaptive Filters

Alternatively, you can represent this same network in abbreviatedform

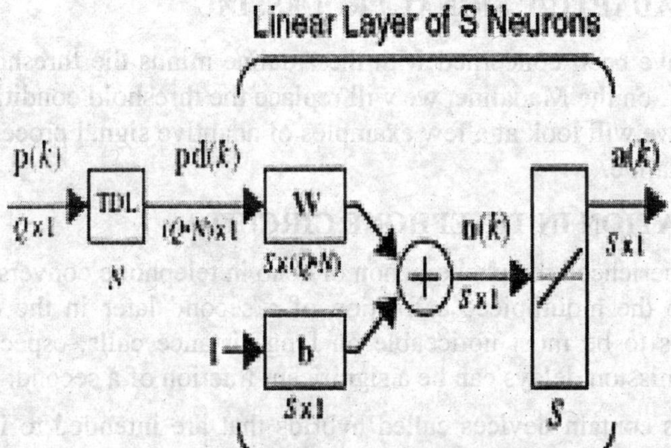

Figure 4.18 Abbreviated Notation

If you want to show more of the detail of the tapped delay line—and there are not too many delays—you can use the following notation:

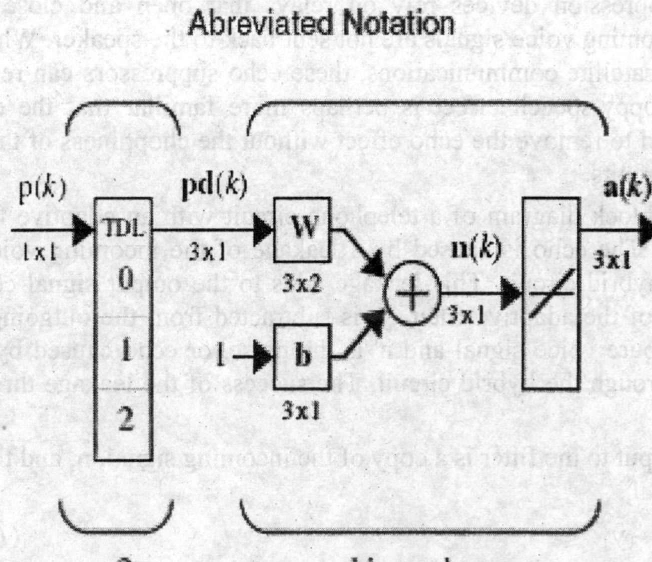

Figure 4.19 Abbreviated Notation with TDL

Here, a tapped delay line sends to the weight matrix:

- The current signal
- The previous signal
- The signal delayed before that

You could have a longer list, and some delay values could be omitted if desired.

The only requirement is that the delays must appears in increasing order as they go from top to bottom.

4.9 APPLICATION OF ADAPTIVE SIGNAL PROCESSING

Up to now, we have been concerned with the Adaline minus the threshold condition on the output. In Section 4.11, on the Madaline, we will replace the threshold condition and examine networks. In this section, we will look at a few examples of adaptive signal processing using only the ALC portion of the Adaline.

4.9.1 ECHO CANCELLATION IN TELEPHONE CIRCUITS

You may have experienced the phenomenon of echo in telephone conversations: you hear the words you speak into the mouthpiece a fraction of a second later in the earphone of the telephone. The echo tends to be most noticeable on long-distance calls, especially those over satellite links where transmission delays can be a significant fraction of a second.

Telephone circuits contain devices called hybrids that are intended to isolate incoming signals from outgoing signals, thus avoiding the echo effect. Unfortunately, these circuits do not always perform perfectly, due to causes such as impedance mismatches, resulting in some echo back to the speaker. Even when the echo signal has been attenuated by a substantial amount, it still may be audible, and hence an annoyance to the speaker.

Certain echo-suppression devices rely on relays that open and close circuits in the outgoing lines so that incoming voice signals are not sent back to the speaker. When transmission delays are long, as with satellite communications, these echo suppressors can result in a loss of parts of words. This choppy-speech effect is perhaps more familiar that the echo effect. An adaptive filter can be used to remove the echo effect without the choppiness of the relays used in other echo suppression circuits.

Figure 4.20 is a block diagram of a telephone circuit with an adaptive filter used as an echo-suppression device. The echo is caused by a leakage of the incoming voice signal to the output line through the hybrid circuit. This leakage adds to the output signal coming from the microphone. The output of the adaptive filter, y, is subtracted from the outgoing signal, $s + n^1$, where s is the outgoing pure voice signal and n^1 is the noise, or echo caused by leakage of the incoming voice signal through the hybrid circuit. The success of the leakage through the hybrid circuit.

Notice that the input to the filter is a copy of the incoming signal, n, and that the error is a copy of the outgoing signal,

$$\varepsilon = s + n^1 - y \tag{4.5}$$

We assume that y is correlated with the noise. n^1, but not with the pure voice signal, s. If the quantity, $n^1 - y$, is some echo still remains in the outgoing signal. Squaring and taking expectation values of both sides of Eq. (4.5) gives

$$(\varepsilon^2 = (s^2) + ((n^1 - y)^2) + 2\,(s(n^1 - y)) \tag{4.6}$$

$$= (s^2) + ((n^1 - y)^2) \tag{4.7}$$

Equation (4.7) follows, since is s is not correlated with either y or n^1, resulting in the last term in Eq. (4.6) being equal to zero.

The signal power, (s^2), is determined by the source of the voice signal-say, some amplifier at the telephone switching station local to the sender. Thus, (s^2) is no directly affected by changes in (ε^2).

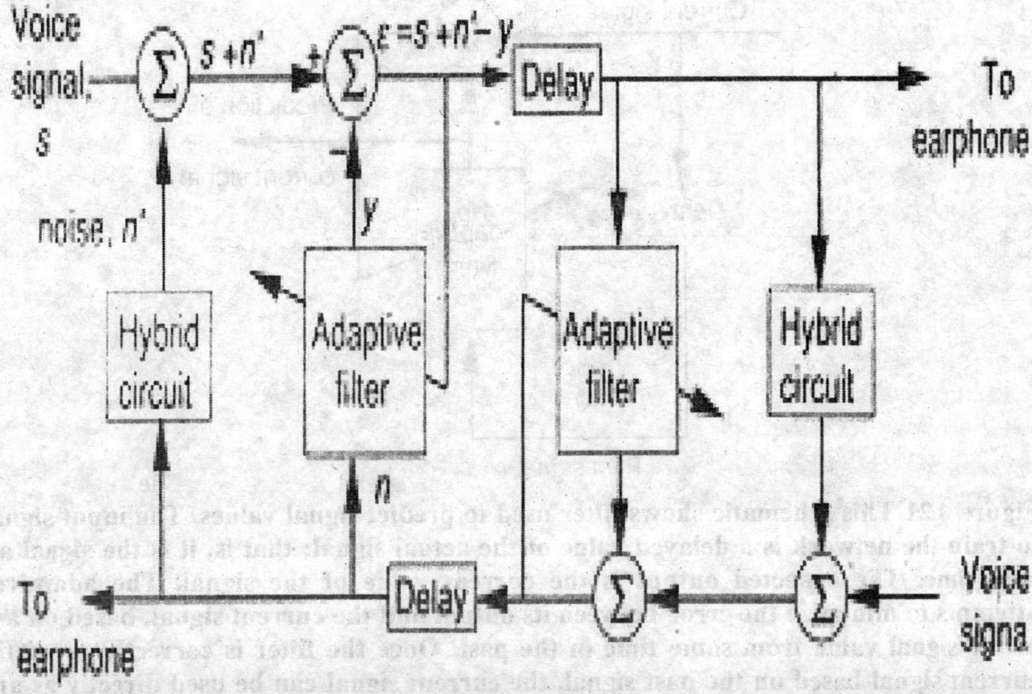

Figure 4.20 This figure is a schematic of a telephone circuit using an adaptive filter to cancel echo. The adaptive filter is depicted as a box; the slanted arrow represents the adjustable weights.

The adaptive filter attempts to minimize (ε^2), and in doing so, minimizes ($(n^1 - y)^2$), the power of the uncanceled noise on the outgoing line. Since there is only one input to the adaptive filter, the device would be configured as a transverse filter. Widrow and Stearns suggest sampling the incoming signal at a rate of 8 KHz and using 128 weight values.

4.9.2 OTHER APPLICATIONS

Rather than go into the details of the many applications that can be addressed by these adaptive filters, we refer you once again to the excellent text by Widrow and Stearns. In this section, we shall simply suggest a few broad areas where adaptive filters can be used in addition to the echo-cancellation application we have discussed.

Figure 4.21 shows an adaptive filter that is used to predict the future value of a signal based on its present value. A second example is shown in Figure 4.22. In this example, the adaptive filter learns to reproduce the output from some plant based on inputs to the system. This configuration has many uses as an adaptive control system. The plant could represent many things, including a human operator. In that case, the adaptive filter could learn how to respond to changing conditions by watching the human operator. Eventually, such a device might result in an automated control system, leaving the human free for more important tasks.[2]

Another useful application of these devices is in adaptive beam-forming antenna arrays. Although the term antenna is usually associated with electromagnetic

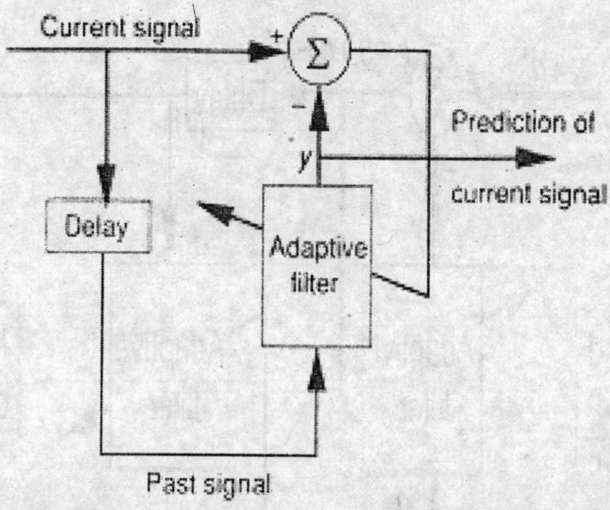

Figure 4.21 This schematic shows filter used to predict signal values. The input signal used to train the network is a delayed value of the actual signal; that is, it is the signal at some past time. The expected output is the current value of the signal. The adaptive filter attempts to minimize the error between its output and the current signal, based on an input of the signal value from some time in the past. Once the filter is correctly predicting the current signal based on the past signal, the current signal can be used directly as an input without the delay. The filter will then make a prediction of the future signal value.

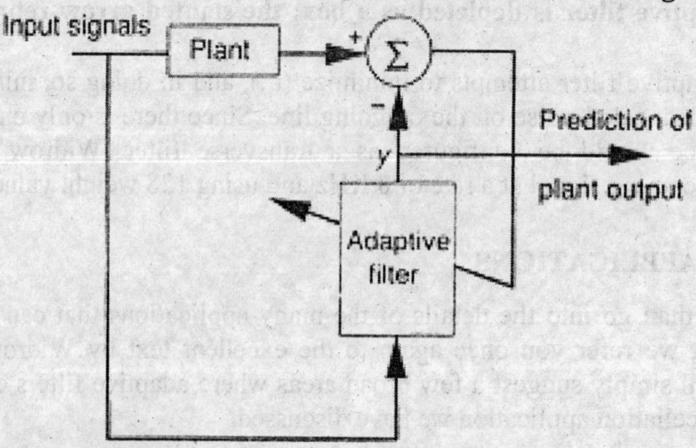

Figure 4.22 This example shows an adaptive filter used to model the output from a system, called the plant. Inputs to the filter are the same as those to the plant. The filter adjusts its weights based on the difference between its output and the output of the plant.

relation, we broaden the definition here to include any spatial array of sensors. The basic task her is to learn to steer the array. At any given time, a signal may be arriving from any given direction, but antennae usually are directional in their reception characteristics. They respond to signals in some directions, but not in others. The antenna array with adaptive filters learns to adjust its directional characteristics in order to respond to the incoming signal no matter what the direction is, while reducing its response to unwanted noise signals coming in from other directions.

Of course, we have only touched on the number of applications for these devices. Unlike many other neural-network architectures, this is a relatively mature device with a long history of success. In the next section, we replace the binary output condition on the ALC circuit so that the latter becomes, once again, the complete Adaline.

4.10 THE MADALINE

It also has some of the same limitations as the perceptron. For example, a two-input Adaline cannot compute the XOR function. Combining Adalines in a layered structure can overcome this difficulty, as we did in Chapter 2 with the perceptron. Such a structure is illustrated in Figure 4.23.

4.10.1 MADALINE ARCHITECTURE

Madaline is the acronym for Many Adalines. Arranged in a multilayered architecture as illustrated in Figure 4.24, the Madaline resembles the general neural-network structure shown in Chapter 1. In this configuration, the Madaline could be presented with a large-dimensional input vector-say, the pixel values from a raster scan. With suitable training, the network could be taught to respond with a binary +1 on one of several output nodes, each of which corresponds to a different category of input image.

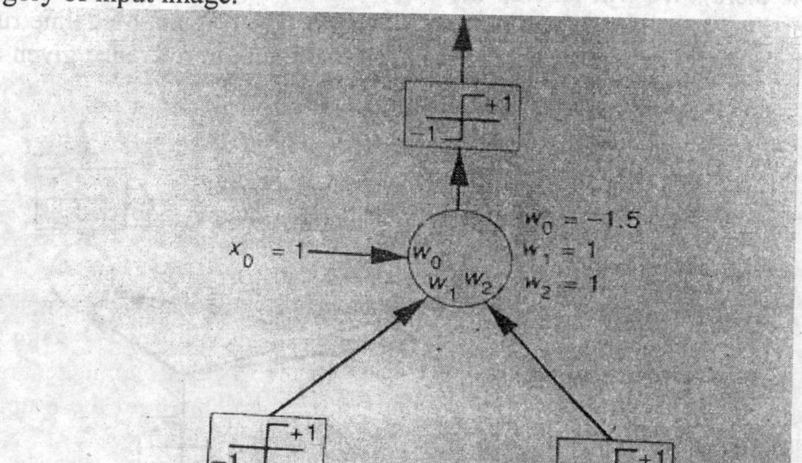

Figure 4.23 Many Adalines (the Madaline) can compute the XOR function of two inputs. Note the addition of the bias terms to each Adaline. A positive analog output from an ALC results in a+1 output from the associated Adaline; a negative analog output results in a -1. Likewise, any inputs to the device that are binary in nature must use ± rather than 1 and 0.

Examples of such categorization are {cat, dog, armadillo, javelina} and {Flogger, Tom Cat, Eagle, Fulcrum}. In such a network, each of four nodes in the output layer corresponds to a single class. For a given input pattern, a node would have a +1 output if the input pattern corresponded to the class represented by that particular node. The other three nodes would have a –1 output. If the input pattern were not a member of any known class, the results from the network could be ambiguous.

To train such a network, we might be tempted to begin with the LMS algorithm at the output layer. Since the network is presumably trained with previously identified input patterns, the desired output vector is known. What we do not know is the desired output for a given node on one of the hidden layers. Furthermore, the LMS algorithm would operate on the analog outputs of the ALC, not on the bipolar output values of the Adaline. For these reasons, a different training strategy has developed for the Madaline.

4.10.2 THE MRII TRAINING ALGORITHM

It is possible to devise a method of training a Madaline-like structure based on the LMS algorithm; however, the method relies on replacing the linear threshold output function with a continuously differentiable function (the threshold function is discontinuous at 0; hence, it is not differentiable there). We will take up the study of this method in the next chapter. For now we consider a method known as Madaline rule II (MRII). The original Madaline rule was an earlier method that we shall not discuss here. Details can be found in reference given at the end of this chapter.

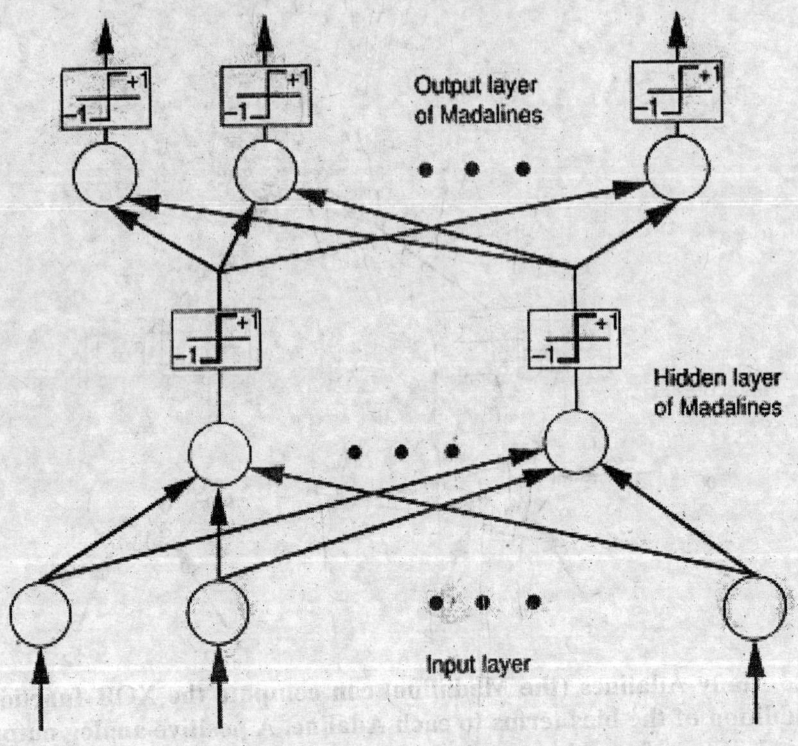

Figure 4.24 Many Adalines can be joined in a layered neural network such as this one.

MRII resembles a trial-and-error procedure with added intelligence in the form of a minimum disturbance principle. Since the output of the network is a series of bipolar units, training amounts to reducing the number of incorrect output nodes for each training input pattern. The minimum disturbance principle enforces the notion that those nodes that can affect the output error while incurring the least change in their weights should have precedence in the learning procedure. This principle is embodied in the following algorithm:

1. Apply a training vector to the inputs of the Madaline and propagate it through to the output units.
2. Count the number of incorrect values in the output layer; call this number the error.
3. For all units on the output layer.

 a. Select the first previously unselected node whose analog output is closest to zero. (This node is the node that can reverse its bipolar output with the change in its weights – hence the term minimum disturbance.

 b. Change the weights on the selected unit such that the bipolar output of the unit changes.

 c. Propagate the input vector forward from the inputs to the outputs once again.

 d. If the weight change results in a reduction in the number of errors, accept the weight change; otherwise, restore the original weights.

4. Repeat step 3 for all layers except the input layer.
5. For all units on the output layer.

 a. Select the previously unselected pair of units whose analog outputs are closest to zero.

 b. Apply a weight correction to both units, in order to change the bipolar output of each.

 c. Propagate the input vector forward from the inputs to the outputs.

 d. If the weight change results in a reduction in the number of errors, accept the weight change; otherwise, restore the original weights.

6. Repeat step 5 for all layers except the input layer.

If necessary, the sequence in steps 5 and 6 can be repeated with triplets of units, or even larger combinations, until satisfactory results are obtained. Preliminary indications are that pairs are adequate for modest-sized networks with up to 25 units per layer.

At the time of this writing, the MRII was still undergoing experimentation to determine its convergence characteristics and other properties. Moreover, a new learning algorithm, MRIII, has been developed. MRIII is similar to MRII, but the individual units have a continuous output function, rather than the bipolar threshold function. In the next section, we shall use a Madaline architecture to examine a specific problem in pattern recognition.

4.10.3 A MADALINE FOR TRANSLATION-INVARIANT PATTERN RECOGNITION

Various Madaline structures have been used recently to demonstrate the applicability of this architecture to adaptive pattern recognition having the properties of translation invariance, rotation invariance, and scale invariance. These three properties are essential to any robust system that would be called on to recognize objects in the field of view of optical or infrared sensors, for example. Remember, however, that even humans do not always instantly recognize objects that have been rotated to unfamiliar orientations, or that have been scaled significantly smaller or larger than their everyday size. The point is that there may be alternatives to training in instantaneous recognition at all angles and scale factors. Be that as it may, it is possible to build neural-network devices that exhibit these characteristics to some degree.

Figure 4.25 shows a portion of a network that is used to implement translation-invariant recognition of pattern. The retina is a 5-by-5-pixel array on which bit-mapped representation of patterns, such as the letters of the alphabet, can be placed. The portion of the network shown is called a slab. Unlike a layer, a slab does not communicate with other slabs in the network, as will be seen shortly. Each Adaline in the slab receives the identical 25 inputs from the retina, and computes a bipolar output in the usual fashion; however, the weights on the 25 Adalines share a unique relationship.

Consider the weights on the top-left Adaline as being arranged in a square matrix duplicating the pixel array on the retina. The Adaline to the immediate right to the

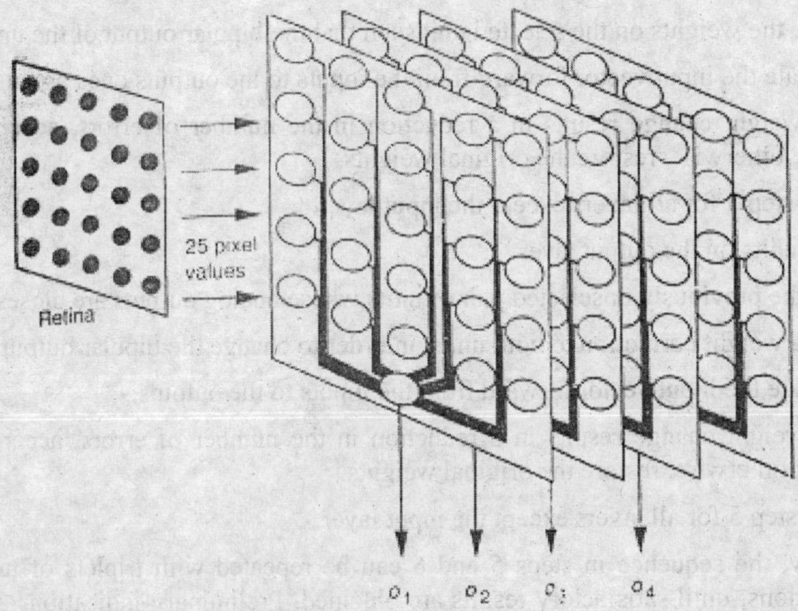

Figure 4.25 This single slab of Adalines will give the same output (either +1 ro -1) for a particular pattern on the retina, regardless of the horizontal or vertical alignment of that pattern on the retina. All 25 individual Adalines are connected to a single Adaline that computes the majority functions; If most of the inputs are +1, the majority element responds with a +1 output. The network derives its translation-invariance properties from the particular configuration of the weights. See the text for details.

top-left pixel has the identical set of weight values, nut translated one pixel to the right: The rightmost column of weights on the first unit wraps around to the left to become the leftmost column on the second unit. Similarly, the unit below the top-left unit also the identical weights, but translated one pixel down. The bottom row of weights on the first unit becomes the top row of the unit under it. This translation continues across each row and down each column in a similar manner. Figure 4.26 illustrates some of these weight matrices. Because of this relationship among the weight matrices, a single pattern on the retina will elicit identical responses from the slab, independent

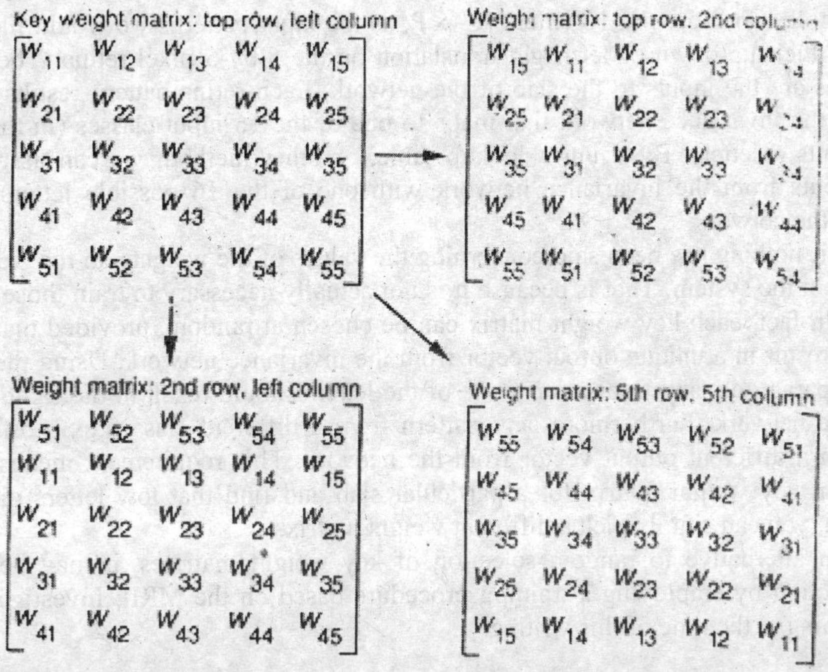

Figure 4.26 The weight matrix in the upper left is the key weight matrix. All other weight matrices on the slab are derived from this matrix. The matrix to the right of the key weight matrix represents the matrix on the Adaline directly to the right of the one with the key weight matrix has wrapped around to become the first column, with the other columns shifting one space to the right. The matrix below the key weight matrix is the one on the Adaline directly below the Adaline with the key weight matrix. The matrix diagonal to the key weight matrix represents the matrix on the Adaline at the lower right of the slab.

of the pattern's translational position on the retina. We encourage you to reflect on this result for a moment (perhaps several moments), to convince yourself of its validity.

The majority node is a single Adaline that computes a binary output based on the outputs of the majority of the Adalines connecting to it. Because of the translational relationship among the weight vectors, the placement of a particular pattern at any location on the retina will result in the identical output from the majority element (we impose the restriction that patterns that extend beyond the retina boundaries will wrap around to the opposite side, just as the various weight matrices are derived from the key weight matrix). Of course, a pattern different from the first may elicit a different response from the majority element. Because only two responses are possible, the slab can differentiate two classes on input patterns. In terms of hyperspace, a slab is capable of dividing hyperspace into two regions.

To overcome the limitation of only two possible classes, the retina can be connected to multiple slabs, each having different key weight matrices (Widrow and Winter's term for the weight matrix on the top-left element of each slab). Given the binary nature of the output of each slab, a system of n slabs could differentiate 2^n different pattern classes. Figure 4.27 shows four such slabs producing a four-dimensional output capable of distinguishing 16 different input pattern classes with translational invariance.

Let's review the basic operation of the translation invariance network in terms of a specific example. Consider the 16 letters A → P, as the input patterns we would like to identify regardless of their up-down or left-right translation on the 5-by-5 pixel retina. These translated retina patterns are the inputs to the slab of the network. Each retina pattern results in an output pattern from the invariance network that maps to one of the 16 input classes (in this case, each class represents a letter). By using a lookup table, or other method, we can associate the 16 possible outputs from the invariance network with one of the 16 possible letters that can be identified by the network.

So far, nothing has been said concerning the values of the weights on the Adalines of the various slabs in the system. That is because it is not actually necessary to train those nodes in the usual sense. In fact, each key weight matrix can be chosen at random, provided that each input-pattern class result in a unique output vector from the invariance network. Using the example of the previous paragraph, any translation f one of the letters should result in the same output from the invariance network. Furthermore, any pattern from a different class (i.e., a different letter) must result in a different output vector from the network. This requirement means that, if you pick a random key weight matrix for a particular slab and find that tow letters give the same output pattern, you can simply pick a different weight matrix.

As an alternative to random selection of key weight matrices, it may be possible to optimize selection by employing a training procedure based on the MRII. Investigations in this area are outgoing at the time of this writing.

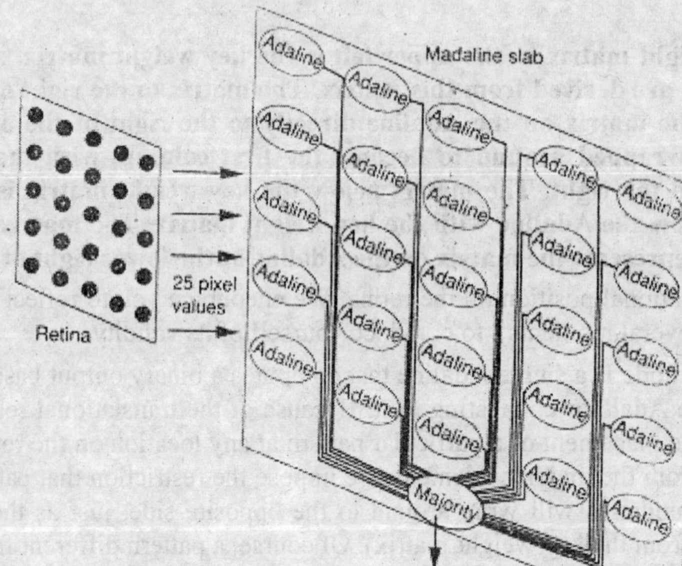

Figure 4.27 Each of the four slabs in the system depicted here will procedure a + 1 or a – 1 output value for every pattern that appears on the retina. The output vector is a four-digit binary number, so the system can potentially differentiate up to 16 different classes of input patterns.

QUESTION BANK

Q1. What is Adaline?
Q2. How Adaline is useful for signal processing?
Q3. What do you signal processing and filters?
Q4. How we can remove the problem of Echo from long distance communication?
Q5. What is Fourier analysis and frequency domain?
Q6. What do you mean digital signal processing?
Q7. What is Adaline? Explain the adaptive linear combiner with the help of diagram?
Q8. Explain the LMS learning rule?
Q9. Explain the various adaptive functions?
Q10. Explain the architecture of adaptive linear network with the help of labeled diagram?
Q11. Draw the diagram of decision boundary of Adaline?
Q12. What is tapped delay line?
Q13. Explain the working of adaptive filter with the of example?
Q14. What is predictive filter? Explain with the help of example?
Q15. Explain the techniques of noise cancellation with the help of proper diagram?
Q16. What do you mean by multiple neuron adaptive filter?
Q17. Draw the abbreviated notation of multiple adaptive filter?
Q18. Explain the techniques of echo cancellation in telephone circuits?
Q19. What are the various application of adaptive filters explain any one of them?
Q20. What is madaline? Explain the architecture of madaline?
Q21. Discuss training algorithm of madaline rule II?
Q22. Explain the translation invariant pattern recognition?

CHAPTER 5

SUPERVISED AND UNSUPERVISED LEARNING

5.1 INTRODUCTION

Supervised learning is a machine learning technique for learning a function from training data. The training data consist of pairs of input objects (typically vectors), and desired outputs. The output of the function can be a continuous value (called regression), or can predict a class label of the input object (called classification). The task of the supervised learner is to predict the value of the function for any valid input object after having seen a number of training examples (i.e. pairs of input and target output). To achieve this, the learner has to generalize from the presented data to unseen situations in a "reasonable" way (see inductive bias). (Compare with unsupervised learning.) The parallel task in human and animal psychology is often referred to as concept learning. The network is supplied with a sequence of both input data and desired (target) output data network is thus told precisely by a "teacher" what should be emitted as output. The teacher can during the learning phase "tell" the network how well it performs ("reinforcement learning") or what the correct behavior would have been ("fully supervised learning"). In supervised learning we have perceptron , Backpropagation network and adaline network described in recent chapters.

Unsupervised learning is a class of problems in which one seeks to determine how the data are organized. It is distinguished from supervised learning (and reinforcement learning) in that the learner is given only unlabeled examples.Unsupervised learning is closely related to the problem of density estimation in statistics. However unsupervised learning also encompasses many other techniques that seek to summarize and explain key features of the data.One form of unsupervised learning is clustering. Another example is blind source separation based on Independent Component Analysis (ICA).

Among neural network models, the Self-Organizing Map (SOM) and Adaptive resonance theory (ART) are commonly used unsupervised learning algorithms. The SOM is a topographic organization in which nearby locations in the map represent inputs with similar properties. The ART model allows the number of clusters to vary with problem size and lets the user control the degree of similarity between members of the same clusters by means of a user-defined constant called the vigilance parameter. ART networks are also used for many pattern recognition tasks, such as automatic target recognition and seismic signal processing. The first version of ART was "ART1", developed by Carpenter and Grossberg(1988).

Self-organizing in networks is one of the most fascinating topics in the neural network field. Such networks can learn to detect regularities and correlations in their input and adapt their future responses to that input accordingly. The neurons of competitive networks learn to recognize groups of similar input vectors. Self-organizing maps learn to recognize groups of similar input vectors in such a way that neurons physically near each other in the neuron layer respond to similar input vectors.

Learning vector quantization (LVQ) is a method for training competitive layers in a supervised manner. A competitive layer automatically learns to classify input vectors. However, the classes that the competitive layer finds are dependent only on the distance between input vectors. If two input vectors are very similar, the competitive layer probably will put them in the same class. There is no mechanism in a strictly competitive layer design to say whether or not any two input vectors are in the same class or different classes.LVQ networks, on the other hand, learn to classify input vectors into target classes chosen by the user.

5.2. COMPETITIVE LEARNING

The prototypic competitive learning ("self-organizing") model is the Kohonen network (named after the Finnish researcher who pioneered the research). A Kohonen network is a two-layered network, much like the Perceptron. But the output layer for a two-neurode input layer can be represented as a two-dimensional grid, also known as the "competitive layer". The input values are continuous, typically normalized to any value between -1 and +1. Training of the Kohonen network does not involve comparing the actual output with a desired output. Instead, the input vector is compared with the weight vectors leading to the competitive layer. The neurode with a weight vector most closely matching the input vector is called the **winning neurode.**

For example, if the input vector is (0.35, 0.8), the winning neurode might have weight vector (0.4, 0.78). The learning rule would adjust the weight vector to make it even closer to the input vector. Only the winning neurode produces output, and only the winning neurode gets its weights adjusted. In more sophisticated models, only the weights of the winning neurode and its immediate neighbors are updated.

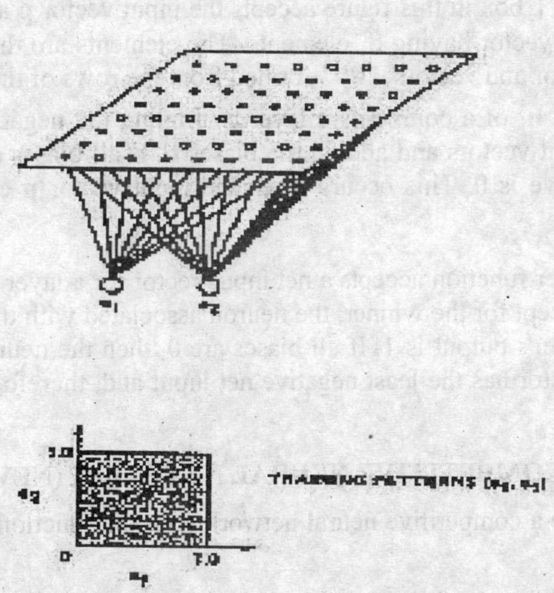

Figure 5.1 Network With Training Patterns

After training, a limited number of input vectors will map to activation of distinct output neurodes. Because the weights are modified in response to the inputs, rather than in response to desired outputs, competitive learning is called **unsupervised** learning, to distinguish it from the **supervised** learning of Perceptrons, Adalines and Backpropagation. In supervised learning, comparison is made between actual outputs and desired outputs supplied by an external supervisor. There is no external supervisor in competitive learning. The neurons in a competitive layer distribute themselves to recognize frequently presented input vectors.

5.2.1 ARCHITECTURE

The architecture for a competitive network is shown below.

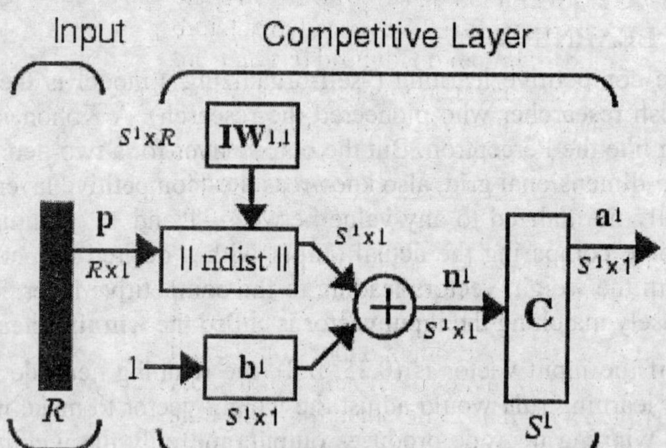

Figure 5.2 Architecture For A Competitive Network

The `||dist||` box in this figure accepts the input vector **p** and the input weight matrix $\mathbf{IW}^{1,1}$, and produces a vector having S_1 elements. The elements are the negative of the distances between the input vector and vectors ${}_i\mathbf{IW}^{1,1}$ formed from the rows of the input weight matrix. Compute the net input $\mathbf{n}^1$ of a competitive layer by finding the negative distance between input vector **p** and the weight vectors and adding the biases **b**. If all biases are zero, the maximum net input a neuron can have is 0. This occurs when the input vector **p** equals that neuron's weight vector.

The competitive transfer function accepts a net input vector for a layer and returns neuron outputs of 0 for all neurons except for the winner, the neuron associated with the most positive element of net input $\mathbf{n}^1$. The winner's output is 1. If all biases are 0, then the neuron whose weight vector is closest to the input vector has the least negative net input and, therefore, wins the competition to output a 1.

5.2.2 CREATING A COMPETITIVE NEURAL NETWORK (NEWC)

You can create a competitive neural network with the function `newc`. A simple example shows how this works.

Suppose you want to divide the following four two-element vectors into two classes.

p = [.1 .8 .1 .9; .2 .9 .1 .8]

```
p =  0.1000  0.8000  0.1000  0.9000
     0.2000  0.9000  0.1000  0.8000
```

There are two vectors near the origin and two vectors near (1,1).

First, create a two-neuron layer with two input elements ranging from 0 to 1. The first argument gives the ranges of the two input vectors, and the second argument says that there are to be two neurons.

```
net = newc([0 1; 0 1],2);
```

The weights are initialized to the centers of the input ranges with the function `midpoint`. You can check to see these initial values as follows:

```
wts = net.IW{1,1}
wts =  0.5000  0.5000
       0.5000  0.5000
```

These weights are indeed the values at the midpoint of the range (0 to 1) of the inputs, as you would expect when using `midpoint` for initialization.

The biases are computed by `initcon`, which gives

```
biases = net.b{1}
biases =  5.4366
          5.4366
```

Now you have a network, but you need to train it to do the classification job.

Recall that each neuron competes to respond to an input vector **p**. If the biases are all 0, the neuron whose weight vector is closest to **p** gets the highest net input and, therefore, wins the competition and outputs 1. All other neurons output 0. You want to adjust the winning neuron so as to move it closer to the input.

5.3 KOHONEN'S SELF-ORGANIZING MAP (SOM)

Kohonon's SOMs are a type of unsupervised learning. The goal is to discover some underlying structure of the data. However, the kind of structure we are looking for is very different than, say, PCA or vector quantization. Kohonen's SOM is called a topology-preserving map because there is a topological structure imposed on the nodes in the network. A topological map is simply a mapping that preserves neighborhood relations.

In the nets we have studied so far, we have ignored the geometrical arrangements of output nodes. Each node in a given layer has been identical in that each is connected with all of the nodes in the upper and/or lower layer. We are now going to take into consideration that physical arrangement of these nodes. Nodes that are "close" together are going to interact differently than nodes that are "far" apart.

What do we mean by "close" and "far"? We can think of organizing the output nodes in a line or in a planar configuration. The goal is to train the net so that nearby outputs correspond to nearby inputs.

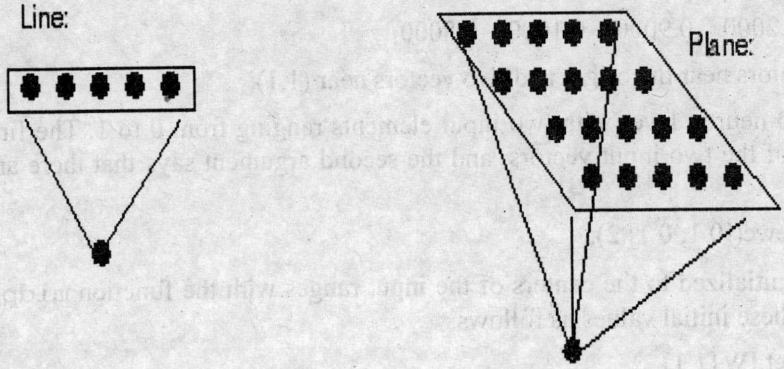

Figure 5.3 Kohonen's Self-Organizing Map

The goal is to train the net so that nearby outputs correspond to nearby inputs.

E.g. if x1 and x2 are two input vectors and t1 and t2 are the locations of the corresponding winning output nodes, then t1 and t2 should be close if x1 and x2 are similar. A network that performs this kind of mapping is called a feature map.In the brain, neurons tend to cluster in groups. The connections within the group are much greater than the connections with the neurons outside of the group. Kohonen's network tries to mimick this in a simple way.

5.3.1 ALGORITHM FOR KOHONON'S SELF ORGANIZING MAP

- Assume output nodes are connected in an array (usually 1 or 2 dimensional)
- Assume that the network is fully connected - all nodes in input layer are connected to all nodes in output layer.
- Use the competitive learning algorithm as follows:
    - Randomly choose an input vector x
    - Determine the "winning" output node i, where w_i is the weight vector connecting the inputs to output node i.
      Note: the above equation is equivalent to $w_i\, x >= w_k\, x$ only if the weights are normalized.
      $|\omega_i - x| \trianglelefteq \omega_k - x| \quad \forall k$
    - Given the winning node i, the weight update is
      $w_k\,(new) = w_k\,(old) + \mu\, \chi\ (i, k)\,(x - w_k)$

where $\chi(i, k)$ is called the neighborhood function that has value 1 when i=k and falls off with the distance $|r_k - r_i|$ between units i and k in the output array. Thus, units close to the winner as well as the winner itself, have their weights updated appreciably. Weights associated with far away output nodes do not change significantly. It is here that the toplogical information is supplied. Nearby units receive similar updates and thus end up responding to nearby input patterns.

The above rule drags the weight vector wi and the weights of nearby units towards the input x.

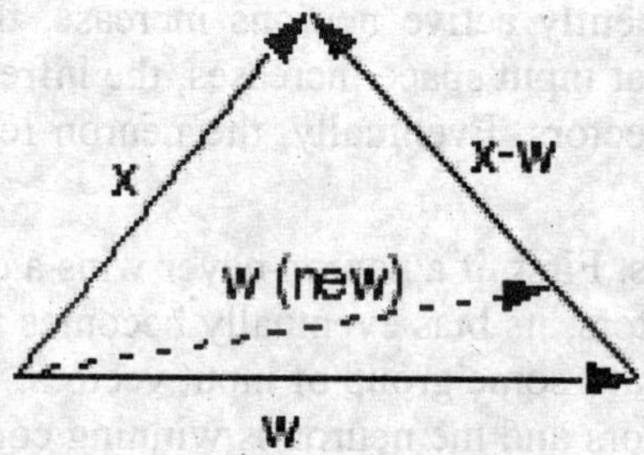

EXAMPLE OF THE NEIGHBORHOOD FUNCTION IS:

$$\chi (I,k) = e^{(-|r_k - r_i|^2)} / (2\sigma^2)$$

where σ^2 is the width parameter that can gradually be decreased over time.

5.3.2 KOHONEN LEARNING RULE (LEARNK)

The weights of the winning neuron (a row of the input weight matrix) are adjusted with the Kohonen learning rule. Supposing that the `i`th neuron wins, the elements of the `i`th row of the input weight matrix are adjusted as shown below.

$$_iIW^{1,1}(q) = {_iIW^{1,1}}(q-1) + \alpha\,(p(q) - {_iIW^{1,1}}(q-1))$$

The Kohonen rule allows the weights of a neuron to learn an input vector, and because of this it is useful in recognition applications.

Thus, the neuron whose weight vector was closest to the input vector is updated to be even closer. The result is that the winning neuron is more likely to win the competition the next time a similar vector is presented, and less likely to win when a very different input vector is presented. As more and more inputs are presented, each neuron in the layer closest to a group of input vectors soon adjusts its weight vector toward those input vectors. Eventually, if there are enough neurons, every cluster of similar input vectors will have a neuron that outputs 1 when a vector in the cluster is presented, while outputting a 0 at all other times. Thus, the competitive network learns to categorize the input vectors it sees.

5.3.3 BIAS LEARNING RULE (LEARNCON)

One of the limitations of competitive networks is that some neurons might not always be allocated. In other words, some neuron weight vectors might start out far from any input vectors and never win the competition, no matter how long the training is continued. The result is that their weights do not get to learn and they never win. These unfortunate neurons, referred to as dead neurons, never perform a useful function. To stop this, use biases to give neurons that only win the competition rarely (if ever) an advantage over neurons that win often. A positive bias, added to the negative distance, makes a distant neuron more likely to win. To do this job a running average of neuron outputs is kept. It is equivalent to the percentages of times each output is 1. This average is used to update the biases with the learning function `learncon` so that the biases of frequently active neurons become smaller, and biases of infrequently active neurons become larger.

As the biases of infrequently active neurons increase, the input space to which those neurons respond increases. As that input space increases, the infrequently active neuron responds and moves toward more input vectors. Eventually, the neuron responds to the same number of vectors as other neurons.

This has two good effects. First, if a neuron never wins a competition because its weights are far from any of the input vectors, its bias eventually becomes large enough so that it can win. When this happens, it moves toward some group of input vectors. Once the neuron's weights have moved into a group of input vectors and the neuron is winning consistently, its bias will decrease to 0. Thus, the problem of dead neurons is resolved.

The second advantage of biases is that they force each neuron to classify roughly the same percentage of input vectors. Thus, if a region of the input space is associated with a larger number of input vectors than another region, the more densely filled region will attract more neurons and be classified into smaller subsections.

5.3.4 TRAINING

Now train the network for 500 epochs. You can use either `train` or `adapt`.

```
net.trainParam.epochs = 500;
net = train(net,p);
```

Note that `train` for competitive networks uses the training function `trainr`. You can verify this by executing the following code after creating the network.

```
net.trainFcn
```

This code produces

```
ans = trainr
```

For each epoch, all training vectors (or sequences) are each presented once in a different random order with the network and weight and bias values updated after each individual presentation.

Next, supply the original vectors as input to the network, simulate the network, and finally convert its output vectors to class indices.

```
a = sim(net,p)
ac = vec2ind(a)
```

This yields

```
ac =   1   2   1   2
```

You see that the network is trained to classify the input vectors into two groups, those near the origin, class 1, and those near (1,1), class 2.

It might be interesting to look at the final weights and biases. They are

```
wts =  0.1000   0.1467
       0.8474   0.8525
biases =  5.4961
          5.3783
```

(You might get different answers when you run this problem, because a random seed is used to pick the order of the vectors presented to the network for training.) Note that the first vector (formed from the first row of the weight matrix) is near the input vectors close to the origin, while the vector formed from the second row of the weight matrix is close to the input vectors near (1,1). Thus, the network has been trained--just by exposing it to the inputs--to classify them.

During training each neuron in the layer closest to a group of input vectors adjusts its weight vector toward those input vectors. Eventually, if there are enough neurons, every cluster of similar input vectors has a neuron that outputs 1 when a vector in the cluster is presented, while outputting a 0 at all other times. Thus, the competitive network learns to categorize the input.

5.4 SELF-ORGANIZING FEATURE MAPS

Self-organizing feature maps (SOFM) learn to classify input vectors according to how they are grouped in the input space. They differ from competitive layers in that neighboring neurons in the self-organizing map learn to recognize neighboring sections of the input space. Thus, self-organizing maps learn both the distribution (as do competitive layers) and topology of the input vectors they are trained on.

The neurons in the layer of an SOFM are arranged originally in physical positions according to a topology function. The function `gridtop`, `hextop`, or `randtop` can arrange the neurons in a grid, hexagonal, or random topology. Distances between neurons are calculated from their positions with a distance function. There are four distance functions, `dist`, `boxdist`, `linkdist`, and `mandist`. Link distance is the most common.

Here a self-organizing feature map network identifies a winning neuron $i*$ using the same procedure as employed by a competitive layer. However, instead of updating only the winning neuron, all neurons within a certain neighborhood $N_{i*}(d)$ of the winning neuron are updated,

using the Kohonen rule. Specifically, all such neurons i $N_{i*}(d)$ are adjusted as follows:

- ${}_iw(q) = {}_iw(q-1) + \alpha(p(q) - {}_iw(q-1))$

  or

- ${}_iw(q) = (1-\alpha)\,{}_iw(q-1) + \alpha p(q)$

Here the neighborhood $N_{i*}(d)$ contains the indices for all of the neurons that lie within a radius d of the winning neuron $i*$.

$N_i(d) = \{j, d_{ij} \le d\}$

Thus, when a vector **p** is presented, the weights of the winning neuron and its close neighbors move toward **p**. Consequently, after many presentations, neighboring neurons have learned vectors similar to each other.

Another version of SOFM training, called the batch algorithm, presents the whole data set to the network before any weights are updated. The algorithm then determines a winning neuron for each input vector. Each weight vector then moves to the average position of all of the input vectors for which it is a winner, or for which it is in the neighborhood of a winner.

To illustrate the concept of neighborhoods, consider the figure below. The left diagram shows a two-dimensional neighborhood of radius d = 1 around neuron 13. The right diagram shows a neighborhood of radius d = 2. These neighborhoods could be written as

$N_{13}(1) = \{8, 12, 13, 14, 18\}$

and

$N_{13}(1) = \{3, 7, 8, 9, 11, 12, 13, 14, 15, 17, 18, 19, 23\}$

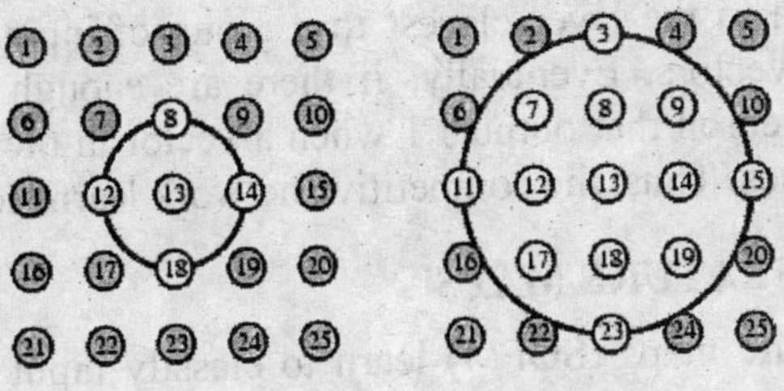

$N_{13}(1)$ $N_{13}(2)$

The neurons in an SOFM do not have to be arranged in a two-dimensional pattern. You can use a one-dimensional arrangement, or three or more dimensions. For a one-dimensional SOFM, a neuron has only two neighbors within a radius of 1 (or a single neighbor if the neuron is at the end of the line). You can also define distance in different ways, for instance, by using rectangular and hexagonal arrangements of neurons and neighborhoods. The performance of the network is not sensitive to the exact shape of the neighborhoods.

5.4.1 ARCHITECTURE

The architecture for this SOFM is shown below.

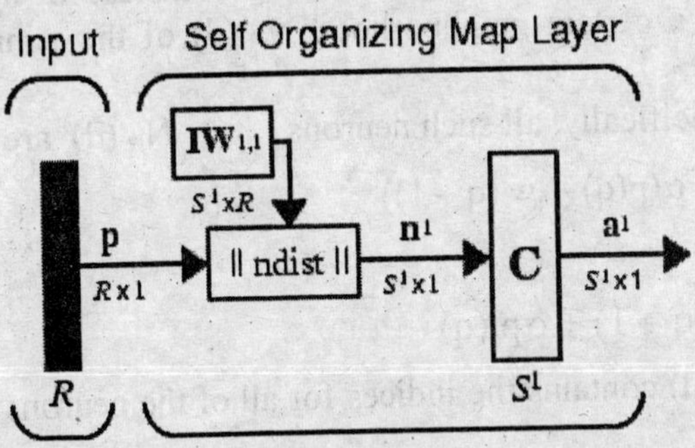

$$n_i^1 = - \| {}_iIW^{1,1} - p \|$$

$$a^1 = \textbf{compet}(n^1)$$

Figure 5.4 Architecture For This SOFM

This architecture is like that of a competitive network, except no bias is used here. The competitive transfer function produces a 1 for output element a^1_i corresponding to i*, the winning neuron. All other output elements in a^1 are 0. Now, however, as described above, neurons close to the winning neuron are updated along with the winning neuron. You can choose from various topologies of neurons. Similarly, you can choose from various distance expressions to calculate neurons that are close to the winning neuron.

5.4.2 CREATING A SELF-ORGANIZING MAP NEURAL NETWORK (NEWSOM)

You can create a new SOM network with the function newsom. This function defines variables used in two phases of learning:

Ordering-phase learning rate

Ordering-phase steps

Tuning-phase learning rate

Tuning-phase neighborhood distance

These values are used for training and adapting.

Consider the following example.

Suppose that you want to create a network having input vectors with two elements that fall in the ranges 0 to 2 and 0 to 1, respectively. Further suppose that you want to have six neurons in a hexagonal 2-by-3 network. The code to obtain this network is

```
net = newsom([0 2; 0 1],[2 3]);
```

Suppose also that the vectors to train on are

```
P = [.1 .3 1.2 1.1 1.8 1.7 .1 .3 1.2 1.1 1.8 1.7;...
0.2 0.1 0.3 0.1 0.3 0.2 1.8 1.8 1.9 1.9 1.7 1.8]
```

You can plot all of this with

```
plot(P(1,:),P(2,:),'.g','markersize',20)
hold on
plotsom(net.iw{1,1},net.layers{1}.distances)
hold off
```

to give

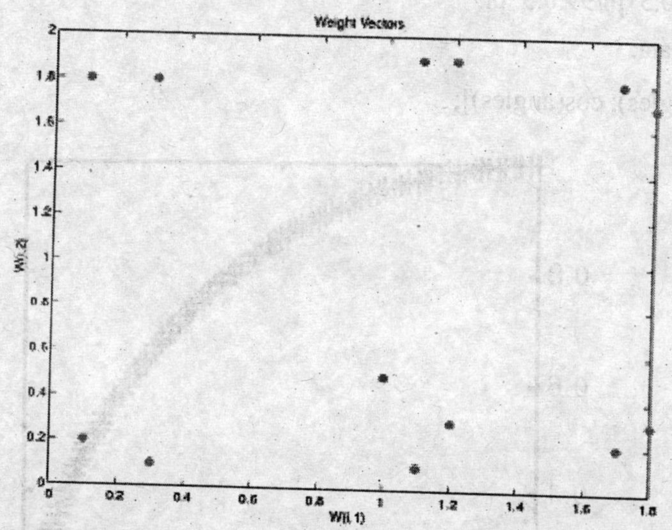

Figure 5.5 Neurons In A Hexagonal 2-By-3 Network

The various training vectors are seen as fuzzy gray spots around the perimeter of this figure. The initialization for `newsom` is `midpoint`. Thus, the initial network neurons are all concentrated at the black spot at (1, 0.5). When simulating a network, the negative distances between each neuron's weight vector and the input vector are calculated (`negdist`) to get the weighted inputs. The weighted inputs are also the net inputs (`netsum`). The net inputs compete (`compete`) so that only the neuron with the most positive net input will output a 1.

5.4.3 TRAINING (LEARNSOMB)

The default learning in a self-organizing feature map occurs in the batch mode (`trainbuwb`). The weight learning function for the self-organizing map is `learnsomb`.

First, the network identifies the winning neuron for each input vector. Each weight vector then moves to the average position of all of the input vectors for which it is a winner or for which it is in the neighborhood of a winner. The distance that defines the size of the neighborhood is altered during training through two phases.

5.4.4 ORDERING PHASE

This phase lasts for the given number of steps. The neighborhood distance starts at a given initial distance, and decreases to the tuning neighborhood distance (1.0). As the neighborhood distance decreases over this phase, the neurons of the network typically order themselves in the input space with the same topology in which they are ordered physically.

5.4.5 EXAMPLES

Two examples are described briefly below. You might try the demonstrations `demosm1` and `demosm2` to see similar examples.

5.4.5.1 ONE-DIMENSIONAL SELF-ORGANIZING MAP

Consider 100 two-element unit input vectors spread evenly between 0° and 90°.

```
angles = 0:0.5*pi/99:0.5*pi;
```

Here is a plot of the data.

```
P = [sin(angles); cos(angles)];
```

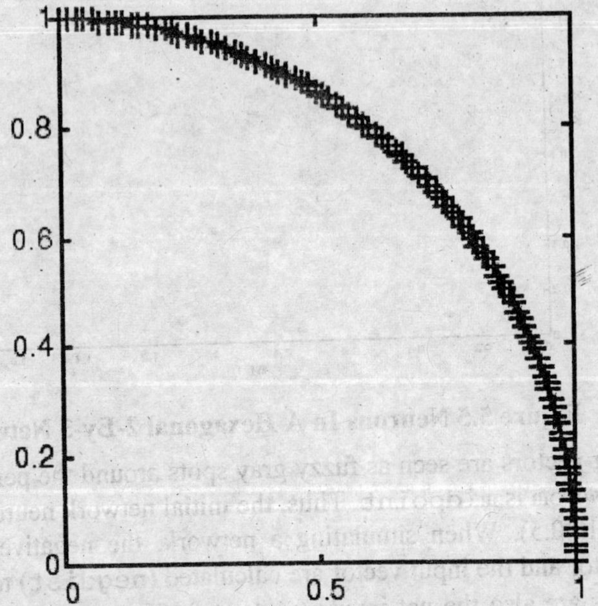

Figure 5.6 One-Dimensional Self-Organizing Map

A a self-organizing map is defined as a one-dimensional layer of 10 neurons. This map is to be trained on these input vectors shown above. Originally these neurons are at the center of the figure.

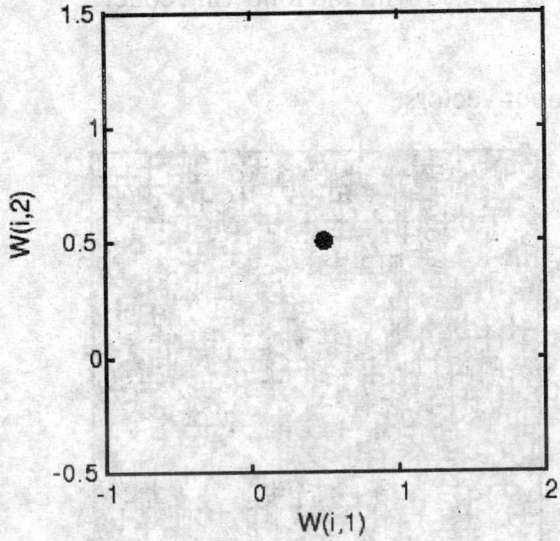

Figure 5.6(A) Neurons Are At The Center

Of course, because all the weight vectors start in the middle of the input vector space, all you see now is a single circle. As training starts the weight vectors move together toward the input vectors. They also become ordered as the neighborhood size decreases. Finally the layer adjusts its weights so that each neuron responds strongly to a region of the input space occupied by input vectors. The placement of neighboring neuron weight vectors also reflects the topology of the input vectors.

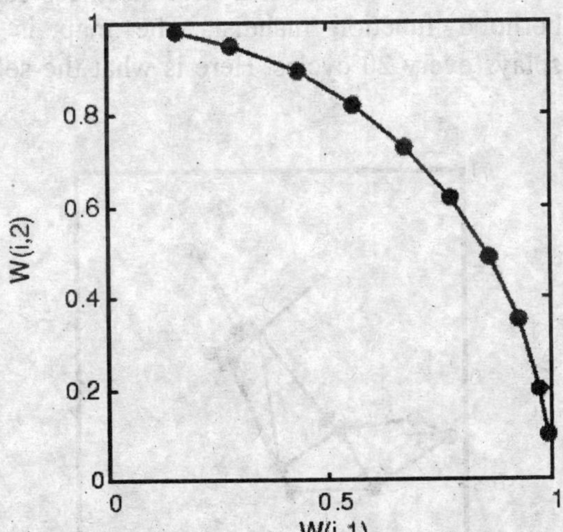

Figure 5.6(B) Input Vectors In A Random Order

Note that self-organizing maps are trained with input vectors in a random order, so starting with the same initial vectors does not guarantee identical training results.

5.4.5.2 TWO-DIMENSIONAL SELF-ORGANIZING MAP

This example shows how a two-dimensional self-organizing map can be trained.

First some random input data is created with the following code:

```
P = rands(2,1000);
```

Here is a plot of these 1000 input vectors.

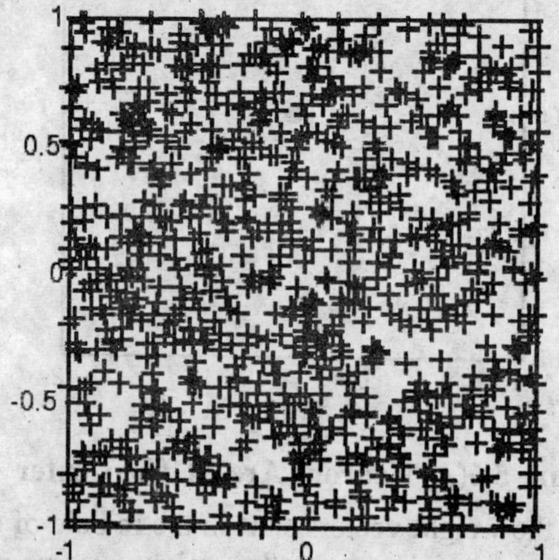

Figure 5.7 Two-Dimensional Self-Organizing Map Can Be Trained Using 1000 Input Vectors

A 5-by-6 two-dimensional map of 30 neurons is used to classify these input vectors. The two-dimensional map is five neurons by six neurons, with distances calculated according to the Manhattan distance neighborhood function mandist. The map is then trained for 5000 presentation cycles, with displays every 20 cycles. Here is what the self-organizing map looks like after 40 cycles.

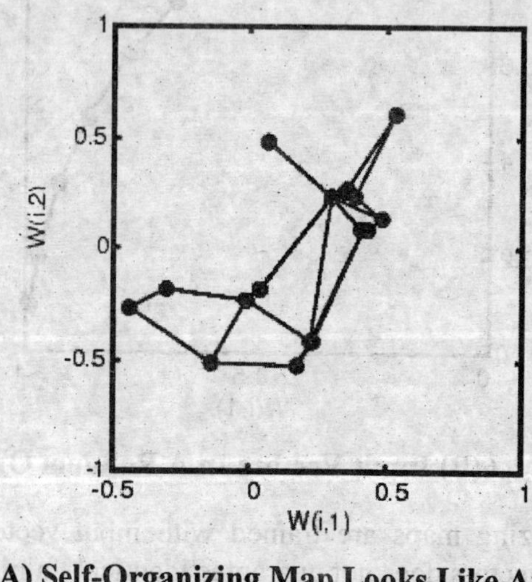

Figure 5.7(A) Self-Organizing Map Looks Like After 40 Cycles

The weight vectors, shown with circles, are almost randomly placed. However, even afteronly 40 presentation cycles, neighboring neurons, connected by lines, have weight vectors close together.

Here is the map after 120 cycles.

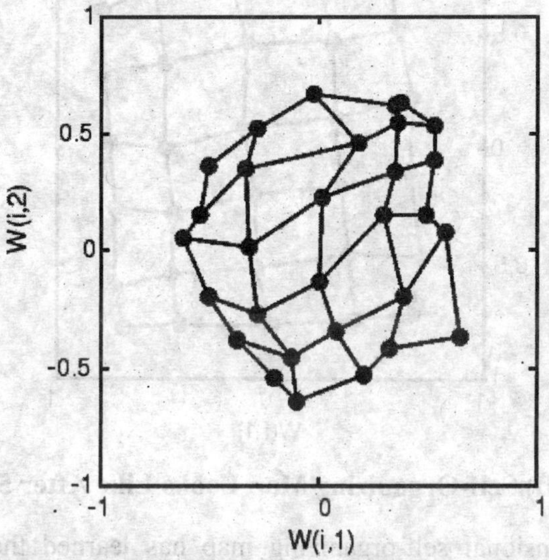

Figure 5.7(B) Self-Organizing Map Looks Like After 120 Cycles

After 120 cycles, the map has begun to organize itself according to the topology of the input space, which constrains input vectors.

The following plot, after 500 cycles, shows the map more evenly distributed across the input space.

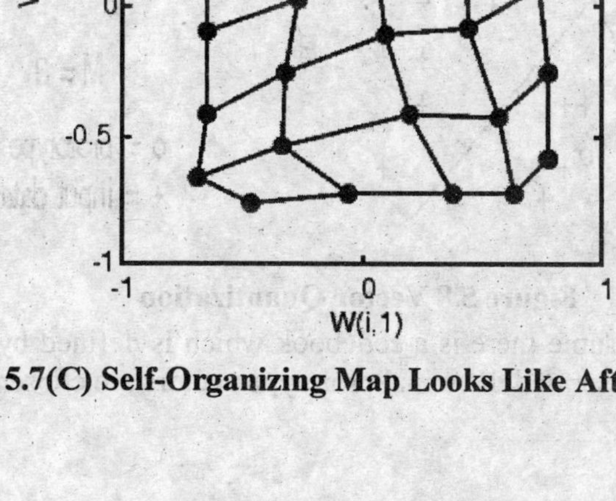

Figure 5.7(C) Self-Organizing Map Looks Like After 500 Cycles

Finally, after 5000 cycles, the map is rather evenly spread across the input space. In addition, the neurons are very evenly spaced, reflecting the even distribution of input vectors in this problem.

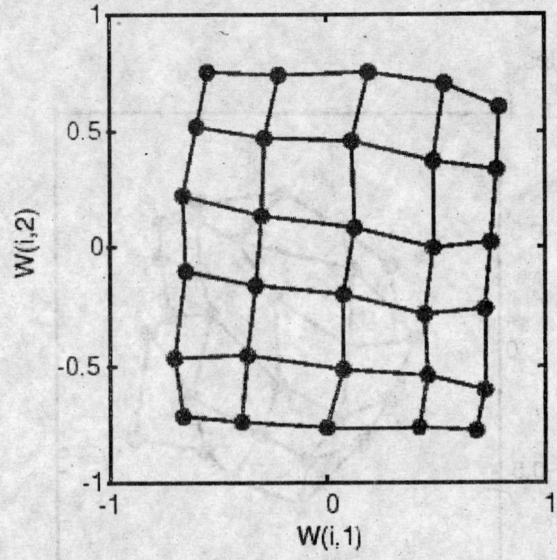

Figure 5.7(D) Self-Organizing Map Looks Like After 5000 Cycles

Thus a two-dimensional self-organizing map has learned the topology of its inputs' space.It is important to note that while a self-organizing map does not take long to organize itself so that neighboring neurons recognize similar inputs, it can take a long time for the map to finally arrange itself according to the distribution of input vectors.

5.5 VECTOR QUANTIZATION (VQ)

Vector quantization is one example of competitive learning. The goal here is to have the network "discover" structure in the data by finding how the data is clustered. The results can be used for data encoding and compression. One such method for doing this is called vector quantization.

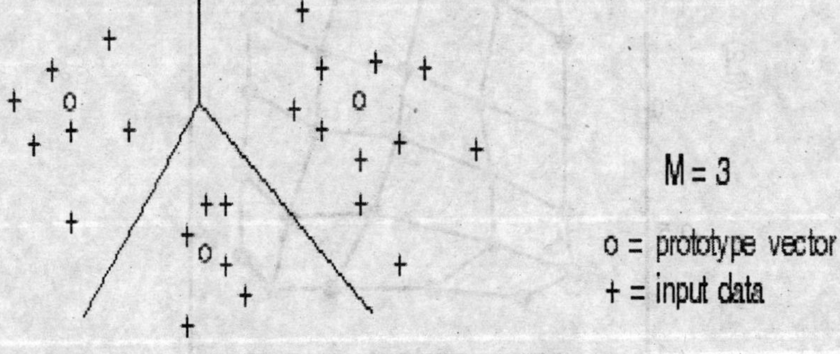

Figure 5.8 Vector Quantization

In vector quantization, we assume there is a codebook which is defined by a set of M prototype vectors. (M is chosen by the user and the initial prototype vectors are chosen arbitrarily).

An input belongs to cluster i if i is the index of the closest prototype (closest in the sense of the normal euclidean distance). This has the effect of dividing up the input space into a Voronoi tesselation

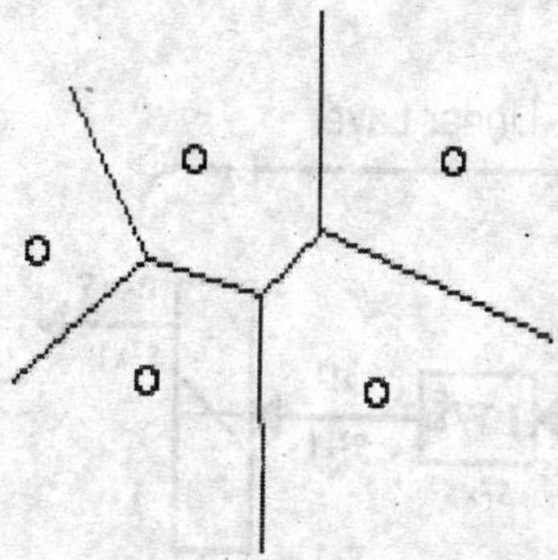

Figure 5.9 Normal Euclidean Distance

5.5.1 IMPLEMENTING VECTOR QUANTIZATION WITH A NETWORK

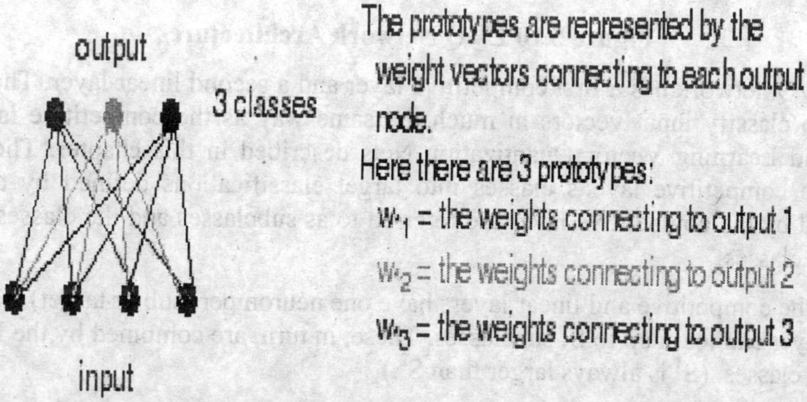

ALGORITHM:

- Choose the number of clusters M
- Initialize the prototypes $w_{*1}, \ldots w_{*m}$ (one simple method for doing this is to randomly choose M vectors from the input data)
- Repeat until stopping criterion is satisfied:
  - Randomly pick an input x
  - Determine the "winning" node k by finding the prototype vector that satisfies $| w_{*k} - x | <= | w_{*i} - x |$ (for all i) note: if the prototypes are normalized, this is equivalent to maximizing w_{*i} x
  - Update only the winning prototype weights according to $w_{*k}(new) = w_{*k}(old) + \square(x - w_{*k}(old))$ This is called the standard competitive learning rule.

5.5.2 LEARNING VECTOR QUANTIZATION NETWORKS

5.5.2.1 ARCHITECTURE

The LVQ network architecture is shown below.

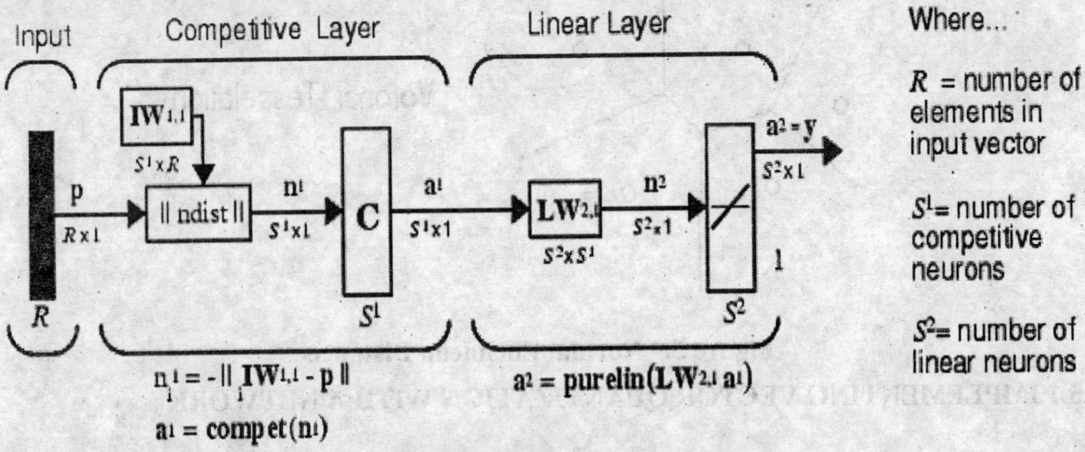

Figure 5.10 LVQ Network Architecture

An LVQ network has a first competitive layer and a second linear layer. The competitive layer learns to classify input vectors in much the same way as the competitive layers of Self-Organizing and Learning Vector Quantization Nets described in this chapter. The linear layer transforms the competitive layer's classes into target classifications defined by the user. The classes learned by the competitive layer are referred to as subclasses and the classes of the linear layer as target classes.

Both the competitive and linear layers have one neuron per (sub or target) class. Thus, the competitive layer can learn up to S^1 subclasses. These, in turn, are combined by the linear layer to form S^2 target classes. (S^1 is always larger than S^2.)

For examplé, suppose neurons 1, 2, and 3 in the competitive layer all learn subclasses of the input space that belongs to the linear layer target class 2. Then competitive neurons 1, 2, and 3 will have $\mathbf{LW}^{2,1}$ weights of 1.0 to neuron $\mathbf{n}^2$ in the linear layer, and weights of 0 to all other linear neurons. Thus, the linear neuron produces a 1 if any of the three competitive neurons (1, 2, or 3) wins the competition and outputs a 1. This is how the subclasses of the competitive layer are combined into target classes in the linear layer.

In short, a 1 in the ith row of $\mathbf{a}^1$ (the rest to the elements of $\mathbf{a}^1$ will be zero) effectively picks the ith column of $\mathbf{LW}^{2,1}$ as the network output. Each such column contains a single 1, corresponding to a specific class. Thus, subclass 1's from layer 1 are put into various classes by the $\mathbf{LW}^{2,1}\mathbf{a}^1$ multiplication in layer 2.

You know ahead of time what fraction of the layer 1 neurons should be classified into the various class outputs of layer 2, so you can specify the elements of $\mathbf{LW}^{2,1}$ at the start. However, you have to go through a training procedure to get the first layer to produce the correct subclass output for each vector of the training set. This training is discussed in Training. First, consider how to create the original network.

5.5.2.2 CREATING AN LVQ NETWORK (NEWLVQ)

You can create an LVQ network with the function `newlvq`,

net = newlvq(PR,S1,PC,LR,LF)

where

PR is an R-by-2 matrix of minimum and maximum values for R input elements.

S^1 is the number of first-layer hidden neurons.

PC is an S^2-element vector of typical class percentages.

LR is the learning rate (default 0.01).

LF is the learning function (default is `learnlv1`).

Suppose you have 10 input vectors. Create a network that assigns each of these input vectors to one of four subclasses. Thus, there are four neurons in the first competitive layer. These subclasses are then assigned to one of two output classes by the two neurons in layer 2. The input vectors and targets are specified by

P = [-3 -2 -2 0 0 0 0 2 2 3; 0 1 -1 2 1 -1 -2 1 -1 0];

and Tc = [1 1 1 2 2 2 2 1 1 1];

It might help to show the details of what you get from these two lines of code.

```
P =-3  -2  -2   0   0   0   0   2   2   3
    0   1  -1   2   1  -1  -2   1  -1   0
Tc = 1   1   1   2   2   2   2   1   1   1
```

A plot of the input vectors follows.

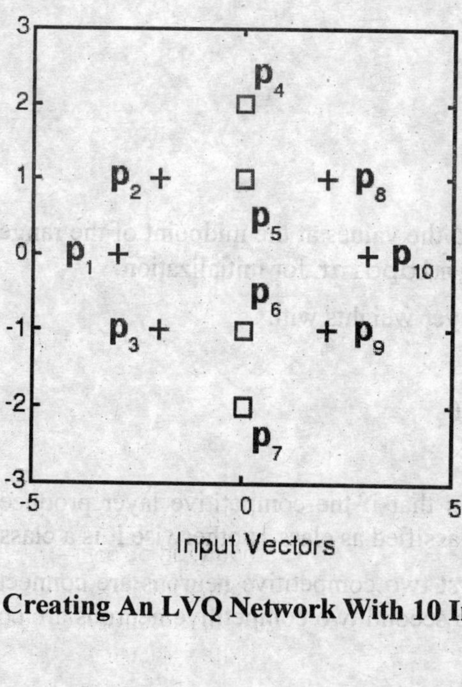

Figure 5.11 Creating An LVQ Network With 10 Input Vectors

As you can see, there are four subclasses of input vectors. You want a network that classifies $\mathbf{p}_1$, $\mathbf{p}_2$, $\mathbf{p}_3$, $\mathbf{p}_8$, $\mathbf{p}_9$, and $\mathbf{p}_{10}$ to produce an output of 1, and that classifies vectors $\mathbf{p}_4$, $\mathbf{p}_5$, $\mathbf{p}_6$, and $\mathbf{p}_7$ to produce an output of 2. Note that this problem is nonlinearly separable, and so cannot be solved by a perceptron, but an LVQ network has no difficulty.

Next convert the `Tc` matrix to target vectors.

```
T = ind2vec(Tc);
```

This gives a sparse matrix `T` that can be displayed in full with

```
targets = full(T)
```

which gives

```
targets =1   1   1   0   0   0   0   1   1   1
         0   0   0   1   1   1   1   0   0   0
```

This looks right. It says, for instance, that if you have the first column of `P` as input, you should get the first column of `targets` as an output; and that output says the input falls in class 1, which is correct. Now you are ready to call `newlvq`.

Call `newlvq` with the proper arguments so that it creates a network with four neurons in the first layer and two neurons in the second layer. The first-layer weights are initialized to the centers of the input ranges with the function `midpoint`. The second-layer weights have 60% (6 of the 10 in `Tc` above) of its columns with a 1 in the first row, (corresponding to class 1), and 40% of its columns will have a 1 in the second row (corresponding to class 2).

```
net = newlvq(P,4,[.6 .4]);
```

Confirm the initial values of the first-layer weight matrix.

```
net.IW{1,1}

ans =   0  0
        0  0
        0  0
        0  0
```

These zero weights are indeed the values at the midpoint of the ranges (-3 to +3) of the inputs, as you would expect when using `midpoint` for initialization.

You can look at the second-layer weights with

```
net.LW{2,1}

ans = 1  1  0  0
      0  0  1  1
```

This makes sense too. It says that if the competitive layer produces a 1 as the first or second element, the input vector is classified as class 1; otherwise it is a class 2.

You might notice that the first two competitive neurons are connected to the first linear neuron (with weights of 1), while the second two competitive neurons are connected to the second linear neuron. All other weights between the competitive neurons and linear neurons have values of 0. Thus, each of the two target classes (the linear neurons) is, in fact, the union of two subclasses (the competitive neurons).You can simulate the network with `sim`. Use the original `P` matrix as input just to see what you get.

```
Y = sim(net,P);
Yc = vec2ind(Y)
Yc =   1   1   1   1   1   1   1   1   1   1
```

The network classifies all inputs into class 1. Because this is not what you want, you have to train the network (adjusting the weights of layer 1 only), before you can expect a good result. The next two sections discuss two LVQ learning rules and the training process.

5.5.3 LVQ1 LEARNING RULE (LEARNLV1)

LVQ learning in the competitive layer is based on a set of input/target pairs.

$$\{p_1, t_1\}, \{p_2, t_2\}, \ldots, \{p_Q, t_Q\}$$

Each target vector has a single 1. The rest of its elements are 0. The 1 tells the proper classification of the associated input. For instance, consider the following training pair.

$$\left\{ p_1 = \begin{bmatrix} 2 \\ -1 \\ 0 \end{bmatrix}, t_1 = \begin{bmatrix} 0 \\ 0 \\ 1 \\ 0 \end{bmatrix} \right\}$$

Here there are input vectors of three elements, and each input vector is to be assigned to one of four classes. The network is to be trained so that it classifies the input vector shown above into the third of four classes.

To train the network, an input vector **p** is presented, and the distance from **p** to each row of the input weight matrix $\mathbf{IW}^{1,1}$ is computed with the function `ndist`. The hidden neurons of layer 1 compete. Suppose that the ith element of $\mathbf{n}^1$ is most positive, and neuron i* wins the competition. Then the competitive transfer function produces a 1 as the i*th element of $\mathbf{a}^1$. All other elements of $\mathbf{a}^1$ are 0.

When $\mathbf{a}^1$ is multiplied by the layer 2 weights $\mathbf{LW}^{2,1}$, the single 1 in $\mathbf{a}^1$ selects the class k* associated with the input. Thus, the network has assigned the input vector **p** to class k* and a^2_{k*} will be 1. Of course, this assignment can be a good one or a bad one, for t_{k*} can be 1 or 0, depending on whether the input belonged to class k* or not. Adjust the i*th row of $\mathbf{IW}^{1,1}$ in such a way as to move this row closer to the input vector **p** if the assignment is correct, and to move the row away from **p** if the assignment is incorrect. If **p** is classified correctly,

$$(a^2_{k*} = t_{k*} = 1)$$

compute the new value of the i*th row of $\mathbf{IW}^{1,1}$ as

$${}_{i*}\mathrm{IW}^{1,1}(q) = {}_{i*}\mathrm{IW}^{1,1}(q-1) + \alpha(p(q) - {}_{i*}\mathrm{IW}^{1,1}(q-1))$$

On the other hand, if **p** is classified incorrectly,

$$(a^2_{k*} = 1 \neq t_{k*} = 0)$$

compute the new value of the i*th row of $\mathbf{IW}^{1,1}$ as

$${}_{i*}\mathrm{IW}^{1,1}(q) = {}_{i*}\mathrm{IW}^{1,1}(q-1) - \alpha(p(q) - {}_{i*}\mathrm{IW}^{1,1}(q-1))$$

You can make these corrections to the i*th row of $\mathbf{IW}^{1,1}$ automatically, without affecting other rows of $\mathbf{IW}^{1,1}$, by back propagating the output errors to layer 1.

Such corrections move the hidden neuron toward vectors that fall into the class for which it forms a subclass, and away from vectors that fall into other classes.

The learning function that implements these changes in the layer 1 weights in LVQ networks is `learnlv1`. It can be applied during training.

5.5.4 TRAINING

Next you need to train the network to obtain first-layer weights that lead to the correct classification of input vectors. You do this with `train` as with the following commands. First, set the training epochs to 150. Then, use `train`:

```
net.trainParam.epochs = 150;
net = train(net,P,T);
```

Now confirm the first-layer weights.

```
net.IW{1,1}
ans =  0.3283   0.0051
      -0.1366   0.0001
      -0.0263   0.2234
            0  -0.0685
```

The following plot shows that these weights have moved toward their respective classification groups.

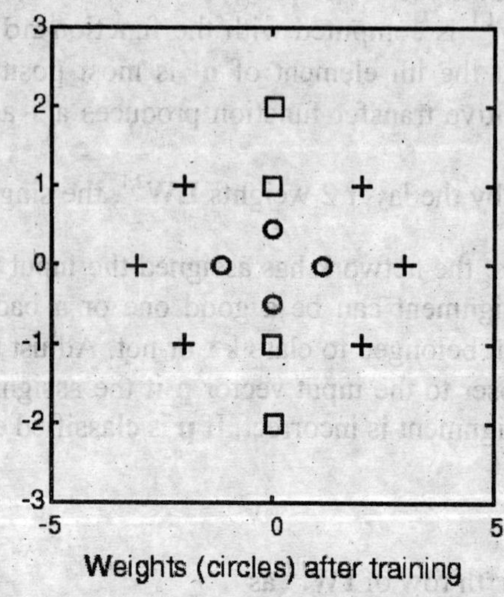

Figure 5.12 Weights After Train Network

To confirm that these weights do indeed lead to the correct classification, take the matrix P as input and simulate the network. Then see what classifications are produced by the network.

```
Y = sim(net,P);
Yc = vec2ind(Y)
```

This gives

```
Yc =   1   1   1   2   2   2   2   1   1   1
```

which is expected. As a last check, try an input close to a vector that was used in training.

```
pchk1 = [0; 0.5];
Y = sim(net,pchk1);
Yc1 = vec2ind(Y)
```

This gives

```
Yc1 =    2
```

This looks right, because `pchk1` is close to other vectors classified as 2. Similarly,

```
pchk2 = [1; 0];
Y = sim(net,pchk2);
Yc2 = vec2ind(Y)
```

gives

```
Yc2 =    1
```

This looks right too, because `pchk2` is close to other vectors classified as 1.

You might want to try the demonstration program `demolvq1`. It follows the discussion of training given above.

5.6 Hebbian Learning

In 1949, Donald Hebb wrote: ``When the axon of cell A is near enough to excite a cell B and repeatedly or persistently takes part in firing it, some growth process or metabolic change takes place in one or both cells such that A's efficiency, as one of the cells firing B, is increased". As a result, a learning method evolved for artificial neural networks, called Hebbian learning, which is an instance of an unsupervised learning procedure. In Hebbian learning, weights between learning nodes are adjusted so that each weight better represents the relationship between the nodes. Nodes which tend to be positive or negative at the same time will have strong positive weights while those which tend to be opposite will have strong negative weights. Nodes that are uncorrelated will have weights near zero.

For example, if two nodes A and B are often simultaneously active, Hebbian learning will increase the connection strength between the two so that excitation of either one tends to cause excitation of the other. On the other hand, if nodes A and C were of opposite activations at all times, then Hebbian learning would gradually decrease the connection in between below zero so that an excited A or C would inhibit the other. Hebbian learning has four features interesting to the cognitive scientist: first it is unsupervised; second it is a local learning rule, meaning that it can be applied to a network in parallel; third it is simple and therefore requires very little computation; fourth it is biologically plausible.

Formally, Hebb's rule for the modification of a weight w_{ij} from neuron i to j with a learning rate η is defined as

$\Delta w_{ij} = \eta ij.$

This rule is not entirely unproblematic, because there exists no bound on the weight of the connection. A common solution to this problem is the introduction of a decay function for each connection. However, given the controlled usage of Hebbian learning in the neural optimal controller constructed here, this step is not necessary.

QUESTION BANK

Q1. What is supervised and unsupervised learning?
Q2. Difference between supervised and unsupervised learning?
Q3. What do you mean competitive learning model?
Q4. Explain the architecture of competitive network?
Q5. How we can create a competitive neural network?
Q6. What is Kohonen's self organizing map?
Q7. Write the algorithm for Kohonen's self organizing map?
Q8. Explain the learning rule of Kohonen's self organizing map?
Q9. What is self organizing features map?
Q10. Explain the architecture of SOFM?
Q11. How can create a self organizing map neural network?
Q12. Explain the example of one dimensional and two dimensional self organizing map?
Q13. What is vector quantization?
Q14. How we can implement vector quantization with a network?
Q15. Explain the architecture of LVQ network?
Q16. How we can create LVQ network with ten input vectors?
Q17. Explain the learning rule of LVQ network?
Q18. How we can train LVQ network?
Q19. What is Hebbian learning?
Q20. Difference between Hebbian and competitive learning?

CHAPTER 6

COUNTER PROPAGATION NETWORK

6.1 INTRODUCTION

Robert Hecht-Nielsen developed the counter-propagation network as a means to combine an unsupervised Kohonen layer with a teachable output layer. This is yet another topology to synthesize complex classification problems, while trying to minimize the number of processing elements and training time. The operation for the counter-propagation network is similar to that of the Learning Vector Quantization network in that the middle Kohonen layer acts as an adaptive look-up table, finding the closest fit to an input stimulus and outputting its equivalent mapping.

The first counter-propagation network consisted of a bi-directional mapping between the input and output layers. In essence, while data is presented to the input layer to generate a classification pattern on the output layer, the output layer in turn would accept an additional input vector and generate an output classification on the network's input layer. The network got its name from this counter-posing flow of information through its structure. Most developers use a uni-flow variant of this formal representation of counter-propagation. In other words. there is only one feedforward path from input layer to output layer.

An example network is shown in Figure 6.1. The uni-directional counter-propagation network has three layers. If the inputs are not already normalized before they enter the network., a fourth layer is sometimes added. The main layers include an input buffer layer, a self-organizing Kohonen layer, and an output layer which uses the Delta Rule to modify its incoming connection weights. Sometimes this layer is called a Grossberg Outstar layer.

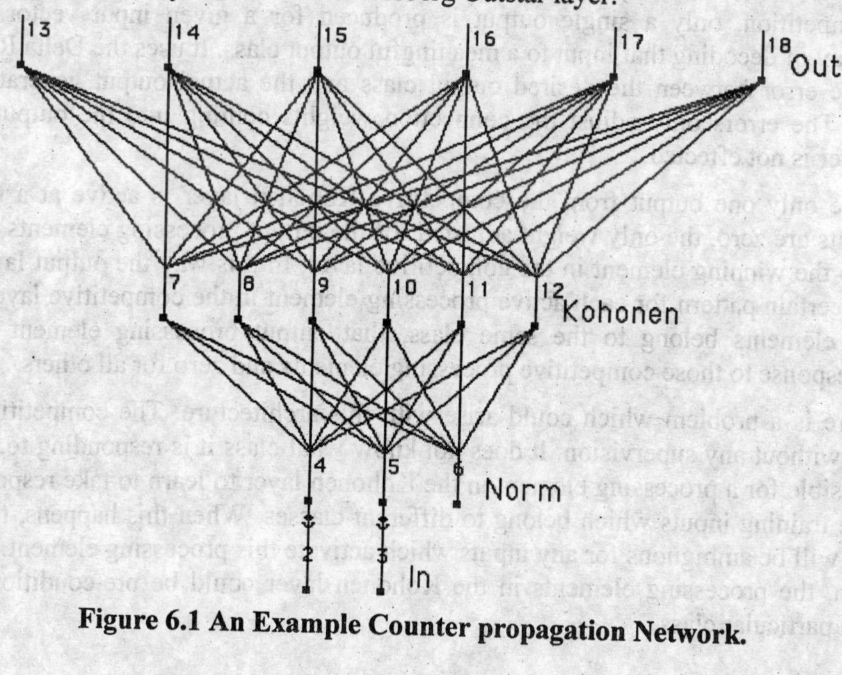

Figure 6.1 An Example Counter propagation Network.

The size of the input layer depends upon how many separable parameters define the problem. With too few, the network may not generalize sufficiently. With too many, the processing time takes too long.

For the network to operate properly, the input vector must be normalized. This means that for every combination of input values, the total "length" of the input vector must add up to one. This can be done with a preprocessor, before the data is entered into the counter-propagation network. Or, a normalization layer can be added between the input and Kohonen layers. The normalization layer requires one processing element for each input, plus one more for a balancing element. This layer modifies the input set before going to the Kohonen layer to guarantee that all input sets combine to the same total.

Normalization of the inputs is necessary to insure that the Kohonen layer finds the correct class for the problem. Without normalization, larger input vectors bias many of the Kohonen processing elements such that weaker value input sets cannot be properly classified. Because of the competitive nature of the Kohonen layer, the larger value input vectors overpower the smaller vectors.

Counter-propagation uses a standard Kohonen paradigm which self-organizes the input sets into classification zones. It follows the classical Kohonen learning law .This layer acts as a nearest neighbor classifier in that the processing elements in the competitive layer autonomously adjust their connection weights to divide up the input vector space in approximate correspondence to the frequency with which the inputs occur. There needs to be at least as many processing elements in the Kohonen layer as output classes. The Kohonen layer usually has many more elements than classes simply because additional processing elements provide a finer resolution between similar objects.

The output layer for counter-propagation is basically made up of processing elements which learn to produce an output when a particular input is applied. Since the Kohonen layer includes competition, only a single output is produced for a given input vector. This layer provides a way of decoding that input to a meaningful output class. It uses the Delta Rule to back-propagate the error between the desired output class and the actual output generated with the training set. The errors only adjust the connection weights coming into the output layer. The Kohonen layer is not effected.

Since only one output from the competitive Kohonen layer is active at a time and all other elements are zero, the only weight adjusted for the output processing elements are the ones connected to the winning element in the competitive layer. In this way the output layer learns to reproduce a certain pattern for each active processing element in the competitive layer. If several competitive elements belong to the same class, that output processing element will evolve weights in response to those competitive processing elements and zero for all others.

There is a problem which could arise with this architecture. The competitive Kohonen layer learns without any supervision. It does not know what class it is responding to. This means that it is possible for a processing element in the Kohonen layer to learn to take responsibility for two or more training inputs which belong to different classes. When this happens, the output of the network will be ambiguous for any inputs which activate this processing element. To alleviate this problem, the processing elements in the Kohonen layer could be pre-conditioned to learn only about a particular class.

6.2 CPN ARCHITECTURE

The counterpropagation network (CPN) is the most recently developed of the models that we have discussed so far in this text. The CPN is not so much a new discovery as it is a novel combination of previously existing network types. Hecht-Nielsen synthesized the architecture from a combination of a structure known as a competitive network and Grossberg's outstar structure. Although the network architecture, as it appears in its originally published form in Figure 6.2, seems rather formidable, we shall see that the operation of the network is quite straightforward.

Given a set of vector pairs, $(x_1, y_1), (x_2, y_2)\ldots\ldots (x_L, y_L)$, the CPN can learn to associate an x vector on the input layer with a y vector at the output layer. If the relationship between x and y can be described by a continuous function, Φ, such that $y = \Phi(x)$, the CPN will learn to approximate this mapping for any value of x in the range specified by the set of training vectors. Furthermore, if the inverse of Φ exists, such that x is a function of y, then the CPN will also learn the inverse mapping, $x = \Phi^{-1}(y)^1$. For a great many cases of practical interest, the inverse function does not exist. In these situations, we can simplify the discussion of the CPN by considering only the forward-mapping case, $y = \Phi(x)$.

In Figure 6.3 we have reorganized the CPN diagram and have restricted our consideration to the forward-mapping case. The network now appears as

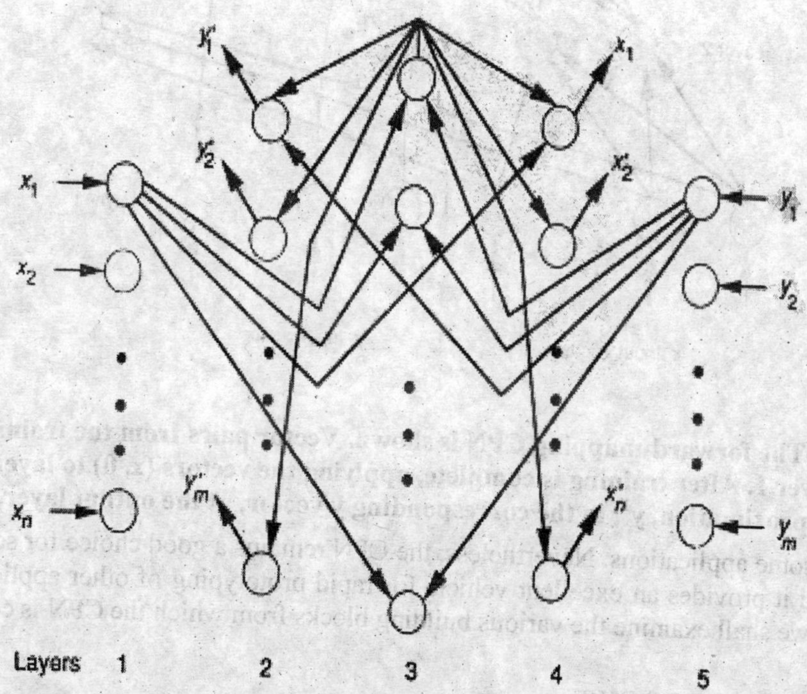

Figure 6.2 This spiderlike diagram of the CPN architecture has five layers: two input layers (1 and 5), one hidden layer (3), and two output layers (2 and 4). The CPN gets its name from the fact that the input vectors on layers 1 and 2 appear to propagate through the network in opposite directions.

A three-layer architecture, similar to, but not exactly like, the backpropagation network discussed in Chapter 3. An input vector is applied to the units on layer 1. Each unit on layer 2 calculates its net-input value, and a competition is held to determine which unit has the largest net-input value. That unit is the only unit that sends a value to the units in the output layer. We shall postpone a detailed discussion of the processing until we have examined the various components of the network.

CPNs are interesting for a number of reasons. By combining existing network types into a new architecture, the CPN hints at the possibility of forming other, useful networks from bits and pieces of existing structures. Moreover, instead of employing a single learning algorithm throughout the network, the CPN uses a different learning procedure on each layer. The learning algorithms allow the CPN to train quite rapidly with respect with respect to other networks that we have studied so far. The tradeoff is that the CPN may not always yield sufficient

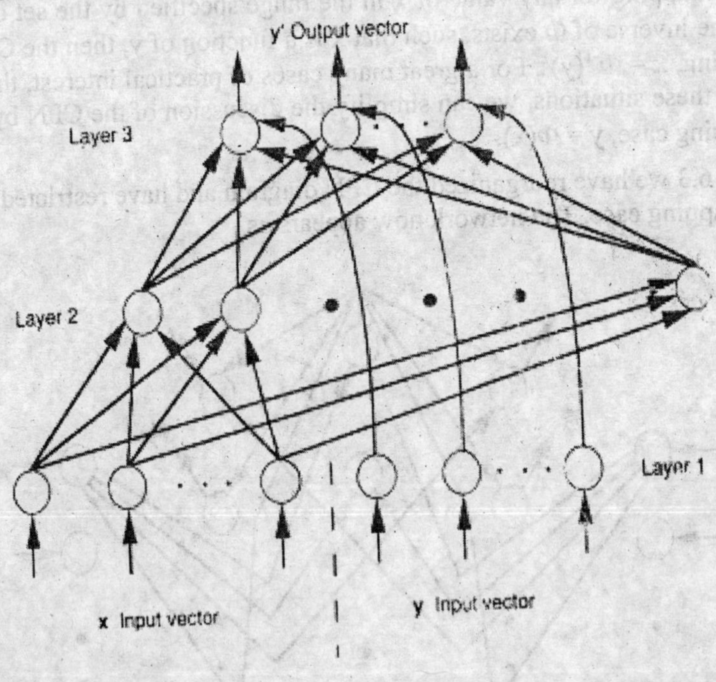

Figure 6.3The forward-mapping CPN is shown. Vector pairs from the training set are applied to layer 1. After training is complete, applying the vectors (x, 0) to layer 1 will result in an approximation, y', to the corresponding y vector, at the output layer, layer 3.

accuracy for some applications. Nevertheless, the CPN remains a good choice for some classes of problems, and it provides an excellent vehicle for rapid prototyping of other applications. In the next section, we shall examine the various building blocks from which the CPN is constructed.

6.3 CPN BUILDING BLOCKS

The PEs and network structures that we shall study in this section play an important role in many of the subsequent chapters in this text. For that reason, we present this introductory material in some detail. There are four major components: an input layer that performs some processing on the input data, a processing element called an instar, a layer of instars knows as a competitive network, and a structure known as an outstar. In section 6.4, we shall return to the discussion of the CPN.

6.3.1 THE INPUT LAYER

Discussions of neural networks often ignore the input-layer processing elements, or consider them simply as pass-through units, responsible only for distributing input data to other processing elements. Computer simulations of networks usually arrange for all input data to be scaled or normalized to accommodate calculations by the computer's CPU. For example, input-value magnitudes may have to be scaled to prevent overflow error during the sum-of-product calculations that dominate most network simulations. Biological systems do not have the benefits of such preprocessing: they must rely on internal mechanisms to prevent saturation of neural activities by large input signals. In this section, we shall examine a mechanism of interaction among processing elements that overcomes this noise-saturation dilemma. Although the mechanism has some neurophysiological plausibility, we shall not examine any of the biological implications of the model.

Examine the layer of processing elements shown in Figure 6.4. There is one input value, I, for each of the n units on the layer. The total input pattern intensity is given by $I = \Sigma_I I_i$. Corresponding to each I_i, we shall define a quantity

$$\theta_I = I_i (\Sigma I_i)^{-1} \tag{6.1}$$

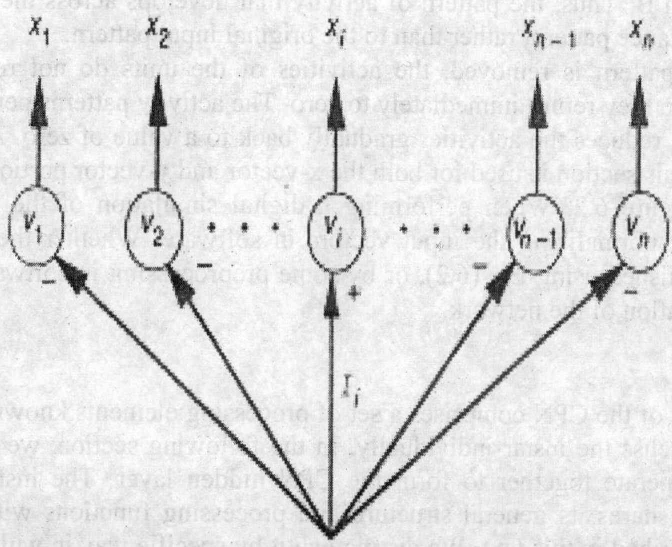

Figure 6.4 This later of input units has n processing elements, $\{v_1, v_2, \ldots, v_n\}$ Each input value, I_i is connected with an excitatory connection (arrow with a plus sign) to its corresponding processing element, v_i. Each I_i is connected also to every other processing element, v_k, $k \neq i$, with an inhibitory connection (arrow with a minus sign). This arrangement is known as on-center, off-surround. The output of the layer is proportional to the normalized reflectance pattern.

The vector, $(\theta_1, \theta_2, \ldots, \theta_n)^t$, is called a reflectance pattern. Notice that this pattern is normalized in the sense that $\Sigma_I \theta_I = 1$.

The reflectance pattern is independent of the total intensity of the corresponding input pattern. For example, the reflectance pattern corresponding to the image of a person's face would be independent of whether the person were being viewed in bright sunlight or in shade. We can usually recognize a familiar person in a wide variety of lighting conditions, even if we have not seen her previously in the identical situation. This experience suggests that our memory stores and recalls reflectance patterns. The outputs of the processing elements in Figure 6.4 are governed by the set of differential equations,

$$x_i = -Ax_i + (B - x_j)\, I_i - x_i \sum_{k \neq i} I_k \qquad (6.2)$$

where $0 < x_i(0) < B$, and $A, B > 0$. Each processing element receives a net excitation (on-center) of $(B - x_i)I_i$ from its corresponding input value. I_i. The addition of inhibitory connections (off-surround), $-x_i\, I_k$, from other units is responsible for preventing the activities activity of the processing element from rising in proportion to the absolute pattern intensity, I_i. Once an input pattern is applied, the processing elements quickly reach an equilibrium state ($x_i = 0$) with

$$x^{eq}_i = \theta_i \frac{BI}{A+1} \qquad (6.3)$$

where we have used the definition of θ_I in Eq. (6.1). The output pattern is normalized, since

$$\Sigma x_i = \frac{BI}{A+I} = B\left(\frac{A+1}{I}\right)^{-1}$$

which is always less than B. Thus, the pattern of activity that develops across the input units is proportional to the reflectance pattern, rather than to the original input pattern.

After the input pattern is removed, the activities of the units do not remain at their equilibrium values, nor do they return immediately to zero. The activity patterns persists for some time while the term $-Ax_i$ reduces the activities gradually back to a value of zero. An input layer of the type discussed in this section is used for both the x-vector and y-vector portions of the CPN input layer shown in Figure 6.2. When performing a digital simulation of the CPN, we can simplify the program by normalizing the input vectors in software. Whether the input-pattern normalization is accomplished using Eq. (6.2), or by some preprocessing in software, depends n the particular implementation of the network.

6.3.2 THE INSTAR

The hidden layer of the CPN comprises a set of processing elements known as instars. In this section, we shall discuss the instar individually. In the following section, we shall examine the set of instars that operate together to form the CPN hidden layer. The instar is a single processing element that shares its general structure and processing functions with many other processing elements described in this text. We distinguish it by specific way in which it is trained to respond to input data.

Let's begin with a general processing element, such as the one in Figure 6.5(a). If the arrow representing the output is ignored, the processing element can be redrawn in the starlike configuration of Figure 6.5(b). The inward-pointing arrows identify the instar structure, but we restrict the use of the term instar to those units whose processing and learning are governed by the equation in this section. The net-input value is calculated, as usual, by the dot product of the input and weight vectors, net = I. w. We shall assume that the input vector, I. and the weight vector, w, have been normalized to a length of 1.

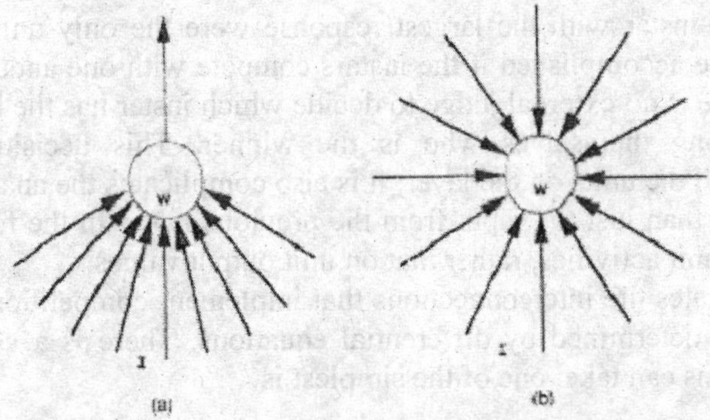

Figure 6.5 This figure shows (a) the general form of the processing element with input vector I, weight vector w, and output value y; and (b) the instar form of the processing element in (a).

The output of the instar is governed by the equation

$$y = -ay + b \text{ net} \tag{6.4}$$

where a, b > 0.

6.3.3 COMPETITIVE NETWORKS

In the previous section; we saw how an individual instar could learn to respond to a certain group of input vectors clustered together in a region of space. Suppose we have several instars grouped in a layer, as shown in Figure 6.6, each of which responds maximally to a group of input vectors in a different region of space. We can say that this layer of instars classifies any input vector, because the instar with the strongest response for any input vector, because the instar with the strongest response for any given input identifies the region f space in which the input vector lies.

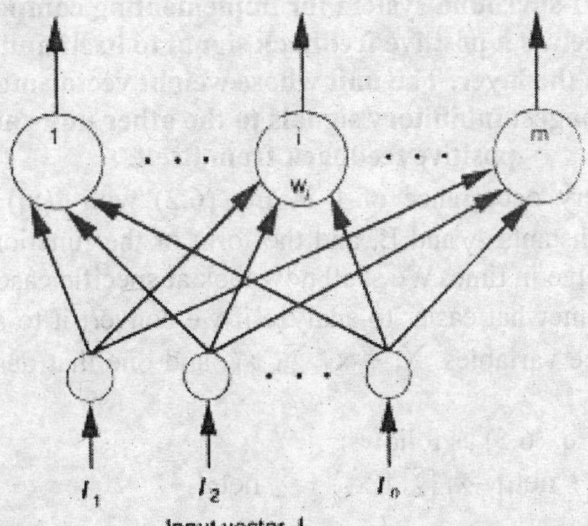

Figure 6.6 A layer of instars arrange in a competitive network. Each unit receives the input vector $I = (I_1, I_2 \ldots \therefore I_n)^t$ and the ith unit has associated with it the weight vector, $w_i = (w_{i1}, w_{i2} \ldots, w_{in})^t$. Net-input values are calculated in the usual way: $net_i = I. w_i$. The winner of the competition is the unit with the largest net input.

Rather than our examining the response of each instar to determine which is the largest, our task would be simpler if the instar with the largest response were the only unit to have a nonzero output. This effect can be accomplished if the instars compete with one another for the privilege of turning on. Since there is no external judge to decide which instar has the largest net input, the units must decide among themselves who is the winner. This decision process requires communication among all the units on the layer; it is also complicates the analysis, since there are more inputs to each unit than just the input from the previous layer. In the following discussion, we shall be focusing on unit activities, rather that on unit output values.

Figure 6.7 illustrates the interconnections that implement competition among the instars. The unit activations are determined by differential equations. There is a variety of forms that these differential equations can take; one of the simplest is

$$x_i = -Ax_i + (B - x_i)\,[f(x_i) + net_i] - x_i\left(\sum_{k\neq i} f(E_k) + \sum_{k\neq i} net_k\right) \quad (6.5)$$

where A, B > 0 and $f(x_i)$ is an function that we shall specify shortly. This equation should be compared to Eq. (6.2).We can convert Eq. (6.2) to

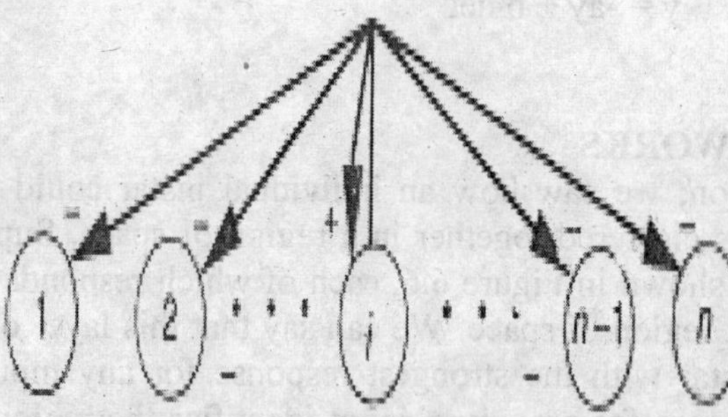

Figure 6.7An on-center off-surround system for implementing competition among a group of instars. Each unit receives a positive feedback signal to itself and sends an inhibitory signal to all other units on the layer. The unit whose weight vector most closely matches the input vector sends the strongest inhibitory signals to the other units and receives the largest positive feedback from itself.

Eq. (6.5) by replacing every occurrence of I_j in Eq. (6.2) with $f(x_j) + net_j$, for all j. The relationship between the constants A and B, and the form of the function, $f(x_j)$, determine how the solutions to Eq.(6.5) evolve in time. We shall now look at specific cases.

Equation (6.5) is somewhat easier to analyze if we convert it to a pair of equations: one that describes the reflectance variables, $X_i = x_i / \sum_k x_k$, and one that describes the total pattern intensity,

$x = \sum_k x_k$. First, rearrange Eq. (6.5) as follows:

$$x_i = -Ax_i + B[f(x_i) + net_i] - x_i\,[\sum f(x_k) + \sum net_k]$$

Next sum over i to get

$$x = -Ax + (B - x)\left(\sum_k f(xX_k) + \sum_k net_k\right) \quad (6.6)$$

Now, substitute xX_i into Eq. (6.5) and use Eq. (6.6) to simplify the result. If we make the definition $g(w) = w^{-1} f(w)$, then we get

$$x X_i = BxX_i \sum_k X_k[g(xX_i) - g(xX_k)] + B(1 - X_i)net_i - BX_i \sum_{k \neq i} net_k \qquad (6.7)$$

We can now evaluate the asymptotic behavior of Eqs. (6.6) nd (6.7). Let's begin with the simple, linear case of f(w) = w. Since g(w) w^{-1} f(w), g(w) = 1 and the first term on the right of Eq. (6.7) is zero. The reflectance variables stabilize at

$$X_i = \frac{net_i}{\Sigma_k net_k}$$

so the activities become

$$x_i = x^{eq} \frac{net_i}{\Sigma_k net_k}$$

where x^{eq} comes from setting Eq. (6.6) equal to zero. This equation shows that the units will accurately register any pattern presented as an input. Now let's look at what happens after the input pattern is removed.

Let $net_i = 0$ for all i. Then, X_i is identically zero for all time and the reflectance variables remain constant. The unit activations now depend only on x, since $x_i = xX_i$. Equation (6.6) reduces to

$$x = (B - A - x)x$$

If $B \leq A$, then $x < 0$ and $x \to 0$. However, if $B > A$, then $x \to B - A$ and the activity pattern becomes stored permanently on the units. This behavior is unlike the behavior of the input units described by Eq. (6.2), where removal of the input pattern always resulted in a decay of the activities. We shall call this storage effect short-term memory (STM). Even though the effect appears to be permanent, we can assume the existence of a reset mechanism that will remove the current pattern so that another can be stored. Figure 6.8 illustrates a simple example for the linear output function.

For our second example, we assume a faster-than-linear output function, $f(w) = w^2$. In this case g(w) = w. Notice that the first term on the right of Eq. (6.7) contains the factor $[g(xX_i) - g(xX_k)]$. For the quadratic output function, this expression reduces to $x[X_i - X_k]$. If $X_i < X_k$ for all values of $k \neq i$, then the first term in Eq. (6.6) is an excitatory term. If $X_i < X_k$ for $k \neq i$, then the first term in Eq. (6.6) becomes an inhibitory term. Thus, this network tends to enhance the activity of the unit with the largest value of X_i. This effect is illustrated in Figure 6.9. After the input pattern is removed, X_i will be greater than zero for only the unit with the largest value of X_i.

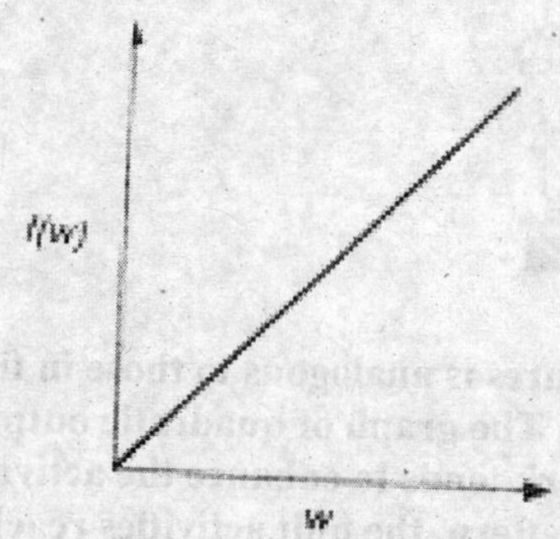

(a)

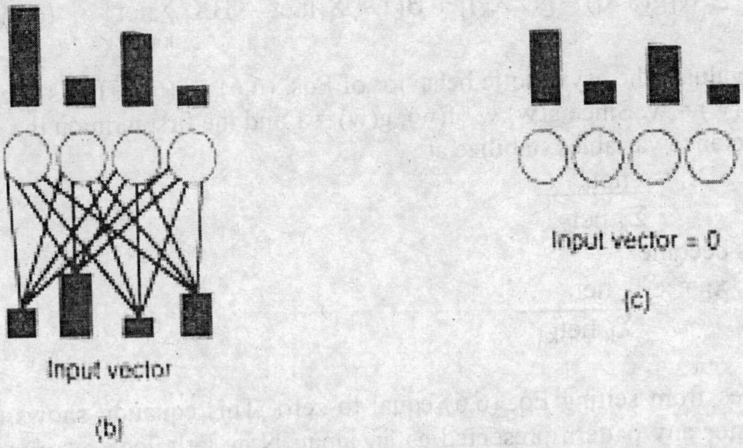

Figure 6.8 This series of figure shows the result of applying a certain input vector to units having a linear output function.(a) The graph of output function ,f(w)=w. (b) This figure shows the result of the sustained application of the input vector. The units reach equilibrium activities as shown .(c) After removal of the input vector , the units reach equilibrium such that the pattern is stored in STM.

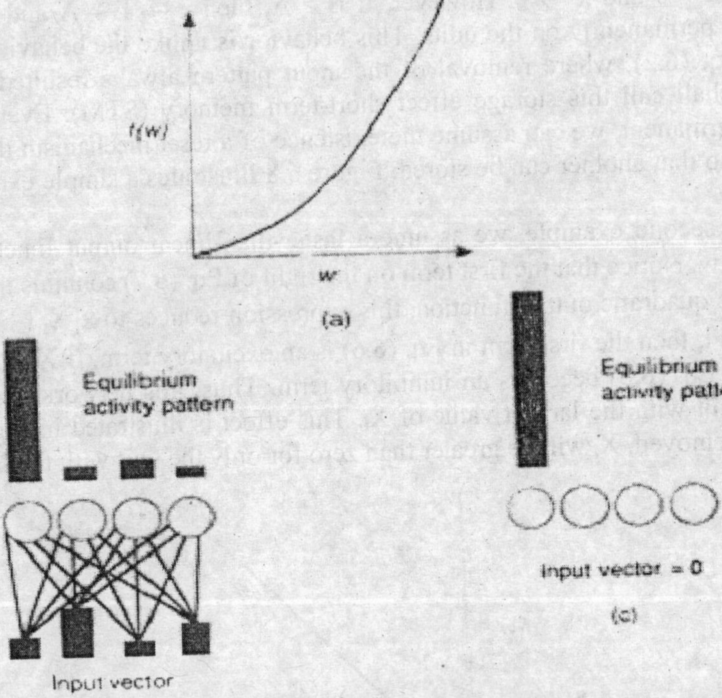

Figure 6.9 This series of figures is analogous to those in fig 6.9. but with units having a quadratic output function. (a) The graph of quadratic output function. (b) While the input vector is present, the network tends to enhance the activity of the unit with the largest activity. For the given input pattern, the unit activities reach the equilibrium values shown. (c) After the input pattern is removed, all activities but the largest decay to zero.

6.3.4 THE OUTSTAR

The final leg of our journey through CPN components brings us to Grossberg's outstar structure. As Figure 6.10 shows, an outstar is composed of all of the units in the CPN outer layer and a single hidden-layer unit. Thus, the outer-layer units participate in several different outstar: one for each unit in the middle layer.

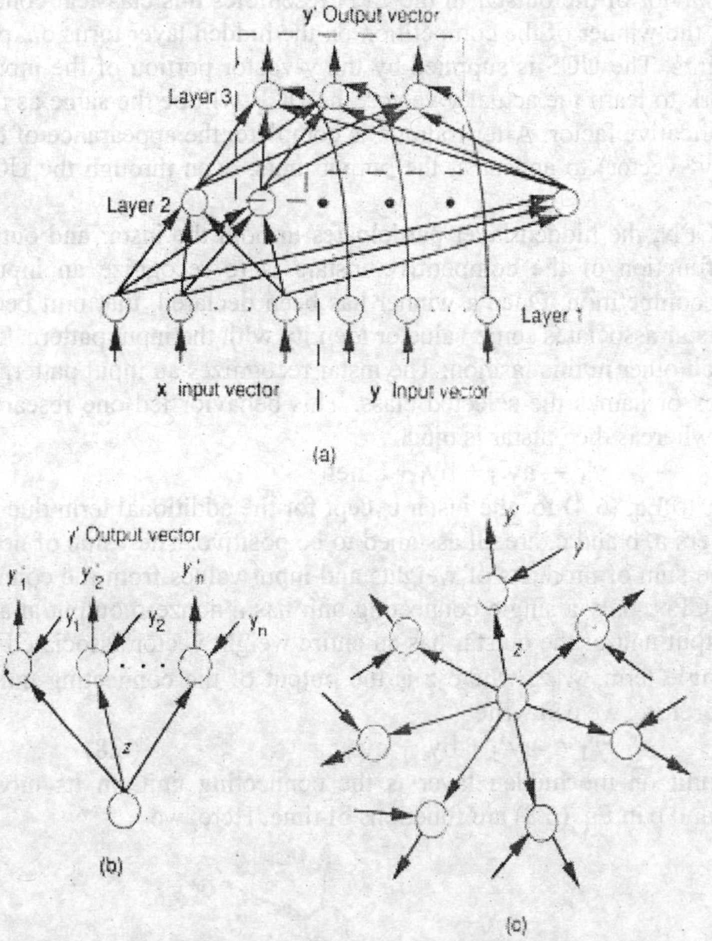

Figure 6.10 This figure illustrates the outstar and its relationship to the CPN architecture. (a) The dotted line encompasses one of the outstar structures in the CPN. The line is intentionally drawn through the middle-layer unit to indicate the dual functionality of that unit. Each middle-layer unit combines with the outer layer to form an individual outstar.(b) A single outstar unit is shown. The output nits of the outstar have two inputs: z, from the connecting unit of the previous layer, and y_i, which is the training input. The training input is present during only the learning period. The output of the outstar is the vector $y' = (y'_1, y'_2, \ldots y'_n)^t$. (c) The outstar is redrawn in a suggestive configuration. Note that the arrows point outward in a configuration that is complementary to the instar.

Grossberg argues that the outstar is the minimal neural architecture capable of classical conditioning. Consider the outstar shown in Figure 6.11. Intially, the conditioned stimulus (CS) (e.g., a ringing bell) is assumed to be unable to elicit a response from any of the units to which it is connected. An unconditioned stimulus (UCS) (the sight of food) can cause an unconditioned response (UCR) (salivation). If the CS is present while the UCS is causing UCR, then the strength of the connection from the CS unit to the UCR unit will also be increased, in keeping with Hebb's theory (see Chapter 1). Later, the CS will be able to cause a conditioned response (CR) (the same as the UCR), even if the UCS is absent.

The behavior of the outstar in the CPN resembles this classical conditioning. During the training period, the winner of the competition on the hidden layer turns on, providing a single CS to the output units. The UCS is supplied by the y-vector portion of the input layer. Because we want the network to learn the actual y vector, the UCR will be the same as the y vector, within a constant multiplicative factor. After training is complete, the appearance of the CS will cause the CR value (the y' vector) to appear at the output units, even through the UCS values will be all zero.

In the CPN, the hidden layer participates in both the instar and outstar structures of the network. The function of the competitive instars is to recognize an input pattern through a winner-take-all competition. Once a winner has been declared, that unit becomes the CS for an outstar. The outstar associates some value or identity with the input pattern. The instar and outstar complement each other in this fashion: The instar recognizes an input pattern and classifies it; the outstar identifies or names the selected class. This behavior led one researcher to note that the instar is dumb, whereas the outstar is bind.

$$y'_I = -ay'_i + by_i + c\ net_i$$

which is similar to Eq. (6.4) for the instar except for the additional term due to the training input, y_i. The parameters a, b and c, are all assumed to be positive. The value of net_i is calculated in the usual way as the sum of products of weights and input values from the connecting units. For the outstar and the CPN, only a single connecting unit has a nonzero output at any given time. Even though each output unit of the outstar has an entire weight vector associated with it, the net input reduces to a single term, $w_{ij}z$, where z is the output of the connecting unit. In the case of the CPN, z = 1. Therefore, we can write

$$y'_I = -ay'_i + by_i + cw_{ij} \qquad (6.8)$$

where the jth unit on the hidden layer is the connecting unit. In its most general form, the parameter a, b, and c in Eq. (6.8) are functions of time. Here, we

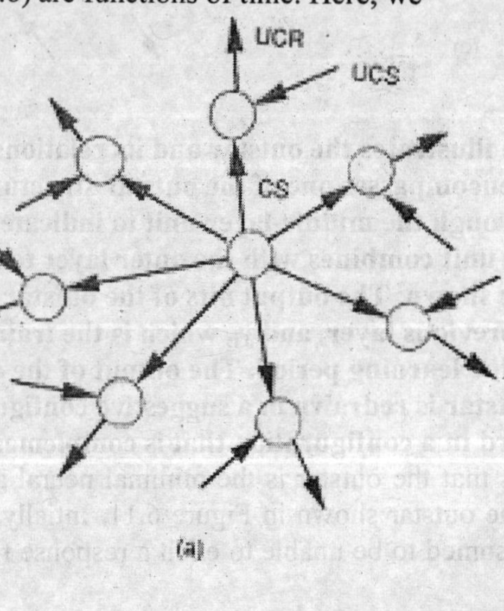

(a)

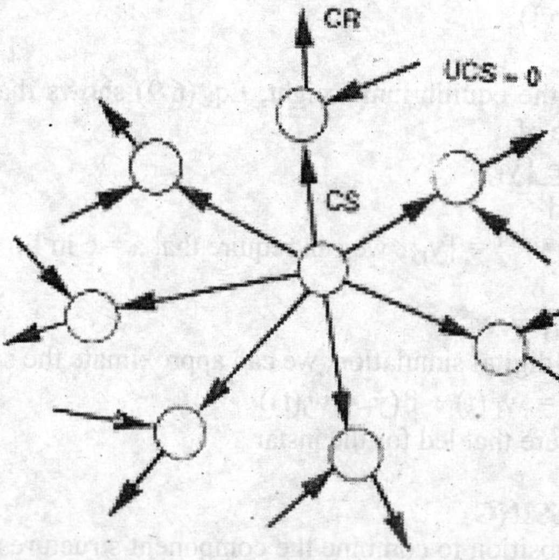

(b)

Figure 6.11 This figure shows an implied classical-conditioning scenario. (a) During the conditioning period, the CS and the UCS excite one of the output units simultaneously. (b) After conditioning, the presence of the CS alone can excite the CR without exciting any of the other output units.

shall consider them to be constants for simplicity. For the remainder of this discussion, we shall drop the subscript from the weight.

After training is complete, no further changes in w_i take place and the training inputs, y_i, are absent. Then, the output of the outstar is

$$y'_l = -ay'_i + cw_i^{eq} \qquad (6.9)$$

where w^{eq}_i is the fixed weight value found during training.

The weights evolve according to an equation almost identical for the instar:

$$w_i = (-dw_i + ey_iz)U(z) \qquad (6.10)$$

Notice that the second term in Eq. (6.10) contains the training input, y_i, not the unit output, y'_l. The U(z) function ensures that no unlearning takes place when there is no training input present, or when the connecting unit is off ($z = 0$). Since both z and U (z) are 1 for the middle-layer unit that wins the competition, Eq. (6.10) becomes

$$w_i = -dw_i + ey_i \qquad (6.11)$$

for the connections from the winning, middle-layer unit. Connections from other middle-layer units do not participate in the learning.

Recall that a given instar can learn to recognize a cluster of input vectors. If the desired CPN outputs (the y_is) corresponding to each vector in the cluster are all identical, then the weights eventually reach the equilibrium values:

$$w_i^{eq} = \frac{e}{d}\, yi$$

If, on the other hand, each input vector in the cluster has a slightly different output value associated with it, then the outstar will learn the average of all of the associated output values:

$$w_i^{eq} = \frac{e}{d}\{y_i\}$$

Using the latter value for the equilibrium weight, Eq. (6.9) shows that the output after training reaches a steady state value of

$$y_i^{leq} = \frac{c}{a}\frac{e}{d}\{y_i\}$$

Since we presumably want $y_i^{leq} = \{y_i\}$, we can require that a = c in Eq. (6.9) and that d = e in Eq. (6.10) Then,

$$y_i^{leq} = \{y_i\} = w_i^{eq} \quad (6.12)$$

For the purpose of digital simulation, we can approximate the solution to Eq. (6.11) by

$$w_i(t+1) = w_i(t) + \beta(y_i - w_i(t)) \quad (6.13)$$

following the same procedure that led for the instar.

6.4 CPN DATA PROCESSING

We are now in a position to combine the component structures from the previous section into the complete CPN. We shall still consider only the forward-mapping CPN for the moment. Moreover, we shall assume that we are performing a digital simulation, so it will now be necessary to model explicitly the interconnect for the input layer or the competitive layer.

6.4.1 FORWARD MAPPING

Assume that all training has occurred and that the network is now in a production mode. We have an input vector, I, and we would like to find the corresponding y vector. the processing is depicted in Figure 6.12 and proceeds according to the following algorithm:

1. Normalize the input vector, $x_i = I_i / (\sqrt{\sum_n I_n^2})$.
2. Apply the input vector to the x-vector portion of layer 1. Apply a zero vector to the y-vector to the y-vector portion of layer 1.
3. Since the input vector is already normalized, the input layer only distributes it to the units on layer 2.
4. Layer 2 is a winner-take-all competitive layer. The unit whose weight vector most closely matches the input vector wins and has an output value of 1. All other units have outputs of 0. The output of each unit can be calculated according to

$$z_i = \begin{cases} 1 & \|net_i\| > \|net_j\| \text{ for all } j \neq i \\ 0 & \text{otherwise} \end{cases} \quad (6.14)$$

5. The single winner on layer 2 excites an outstar.

Each unit in the outstar quickly reaches an equilibrium value equal to the value of the weight on the connection from the winning layer 2 unit [see Eq. (6.12)]. If the ith unit wins on the middle layer, then the output layer produces an output vector $y' = (w_{1i}, w_{2i}, \ldots w_{mi})^t$, where m represents the number of units on the output layer. A simple way to view this processing is to realize that the equilibrium output of the outstar is equal to the outstar's net input.

$$Y_k^{leq} = \sum_j w_{kj} z_j \quad (6.15)$$

Since $z_j = 0$ unless j = i, then $y_k^{leq} = w_{ki} z_i = w_{ki}$, which is consistent with the results obtained in Section 6.1.

This simple algorithm used equilibrium, er asymptotic, values of node activities and outputs. We thus avo the need to solve numerically all the corresponding differential equations.

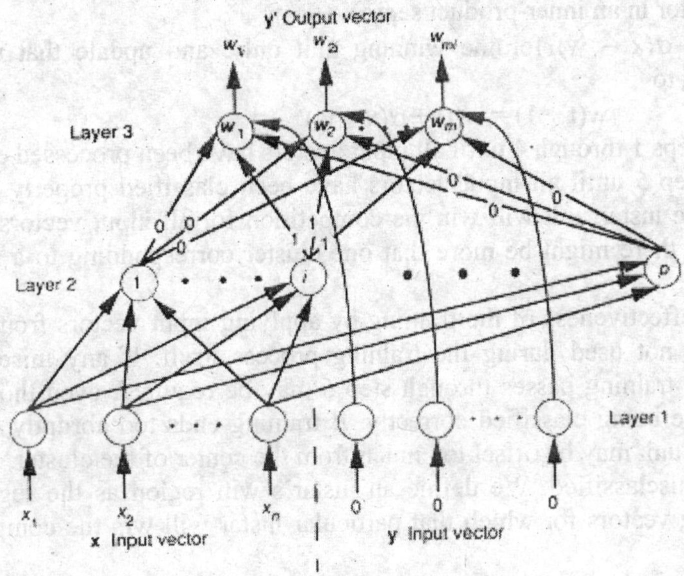

Figure 6.12 This figure shows a summary of the processing done on an input vector by the CPN. The input vector $(x_1, x_2, \ldots, x_n)^t$ is distributed to all units on the competitive layer. The ith unit wins the competition and has an output of 1; all other competitive units have an output of 0. This competition effectively selects te proper output vector by exciting a single connection to each of the outstar units on the output layer.

6.4.2 TRAINING THE CPN

Here again, we assume that we are performing a digital simulation of the CPN. Although this assumption does not eliminate the need to find numerical solutions to the differential equations, we can still take advantage of prenormalized input vectors and an external judge to determine winners on the competitive layer. We shall also assume that a set of training vectors has been defined adequately. We shall have more to say on that subject in a later section.

Because there are two different learning algorithms in use in the CPN, we shall look at each one independently. In fact, it is a good idea to train the competitive layer completely before beginning to train the output layer.The competitive-layer units train according to the instar learning algorithm described in Section 6.2. Since there will typically be many instars on the competitive layer, the iterative training process described earlier must be amended slightly. Here, as in Section 6.2, we assume that a cluster of input vectors forms a single class. Now, however, we have the situation where we may have several clusters of vectors, each cluster representing a different class. Our learning procedure must be such that each instar learns (wins the competition) for all the vectors in a single cluster. To accomplish the correct classification for each class of input vectors, we must proceed as follows:

1. Select an input vector from among all the input vectors to be used for training. The selection should be random according to the probability distribution of the vectors.
2. Normalize the input vector and apply it to the CPN competitive layer.

3. Determine which unit wins the competition by calculating the net-input value for each unit and selecting the unit with the largest (the unit whose weight vector is closest to the input vector in an inner-product sense).
4. Calculate $\alpha(x - w)$ for the winning unit only, and update that unit's weight vector according to
$$w(t+1) = w(t) + \alpha(x - w)$$
5. Repeat steps 1 through 4 until all input vectors have been processed once.
6. Repeat step 5 until all input vectors have been classified properly. When this situation exists, one instar unit will win the competition for all input vectors in a certain cluster. Note that there might be more that one cluster corresponding to a single class of input vectors.
7. Test the effectiveness of the training by applying input vectors from the various classes that were not used during the training process itself. If any misclassifications occur, additional training passes through step 6 may be required, even thought all the training vectors are being classified correctly. If training ends too abruptly, the win region of a particular unit may be offset too much from the center of the cluster, and outlying vectors may be misclassified. We define an instar's win region as the region of vector space containing vectors for which that particular instar will win the competition. (See Figure 6.13)

An issue that we have overlooked in out discussion is the question of initialization of the weight vectors. For all but the simplest problems, random initial weight vectors will not be adequate. We already hinted at an initialization method earlier: Set each weight vector equal to a representative of one of the clusters. We shall have more to say on this issue in the next section.

Once satisfactory results have been obtained on the competitive layer, training of the outstar layer can occur. There are several ways to proceed based on the nature of the problem.

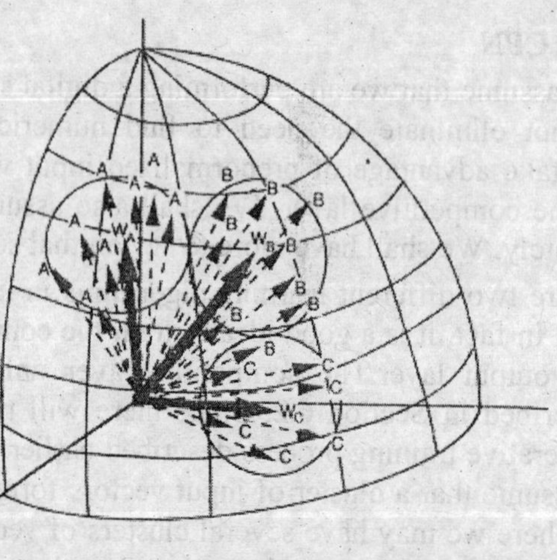

Figure 6.13 In this drawing, three clusters of vectors represent three distinct classes: A, B and C. Normalized, these vectors end on the unit hypersphere. After training, the weight vectors on the competitive layer have settled near the centroid of each cluster. Each weight vector has a in region represented, although not accurately, by the circles drawn on the surface of the sphere around each cluster. Note that one of the B vectors encroaches into C's win region indicating that erroneous classification is possible in some cases.

Suppose that each cluster of input vectors represents a class, and all of the vectors in a cluster map to the identical output vector. In this case, no iterative training algorithm is necessary. We need only to determine which hidden unit wins for a particular class. Then, we simple assign the weight vector on the appropriate connections to the output layer to be equal to the desired output vector. that is, if the ith hidden unit wins for all input vectors of the call for which A is the desired output vector, then we set $w_{ki} = A_k$, where w_{ki} is the weight on the connection from the ith hidden unit to the kth output unit.

If each input vector in a cluster maps to a different output vector, then the outstar learning procedure will enable the outstar to reproduce the average of those output vectors when any member of the class is presented to the inputs of the CPN. If the average output vector for each class is known or can be calculated in advance, then a simple assignment can be made as in the previous paragraph: Let $w_{ki} = \langle A_k \rangle$.

If the average of the output vectors is not known, then an iterative procedure can be used based on Eq. (6.13).

1. Apply a normalized input vector, x_k, and its corresponding output vector, y_k, to the x and y inputs of the CPN, respectively.
2. Determine the winning competitive-layer unit.
3. Update the weights on the connections from the winning competitive unit to the output units according to Eq. (6.13): $w_i(t+1) = w_i(t) + \beta(y_{ki} - w_i(t))$
4. Repeat steps 1 through 3 until all vectors of all classes map to satisfactory outputs.

6.5 AN IMAGE-CLASSIFICATION EXAMPLE

In this section, we shall look at an example of how the CPN can be used to classify images into categories. In addition, we shall see how a simple modification of the CPN will allow the network to perform some interpolation at the output layer.

The problem is to determine the angle of rotation of the principal axis of an object in tow dimensions, directly from the raw video image of the object. In this case, the object is a model of the Space Shuttle that can be rotated 360 degrees about a single axis of rotation. Numerical algorithms as well as pattern-matching techniques exist that will solve this problem. The neural-network solution possesses some interesting advantages, however, that may recommend it over these traditional approaches.

Figure 6.14 shows a diagram of the system architecture for the spacecraft orientation system. The video camera, television monitor, and robot all interface to a desktop computer that simulates the neural network and hoses a video frame-grabber board. The architecture is an example of how a neural network can be embedded as a part of an overall system.

The system uses CPN having 1026 input units (1024 for the image and 2 for the training inputs), 12 hidden units, and 2 output units. The units on the middle layer learn to divide the input vectors into different classes. There are 12 units in this layer, and 12 different input vectors are used to train the network. These 12 vectors represent images of the shuttle at 30-degree increments (0°, 30°, ...330°). Since there are 12 categories and 12 training vectors, training of the competitive layer consists of setting each unit's weight equal to one of the (normalized) input vectors. The output layer units learn to associate the correct sine and cosine values with each of the classes represented on the middle layer.

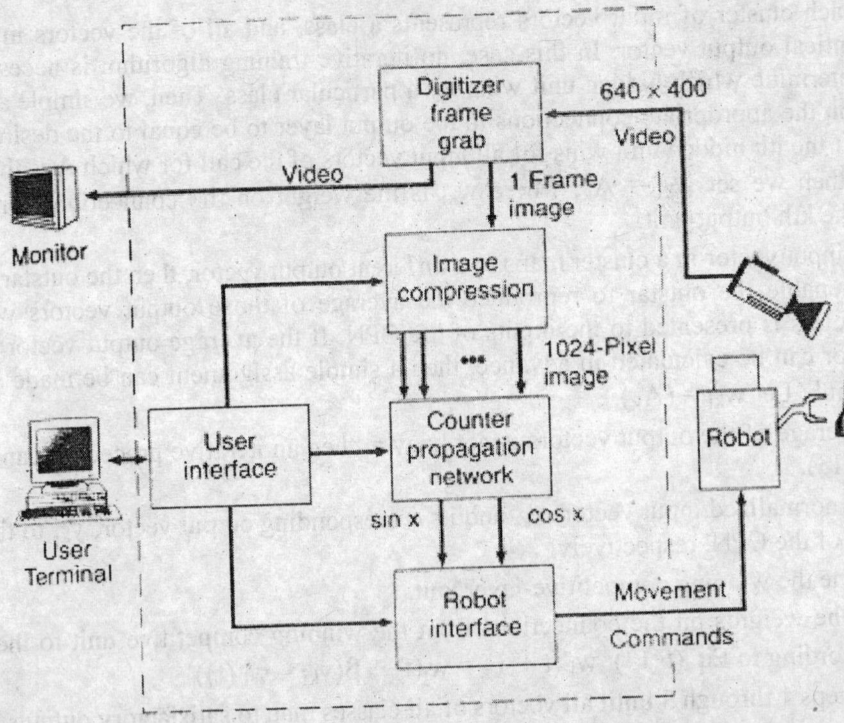

Figure 6.14 The system architecture for the spacecraft orientation system is shown. The video camera and frame-grabber capture a 256-by-256-pixel image of the model. That image is reduced to 32-by-32 pixels by a pixel-averaging technique and is then threshold to produce a binary image. The resulting 1024-component vector is used as the input to the neural network, which responds by giving the sine and cosine of the rotation angle of the principal axis of the model. These output values are converted to an angle that is sent as part of a command string to a mechanical robot assembly. The command sequence causes the robot to reach out and pick up the model. The angle is used to roll the robot's wrist to the proper orientating, so that the robot can grasp the model perpendicular to the long axis.

It would seem that this network is limited to classifying all input patterns into only one of 12 categories. An input pattern representing a rotation of 32 degrees, for example, probably would be classified as a 30-degree pattern by this network. One way to remedy this deficiency would be to add more units on the middle layer, allowing for a finer categorization of the input images. An alternative approach is to allow the output units to perform an interpolation for patterns that do not match one of the training patterns to within a certain tolerance. For this intrpolative scheme to be accomplished, more than one unit on the competitive layer must share in winning for each input vector.

Recall that the output-layer units calculate their output values according to Eq. (6.15): $y^1_k = \sum_j w_{kj} z_j$. In the normal case, where the ith hidden unit wins, $y^1_k = w_{ki}$, since $z_j = 0$ otherwise. Suppose two competitive units shared in winning-the ones with the two closest matching patterns. Further, let the output of those units be proportional to how close the input pattern is; that is $z_j \propto \cos \theta_j$ for the two wining units. If we restrict the total outputfrom the middle layer to unity, then the output values from the output layer would be

$$y'_k = w_{ki}z_i + w_{kj}z_j$$

where the ith and jth units on the middle layer were the winners, and

$$z_i + z_j = 1$$

The network output is a linear interpolation of the output that would be obtained from the two patterns that exactly matched the two hidden units that shared the victory.

Using the technique, the network will classify successfully input patterns representing rotation angles it had never seen during the training period. In our experiments, the average error was approximately ±3°. However, since a simple linear interpolation scheme is used, the error varied from almost 0 to as mush as 10 degrees. Other interpolation schemes could result in considerably higher accuracy over the entire range of input patterns.

One of the benefits of using the neural-network approach to pattern matching is robustness in the presence of noise or of contradictory data. An example is shown in Figure 6.15, where the network was able to respond correctly, even though a substantial portion of the image was obscured.

It is unlikely that someone would use a neural network for a simple orientation determination. The methodology can be extended to more realistic cases, however, where the object can be rotated in three dimensions. In such cases, the time required to construct and train a neural network may be significantly less than the time required for development of algorithms that perform the identical tasks.

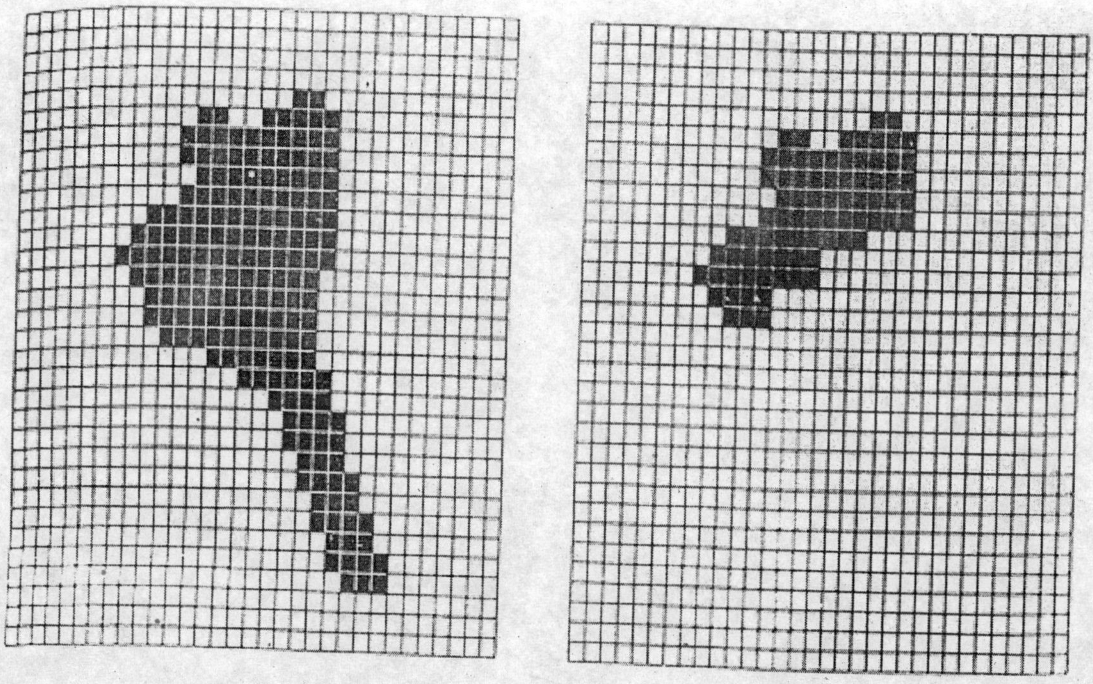

(a) (b)

Figure 6.15 These figures show 32-by-32-pixel arrays of two different input vectors for the spacecraft-orientation system. (a) This is a bit-mapped image or the space-shuttle model at an angle of 150° as measured clockwise from the vertical. (b) The obscured image was used as an input vector to the spacecraft-orientation system.

QUESTION BANK

Q1. What is counter propagation network?
Q2. Explain the architecture of CPN?
Q3. Draw the spider like diagram of CPN architecture and explain it?
Q4. Explain the CPN building block in detail?
Q5. What is instar?
Q6. What is outstar? Explain the function of outstar in CPN building block with the help of diagram?
Q7. Explain the processing of CPN data?
Q8. How we can train the Counter propagation network?
Q9. How CPN can be use to classify images of different categories?
Q10. Explain the system architecture for the space craft orientation system?

CHAPTER 7

ADAPTIVE RESONANCE THEORY

7.1 INTRODUCTION

One of the nice features of human memory is its ability to learn many new things without necessarily forgetting things learned in the past. A frequently cited example is the ability to recognize your parents even if you have not seen them for some time and have learned many new faces in the interim. It would be highly desirable if we could impart this same capability to an Artificial Neural Networks. Most neural networks will tend to forget old information if we attempt to add new information incrementally. When developing an artificial neural network to perform a particular pattern-classification operation, we typically proceed by gathering a set of exemplars, or training patterns, then using these exemplars to train the system.

During the training, information is encoded in the system by the adjustment of weight values. Once the training is deemed to be adequate, the system is ready to be put into production, and no additional weight modification is permitted. This operational scenario is acceptable provided the problem domain has well-defined boundaries and is stable. Under such conditions, it is usually possible to define an adequate set of training inputs for whatever problem is being solved. Unfortunately, in many realistic situations, the environment is neither bounded nor stable. Consider a simple example. Suppose you intend to train a backpropagation to recognize the silhouettes of a certain class of aircraft. The appropriate images can be collected and used to train the network, which is potentially a time-consuming task depending on the size of the network required. After the network has learned successfully to recognize all of the aircraft, the training period is ended and no further modification of the weights is allowed. If, at some future time, another aircraft in the same class becomes operational, you may wish to add its silhouette to the store of knowledge in your neural network. To do this, you would have to retrain the network with the new pattern plus all of the previous patterns. Training on only the new silhouette could result in the network learning that pattern quite well, but forgetting previously learned patterns. Although retraining may not take as long as the initial training, it still could require a significant investment.

The adaptive resonance theory (ART) has been developed to avoid the stability-plasticity dilemma in competitive networks learning. The stability-plasticity dilemma addresses how a learning system can preserve its previously learned knowledge while keeping its ability to learn new patterns. ART architecture models can self-organize in real time producing stable recognition while getting input patterns beyond those originally stored. ART is a family of different neural architectures. The first and most basic architecture is ART1 (Carpenter and Grossberg, 1987). ART1 can learn and recognize binary patterns. ART2 (Carpenter and Grossberg, 1987) is a class of architectures categorizing arbitrary sequences of analog input patterns. ART is used in modeling such as invariant visual pattern recognition (Carpenter et al 1989) where biological equivalence is discussed (Carpenter and Grossberg 1990).

An ART system consists of two subsystems, an attentional subsystem and an orienting subsystem. The stabilization of learning and activation occurs in the attentional subsystem by matching bottom-up input activation and top-down expectation. The orienting subsystem controls the attentional subsystem when a mismatch occurs in the attentional subsystem. In other words, the orienting subsystem works like a novelty detector.

An ART system has four basic properties. The first is the self-scaling computational units. The attentional subsystem is based on competitive learning enhancing pattern features but suppressing noise. The second is self-adjusting memory search. The system can search memory in parallel and adaptively change its search order. Third, already learned patterns directly access their corresponding category. Finally, the system can adaptively modulate attentional vigilance using the environment as a teacher. If the environment disapproves the current recognition of the system, it changes this parameter to be more vigilant.

7.2 MOTIVATION

Adaptive resonance theory nets are designed to allow the user to control the degree of similarity of patterns placed on the same cluster. However, since input pattern may differ in their level of detail (number of components that are nonzero), the relative similarity of an input pattern to the weight vector for a cluster unit, rather then the absolve difference between the vector, is used. (A difference in one component is more significant in patterns that have very few nonzero components than it is in patterns with many nonzero components). As the net trained, each training pattern may be presented several times. A patterns may be placed on one cluster unit the first time it is presented and then placed on a different cluster when it is presented later (due to changes in the weights for the first cluster if it has learned other patterns in the meantime). A stable net will not return a pattern to a previous cluster, in other words, a pattern oscillating among different cluster unit at different stages of training indicated an unstable net.

Some nets achieves stability by reducing the learning rate as the same set of training patterns is presented many times. However, this does not allow the net to learn readily a new pattern that is presented for the first time after a number of training epochs have already taken place. The ability of a net to respond to (learn) a new pattern equally well at any stage of learning is called plasticity. Adaptive resonance theory nets are designed to be both stable and plastic.

Also, attention has been paid to structuring ART nets so that neural processes can control the rather intricate operation of these nets. This requires a number of neurons in addition to the input units, cluster unit's, and unit for the comparison of the input signal with the cluster unit's weights.

7.3 BASIC ARCHITECTURE

The basic architecture of an adaptive resonanceneural net involves three groups of neurons; an it processing field (called the F_1 layer), the cluster units (the F_2layer), and a mechanism to control the degree of similarity of patterns placed on the same cluster (a reset mechanism). The F_1 layer can be considered to consist of two parts; the input portion (especially in ART2). The interface portion combines signal from the input portion and the F_2 layer, for use in comparing the similarity of the input signal to the weight vector for the cluster unit that has been selected as a candidate for learning.. We Shall denote the input portion of the F_1, layer as F_2 (a) and the interface portion as F_1 (b).

To control the similarity of patterns placed on the same cluster, there are two sets of connection (each with its own weight) between each unit.in the interface portion of the input field and each cluster unit. The F_1 (b) layer is connected to theF_2 layer by bottom-up weights; the bottom-up weight on the connection from the ithF_1 unit to the jth F_2 unit is designated b_{ji}. The F_2 layer is connected to the F_1(b) layer by top-down weight; the top-down weight on the connection from the jth F_2 unit to the jth F_1 unit is designated t_{ji}.

The F_2 layer is a competitive layer: The cluster unit with the largest net becomes the candidate to learn the input pattern. The activation of all other F_2 unit are set to zero, the interface units now combine information from the input and cluster units Whether or not this cluster unit is allowed to learn the input pattern depends on how similar it top-down weight vector is to the input vector. This decision is made by the reset unit. based on signals it receives from the input (a) and interface (b) portions of the F_1 layer. If the cluster unit is not allowed to learn, it is inhibited and a new cluster unit is selected as the candidate.

The supplemental units needed to control the processing of information in the ART nets described forART1 and ART2 in sections 7.4 and 7.5 respectively..

7.3.1 BASIC OPERATION

It is difficult to describe even the basic architecture of adaptive resonance theory nets without discussing the operation of the nets. Details of the operation of ART1 and ART2 are presented later in this chapter.

A learning trial in ART consist of the presentation of one input pattern. Before the pattern is presented, the activations of all units in the net are set to zero. All F_2 units are inactive. (Any F_2 units that had been inhibited on the previous learning trial are again available to complete.) Once a pattern is presented, it continues to send its input signal
until the learning trial is completed. The degree of similarity required for pattern to be assigned to the same cluster unit is controlled by a user-specified parameter, known as the vigilance parameter.

Although the detail of the reset mechanism for ART21 and ART2 differ, its function is to control the state of each node in the F_2 layer. At any time, an F_2 node is in one of three states.
Active ("on ," activation = d; d = 1 for ART1, 0 < d < 1 for ART2),
Inactive ("off," activation = 0, but available to participate in competition or
Inhibited ("off," activation = 0, and prevented from participating in any further competition during the presentation of the current input vector).
A summary of the steps that occur in ART nets in general is as follows.

Step 0 Initialize parameters.
Step 1. While stopping condition is false, do steps 2-9,
Step 2. For each input vector, do steps 3-8.
Step 3. Process F_1 layer.
Step 4. While reset condition is true, do steps 5-7
Steps 5.Find candidate unit to learn the current input pattern F_2 units (which is not inhibited) with largest input.
Step 6. F_1 (b) units combine their input from F_1 (a) and F_2.
Step 7. Test reset condition (detail differ for ART1 and ART2):
If reset is true, then the current candidate unit is rejected (inhibited) ; return to step 4.
If reset is false, then the current candidate unit is accepted for learning; proceed to step 8.
Sec. 7.1 Introduction
Step 8. Learning Weights change according to different equations.

Step 9. Text stopping condition.

The calculations in Step 2 constitute a "learning trial," i.e., one presentation of one pattern. Although ART does not require that all training patterns be presented in the same prodder, or even that all patterns be presented with the same frequency, we shall refer to the calculations of step 1 (one presentation of each training pattern) as an epoch. Thus, foregoing algorithmic structure, while convenient, is not the most general from for ART. The learning process may involve many weight updates and/or many epochs.

7.3.2 LEARNING

In adaptive resonance theory, the change in the activations of units and in weights are governed y coupled differential equations. The net is a continuously changing (dynamical) system, but the process can be simplified because the activations are assumed to change much more rapidly than the weights. Once an acceptable cluster unit has been selected for learning, the bottom-up and top-down signals are maintained for an extended period, during which time the weight changes occur. This is the "reasonable" that gives the net its name.

Two types of learning that differ both in their theoretical assumptions and n their performance characteristics can be sued for ART nets. In the fast learning mode, it is assumed that weight updates during resonance occur rapidly, relative to the length of time a pattern is presented on any particular trail. Thus, in fast learning, the weights reach equilibrium on each trail. In the slow learning mode the weight changes occur slowly relative to the duration of a learning trail; the weights do not reach equilibrium on a particular trail. Many more presentations of the patterns are required for slow learning that for fast learning, but fewer calculations occur on each learning trail in slow learning. In order to achieve the performance characteristics of slow learning to the fullest extent, we shall assume that only one weight update, with a relatively small learning rate, occurs on each learning trial in the slow learning mode.

In fast learning, the net is considered stabilized when each pattern chooses the correct cluster unit when it is presented (without causing any unit to reset). For ART1, because the patterns are binary, the weights associated with each cluster unit also stabilize in the fast learning mode. The resulting weight vectors are appropriate for the type of input patterns used in ART1. Also, the equilibrium weights are easy to determine, and the iterative solution of the differential equations that control the weight updates is not necessary. This is the form of learning that is typically used for ART1 and is the nly algorithm we consider.

In general, for ART2, the weights produced by fast learning continue to change each time a pattern is presented. The net stabilizers after only a few presentations of each training pattern. However, since the differential equations for the weight updates depend on the activation of units whose activations change during the resonance process, it is not as straightforward to find the equilibrium weights immediately for ART2 as it is for ART1. The process of solving the weight update equations by letting the net iterate as resonance occurs is illustrated in several examples.

In the slow learning mode, weight changes do not reach equilibrium during any particular learning trial and more trials are required before the net stabilizes [Carpenter & Gross berg, 1987a, 1987b].Although slow learning is theoretically possible for ART1, it is not typically used in this form. For ART2, however, the weight produced by slow learning may be much more appropriate than those produced by fast learning for certain types of data.

7.4 ART1

ART1 is designed to cluster binary input vectors, following for great variation the number of nonzero components, and direct user control of the degree of similarity among patterns placed on the same cluster unit. The architecture of an ART1 net consists of two field units---- the F_1 unit and the F_2 (cluster) units----- together with a reset unit to control the degree of similarity of patterns placed on the same cluster unit. (For convenience, we have expanded the description of the F_1 units from the original presentation of the net in Carpenter and Grossberg (1987a) to include an explicit set of input units, the F_1(a) units, as well as the F_1(b) units, which exchange information with the F_2 units.) The F_1 and F_2 layers are connected by two sets of weighted pathways, In addition, several supplemental units are included in the net to provide for neural control of the learning process.

The learning process is designed so that it is not required either that patterns be presented in a fixed order or that the number of patterns to be clustered be known in advance (i.e., more patterns can be added to the data set during the training process if desired) . Updates for both the bottom-up and top-down weight are controlled by differential equations. However, it is assumed that the ART1 net is being operated in the fast learning mode, in which the weights reach equilibrium during each learning trial (presentation of a pattern).Since the activation of the F_1units do not change during this resonance phase, the equilibrium weights can be determined exactly, and the iterative solution of the differential equations is not necessary.

7.4.1 ARCHITECTURE

The architecture of ART1 consists of computational units and supplemental units.

7.4.2 COMPUTATIONAL UNITS

The architecture of the computational units for ART1 consists of F_1 units (input and interface units), F_2 units (cluster units), and a reset unit that implements user control over the degree of similarity of patterns placed on the same cluster. This main portion of the ART1 architecture is illustrated in Figure 7.1.

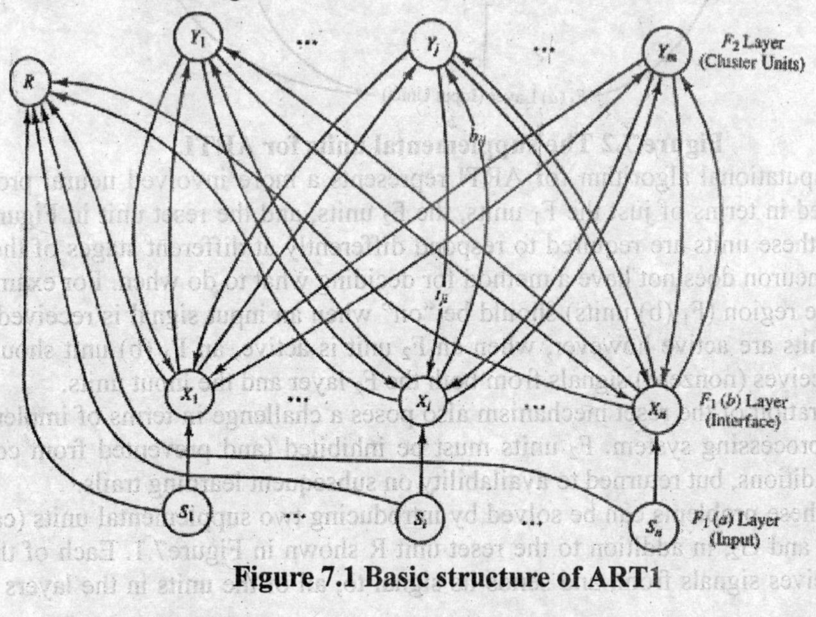

Figure 7.1 Basic structure of ART1

Each unit in the F_1(a) (input) layer is connected to the corresponding unit in the F_1 (b) (interface) layer. Each unit in the F_1 (a) and F_1(b) layer is connected to the reset unit, which in turn is connected to every F_2 unit. Each unit in the F_1(b) layer is connected to each unit the F_2 (cluster) layer by two weighted pathways. The F_1 (b) unit X_i is connected to the F_2 unit Y_j by bottom-up weights b_{ij}. Similarly, unit Y_j is connected to unit X_i by top-down weights t_{ij}. Only one representative weight b_{ij} is indicated on the connections between the F_1 and F_2 layer; similarly, t_{ji} is a representative weight for the connections between the F_2 and F_1layer. The F_2 layer is a competitive layer in which only the uninhibited node with the largest net input has a nonzero activation.

7.4.3 SUPPLEMENTARY UNITS

The supplemental units shown in Figure 7.2 are important from a theoretical point of view. They provide a mechanism by which the computations performed by the algorithm can be accomplished using neural network principles. However, this theoretical discussion of the necessary supplemental units is not required to be able to use the computational algorithm. The reader may proceed directly to the algorithm if desired.

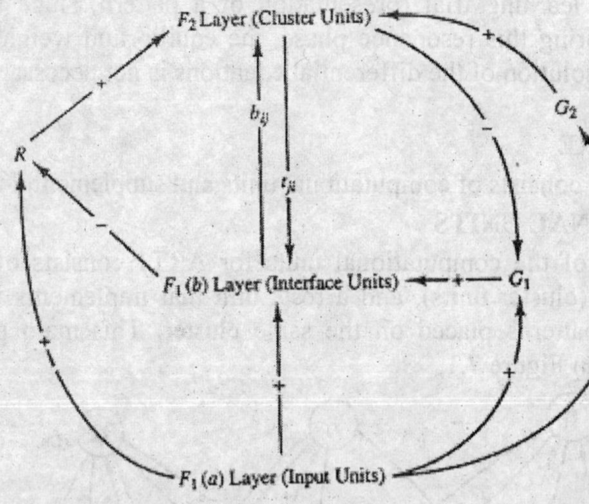

Figure 7.2 The supplemental units for ARTI.

The computational algorithm for ARTI represents a more involved neural process than can be represented in terms of just the F_1 units, the F_2 units, and the reset unit in Figure7.1. The difficulty is that these units are required to respond differently at different stages of the process, and a biological neuron does not have a method for deciding what to do when. For example, units in the F_1 interface region (F_1 (b) units) should be "on" when an input signal is received (from F_1 (a)) and no F_2 units are active however, when an F_2 unit is active, an F_1 (b) unit should remain "on" only if it receives (nonzero) signals from both the F_2 layer and the input units.

The operation of the reset mechanism also poses a challenge in terms of implementation within a neural processing system. F_2 units must be inhibited (and prevented from competing) under certain conditions, but returned to availability on subsequent learning trails.

Both of these problems can be solved by introducing two supplemental units (called gain control units) G_1 and G_2, in addition to the reset unit R shown in Figure7.1. Each of these three special units receives signals from, and sends its signal to, all of the units in the layers indicated in Figure 7.2. Excitatory signals are indicated by "+" and inhibitory signals by " –", A signal is sent whenever any unit in the designated layer is "on."

Each unit in either the F_1 (b) (interface region) or F_2 layer of the ART1 net has three sources from which it can receive a signal. F_1 (b) interface units can receive signals from an F_1 (a) unit (an input signal), from an F_2 node (a top-down signal), or from the G_1 unit. Similarly, an F_2 unit can receive signal from the F_1 interface units, unit R, r the G_2 unit. An F_1 (b) (interface) or F_2 unit must receive two excitatory signals in order to be "on." Since there are three possible sources of signals, this requirement is called the two-thirds rule.

The F_1 (b) (interface) nodes are required to send a signal (to the F_2 nodes and the reset unit) whenever an input vector is presented and no F_2 node is active. However, after an F_2 node has been chosen in the competition, it is necessary that only the F_1 (b) nodes whose top-down signal and input signal match remain active. This is accomplished through the use of the G_1 and G_2 units and the two-thirds rule. The G_1 unit is inhibited whenever any F_2 units is on. When no F_2 unit is on, each F_1 interface unit receives a signal from the G_1 unit; in this case, all of the units that receive a positive input signal from the input vector that is presented will fire. In a similar manner, the G_2 unit controls the firing of the F_2 units; they must obey a two-thirds rule, too. The two-thirds rule also plays a role in the choice of parameters and initial weights, considered in next Section .

The reset unit R controls the vigilance matching. As indicated in Figure 7.2 when any unit in the F_1 (a) input layer is on, an excitatory signal is sent to unit R. The strength of that signal depends on how many F_1 (input) units are on. However, R also receives inhibitory signals from the F_1 interface units that are on. If enough F_1 (b) interface units are on (as determined by the vigilance parameter set by the user), unit R is prevented from firing. If unit R does fire, it inhibits any F_2 unit that is on. This forces the F_2 layer to choose a new winning node.

7.4.4 ALGORITHM

In the first two parts of this section, we provide a description of the training process for ART1 (using fast learning) and a step-by-step algorithm for the training. A discussion of the choice of parameter values and initial weights follows the training algorithm. the notation we use is as follows:

n	number of components in the input vector.
m	maximum number of clusters that can be formed.
b_{ij}	bottom-up weights (from F_1 (b) unit X_i to F_2 unit Y_j).
t_{ji}	top-down weights (from F_2 unit Y_j to F_1 unit X_i).
p	vigilance parameter.
s	binary input vector (an n-tuple).
x	activation vector for F_1 (b) layer (binary).
$\|\|x\|\|$	norm of vector x, defined as the sum of the components x_i.

7.4.5 DESCRIPTION

A binary input vector s is presented to the F_1 (a) layer, and the signals are sent to the corresponding X units. These F_1 (b) units then broadcast to the F_2 layer over connection pathways with bottom-up weights. Each F_2 unit computes its net input, and the units compete for the right to be active. The unit with the largest net input sets its activation to 1; all other have an activation of 0. We shall denote the index of the winning unit as J. this winning unit becomes the candidate to learn the input pattern. A signal is then sent down from F_2 to F_1 (b) (multiplied by the top-down weights). The X units (in the interface portion of the F_1 layer) remain "on" only if they receive nonzero signals from both the F_1 (a) and F_1 units.

The norm of the vector x (the activation vector for the interface portion of F_1) gives the number of components in which the top-down weight vector for the winning F_2 unit t_j and the input vector s are both 1. (This quantity is sometimes referred to as the match.) If the ratio of $||x||$ to $||s||$ is greater than r equal to the vigilance parameter, the weights (top down and bottom up) for the winning cluster unit are adjusted.

However, if the ratio is less than the vigilance parameter, the candidate unit is rejected, and another candidate unit must be chosen. The current winning cluster unit becomes inhibited, so that it cannot be chosen again as a candidate on this learning trail, and the activations of the F_1 units are reset to zero. The same input vector again sends its signal to the interface units, which again sent this as the bottom-up signal to the F_2 layer, and the competition is repeated (but without the participation of any inhibited units).

The process continues until either a satisfactory match is found (a candidate is accepted) or all units are inhibited. The action to be taken if all units are inhibited must be specified by the user. It might be appropriate to reduce the value of the vigilance parameter, allowing less similar patterns to be placed on the same cluster, or to increase the number cluster units, or simply to designate the current input pattern as an outlier that could not be clustered.

In the theoretical formulation of the ART process, learning occurs during the resonance phase, in which the signals continue t flow throughout the net Care is taken in setting the parameter values so that a reset cannot suddenly occur as the weights change, nor will a new winning unit be chosen after a candidate unit is accepted for learning (see Section). The algorithm given shortly uses these equilibrium values in Step 8.

At the end of each presentation of a pattern (normally, after the weights have been adjusted), all cluster units are returned to inactive status (zero activations, but available to participate in the next competition).

The use of the ratio of the match to the norm of the input vector in the reset calculations described allows an ART1 net to respond to relative differences. This reflects the fact that a difference of one component in vector with only a few nonzero components is much more significant than a difference of one component in vectors with many nonzero components.

7.4.6 TRAINING ALGORITHM

The training algorithm for an ART1 net is presented next. A discussion of the role of the parameters and an appropriate choice of initial weights follows.

Step 0. Initialize parameters:

$L > 1,$

$0 < p \leq 1.$

Initialize weights:

$$0 < b_{ij}(0) < \frac{L}{L - 1 + n},$$

$$t_{ij}(0) = 1.$$

Step 1. While stopping condition is false, do steps 2-13.

Step 2. For each training input, do Steps 3-12.

Step 3 **Set activations of all F_2 units to zero.**

Set activations of $F_1(a)$ units to input vector s.

Step 4. Compute the norm of s:

$$||s|| = \sum_i s_i.$$

Step 5 Send input signal from F_1 (a) to the F_1 (b) layer:

$$x_i = s_i.$$

Step 6. For each F_2 node that is not inhibited:

If $y_j \neq -1$, then

$$y_j = \sum_i b_{ij} x_i.$$

Step 7 While reset is true, do Steps 8-11.

Step 8. Find J such that $y_j \geq y_j$ for all nodes j.

If $y_j = -1$, then all nodes are inhibited and this pattern cannot be clustered.

Step 9. Recomputed activation x of F_1 (b):

$$x_i = d_i t_{ji}.$$

Step 10. Compute the norm of vector x:

$$||x|| = \sum_i x_i.$$

Step 11. Test for reset:

If $\frac{||x||}{||s||} < p$, then

$y_j = -1$ (inhibit node J) (and continue, executing Step 7 again).

If $\frac{||x||}{||s||} \geq p$,

Step 12. Update the weights for node J (fast learning):

$$b_{ij}\,(new) = \frac{Lx_i}{L - 1 + ||x||},$$

$$t_{ji}(new) = x_i.$$

Step 13. Test for stopping condition.

Comments. Step 3 removes all inhibitions from the previous learning trail (presentation of a pattern).

Setting y = - 1 for an inhibited node (in step 6) will prevent that node from being a winner. Since all weights and signals in the net are nonnegative a unit with a negative activation can never have the largest activation.

In step 8, in case of a tie, take J to be the smallest such index.

In step 9, unit X_i is "on" only if it receives both an external signal s_i and a signal sent down from F_2 to F_1, t_{ji}.

The stopping condition in Step 13 might consist of any of the following:

No weight changes,

No units reset, or

Maximum number of epochs reached.

The ART1 training process is often described in terms of setting the activation of the winning F_2 unit 1 and all others to 0. However, it is easy to implement the algorithm without making explicit use of those activations, so in the interest of computational simplicity, they are omitted here.

The user must specify the desired action to be taken in the event that all the F_2 nodes are inhibited in Step 8. The possibilities include adding more cluster units, reducing the vigilance, and classifying the pattern as an outlier that cannot be clustered (with the given parameters).

Notes that t_{ij} is either 0 or 1, and once it is set to 0 during learning, it can never be set back to 1 (which provides the stable learning mentioned before).

7.4.7 PARAMETERS

User-defined parameters with restrictions indicated for permissible values [Carpenter & Grossberg, 1987a] and sample values [Lippmann, 1987] are as follows:

PARAMETER	PERMISSIBLE RANGE	SAMPLE VALUE
L	$L > 1$	2
p	$0 < p \leq 1$ (vigilance parameter)	.9
b_{ij}	$0 < b_{ij}(0) < \dfrac{L}{L-1+n}$ (bottom-up weights)	$\dfrac{1}{1+n}$.
t_{ji}	$t_{ji}(0) = 1$ (top-down weights)	1

The derivation of the restrictions on the initial bottom-up and top-down weights is given in Section 7.2.4. Larger values for the initial bottom-up weights may encourage the net to form more clusters. The sample values of $b_{ij}(0)$ (one-half of the maximum allowed value for $L = 2$) are used in the examples of Section 7.2.3.

The equilibrium weights, which are used in the ART1 algorithm are derived in Section 7.2.4. The algorithm uses fast learning, which assumes that the input pattern is presented for the long enough period of time for the weights to reach equilibrium. Since none of the activations of the F_1 units change during resonance, it is not necessary actually to perform the iterations to solve the weight-update differential equations numerically.

Several values of p are illustrated in the examples of next Section.

7.5 ART2

ART2 is designed to perform for continuous-valued input vectors the same type of tasks as ART1 does for binary-valued input vectors. The differences between ART2 and ART1 reflect the modifications needed to accommodate patterns with continuous-valued components. The more complex F_1 field f ART2 is necessary because continuous-valued input vectors may be arbitrarily close together. The F_1 field in ART2 includes a combination of normalization and noise suppression, in addition to the comparison of the bottom-up and top-down signals needed for the reset mechanism. The learning process for ART2 is summarized and discussed in more detail.

There are two types of continuous-valued inputs for which ART2 may be used. The first might be called "noisy binary" signals. These consist of patterns whose information is conveyed primarily by which components are "on" or "virtually off," rather than by the differences in the magnitude of the components that are positive. The equilibrium weights found by the fast learning mode are suitable for this type of data. However, it is not as easy to find equilibrium weights in ART2 as it is for ART1, because the differences equations for the weight updates depend on activations in the F_1 layer, which are changing as learning progress.

For patterns in which the range of values of the components carries significant information and the weight vector for a cluster unit is to be interpreted as an exemplar for the patterns placed on that unit, the slow learning mode may be more appropriate. We can think of this second type of data as "truly continuous." Both forms of learning are included in the algorithm.

7.5.1 ARCHITECTURE

A typical ART2 architecture [Carpenter & Grossberg, 1987b] is illustrated in Figure 7.4. The F_1 layer consists of six types of units (the W, X, U, V, P, and Q units). There are n units of each of these types (where n is the dimension of an input pattern). Only one unit of each type is shown in the figure. A supplemental unit between the W and X units receives signals from all of the W units, computes the norm of the vector w, and sends this (inhibitory0 signal to each of the X units. Each of these also receives an excitatory signal from the corresponding W unit. Detail of this portion of the net is shown in Figure 7.4.

A similar supplemental unit performs the same role between the P and Q units, and another does so between the V and U units. Each X unit is connected to the corresponding V unit, and each Q unit is connected to the corresponding V unit also. The symbols on the connection paths between the various units in the F_1 layer in Figure 7.4 indicate the transformation that occurs to the signal as it passes from one type of unit to the next; they do not indicate multiplication by the given quantity. However, the connections between units P_i (of the F_1 layer) and Y_j (0f the F_2 layer) do show the weights that multiply the signal transmitted over those paths. The activation of the winning F_2 unit is d, where $0 < d < 1$. The activation function applied to x and q will be discussed later. The symbol ---→ indicates normalization; i.e. the vector q of activations of the Q units is just the vector p of activations of the P units,, normalized to approximately unit length.The action of the F_2 layer (units Y_j in Figure7.4) is essentially unchanged from the action in ART1. The units complete in a winner-take-all mode for the right to learn each input pattern. As in ART1, learning occurs only if the top-down weight vector for the winning unit is sufficiently similar to the input vector. The test for reset in ART1 and ART 2 differ. (See the algorithm for details of the test used in ART2.)

The U units perform a similar role to the input phase of the F_1 layer in ART1. However, in ART2 some processing of the input vector is necessary because the magnitudes of the real-values input vectors may vary more than for the binary input vectors of ART1. ART2 treats small components as noise and does not distinguish between patterns that are merely scaled versions of each other. The P units play the role of the interface F_1 units in the ART1 architecture. The role of the supplemental units in ART1 has been incorporated within the F_1 layer.

Figure 7.5 presents an expanded diagram of the F_1 layer of the ART2 net illustrated in Figure 7.3. In keeping with the diagrams for other nets (in other chapters), only weights are shown on the connections between units. (IF no weight is indicated, the signal transverses that pathway without modification.)

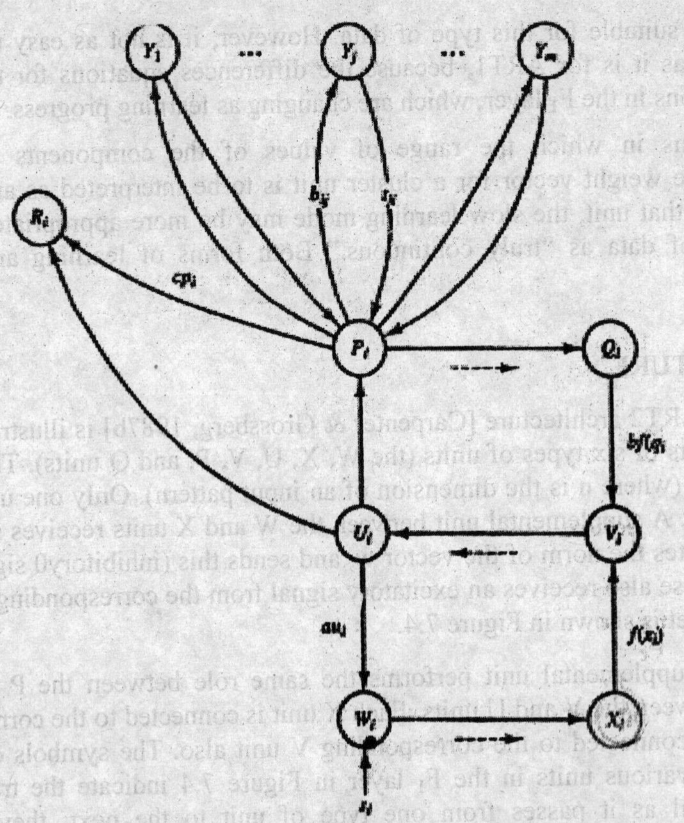

Figure 7.3 Typical ART2 architecture [Carpenter & Grossberg, 1987b]

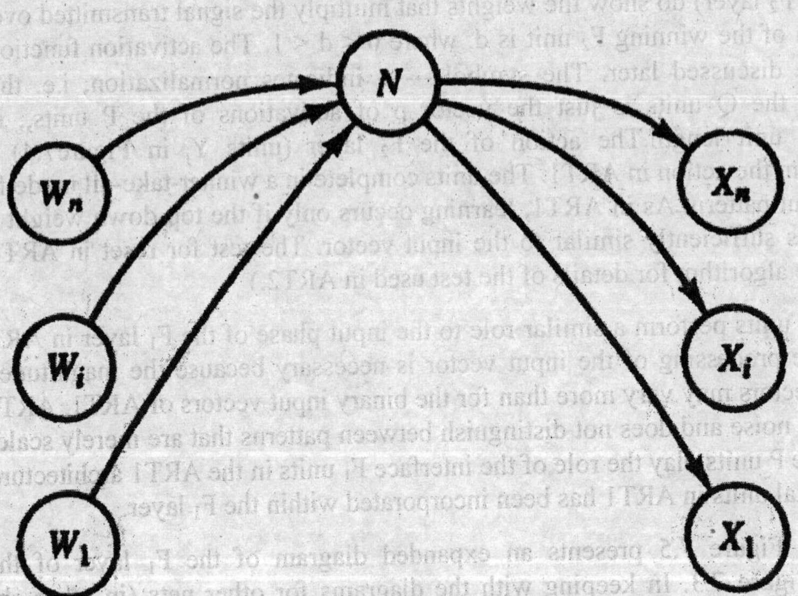

Figure 7.4 Detail of connections from W units to X units, showing the supplemental unit N to perform normalization.

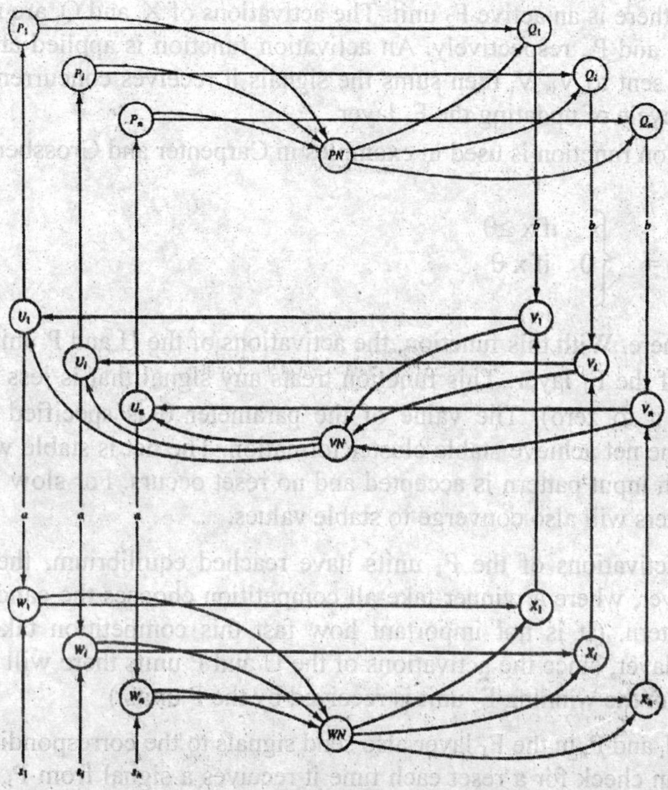

Figure 7.5 Expanded diagram of the F_1 layer of a typical ART2 architecture. Units X_i and Q_i apply an activation function to their net input; this function suppresses any components of the vectors of activations at those levels that fall below the user-selected value θ. The connection paths from U to W and from Q to V have fixed weights a and b, respectively.

7.5.2 ALGORITHM

This section provides a description of the training algorithm for ART2 (for both fast and slow learning), a step-by-step statement of the algorithm, and a summary of the basic information about the parameters and choice of initial weights necessary to implement the algorithm. illustrate the influence of some of these parameters. Derivations of the restrictions on the choice of parameter values and initial weights are given.

7.5.3 DESCRIPTION

A learning trial consists of one presentation of one input pattern. The input signal $s = (s_1,\ldots,s_i,\ldots s_n)$ continues to be sent while all of the actions to be described are performed. At the beginning of a learning trial, all activations are set to zero.

The computation cycle (for a particular learning trial) within the F_1 layer can be thought of as originating with the computation of the activation of unit U_i (the activation of unit V_i normalized to approximately unit length). Next, a signal is sent from each unit U_i to its associated units W_i and P_i. The activations of units W_i and P_i are then computed. Unit W_i sums the signal it receives from U_i and the input signal s_i. P_i sums the signal it receives from U_i and the top-down signal it receives if there is an active F_2 unit. The activations of X_i and Q_i are normalized versions of the signals at W_i and P_i, respectively. An activation function is applied at each of these units before the signal is sent to V_i, V_i then sums the signals it receives concurrently from X_i and Q_i; this completes one cycle of updating the F_1 layer.

The activation function is used in examples in Carpenter and Grossberg's (1987b)

$$f(x) = \begin{cases} x & \text{if } x \geq \theta \\ 0 & \text{if } x \; \theta \end{cases}$$

original paper and here. With this function, the activations of the U and P units reach equilibrium after two updates of the F_1 layer. This function treats any signal that is less than θ as noise and suppresses it (sets it to zero). The value of the parameter θ is specified by the user. Noise suppression helps the net achieve stable cluster formation. The net is stable when the first cluster unit chosen for each input pattern is accepted and no reset occurs. For slow learning, the weight vectors for the clusters will also converge to stable values.

After the activations of the F_1 units have reached equilibrium, the P units send their signals to the F_2 layer, where a winner-take-all competition chooses the candidate cluster unit to learn the input pattern. (It is not important how fast this competition takes place relative to iterations in the F_1 layer, since the activations of the U and P units there will not change until the top-down signal from the winning F_2 unit is received by the P units.)

The units U_i and P_i in the F_1 layer also send signals to the corresponding reset unit R_i. The reset mechanism can check for a reset each time it receives a signal from P_i, since the necessary computations are based on the value of that signal and the most recent signal the unit R_i had received from U_i. However, this needs to be done only when P_i first receives a top-down signal, since parameter values are chosen such that no reset will occur if no F_2 unit is active, or after learning has started. The reset mechanism will be considered in more detail.

After the conditions for reset have been checked, the candidate cluster unit either will be rejected as not similar enough to the input pattern or will be accepted. If the cluster unit is rejected, it will become inhibited (prevented from further participation in the current learning trial), and the cluster unit with the next largest net input is chosen as the candidate. This process continues until an acceptable cluster unit is chosen (or the supply of available cluster units is exhausted). When a candidate cluster unit is chosen that passes the reset conditions, learning will occur.

In slow learning, only one iteration of the weight update equations occurs on each learning trial. A large number of presentations of each pattern is required, but relatively little computation is done on each trial. For convenience, these repeated presentations are treated as epochs in the algorithm that follows. However, there is no requirement that the patterns be presented in the same order or that exactly the same patterns be presented on each cycle through them.

In the fast learning mode, the weight updates (alternating with updates of the F_1 layer activations) continue until the weights reach equilibrium on each trial. Only a few epochs are required, but a large number of iterations through the weight-update-F_1-update portion of the algorithm must be performed on each learning trial (presentation of a pattern). In fast learning, the placement of the patterns on clusters stabilizers (no reset occurs), but the weights will change for each pattern presented.

7.5.4 TRAINING ALGORITHM

The algorithm that follows can be used for either fast learning or slow learning. In fast learning, iterations of weight change followed by updates of F_1 activations proceed until equilibrium is reached. In slow learning, only one iteration of the weight-update step is performed, but a large number of learning trial is required in order for the net to stabilize,. [Carpenter & Grossberg, 1987b]. Fast learning and slow learning are compared in the examples in Section .

Calculations for Algorithm. The following calculation are repeated at several steps of eh algorithm and will be referred to as "update F_1 activations." Unit J is the winning F_2 node after competition. If no winning unit has been chosen, d will be zero of all units. Note that the calculations for w_i and p_i can be done in parallel, as can the calculations for x_i and q_i.

The update F_1 activations are:

$$u_i = \frac{v_i}{e + ||v||},$$

$$w_i = s_i + au_i, \qquad p_i = u_i\, dt_{ji},$$

$$x_i = \frac{w_i}{e + ||w||}, \qquad q_i = \frac{p_i}{e + ||p||}$$

$$v_i = f(x_i) + bf(q_i).$$

The activation function is

$$f(x) = \begin{cases} x & \text{if } x \geq \theta \\ 0 & \text{if } x < \theta \end{cases}$$

Algorithm

Step 0. Initialize parameters:

$a, b, \theta, c, d, e, \alpha, \rho.$

Step 1. Do Steps 2-12 N_EP times.

(Perform the specified number of epochs of training.)

Step 2. For each input vector s, do Steps 3-11.

Step 3. Update F_1 unit activations:

$$u_i = 0, \qquad x_i = \frac{s_i}{e + ||s||},$$

$$w_i = s_i, \qquad q_i == 0,$$

$$p_i = 0, \qquad v_i = f(x_i).$$

Update F_1 unit activations again:

$$u_i = \frac{v_i}{e + ||v||},$$

$w_i = s_i + au_i,$

$p_i = u_i,$

$x_i = \dfrac{w_i}{e + ||w||},$

$q_i = \dfrac{p_i}{e + ||p||},$

$v_i = f(x_i + bf(q_i).$

Step 4. Compute signals to F_2 units:

$$y_i = \sum_i b_{ij} p_i$$

Step 5. While reset is true, do Steps 6-7.

Step 6. Find F_2 unit Y_j with largest signal. (Define J such that $Y_j \geq y_j$ for $j = 1,\ldots.m.$)

Step 7. Check for reset:

$u_i = \dfrac{v_i}{e + ||v||},$

$p_i = u_i + dt_{ji},$

$r_i = \dfrac{u_i + cp_i}{e + ||u|| + c||p||}.$

If $||r|| < p - e$, then

$y_j = -1$ (inhibit J)

(reset is true; repeat Step 5);

If $||r|| \geq p - e$, thenm

$w_i = s_i + au_i,$

$x_i = \dfrac{w_i}{e + ||w||},$

$q_i = \dfrac{p_i}{e + ||p||},$

$v_i = f(x_i) + bf(q_i).$

Reset is false; proceed to Step 8.

Step 8. Do steps 9-11 N_IT times.

(Perform the specified number of learning iterations.)

Step 9. Update weights for winning unit J:

$t_{ji} = \alpha du_i + \{1 + \alpha d(d - 1)\}t_{ji}$

$b_{ij} = \alpha du_i + \{1 + \alpha d(d - 1)\}b_{ij}$

Step 10. Update F_i activations:

$u_i = \dfrac{v_i}{e + ||v||},$

$w_i = s_i + au_i,$

$p_i = u_i\, dt_{ji},$

$x_i = \dfrac{w_i}{e + ||w||},$

$q_i = \dfrac{p_i}{e + ||p||},$

$v_i = f(x_i) + bf(q_i)$.

Step 11. Test stooping condition for weight updates.

Step 12. Test stopping condition for number of epochs.

Comments. In the preceding algorithms, we have made use of the following facts:

1. Reset cannot occur during resonance (Step 8).
2. A new winning unit cannot be chosen during resonance.

We have not used the facts that:

1. Typically, in slow learning N_IT = 1, and Step 10can be omitted.
2. In fast learning, for the pattern learned by a cluster, u will be parallel to t throughout the training cycle and the equilibrium weights will be

$$t_{ji} = \frac{1}{1-d} u_i;$$

$$b_{ij} = \frac{1}{1-d} u_i;$$

Other possible stopping conditions are as follows:

Repeat Step 8 until the weight changes are below some specified tolerance. For slow learning, repeat Step 1 until the weight changes are below some specified tolerance. For fast learning, repeat Step 1 until the placement of patterns on the cluster units does not change from on epoch to next.

Steps 3 through 11 constitute on learning trial (one presentation of a pattern). It will be convenient (especially in describing the implementation of fast learning and slow learning using this algorithm) to refer to the performance of a learning trial for each input pattern as an epoch. It is not necessary that the patterns be presented in the same order on each epoch. Note that the action of updating the F_1 activations during the extended resonance phase of the fast learning mode (the computations in Step 8) causes the values of the u_i that appear in the weight update equations to change as learning progress.

7.5.5 CHOICES

Parameters. A summary of the role of the various parameters used in the algorithm is given here. Derivations of some of these restrictions are given. The parameters and their roles are as follows:

n Number of input units (F_1 layer);

m number of cluster units (F_2 layer);

a, b fixed weights in the F_1 layer; sample values are a = 10. Setting either a = 0 or b = 0 produces instability in the net; other than that, the net is not particularly sensitive to the values chosen.

c fixed weight used in testing for reset; a sample value is c = 1. A small c gives larger effective range of the vigilance parameter .

d activation of winning F_2 unit; a sample value is d = .9. Note that c and d must be chosen to satisfy the inequality

$$\frac{cd}{1-d} \leq 1$$

(in order to prevent a reset from occurring during a learning trial). T ratio should be chosen close to 1 to achieve a larger effective range for vigilance.

e a small parameter introduced to prevent division by zero when the norm of a vector is zero. This value prevents the normalization to unity from being exact. A value of zero is typically used in the hand computations and derivations that follow and may be used in the algorithm if the normalization step is skipped when the vector is zero.

θ noise suppression parameter, a sample value is $\theta = 1/\sqrt{n}$. The sample value may be larger than desired in some applications. Components of the normalized input vector (and other vector in the F_1 loop) that are less than this value are set to zero.

α learning rate. A smaller value will slow the learning in either the fast or the slow learning mode. However, a smaller value will ensure that the weights (as well as the placement of patterns on clusters) eventually reach equilibrium in the slow learning mode.

ρ vigilance parameter. Along with the initial bottom-up weights, this parameter determines how many clusters will be formed. Although theoretically, values from 0 to 1 are allowed, only values between approximately 0.7 and 1 perform any useful role in controlling the number of clusters. (Any value less than 0.7 will have the same effect as setting ρ to zero.) Some choices of vales for c and d will restrict the effective range of values for ρ even further.

Initial Weights. The initial top-down weights for the ART2 net are as follows:

$t_{ij}(0)$ initial top-down weights (must be small to ensure that no reset will occur for the first pattern placed on a cluster unit);

$$t_{ji}(0) = 0.$$

$b_{ij}(0)$ intial bottom-up weights; must be chosen to satisfy the inequality

$$b_{ij}(0) \le \frac{1}{(1-d)\sqrt{n}},$$

to prevent the possibility of a new winner being chosen during "resonance" as the weights change. Larger values of b_{ij} encourage the net to form more clusters. .

Learning Mode. Fast learning and slow learning differ not only in the theoretical assumption on which they are based (in terms of the speed of learning relative to the duration of presentation of a pattern during any one learning trial), but also in the performance characteristics of the clusters and weight vectors formed when they are used. Some differences in the performance of fast and slow learning are summarized here and are illustrated in the examples of the next section.

Fast learning results in weight vectors that have some of the same characteristics as the weights found by ART1. Typically, a component of the weight vector for a particular cluster unit that is set to zero during a learning trial will not become nonzero during a subsequent learning trial. Furthermore, if a pattern being learned by a cluster has one or more components that are zero after noise suppression is applied, the corresponding components of the weight vector will be set to zero during learning. However, the weights of the nonzero components will change on each learning trial to reflect the relative magnitudes of the nonzero components of the current input vector. this suggest that fast learning may be more appropriate for data in which the primary information is contained in the pattern of components that are "small" or "large," rather than for data in which the relative sizes of the nonzero components is important.

Slow learning requires many epochs of training, with only one weight update iteration performed on each learning trial. The weight vector for each cluster is the average of the pattern it has learned, which may make the weight vector a more suitable exemplar for the cluster for certain types of applications. The weights reach equilibrium (to within a tolerance determined by the learning rate). In some applications, slow learning may also produce clustering that is less influenced by the order of presentation of the pattern than the clustering produced by fast learning.

7.6 SIMPLE ARCHITECTURE OF ART

Grossberg introduced a model for explaining biological phenomena. The model has three crucial properties: a normalization of the total network activity. Biological systems are usually very adaptive to large changes in their environment. For example, the human eye can adapt itself to large variations in light intensities; contrast enhancement of input patterns. The awareness of subtle differences in input patterns can mean a lot in terms of survival. Distinguishing a hiding panther from a resting one makes all the difference in the world. The mechanism used here is contrast enhancement;

Short-term memory (STM) storage of the contrast-enhanced pattern. Before the input pattern can be decoded, it must be stored in the short-term memory. The long-term memory (LTM) implements an arousal mechanism (i.e., the classi cation), whereas the STM is used to cause gradual changes in the LTM.

The system consists of two layers, F1 and F2, which are connected to each other via the LTM

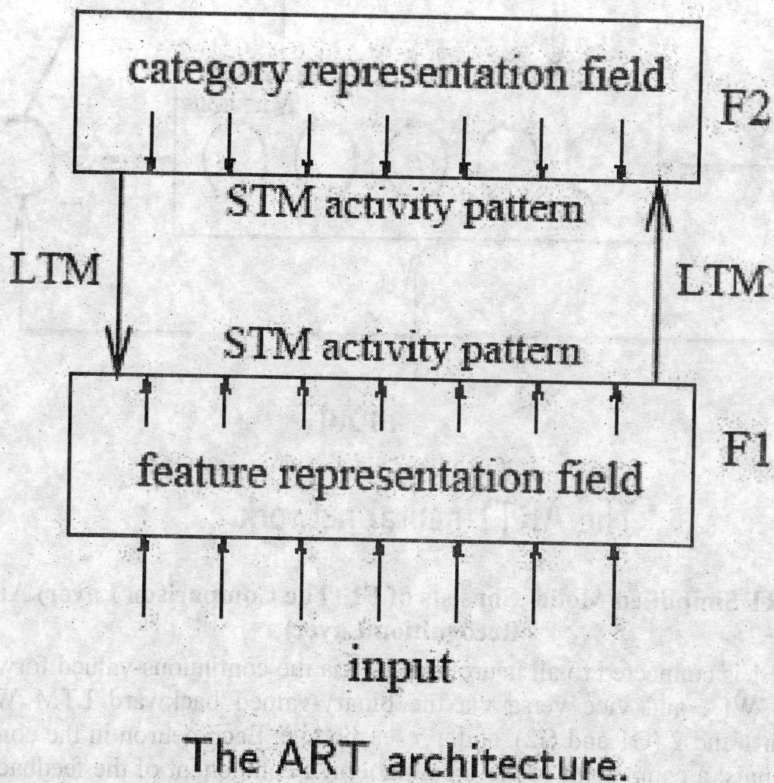

Figure 7.6 Simple Architecture Of ART

The input pattern is received at F1, whereas classi cation takes place in F2. As mentioned before, the input is not directly classified. First a characterisation takes place by means of extracting features, giving rise to activation in the feature representation field. The expectations, residing in the LTM connections, translate the input pattern to a categorisation in the category representation field. The classi cation is compared to the expectation of the network, which resides in the LTM weights from F2 to F1. If there is a match, the expectations are strengthened, otherwise the classification is rejected.

7.7 ART: THE SIMPLIFIED NEURAL NETWORK MODEL

The ART simplified model consists of two layers of binary neurons (with values 1 and 0), called F1 (the comparison layer) and F2 (the recognition layer)

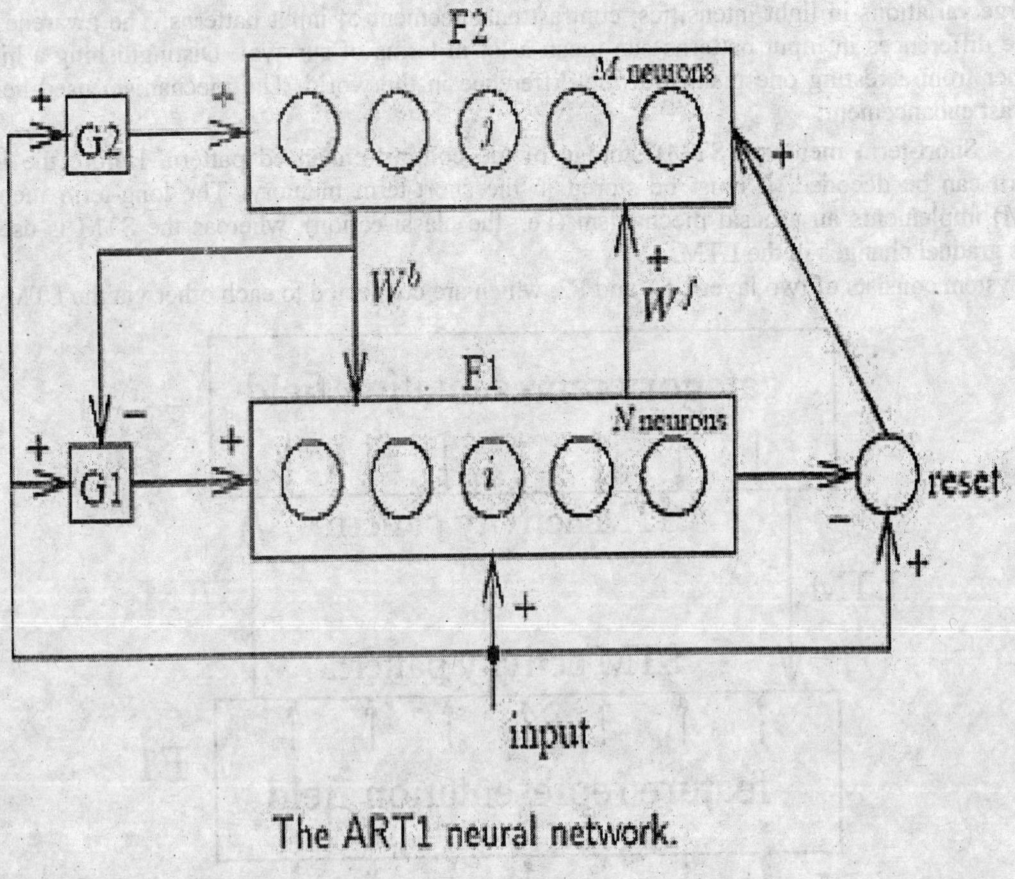

Figure7.7 ART Simplified Model Consists of F1 (The Comparison Layer) And F2 (The Recognition Layer)

Each neuron in F1 is connected to all neurons in F2 via the continuous-valued forward long term memory (LTM) Wf , and vice versa via the binary-valued backward LTM Wb. The other modules are gain 1 and 2 (G1 and G2), and a reset module. Each neuron in the comparison layer receives three inputs: a component of the input pattern, a component of the feedback pattern, and a gain G1. A neuron outputs a 1 if and only if at least three of these inputs are high: the 'two-thirds rule.' The neurons in the recognition layer each compute the inner product of their incoming (continuous-valued) weights and the pattern sent over these connections. The winning neuron then inhibits all the other neurons via lateral inhibition. Gain 2 is the logical 'or' of all the elements in the input pattern x. Gain 1 equals gain 2, except when the feedback pattern from F2 contains any 1; then it is fórced to zero. Finally, the reset signal is sent to the active neuron in F2 if the input vector x and the output of F1 differ by more than some vigilance level.

7.8 OPERATION

The network starts by clamping the input at F1. Because the output of F2 is zero, G1 and G2 are both on and the output of F1 matches its input.The pattern is sent to F2, and in F2 one neuron becomes active. This signal is then sent back over the backward LTM, which reproduces a binary pattern at F1. Gain 1 is inhibited, and only the neurons in F1 which receive a 'one' from both x and F2 remain active. If there is a substantial mismatch between the two patterns, the reset signal will inhibit the neuron in F2 and the process is repeated.

1. Initialisation:

$$\mathbf{w}_{ji}^{b}(0) = 1$$

$$\mathbf{w}_{ij}^{f}(0) = \frac{1}{1+N}$$

where N is the number of neurons in F1, M the number of neurons in F2, $0 < i < N$, and $0 \leq j < M$. Also, choose the vigilance threshold ρ, $0 \leq \rho \leq 1$;

2. Apply the new input pattern x:

3. compute the activation values y0 of the neurons in F2:

$$y_i' = \sum_{j=1}^{N} w_{ij}{}^{f}(t)\, x_i;$$

4. select the winning neuron k $(0 \leq k < M)$:

5. vigilance test: if

$$\frac{\mathbf{w}_k{}^{b}(t)\cdot\mathbf{x}}{\mathbf{x}\cdot\mathbf{x}} > \rho,$$

where . denotes inner product, go to step 7, else go to step 6. Note that w_K^{b} essentially is the inner product x^{*} . x,which will be large if x^{*} and xnear to each other;

6. neuron k is disabled from further activity. Go to step 3;

7. Set for all l, $0 \leq l < N$:

$$w_{kl}{}^{b}(t+1) = w_{kl}{}^{b}(t)\, x_l,$$

$$w_{lk}{}^{f}(t+1) = \frac{w_{kl}{}^{b}(t)\, x_l}{\frac{1}{2} + \sum_{i=1}^{N} w_{ki}{}^{b}(t)\, x_i};$$

8. re-enable all neurons in F2 and go to step 2.

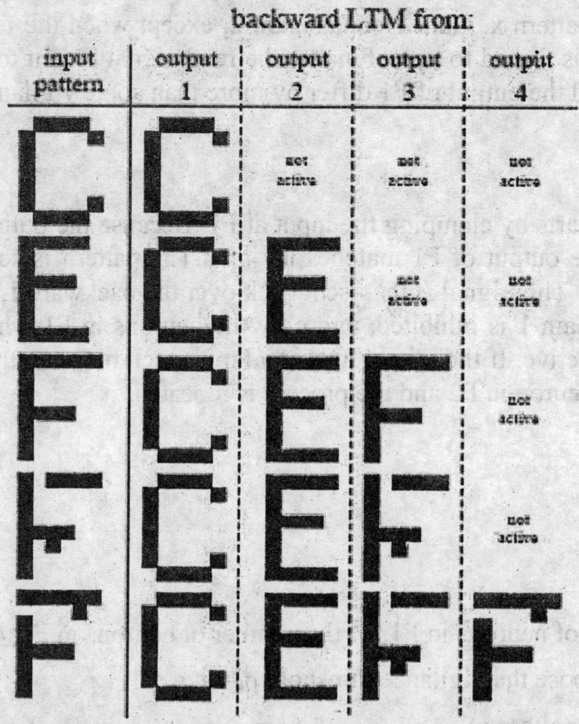

Figure 7.8 Carpenter Grossberg Network For Letter Patterns

An example of the behaviour of the Carpenter Grossberg network for letter patterns. The binary input patterns on the left were applied sequentially. On the right the stored patterns (i.e., the weights of Wb for the first four output units) are shown.

7.9 ART: THE ORIGINAL MODEL

In later work, Carpenter and Grossberg (Carpenter & Grossberg, 1987a, 1987b) present several neural network models to incorporate parts of the complete theory. We will only discuss the first model, ART1. The network incorporates a follow-the-leader clustering algorithm (Hartigan, 1975). This algorithm tries to fit each new input pattern in an existing class. If no matching class can be found, i.e., the distance between the new pattern and all existing classes exceeds some threshold, a new class is created containing the new pattern. The novelty in this approach is that the network is able to adapt to new incoming patterns, while the previous memory is not corrupted. In most neural networks, such as the backpropagation network, all patterns must be taught sequentially; the teaching of a new pattern might corrupt the weights for all previously learned patterns. By changing the structure of the network rather than the weights, ART1 overcomes this problem.

7.10 THE ART NETWORK STRUCTURE

The ART network consists of 2 layers:

(I) a Comparison Layer (CL)

(II) a Recognition Layer (RL), which are interconnected.

In addition, the network consists of two Gain elements, one, (G1) feeding its output g1 to the Comparison layer and the second, (G2) feeding its output g2 to the Recognition Layer, and thirdly, a Reset element where the comparison, as performed in the Comparison Layer, is evaluated with respect to a preselected tolerance value ("vigilance" value). See Fig. 7.7.

7.10. (A) THE COMPARISON LAYER (CL)

A binary element x_j of the m-dimensional input vector x is inputted into the jth (j = 1 . . . m; m = dim(x)) neuron of the CL. The jth neuron is also inputted by a weighted sum. (p_j) of the recognition-output vector r from the RL where

$$p_j = \sum_{i=1}^{m} t_{ij} r_i \tag{7.1}$$

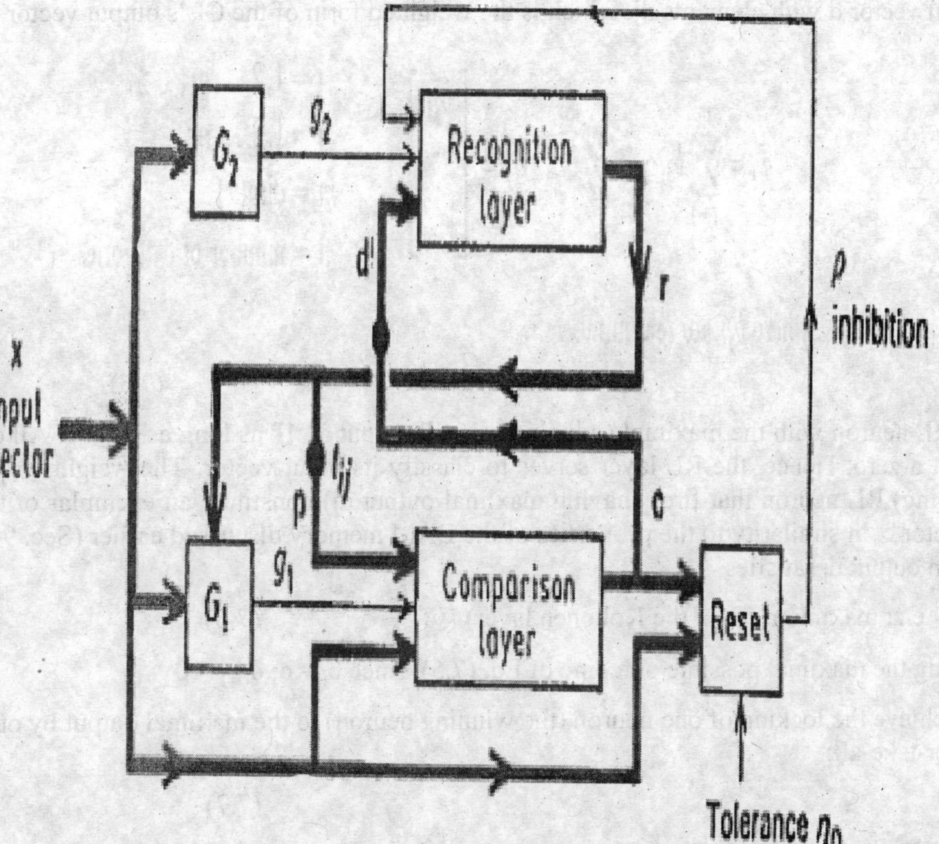

Fig. 7.9 ART network schematic.

r_i being the ith component of the m-dimensional recognition-output vector r of the RL layer and n being the number of categories to be recognized.

Furthermore, all CL neurons receive the same g1 scalar output of the same element G1. The m-dimensional (m = dim(x)) binary comparison-layer output vector c of the CL layer initially equals the input vector, namely, at the initial iteration

$c_j(0) = x_j(0)$ (7.2)

Also, initially:

$g_1(0) = 1$ (7.3)

The CL's output vector c satisfies a (two-thirds) majority rule requirement s.t. its output is

$c_j = 1$

only if at least two of this (CL) neuron's three inputs are 1. Hence, Eqs. (7.2), (7.3) imply, by the "two-thirds majority" rule, that initially

$c(0) = x(0)$ (7.4)

since initially no feedback exists from the RL layer, while g1 (0) = 1.

7.10 (B) THE RECOGNITION LAYER (RL)

The RL layer serves as a classification layer. It receives as its input an n-dimensional weight vector d with elements dj, which is the weighted form of the CL's output vector c; s.t.

$$d_j = \sum_{i=1}^{m} b_{ji} c_i = \mathbf{b}_j^T \mathbf{c}; \quad \mathbf{b}_j \triangleq \begin{bmatrix} b_{j1} \\ \vdots \\ b_{jm} \end{bmatrix}; \quad \begin{array}{l} i = 1,2,\ldots m; \\ j = 1,2,\ldots n; \\ m = \dim(x) \\ n = \text{number of categories} \end{array}$$

where b_{ji} are real numbers.

(7.5)

The RL neuron with the maximal (winning) dj will output a "1" as long as g2 = 1. All others will output a zero. Hence, the RL layer serves to classify its input vector. The weights b_{ij} of the jth (winning) RL neuron that fires (having maximal output dj) constitute an exemplar of the pattern of vector c, in similarity to the properties of the BAM memory discussed earlier (Sec. 9.3), noting that an output d_j satisfies

$d_j = c^T c$ at maximum (as in the Kohonen layer) (7.6)

d_j being the maximal possible outcome of Eq. (7.5), since $b_j = c$; $d_{i \neq j} = 0$

We achieve the locking of one neuron (the winning neuron) to the maximal output by outputting a winner-take-all:

$r_j = 1$ (7.7)

while all other neurons yield

$r_{i \neq j} = 0$ if $p = 0$ (no inhibition) (7.8)

For this purpose an interconnection scheme is employed in the RL that is based on lateral inhibition. The lateral inhibition interconnection is as in Fig. 7.10, where the output r of each neuron (i) is connected via an inhibitory (negative) weight matrix $L = \{l_{ij}\}$, $i \neq j$, where $l_{ij} < 0$ to any other neutron (j). Hence, a neuron with a

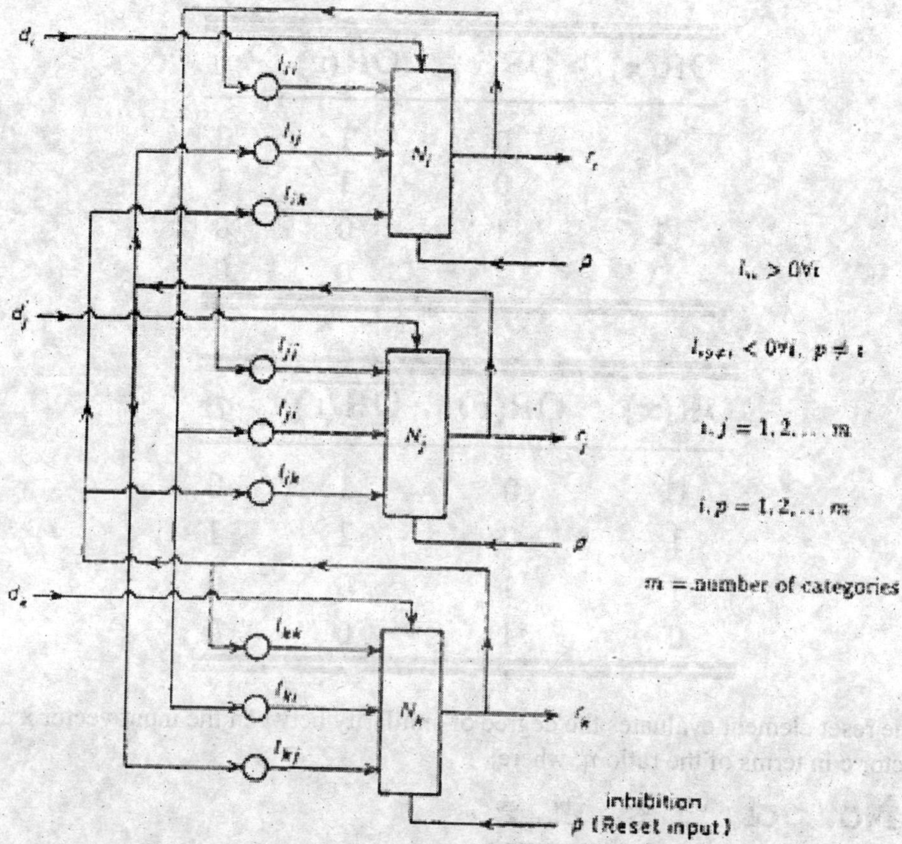

Fig. 7.10 Lateral inhibition in an RL layer of an ART network.

large output inhibits all other neurons. Furthermore, positive feedback ljj > 0 is employed such that each neuron's output rj is fed back with a positive weight to its own input to reinforce its output if it is to fire (to output a "one"). This positive reinforcement is termed as adaptive resonance to motivate the resonance term in "ART".

7.10 (C) GAIN AND RESET ELEMENTS

The gain elements feed the same scalar output to all neurons concerned as in Fig. 7.9, g1 being inputted to the CL neurons and g2 to RL neurons, where:

$$g_2 = OR(x) = OR(x_1....x_N)$$

$$g_1 = \overline{\overline{OR(r)}} \cap OR(x)$$

$$= \overline{OR(r_1.....r_N)} \cap OR\,(x_1...x_N) = g_2 \cap \overline{OR(r)} \qquad (7.9)$$

Hence, if at least one element of x is 1 then g2 = 1. Also, if any element of g2 = 1 but also no elements of r is 1 then gl = 1, else gl = 0. (See Table5.1). Note that the overhead bar denotes negation, whereas fl denotes a logical "and" (intersection). Also, note that if OR(x) is zero, then OR(r) is always zero, by the derivation of r as above.

OR(x)	OR(r)	$\overline{OR(r)}$	g_1
0	0	1	0
1	0	1	1
1	1	0	0
0	1	0	0

OR(x)	OR(r)	$\overline{OR(r)}$	g_1
0	0	1	0
1	0	1	1
1	1	0	0
0	1	0	0

Finally, the reset element evaluates the degree of similarity between the input vector x and the CL output vector c in terms of the ratio η, where:

$$\eta = \frac{\text{No. of "1"s in c}}{\text{No. of "1"s in x}} \qquad (7.10)$$

Subsequently, if

$$\eta < \eta_o \qquad (7.11)$$

η_0 being a pre-set initial tolerance (vigilance) value, then a reset signal (p) is outputted to inhibit the particular RL neuron that has fired at the given iteration. See Fig. A reset factor based of the Hamming distance between vectors c and x can also be considered.

7.11 SETTING-UP OF THE ART NETWORK

7.11 (A) INITIALIZATION OF WEIGHTS

The CL weight matrix B is initialized [Carpenter and Grossberg, 1987a] as follows:

$$b_{ij} < \frac{E}{E+m-1} \quad \forall_{i,}\, j \qquad (7.12)$$

Where

$$m = \dim(x)$$

$$E > 1 \text{ (typically } E = 2)$$

The RL weight matrix T is initialized such that

$$t_{ij} = 1 \quad \forall_{i,}\, j \qquad (7.13)$$

The tolerance level η_0 (vigilance) is chosen as

$$0 < \eta_0 < 1 \quad (7.14)$$

A high η_0 yields fine discrimination whereas a low η_0 allows grouping of more dissimilar patterns. Hence, one may start with lower η_0 and raise it gradually.

7.11 (B) TRAINING

The training involves the setting of the weight matrices B (of the RL) and T (of the CL) of the ART network.

Specifically, the network may first be exposed for brief periods to successive input vectors, not having time to converge to any input vector but only to approach some settings corresponding to some averaged x.

The parameters bij of vector bj of B are set according to:

$$b_{ij} = \frac{Ec_i}{E + 1 + \sum_k c_k} \quad (7.15)$$

where E> 1 (usually, E = 2)

ci = the ith component of vector c where j corresponds to the winning neuron. Furthermore, the parameter t_{ij} of T are set such that

$$t_{ij} = c_i \;\; \forall_i = 1 \ldots m; \;\; m = \dim(x) \quad (7.16)$$

j denoting the winning neuron.

7.12 NETWORK OPERATION

Initially, at iteration 0, x = 0. Hence, by Eq. (7.9), g2(0) = 0 and g1(0) = 0 Consequently c(0) = 0 by Eq. (4).

Also, since g2(0) = 0, the output vector r to the CL is, by the majority 2/3 rule that governs both layers is: r(0) = 0.

Subsequently, when a vector $x \neq 0$ is being applied, no neuron has an advantage on any other. Since now $x \neq 0$ then g2 = 1 and thus also g1 = 1 (due to r(0) = 0). Hence

$$c = x \quad (7.17)$$

by the majority rule described earlier.

Subsequently, by Eqs. (7.5), (7.6) and the properties of the RL, the jth of the RL neuron, which best matches vector c will be the only RL neuron to fire (to output a one). Hence $r_j = 1$ and $r_{i \neq j} = 0$ to determine vector r at the output of the RL. Note that if several neurons have same d then the first one will be chosen (lowest j).

Now r as above is fed back to the CL such that it is inputted to the CL neurons via weights t_{ij}. The m-dimensional weight vector p at the input of the CL thus satisfies namely

$p_j = t_j$; t_j denoting a vector of T (7.18a)

for winning neuron, and

$$p_j = 0 \quad (7.18b)$$

otherwise

Notice that $r_j = 1$ and t_{ij} are binary values. The values t_{ij} of T of the CL are set by the training algorithm to correspond to the real weight matrix B (with elements b_{ij}) of the RL.

Since now $r \neq 0$, then g1 becomes 0 by Eq. (7.9) and by the majority rule, the CL neurons which receive that non-zero components of x and of p will fire (to output a "one" in the CL's output vector c). Hence, the outputs of the RL force these components of c to zero where x and p do not have matching "ones".

If classification is considered by the reset element to be adequate, then classification is stopped. Go to (f), else: A considerable mismatch between vectors p and x will result in a considerable mismatch (in terms of "one's") between vectors x and c. This will lead to a low η as in Eq. (7.10) as computed by the reset element of the network such that $\eta < \eta o$. This, in turn, will inhibit the firing neuron of the

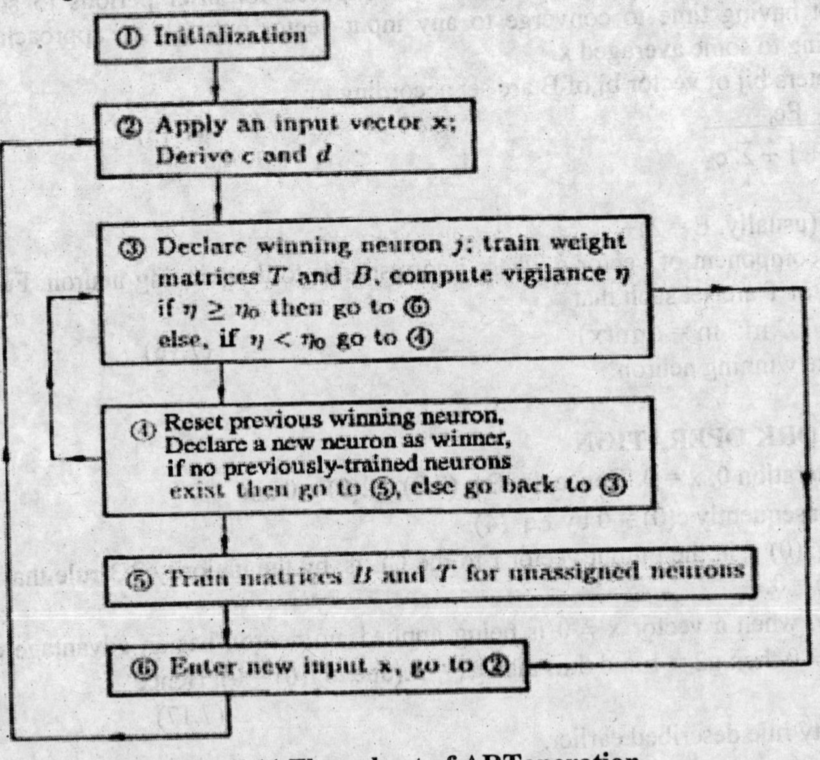

Fig 7.11 Flow-chart of ARToperation.

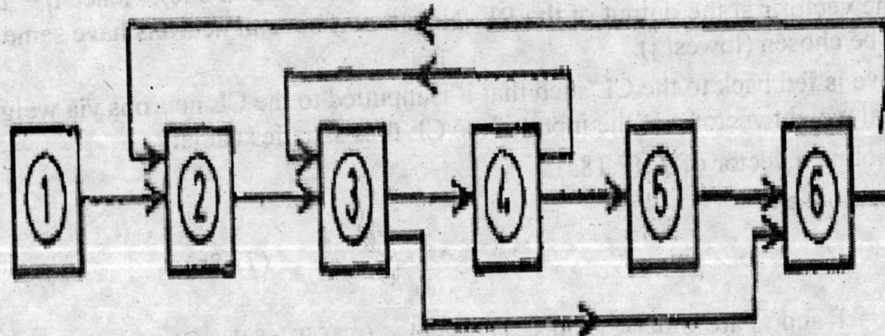

Fig 7.12 Simplified ART flow chart (encircled numbers: as in Fig. 7.8).

RL. Since now $\eta < \eta_O$., then also all elements of r = 0. Hence, g1 = 1 and x = c by the majority rule. Consequently, as long as neurons that are weighted still exist, a different neuron in the RL will win (the last winner being now inhibited), go to (c). (If at this iteration the reset element still considers the fit (classification) to be inadequate, the cycle is repeated. Now either a match will eventually be found:

In that case the network will enter a training cycle where the weights vectors t_j and b_j associated with the firing RL neuron are modified to match the input x considered.) Alternatively, if no neuron matches the input within the tolerance, then go to (e).

Now, a previously unassigned neuron is assigned weights vectors t_j, and b_j to match the input vector x. In this manner, the network does not lose (forget) previously learned patterns, but is also able to learn new ones, as does a biological network.

Apply new input vector.

The procedure above is summarized in Fig. 7.8. The categories (classes, patterns) which have been trained to be recognized are thus in terms of vectors (columns tj) of the weights matrix T; j denoting the particular category (class) considered, and j = 1, 2,.. . , n, where n is the total number of classes considered.

7.13 PROPERTIES OF ART

One can show [Carpenter and Grossberg, 1987a] that the ART network has several features that characterize the network, as follows:

Once the network stabilizes (weights reach steady state), the application of an input vector x, that has been used in training, will activate the correct RL neuron without any search (iterations). This property of direct access is similar to the rapid retrieval of previously learned patterns in biological networks.

The search process stabilizes at the winning neuron.

The training is stable and does not switch once a winning neuron has been identified.

The training stabilizes in a finite number of iterations.

To proceed from binary patterns (0/1) to patterns with different shades of gray, the authors of the ART-I network above developed the ART-II network [Carpenter and Grossberg, 1987b] which is not discussed here but which follows the basic philosophy of the ART-I network described above while extending it to continuous inputs.

The above indicates that the ART network; have many desirable features of biological networks, such as its being unsupervised, plastic, stable and of a finite number of iterations, and having immediate recall of previously learned patterns. The main shortcoming of the ART-I network is that a missing neuron destroys the whole learning process (since x and c must be of the same dimension). This contrasts an important property of biological neural networks. Whereas many of the properties of the ART network outlined above were missing in the previous networks, the latter shortcoming is not fundamental to the networks of the earlier chapters. It also leads us to consider the neural network designs of the next chapters, specifically, the Cognitron/Neocognitron neural network design and the LAMSTAR network design, which (among other things) avoid the above shortcoming.

QUESTION BANK

Q1. What do you mean by Adaptive resonance theory?
Q2. What are the various motivation of ART?
Q3. Explain the basic architecture of Adaptive resonance theory in detail?
Q4. Explain the basic operation of ART nets?
Q5. What is ART1? Explain the architecture of ART?
Q6. Write steps to train the ART1 network?
Q7. What is ART2? How it is different from ART1?
Q8. Explain the architecture of ART2 and also draw its diagram?
Q9. Write steps to train a ART network?
Q10. Explain the simple architecture of ART having LTM and STM activity pattern?
Q11. Draw the ART simplified model consist of comparison layer and recognition layer?
Q12. Explain the basic operation of two layer ART network?
Q13. Explain the structure of ART network?
Q14. How we can set up ART network?
Q15. Draw flow chart of ART operation?
Q16. What are the various properties of ART networks?

CHAPTER 8

NEOCOGNITRON

8.1 INTRODUCTION

Artificial neural network architectures such as backpropagation tend to have general applicability. We can use a single network type in many different applications by changing the network's size, parameters, and training sets. In contrast, the developers of the neocognitron set out to tailor architecture for a specific application: recognition of handwritten characters. Such a system has a great deal of practical application, although, judging from the introductions to some of their papers, Fukushima and his coworkers appear to be more interested in developing a model of the brain .To that end, their design was based on the seminal work performed by Hubel and Weisel elucidating some of the functional architecture of the visual cortex. We could not begin to provide a complete accounting of what is known about the anatomy and physiology of the mammalian visual system. Nevertheless, we shall present a brief and highly simplified description of some of that system's features as an aid to understanding the j basis of the neocognitron design.

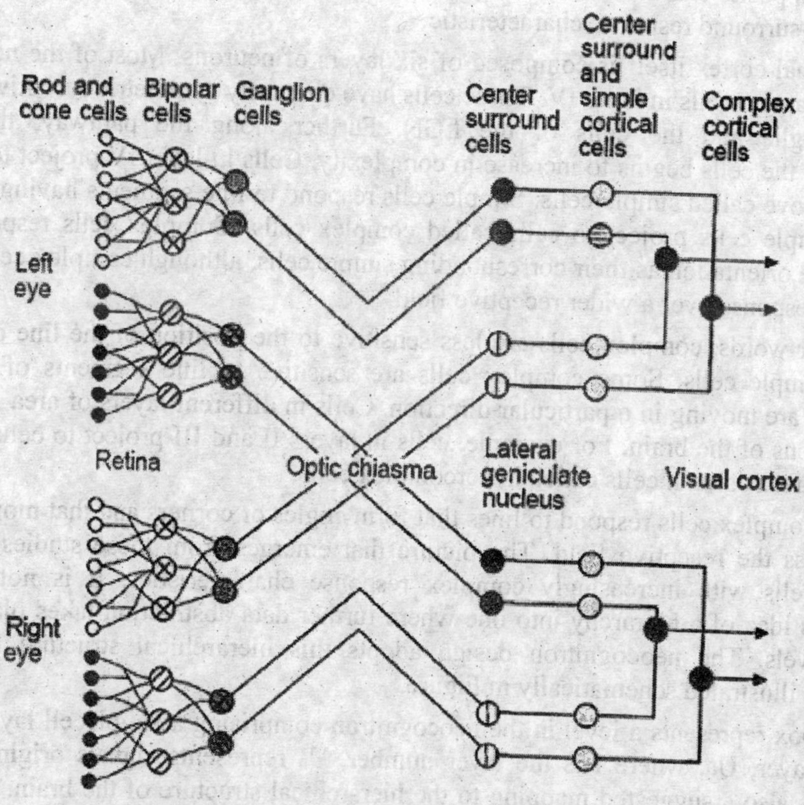

Figure 8.1 Visual pathways from the eye to the primary visual cortex are shown

Some nerve fibers from each eye cross over into the opposite hemisphere of the brain, where they meet nerve fibers from the other eye at the LGN. From the LGN, neurons project back to area 17. From area 17, neurons project into other cortical areas, other areas deep in the brain, and also back to the LGN.

Figure shows the main pathways for neurons leading from the retina back to the area of the brain known as the viiual, or striate, cortex. This area is also known as area 17. The optic nerve ii made up of axons from nerve cells called retinal ganglia. The ganglia receive stimulation indirectly from the light-receptive rods and cones through several intervening neurons. Hubel and Weisel used an amazing technique to discern the function of the various nerve cells in the visual system. They used microelectrodes to record the response of individual neurons in the cortex while stimulating the retina with light. By applying a variety of patterns and shapes, they were able to determine the particular stimulus to which a neuron was most sensitive. The retinal ganglia and the cells of the lateral geniculate nucleus (LGN) appear to have circular receptive fields.

They respond most strongly to circular spots of light of a particular size on a particular part of the retina. The part of the retina responsible for stimulating a particular ganglion cell is called the receptive field of the ganglion. Some of these receptive fields give an excitatory response to a centrally located spot of light, and an inhibitory response to a larger, more diffuse spot of light. These fields have an on-center off-surround response characteristic. Other receptive fields have the opposite characteristic, with an inhibitory response to the centrally located spot—an off-center on-surround response characteristic.

The visual cortex itself is composed of six layers of neurons. Most of the neurons from the LGN terminate on cells in layer IV. These cells have circularly symmetric receptive fields like the retinal ganglia and the cells of the LGN. Further along the pathway, the response characteristic of the cells begins to increase in complexity. Cells in layer IV project to a group of cells directly above called simple cells. Simple cells respond to line segments having a particular orientation. Simple cells project to cells called complex cells. Complex cells respond to lines having the same orientation as their corresponding simple cells, although complex cells appear to integrate their response over a wider receptive field.

In other words, complex cells are less sensitive to the position of the line on the retina than are the simple cells. Some complex cells are sensitive to line segments of a particular orientation that are moving in a particular direction. Cells in different layers of area 17 project to different locations of the brain. For example, cells in layers II and III project to cells in areas 18 and 19. These areas contain cells called hypercomplex cells.

Hypercomplex cells respond to lines that form angles or corners and that move in various directions across the receptive field. The picture that emerges from these studies is that of a hierarchy of cells with increasingly complex response characteristics. It is not difficult to extrapolate this idea of a hierarchy into one where further data abstraction takes place at higher and higher levels. The neocognitron design adopts this hierarchical structure in a layered architecture, as illustrated schematically in Figure.

Each box represents a level in the neocognitron comprising a simplecell layer, usi, and a complex-cell layer, Ua, where i is the layer number. U_0 represents signals originating on the retina. There is also a suggested mapping to the hierarchical structure of the brain. The network concludes with single cells that respond to complex visual stimuli.

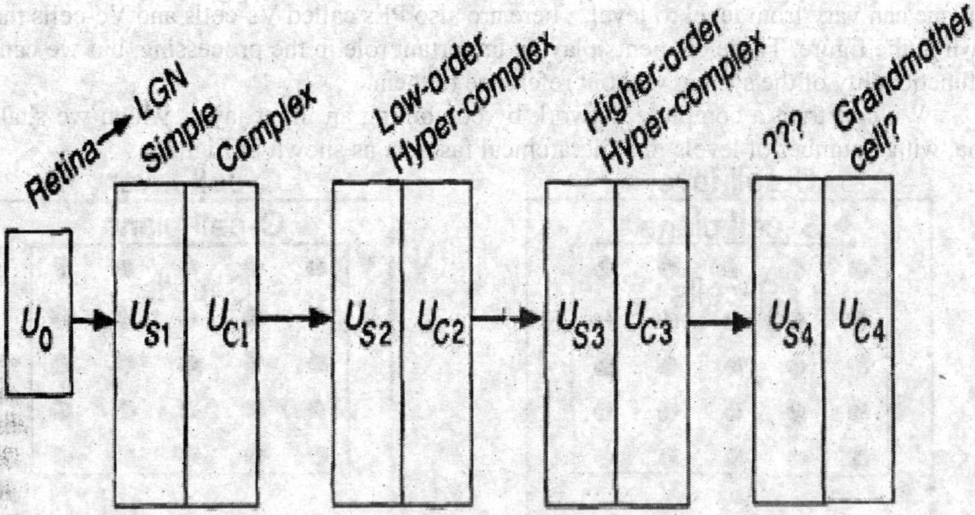

Figure 8.2 The neocognitron hierarchical structure is shown

These final cells are often called grandmother cells after the notion that there may be some cell in your brain that responds to complex visual stimuli, such as a picture of your grandmother. We remind you that the description of the visual system that we have presented here is highly simplified. There is a great deal of detail that we have omitted. The visual system does not adhere to a strict hierarchical structure as presented here. Moreover, we do not subscribe to the notion that grandmother cells per se exist in the brain. We know from experience that strict adherence to biology often leads to a failed attempt to design a system to perform the same function as the biological prototype: Flight is probably the most significant example. Nevertheless, we do promote the use of neurobiological results if they prove to be appropriate. The neocognitron is an excellent example of how neurobiological results can be used to develop a new network architecture.

8.2 NEOCOGNITRON ARCHITECTURE

The neocognitron design evolved from an earlier model called the cognitron, and there are several versions of the neocognitron itself. The one that we shall describe has nine layers of PEs (Processing elements), including the retina layer. The system was designed to recognize the numerals 0 through 9, regardless of where they are placed in the field of view of the retina. Moreover, the network has a high degree of tolerance to distortion of the character and is fairly insensitive to the size of the character. This first architecture contains only feedforward connections.

The PEs of the neocognitron are organized into modules that we shall refer to as levels. A single level is shown in Figure 8.3. Each level consists of two layers: a layer of simple cells, or S-cells, followed by a layer of complex cells, or C-cells. Each layer, in turn, is divided into a number of planes, each of which consists of a rectangular array of PEs. On a given level, the S-layer and the C-layer may or may not have the same number of planes. All planes on a given layer will have the same number of PEs; however, the number of PEs on the S-planes can be different from the number of PEs on the C-planes at the same level. Moreover, the number of PEs per plane can vary from level to level. There are also PEs called Vs-cells and Vc-cells that are not shown in the figure. These elements play an important role in the processing, but we can describe the functionality of the system without reference to them.

We construct a complete network by combining an input layer, which we shall call the retina, with a number of levels in a hierarchical fashion, as shown in Figure

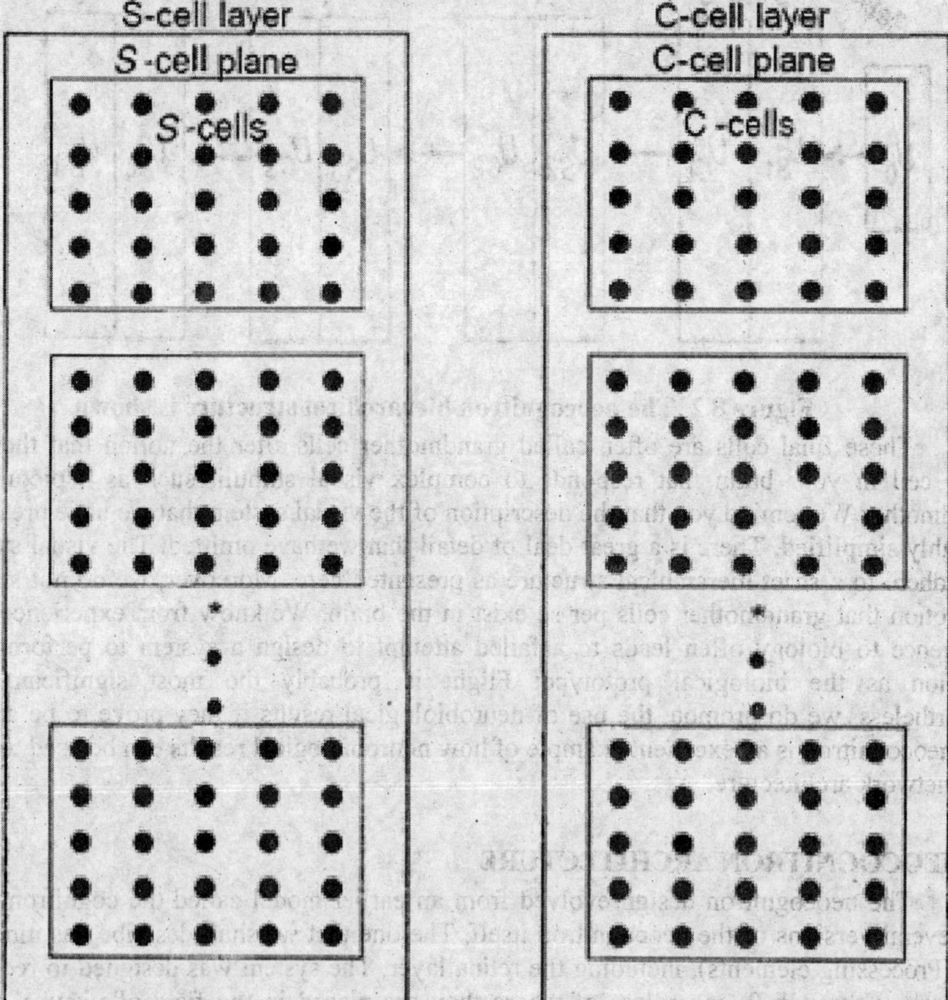

Figure 8.3 A single level of a neocognitron is shown

Each level consists of two layers, and each layer consists of a number of planes. The planes contain the PEs in a rectangular array. Data pass from the S-layer to the C-layer through connections that are not shown here. In neocognitrons having feedback, there also will be connections from the C-layer to the S-layer. That figure shows the number of planes on each layer for the particular implementation that we shall describe here. We call attention to the fact that there is nothing, in principle, that dictates a limit to the size of the network in terms of the number of levels.

The interconnection strategy is unlike that of networks that are fully interconnected between layers, such as the backpropagation network.

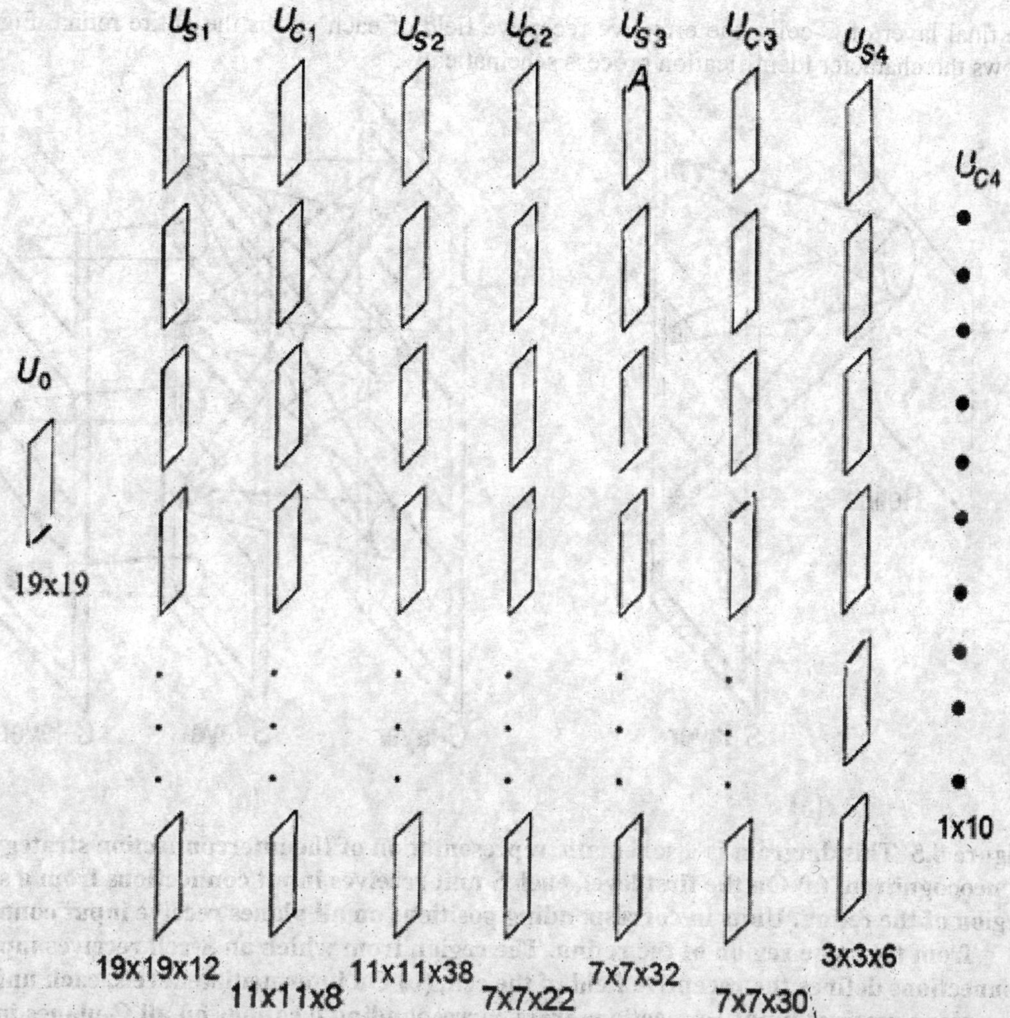

Figure 8.4 shows a schematic illustration of the way units are connected in the neocognitron

The figure 8.4 shows the basic organization of the neocognitron for the numeral-recognition problem. There are nine layers, each with a varying number of planes. The size of each layer, in terms of the number of processing elements, is given below each layer. For example, layer Uc2 has 22 planes of 7 x 7 processing elements arranged in a square matrix. The layer of C-cells on the final level is made up of 10 planes, each of which has a single element. Each element corresponds to one of the numerals from 0 to 9. The identification of the pattern appearing on the retina is made according to which C-cell on the final level has the strongest response.

As we look deeper into the network, the S-cells respond to features at higher levels of abstraction; for example, corners with intersecting lines at various angles and orientations. The C-cells integrate the responses of groups of Scells. Because each S-cell is looking for the same feature in a different location, the C-cells' response is less sensitive to the exact location of the feature on the input layer. This behavior is what gives the neocognitron its ability to identify characters regardless of their exact position in the field of the retina. By the time we have reached the final layer of C-cells, the effective receptive field of each cell is the entire retina. Figure 8.6 shows the character identification process schematically.

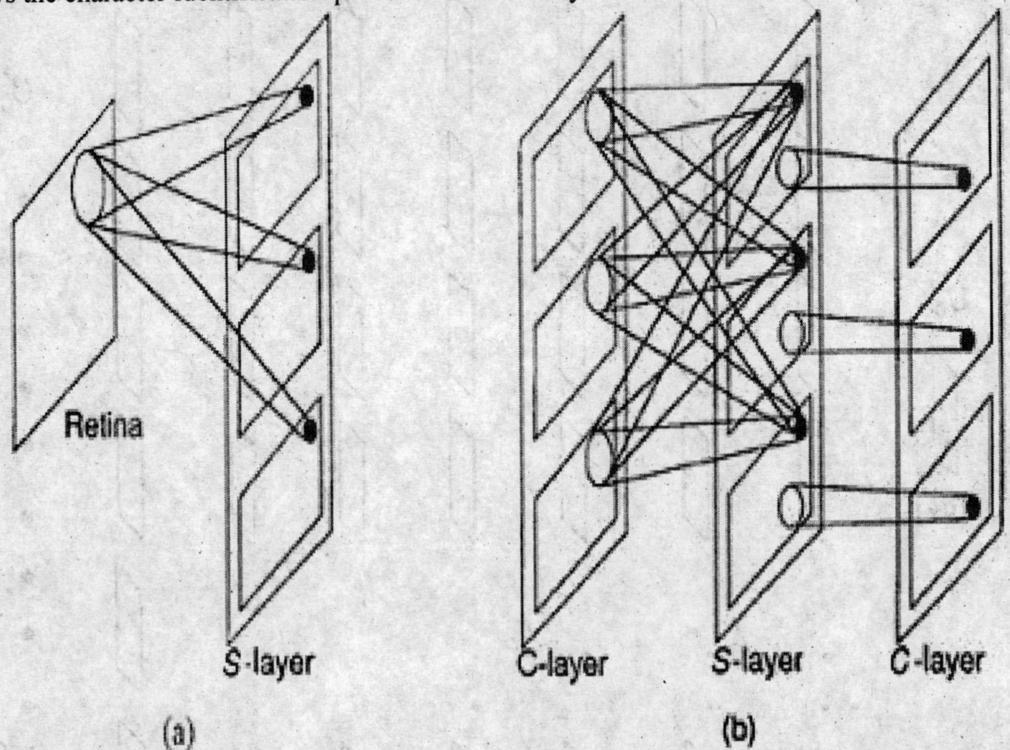

Figure 8.5 This diagram is a schematic representation of the interconnection strategy of the neocognitron. (a) On the first level, each S unit receives input connections from a small region of the retina. Units in corresponding positions on all planes receive input connections from the same region of the retina. The region from which an S-cell receives input connections defines the receptive field of the cell, (b) On intermediate levels, each unit on a s-plane receives input connections from corresponding locations on all C-planes in the previous level. C-cells have connections from a region of S-cells on the S level preceding it. If the number of C-planes is the same as that of S-planes at that level, then each C-cell has connections from S-cells on a single s-plane. If there are fewer C-planes than S-planes, some C-cells may receive connections from more than one S-plane

Each cell in a plane on the first S-layer receives inputs from a single input layer—namely, the retina. On subsequent layers, each S-cell plane receives inputs from each of the C cell planes immediately preceding it. The situation is slightly different for the C-cell planes. Typically, each cell on a C-cell plane examines a small region of S-cells on a single S-cell plane. For example, the first C-cell plane on layer 2 would have connections to only a region of S-cells on the first S-cell plane of the previous layer. Reference back to Figure D reveals that there is not necessarily a one-to-one correspondence between C-cell planes and S-cell planes at each layer in the system. This discrepancy occurs because the system designers found it advantageous to combine the inputs from some S-planes to a single C-plane if the features that the S-planes were detecting were similar. This tuning process is evident in several areas of the network architecture and processing equations.

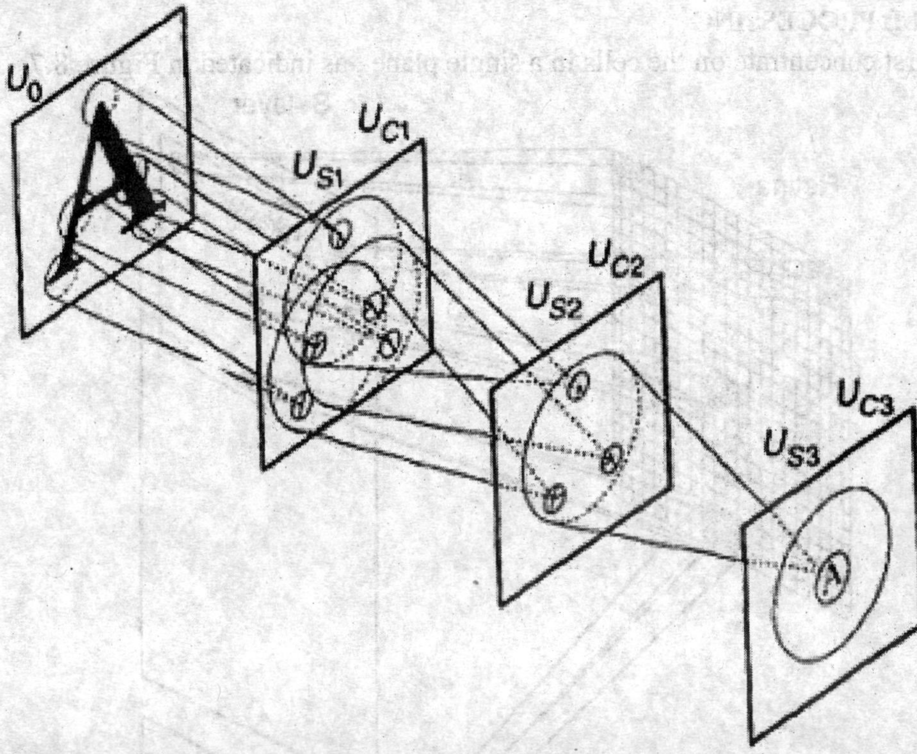

Figure 8.6 This figure illustrates how the neocognitron performs its character-recognition function

The neocognitron decomposes the input pattern into elemental parts consisting of line segments at various angles of rotation. The system then integrates these elements into higher-order structures at each successive level in the network. Cells in each level integrate the responses of cells in the previous level over a finite area. This behavior gives the neocognitron its ability to identify characters regardless of their exact position or size in the field of view of the retina. The weights on connections to S-cells are determined by a training process. Unlike in many other network architectures (such as backpropagation), where each unit has a different weight vector, all S-cells on a single plane share the same weight vector. Sharing weights in this manner means that all S-cells on a given plane respond to the identical feature in their receptive fields, as we indicated. Moreover, we need to train only one S-cell on each plane, then to distribute the resulting weights to the other cells. The weights on connections to C-cells are not modifiable in the sense that they are not determined by a training process. All C-cell weights are usually determined by being tailored to the specific network architecture. As with Splanes, all cells on a single C-plane share the same weights. Moreover, in some implementations, all C-planes on a given layer share the same weights.

8.3 NEOCOGNITRON DATA PROCESSING

In this section we shall discuss the various processing algorithms of the neocognitron cells. First we shall look at the S-cell data processing including the method used to train the network. Then, we shall describe processing on the C-layer.

8.3.1 S-CELL PROCESSING

We shall first concentrate on the cells in a single plane , as indicated in Figure 8.7

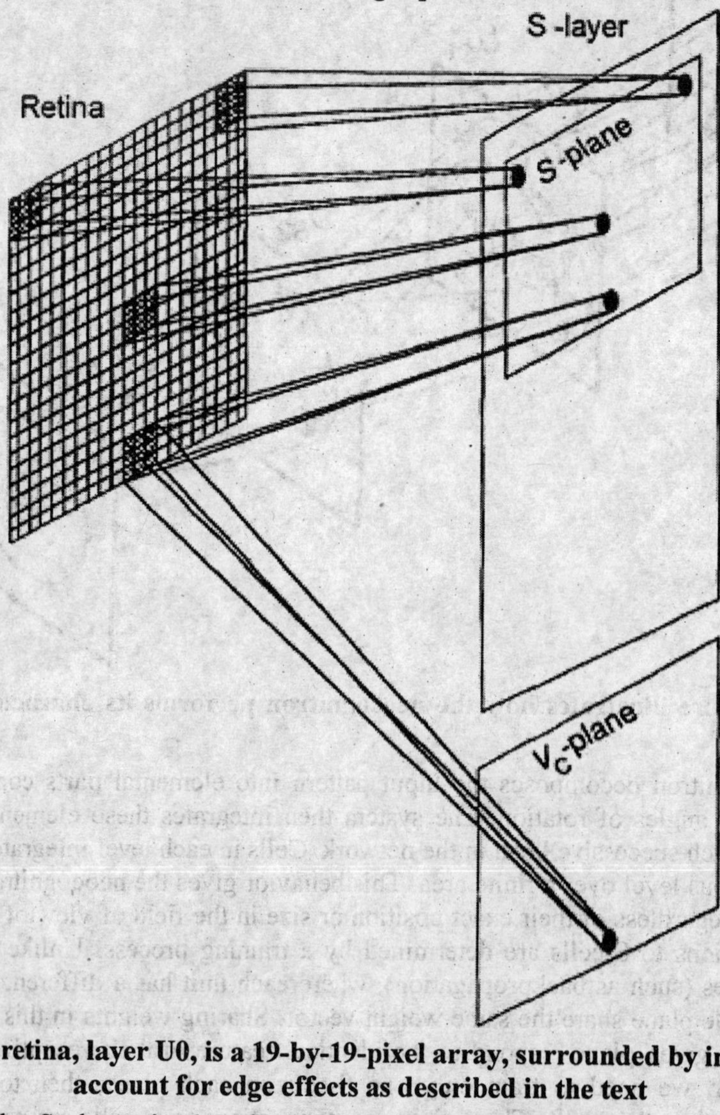

Figure 8.7 The retina, layer U0, is a 19-by-19-pixel array, surrounded by inactive pixels to account for edge effects as described in the text

One of the S-planes is shown, along with an indication of the regions of the retina scanned by the individual cells. Associated with each S-layer in the system is a plane of vrcells. These cells receive input connections from the same receptive field as do the S-cells in corresponding locations in the plane. The processing done by these Vc-cells is described in the text.

We shall assume that the retina, layer Uo, is an array of 19 by 19 pixels. Therefore, each Usi plane will have an array of 19 by 19 cells. Each plane scans the entire retina for a particular feature. As indicated in the figure, each cell on a plane is looking for the identical feature but in a different location on the retina. Each S-cell receives input connections from an array of 3 by 3 pixels on the retina. The receptive field of each S-cell corresponds to the 3 by 3 array centered on the pixel that corresponds to the cell's location on the plane. When building or simulating this network, we must make allowances for edge effects. If we surround the active retina with inactive pixels (outputs always set to zero), then we can automatically account for cells whose fields of view are centered on edge pixels. Neighboring S-cells scan the retina array displaced by one pixel from each otlier. In this manner, the entire image is scanned from left to right and top to bottom by the cells in each Splane.

A single plane of Vc-cells is associated with the S-layer, as indicated in Figure 8.7 . The Vc-plane contains the same number of cells as does each Splane. Vc-cells have the same receptive fields as the S-cells in corresponding locations in the plane. The output of a Vc-cell goes to a single S-cell in every plane in the layer. The S-cells that receive inputs from a particular Vc-cell are those that occupy a position in the plane corresponding to the position of the Vc-cell. The output of the Vc-cell has an inhibitory effect on the S-cells. Figure8.8 shows the details of a single S-cell along with its corresponding inhibitory cell.

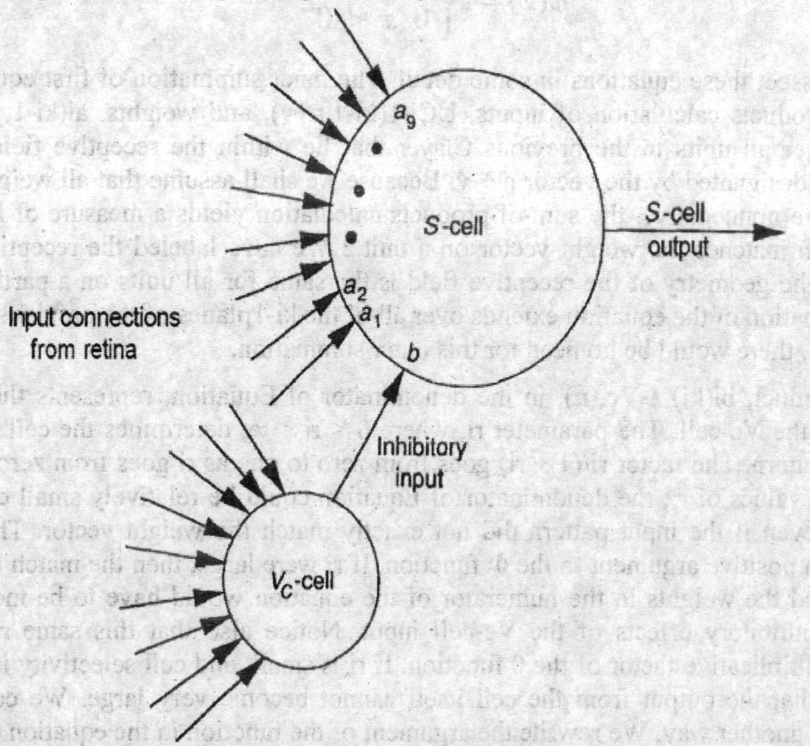

Figure 8.8 A Single 5-Cell And Corresponding Inhibitory Cell On The Us\ Layer Are Shown

Each unit receives the identical nine inputs from the retina layer. The weights, a,, on the S-cells determine the feature for which the cell is sensitive. Both the a, weights on connections from the retina, and the weight, b, from the Vr-cells are modifiable and are determined during a training process, as described in the text. Up to now, we have been discussing the first S-layer, in which cells receive input connections from a single plane (in this case the retina) in the previous layer. For what follows, we shall generalize our discussion to include the case of layers deeper in the network where an S-cell will receive input connections from all the planes on the previous C-layer. Let the index k refer to the kth plane on level: 1. We can label each cell on a plane with a two-dimensional vector, with n indicating its position on the plane; then, we let the vector v refer to the relative position of a cell in the previous layer lying in the receptive field of unit n. With these definitions, we can write the following equation for the output of any 5-cell:

$$U_{S_l}(k_l, \mathbf{n}) =$$

$$r_l \cdot \phi\left[\frac{1+\sum_{k_{l-1}=1}^{K_{l-1}}\sum_{\mathbf{v}\in A_l} a_l(k_{l-1},\mathbf{v},k_l)\cdot U_{C_{l-1}}(k_{l-1},\mathbf{n}+\mathbf{v})}{1+\frac{r_l}{1+r_l}b_l(k_l)\cdot V_{C_l}(\mathbf{n})}-1\right]$$

where the function Φ is a linear threshold function given by

$$\phi(x) = \begin{cases} x & x \geq 0 \\ 0 & x < 0 \end{cases}$$

Let's dissect these equations in some detail. The inner summation of first equation is the usual sum-of-products calculation of inputs, UCi-1(ki-1,n+v), and weights, ai(ki-1, v. ki). The sum extends over all units in the previous Clayer that lie within the receptive field of unit n. Those units are designated by the vector n + v. Because we shall assume that all weights and cell output values are nonnegative, the sum-of-products calculation yields a measure of how closely the input pattern matches the weight vector on a unit.2 We have labeled the receptive field Ai, indicating that the geometry of the receptive field is the same for all units on a particular layer. The outer summation of the equation extends over all of the ki-1planes of the previous C-layer. In the case of Us1 , there would be no need for this outer summation.

The product, bi(ki) • Vc,(n), in the denominator of Equation, represents the inhibitory contribution of the Vc-cell. The parameter ri, where 0 < ri < ∞, determines the cell's selectivity for a specific pattern. The factor ri/(1 + ri) goes from zero to one as ri goes from zero to infinity. Thus, for small values of r;, the denominator of Equation could be relatively small compared to the numerator even if the input pattern did not exactly match the weight vector. This situation could result in a positive argument to the Φ function. If ri were large, then the match between the input pattern and the weights in the numerator of the equation would have to be more exact to overcome the inhibitory effects of the Vc-cell input. Notice also that this same ri parameter appears as a multiplicative factor of the 0 function. If ri is small, and cell selectivity is small, this factor ensures that the output from the cell itself cannot become very large. We can view the function of r; in another way. We rewrite the argument of the function in the equation as

$$\frac{e-[r_l/(1+r_l)]h}{1+[r_l/(1+r_l)]h}$$

where e is the net excitatory term and h is the net inhibitory term. According to function

$$\phi(x) = \begin{cases} x & x \geq 0 \\ 0 & x < 0 \end{cases}$$

the S-cell output will be nonzero only if

$$e - \frac{r_l}{1 + r_l}h > 0$$

Or

$$\frac{e}{h} > \frac{r_l}{1 + r_l}$$

Thus, the quantity ri determines the minimum relative strength of excitation versus inhibition that will result in a nonzero output of the unit. As r; increases, ri/(l + ri) → 1. Therefore, a larger ri requires a larger excitation relative to inhibition for a nonzero output.

Notice that neither of the weight expressions, ai(ki-1,v,ki), or bi(ki) depend explicitly on the position, n, of the cell. Remember that all cells on a plane share the same weights, even the bi(ki) weights, which we did not discuss previously.

We must now specify the output from the inhibitory nodes. The Vc-cell at position n has an output value of

$$V_{C_l}(\mathbf{n}) = \sqrt{\sum_{k_{l-1}=1}^{K_{l-1}} \sum_{\mathbf{v} \in A_l} c_l(\mathbf{v}) \cdot U_{C_{l-1}}^2(k_{l-1}, \mathbf{n} + \mathbf{v})}$$

where ci(v) is the weight on the connection from a cell at position v of the Vc -cell's receptive field. These weights are not subject to training. They can take the form of any normalized function that decreases monotonically as the magnitude of v increases.

8.3.2 TRAINING WEIGHTS ON THE S-LAYERS

In principle, training proceeds as it does for many networks. First, an input pattern is presented at the input layer and the data are propagated through the network. Then, weights are allowed to make incremental adjustments according to the specified algorithm. After weight updates have occurred, a new pattern is presented at the input layer, and the process is repeated with all patterns in the training set until the network is classifying the input patterns properly.In the neocognitron, sharing of weights on a given plane means that only a single cell on each plane needs to participate in the learning process. Once its weights have been updated, a copy of the new weight vector can be distributed to the other cells on the same plane. To understand how this works, we can think of the 5-planes on a given layer as being stacked vertically on top of one another, aligned so that cells at corresponding locations are directly on top of one another. We can now imagine many overlapping columns running perpendicular to this stack. These columns define groups of S-cells, where all of the members in a group have receptive fields in approximately the same location of the input layer.

8.3.2.1 UNSUPERVISED TRAINING

With this model in mind, we now apply an input pattern and examine the response of the S'-cells in each column. To ensure that each 5-cell provides a distinct response, we can initialize the a; weights to small, positive random values. The bi weights on the inhibitory connections can be initialized to zero. We first note the plane and position of the S-cell whose response is the strongest in each column. Then we examine the individual planes so that, if one plane contains two or more of these S-cells, we disregard all but the cell responding the strongest. In this manner, we will locate the S-cell on each plane whose response is the strongest, subject to the condition that each of those cells is in a different column. Those S-cells become the prototypes, or representatives, of all the cells on their respective planes. Likewise, the strongest responding Vf-cell is chosen as the representative for the other cells on the Vc-plane. Once the representatives are chosen, weight updates are made according to the following equations:

$$\Delta a_l(k_{l-1}, \mathbf{v}, \hat{k}_l) = q_l c_{l-1}(\mathbf{v}) U_{C_{l-1}}(k_{l-1}, \hat{\mathbf{n}} + \mathbf{v})$$

$$\Delta b_l(\hat{k}_l) = q_l V_{C_{l-1}}(\hat{\mathbf{n}})$$

where qi is the learning rate parameter, ci-1(v), is the monotonically decreasing function as described in the previous section, and the location of the representative for plane ki is A. Notice that the largest increases in the weights occur on those connections that have the largest input signal, Uci-1(ki-1, n + v). Because the 5-cell whose weights are being modified was the one with the largest output, this learning algorithm implements a form of Hebbian learning.

Notice also that weights can only increase, and that there is no upper bound on the weight value. Once the cells on a given plane begin to respond to a certain feature, they tend to respond less to other features. I\fter a short time, each plane will have developed a strong response to a particular feature. Moreover, as we look deeper into the network, planes will be responding to more complex features.

8.4. EXAMPLE - ABILITIES OF THE NEOCOGNITRON

On this simple example we will demonstrate abilities of the neocognitron at recognition of presented patterns. The black-box in this example contains neocognitron network which can distinguish between two different types of patterns (between digit zero and digit one). For the learning of the network we have used patterns shown in figure 8.9.

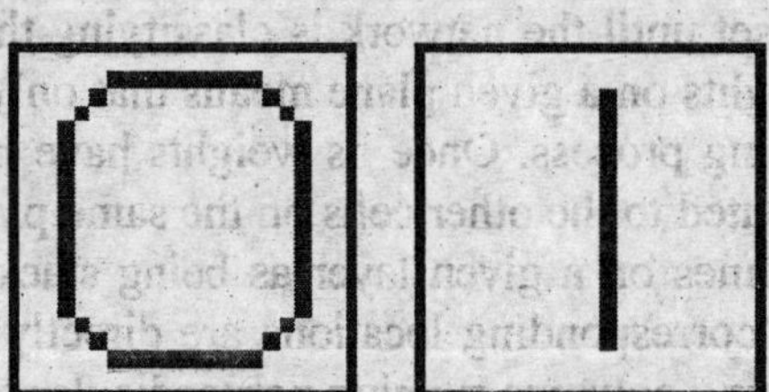

Figure 8.9 Patterns 0 And 1 Used For Learning

By the learning of the neocognitron to distinguish between these two types of patterns we have created two different categories in the network. In the future the network will respond on every presented pattern with a pair of values. Each of these values is a measure of belonging of presented pattern into one of two created categories. Click on one of the prepared patterns. The network processes it and assigns it to one of the categories. Notice, that the network assigns patterns which have not been presented during learning to the correct category, too. These patterns were produced by distortion of patterns used for learning, shown in figure 8.9.

8.4.1. BASIC PRINCIPLE OF THE NEOCOGNITRON

Hierarchical feature extraction is the basic principle of the neocognitron. For easier understanding of this principle we will explain terms feature and feature extraction firstly.

Hierarchical feature extraction consists in distribution of extracted features to several stages. The simplest features (usually only rotated lines) are extracted in the first stage and in each of the following stages the more complex features are extracted. In this process it is important fact that only informations obtained in the previous stage are used for feature extraction in the certain stage. Hierarchy of features which we can use for recognition of digit zero in the neocognitron is illustrated schematically in figure 8.10. Joining between features in adjoining stages represents what features from previous layer are used during extraction of the certain feature.

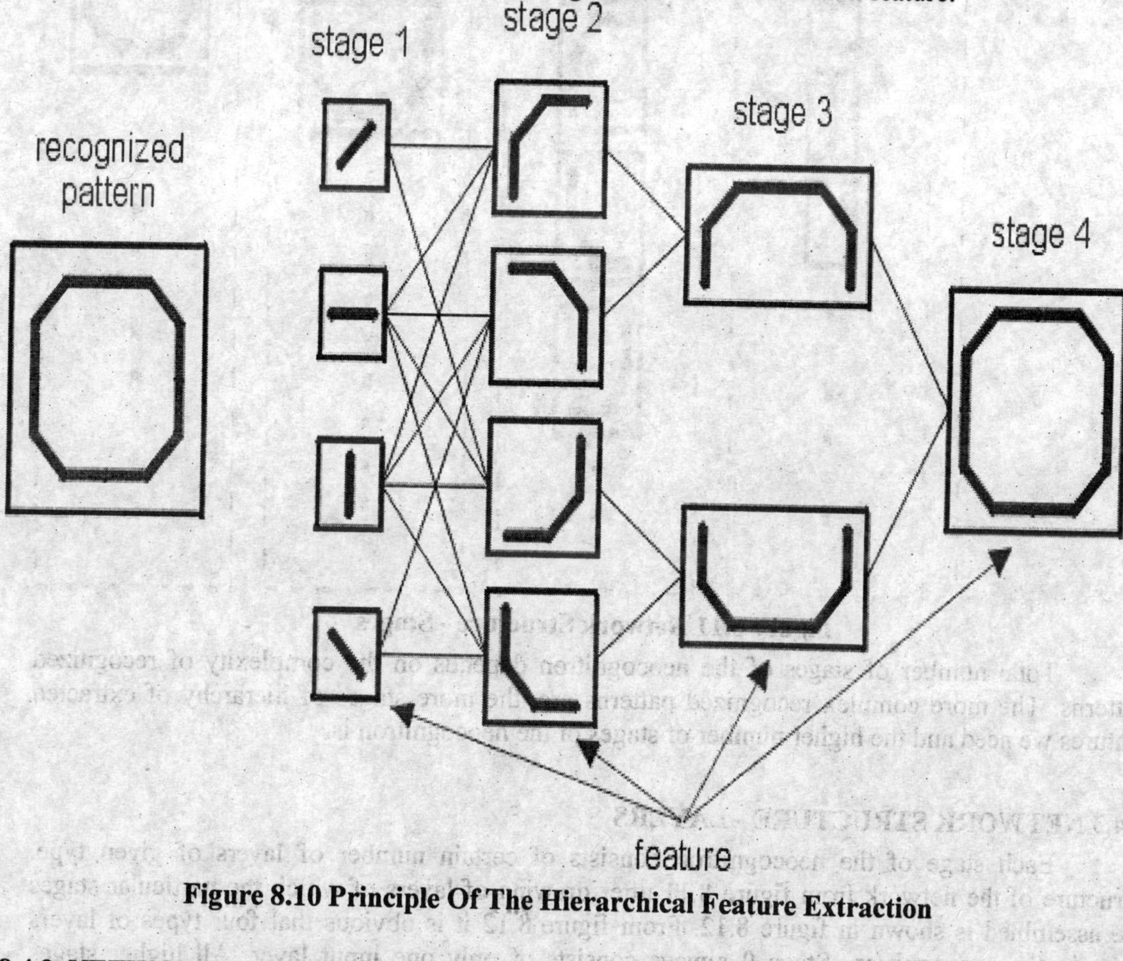

Figure 8.10 Principle Of The Hierarchical Feature Extraction

8.4.2. NETWORK STRUCTURE - STAGES

Structure of the neocognitron arises from a hierarchy of extracted features. One appropriate stage of the neocognitron is created for each stage of the hierarchy of extracted features. The network however contains one additional stage, labeled as stage 0, which is not used, in contrast to higher stages, for feature extraction.

All the stages of the neocognitron and a part of features extracted by them, which corresponds to hierarchy in figure 8.10, are shown in figure 8.11.

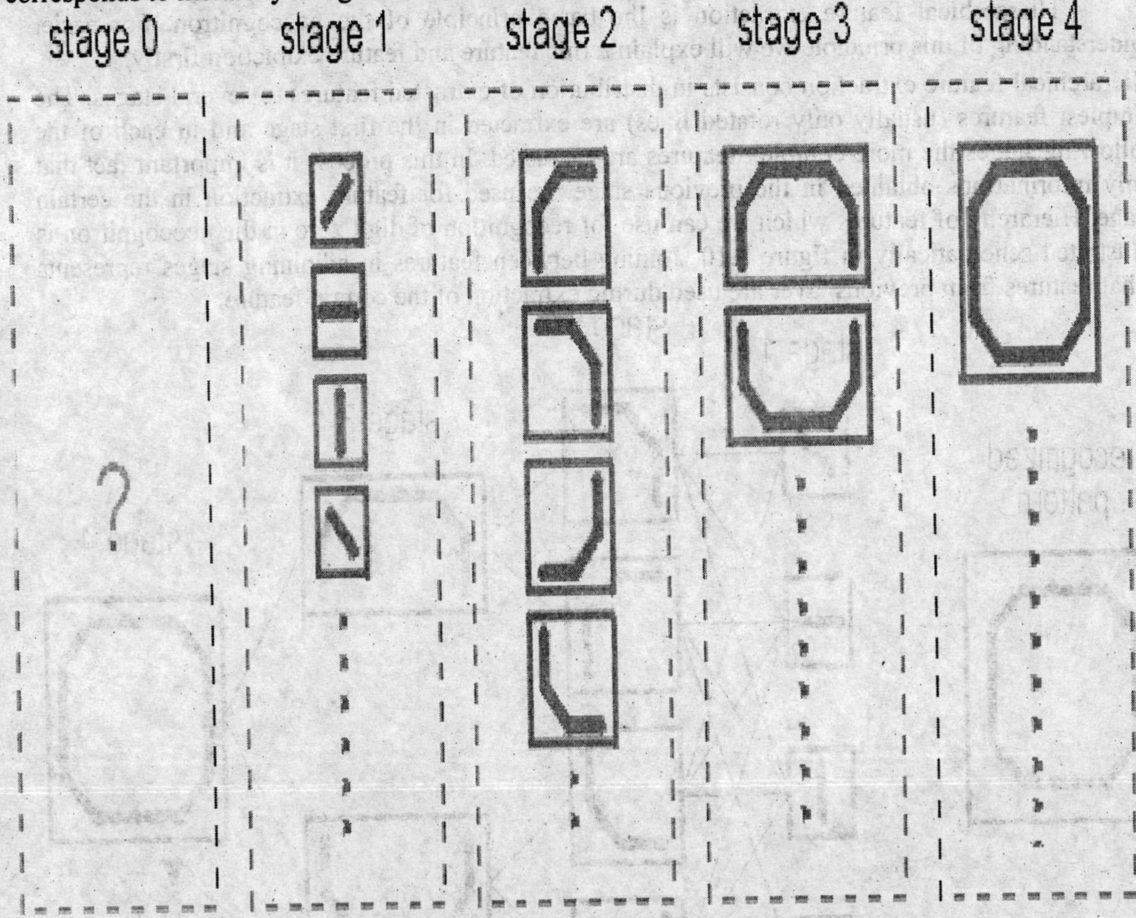

Figure 8.11 Network Structure - Stages

Total number of stages of the neocognitron depends on the complexity of recognized patterns. The more complex recognized patterns are, the more stages of hierarchy of extracted features we need and the higher number of stages of the neocognitron is.

8.4.3 NETWORK STRUCTURE - LAYERS

Each stage of the neocognitron consists of certain number of layers of given type. Structure of the network from figure 8.11 after drawing of layers of which the particular stages are assembled is shown in figure 8.12. From figure 8.12 it is obvious that four types of layers exist in the neocognitron. Stage 0 always consists of only one input layer. All higher stages consist of one S-layer, one V-layer and one C-layer. In figure 8.12 we have also established ordinarily used notation of layers in the neocognitron. We will use this notation, described in table 1, in the following text as well.

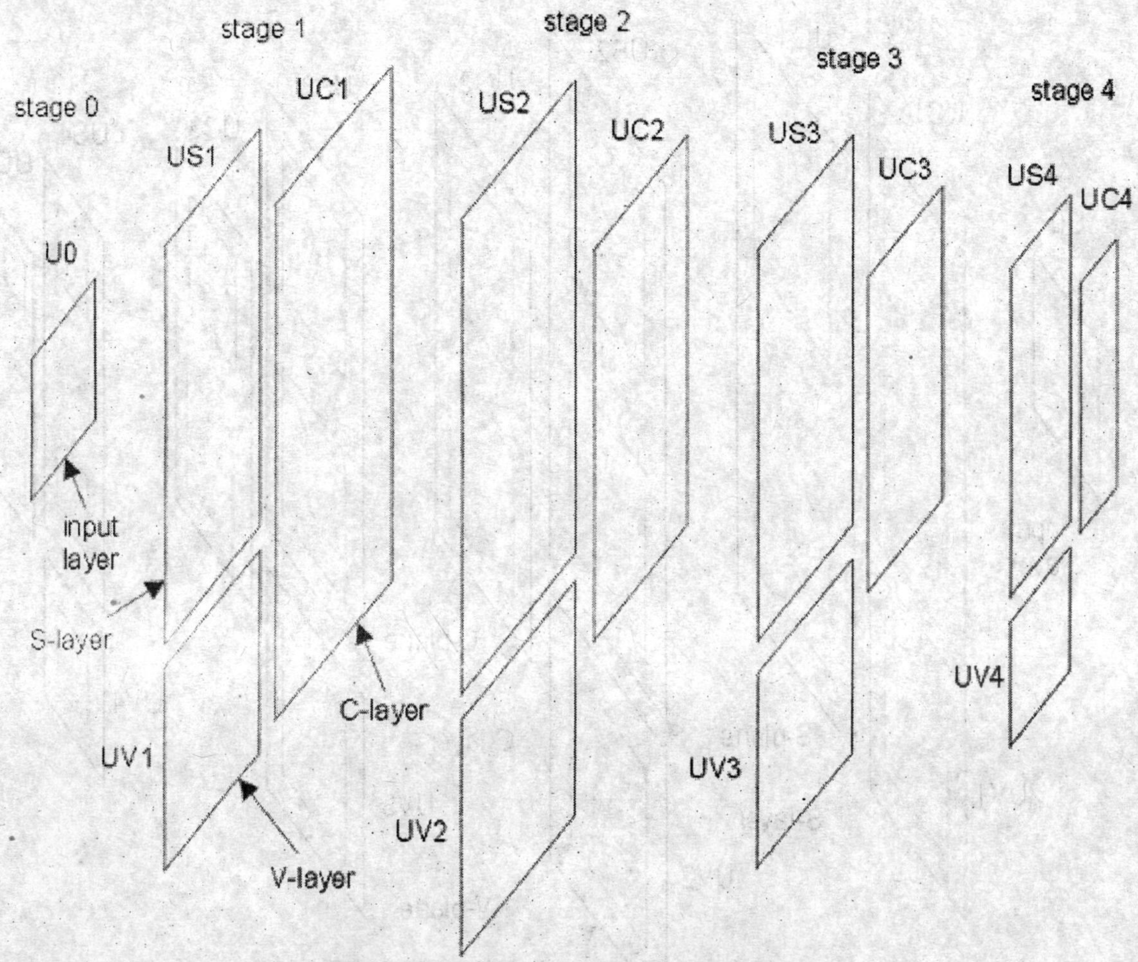

Figure 8.12 Network Structure - Layers

Symbol	Denotes
U0	input layer
USl	S-layer in the l-th stage of the network
UVl	V-layer in the l-th stage of the network
UCl	C-layer in the l-th stage of the network

Tab.1 - Notation Used For Layers In The Neocognitron

8.4.4. NETWORK STRUCTURE - CELL PLANES

Each layer in the neocognitron consists of certain number of cell planes of the same type. Input layer is exception from this rule. For the input layer the term cell plane is not established. Number of cell planes in each S-layer and C-layer depends on the number of features extracted in corresponding stage of the network. Each V-layer always consists of only one cell plane. Structure of the network from figure 8.12 after drawing of cell planes from which the particular layers are assembled is shown in figure 8.13. From figure 8.13 it is obvious that three types of cell planes exist in the neocognitron - S-planes, V-planes and C-planes.

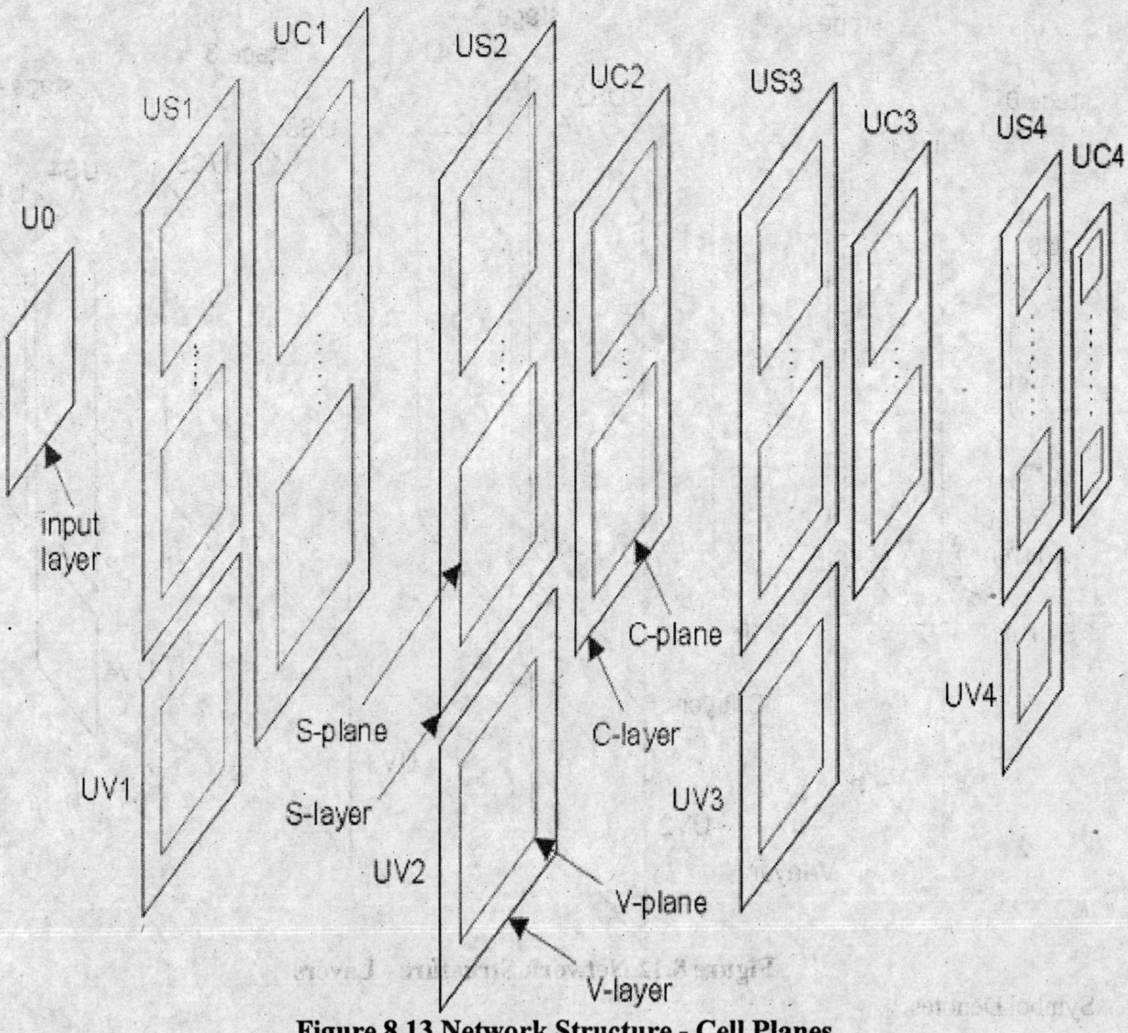

Figure 8.13 Network Structure - Cell Planes

8.4.5. NETWORK STRUCTURE - CELLS

Now we have come to the ground of the neocognitron which is cell. The neocognitron is made of large amount of cells of several distinct types which are organized in cell planes, layers and stages. All the cells, regardless of their type, process and generate analog values. From figure 8.14 it is obvious that each S-plane, V-plane, C-plane and input layer consists of array of cells of the certain type. Size of cell arrays is the same for all cell planes in one layer and it decreases with increasing of the network stage. Each C-plane in the highest stage of the network contains only one cell. Its output value indicates a measure of belonging of presented pattern into the category represented by this cell. Size of cell array in each V-plane is the same as size of cell arrays in S-planes in the same stage of the network.

From figure 8.14 it is obvious that four types of cells exist in the neocognitron - receptor cells, S-cells, V-cells and C-cells.

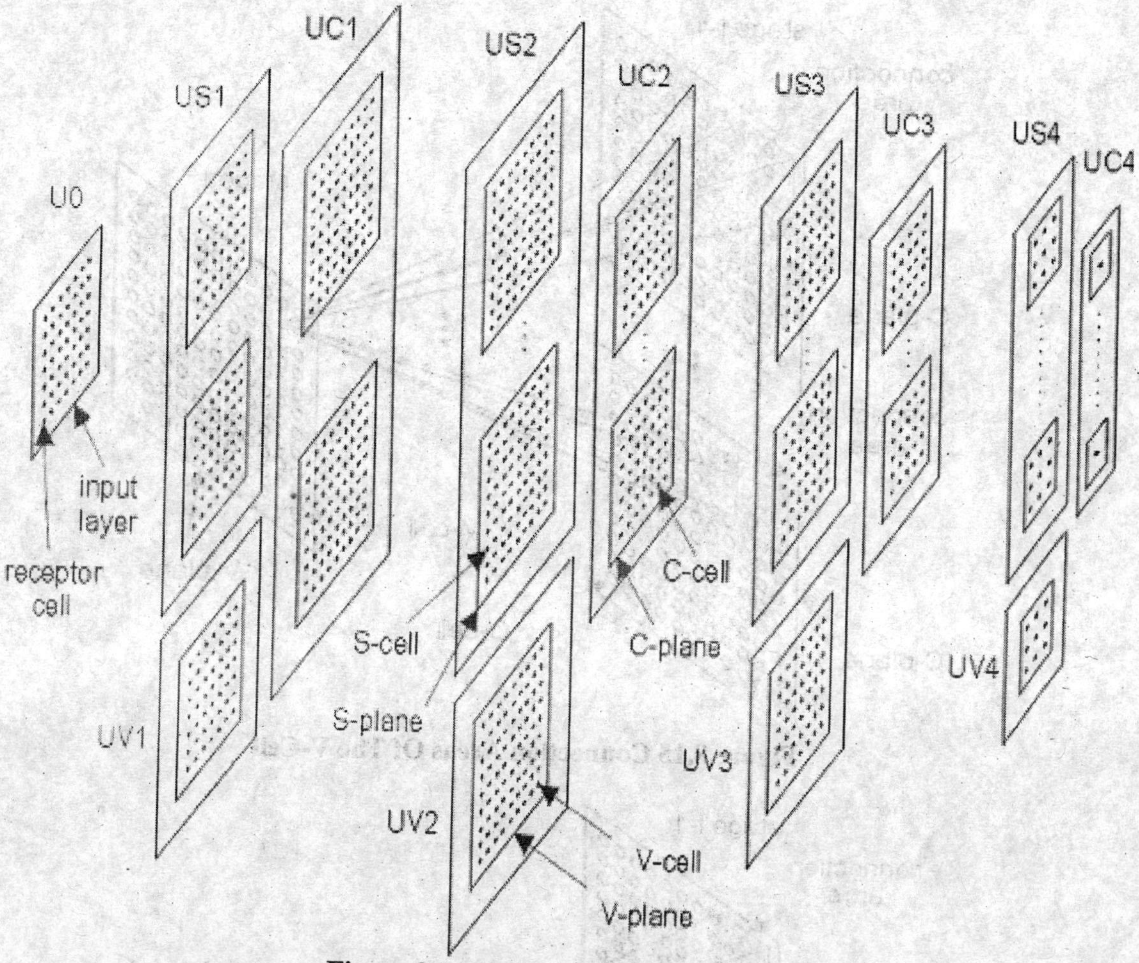

Figure 8.14 Network Structure - Cells

8.4.6. V-CELL FUNCTION

Each V-cell in the neocognitron evaluates outputs of C-cells (or receptor cells) from the certain connection areas from previous C-layer (or input layer). Size of connection areas is the same for all V-cells and S-cells in one stage of the network and it is determined at construction of the network. One V-cell connection areas of size 3 by 3 cells are shown in figure 8.15.

V-cell output value represents average activity of cells from connection areas and it is used for inhibition of corresponding S-cell activity. Exact specification of V-cell function is described in mathematical description of its behaviour.

8.4.7. S-CELL FUNCTION

Each S-cell in the neocognitron evaluates outputs of C-cells (or receptor cells) from the certain connection areas from previous C-layer (or input layer). Size of connection areas is the same for all S-cells in one S-layer and it is determined at construction of the network. One S-cell connection areas of size 3 by 3 cells are shown in figure 8.16.

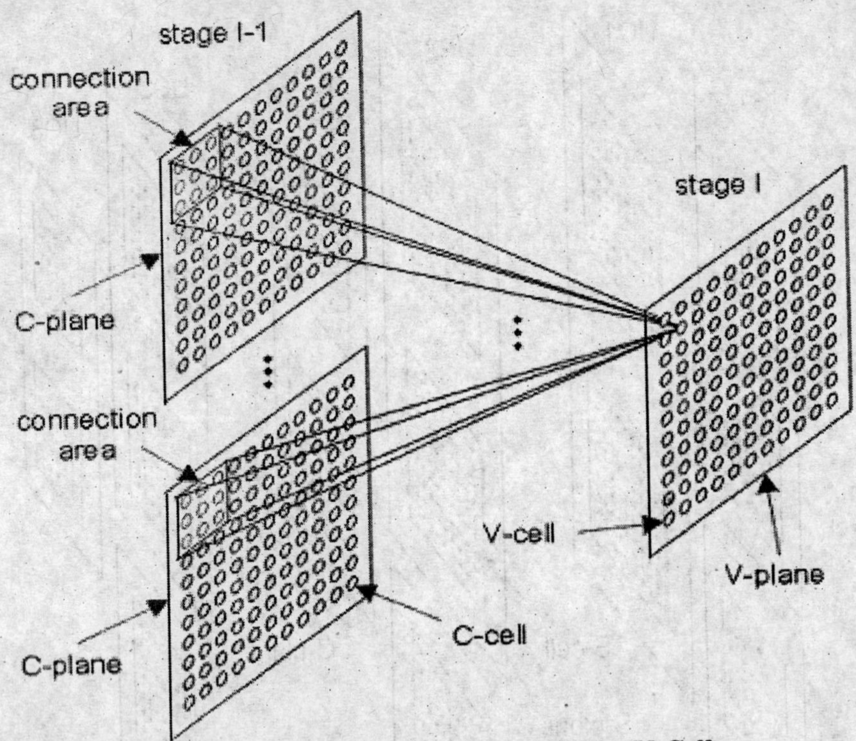

Figure 8.15 Connection Areas Of The V-Cell

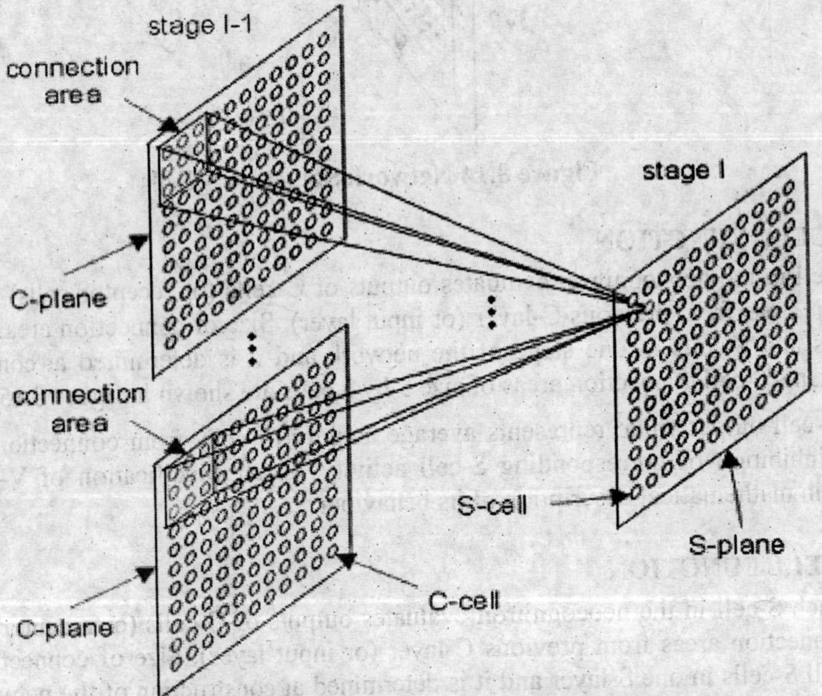

Figure 8.16 Connection Areas Of The S-Cell

Function of each S-cell is to extract the certain feature at the certain position in the input layer (i.e. in its receptive field). For extraction of this feature an S-cell uses only informations obtained from its connection areas and information about average activity in these areas obtained from corresponding V-cell. All S-cells in one S-plane always extract the same feature.

The feature extracted by S-cell is determined by weights for this cell. Weights and method for their adjusting will be described later in detail. For a better conception about function of weights we can compare them to a mask which is used at determination about feature presence for now. The meaning of weights is obvious best for cells from layer US1.

Each S-cell in this layer has only one connection area and this area is S-cell's receptive field at the same time. So weights (mask if you want) contain directly representation of the certain feature. In higher S-layers correspondency between extracted feature and its representation by the weights is already not so obvious. Cell plane of S-cells designated for extraction of feature corresponding to vertical line is shown in figure 8.17.

S-cell is activated only if this feature is present in S-cell's receptive field (it is identical with connection area here). When incorrect feature is presented the cell becomes inactive.

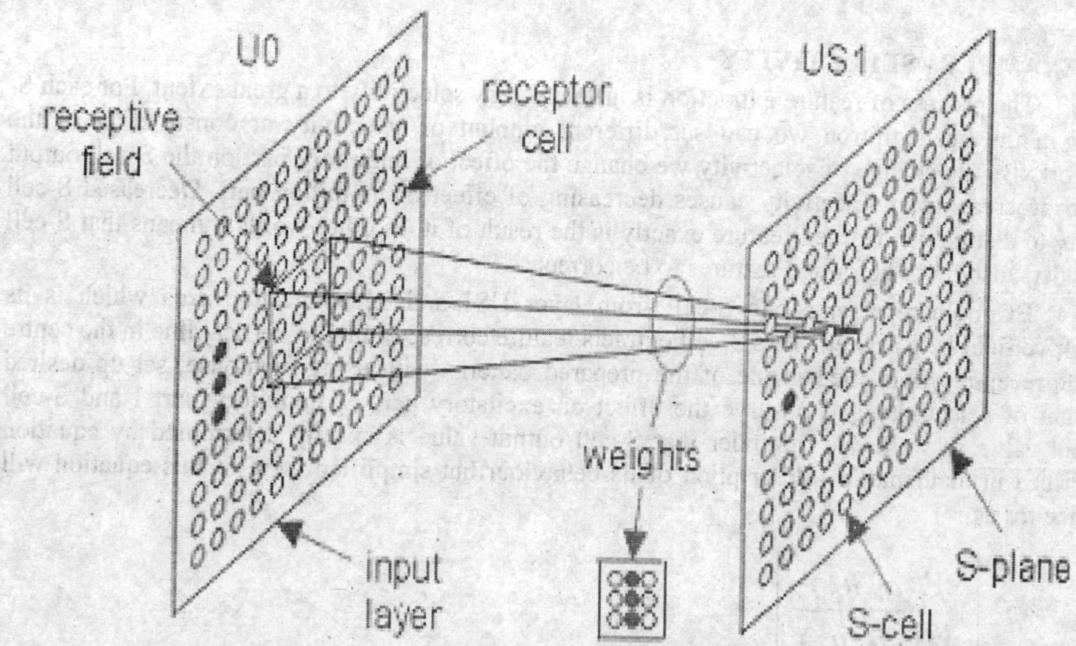

Figure 8.17 S-Cell Function

S-cell output value is determined exactly by the equation described in mathematical description. However, for understanding of S-cell function simplified equation is sufficient :

$$u_S = \varphi^* \left[\frac{\mathrm{E}(a,\ u_C)}{\mathrm{I}(r,\ b,\ u_V)} \right]$$

The symbols used in this equation have the following meaning : Symbol Denotes

us S-cell output value

φ^* non-linear function

E excitatory part

a a-weights

uc output values of C-cells from connection areas

I inhibitory part

r selectivity

b b-weight

uv V-cell output value

The S-cells ability to extract not only learned features but also deformed representations of these features is influenced by the choice of parameter denoted as selectivity to a great extent. On the following example we will demonstrate how selectivity affects the process of feature extraction in the neocognitron.

8.5. EXAMPLE - SELECTIVITY

The process of feature extraction is influenced by selectivity to a great extent. For each S-layer in the neocognitron we can set different amount of selectivity at construction of the network. By the change of selectivity we change the effect of inhibitory part on the S-cell output value. Decreasing of selectivity causes decreasing of effect of inhibition part. Decreased S-cell ability to distinguish learned feature exactly is the result of it. In other words it means that S-cell considers also more deformed features to be correct.

Example represents one S-cell from layer US1 and its connection area which is its receptive field here as well. This S-cell extracts feature corresponding to vertical line in the centre of the receptive field. Select one of the prepared patterns with using of mouse, set up desired amount of selectivity and observe the effect on excitatory part E, inhibitory part I and S-cell output value as well. We reminder that S-cell output value is exactly determined by equation described in mathematical description of its behaviour but simplified form of this equation will suffice for us :

$$u_S = \varphi^* \left[\frac{\mathrm{E}(a,\ u_C)}{\mathrm{I}(r,\ b,\ u_V)} \right]$$

8.5.1. C-CELL FUNCTION

Each C-cell in the neocognitron evaluates outputs of S-cells from the certain connection area from one of S-planes from previous S-layer. Number of S-planes, however, can be greater in some cases. Size of connection areas is the same for all C-cells in one C-layer and it is determined at construction of the network. One C-cell connection area of size 5 by 5 cells is shown in figure 8.18. C-cell output value depends on activity of S-cells from connection area. The greater number of active S-cells is or the greater their activities are the greater C-cell output value is.

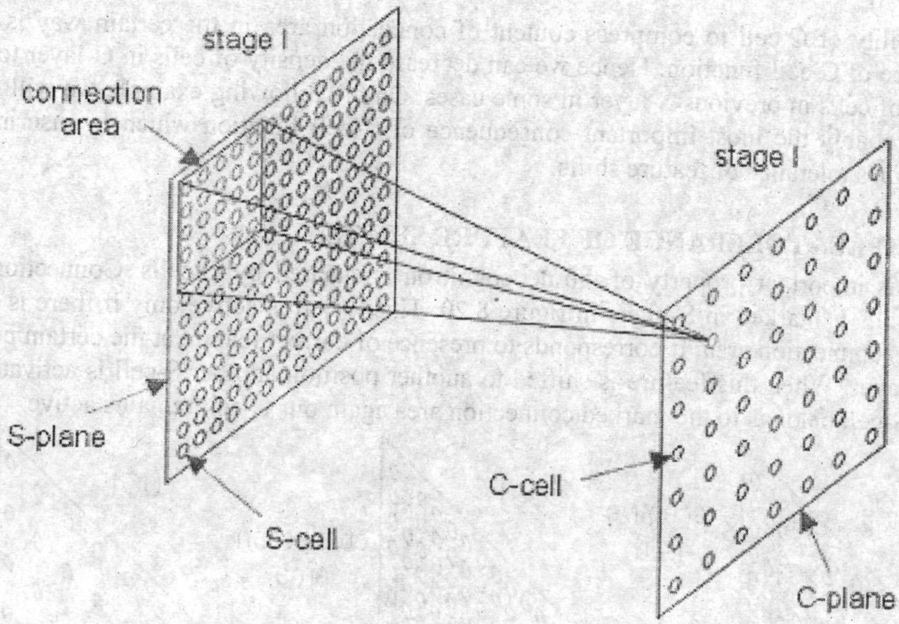

Figure 8.18 Connection Area Of The C-Cell

C-cell function is exactly described in mathematical description. For C-cell to be active it is sufficient that at least one active S-cell is present in its connection area. With regard to overlapping of neighbouring C-cell connection areas activity of one S-cell affects activity of greater number of C-cells. In consequence of that C-plane contains a blurred representation of S-plane content. This is obvious from figure 8.19 as well where one active S-cell and all C-cells influenced by it are marked.

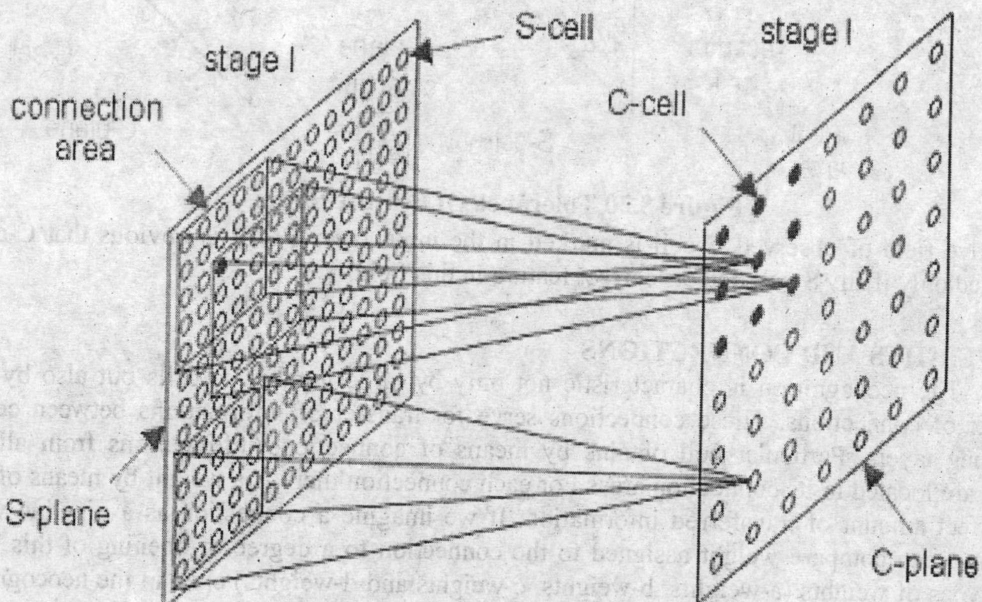

Figure 8.19 C-Cell Function

Ability of C-cell to compress content of connection area in the certain way is the next consequence of C-cell function. Hence we can decrease the density of cells in C-layer to the half of density of cells in previous S-layer in some cases. On the following example we will show the last and probably the most important consequence of C-cell function which is ensuring of the neocognitron's tolerance of feature shifts.

8.6. EXAMPLE - TOLERANCE OF FEATURE SHIFTS

This important property of the neocognitron is ensured by C-cells. Connection area of one of C-cells is marked in S-plane in figure 8.20. This C-cell is active only if there is an active S-cell in its connection area. It corresponds to presence of correct feature at the certain position in the input layer. When this feature is shifted to another position another S-cell is activated. If the activated S-cell belongs to the marked connection area again our C-cell remains active.

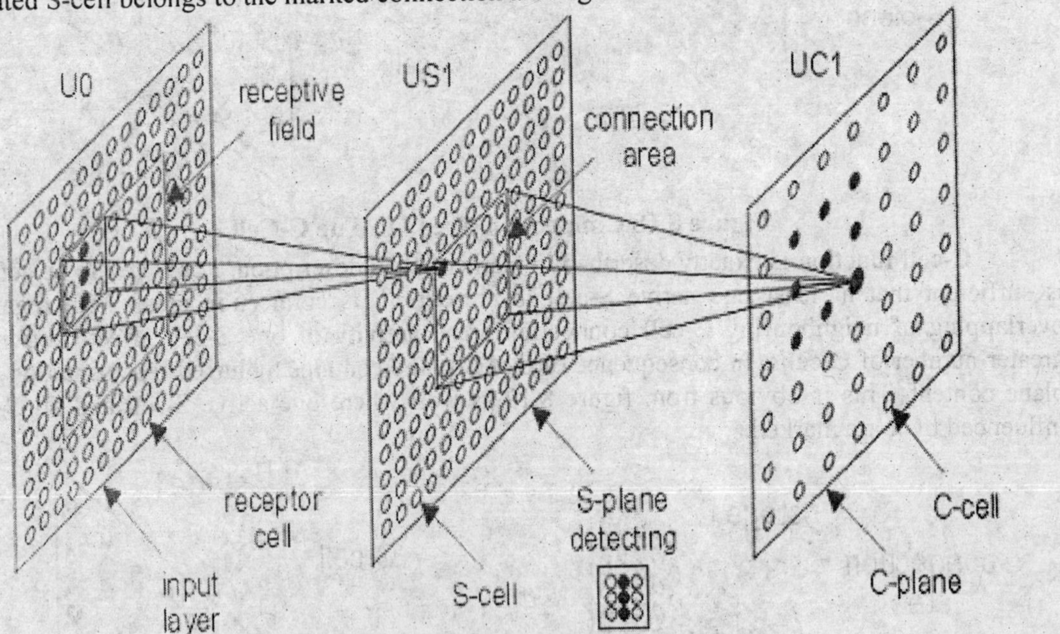

Figure 8.20 Tolerance Of Feature Shifts

Receptive field of observed C-cell is marked in the input layer U0. It is obvious that C-cell is activated only if any S-cell detects correct feature in this field.

8.7. WEIGHTS AND CONNECTIONS

The neocognitron is characteristic not only by large number of cells but also by large number of connections. These connections serve for transfer of informations between cells in adjoining layers. Particular cell obtains by means of connections informations from all cells which are located in its connection areas.For each connection there is a weight by means of it we can affect amount of transferred information. If we imagine a connection as a pipeline with a valve we can compare weight assigned to the connection to a degree of opening of this valve. Four types of weights (a-weights, b-weights, c-weights and d-weights) exist in the neocognitron. Each of these types of weights is used for connections between two layers of different types. It is shown schematically in figure 8.21.

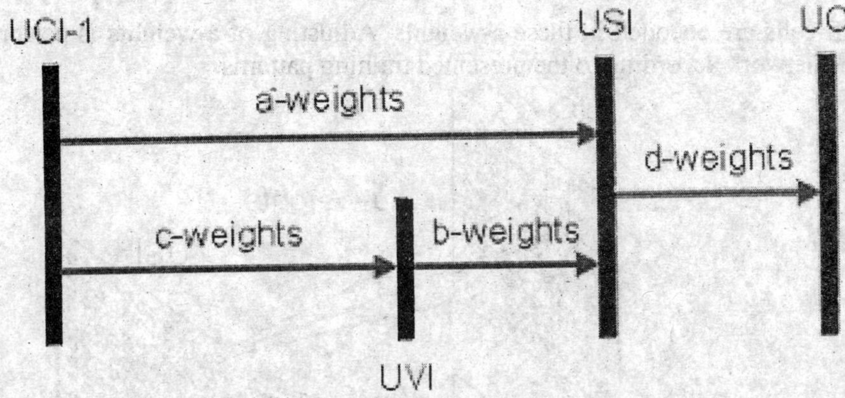

Figure 8.21 Weights In The Neocognitron

Weight sharing is the next term being connected with weights. By this term we designate the fact that all cells in one cell plane use the same weights for connections leading from cells in their connection areas. By the means of weight sharing it is guaranteed that all cells from one cell plane always extract the same feature.

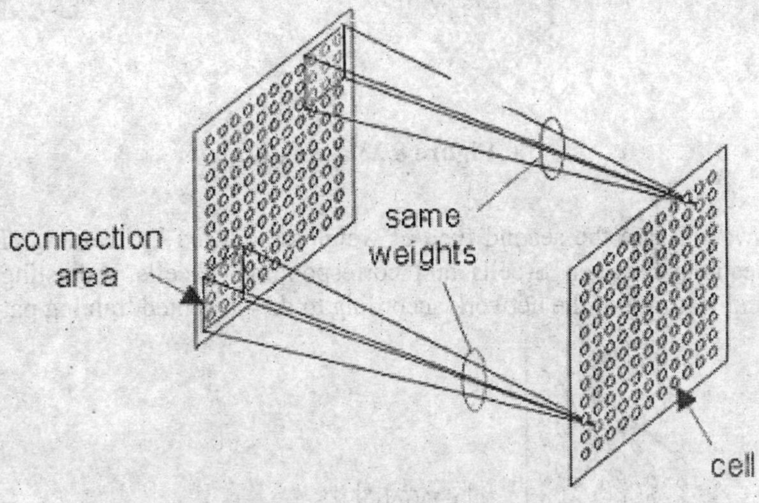

Figure 8.22 Weight Sharing

We can split the weights shown in figure 8.21 according to the way which they are adjusted :

weights modified by learning

1. a-weights
2. b-weights

Fixed Weights

3. c-weights
4. d-weights

1. a-weights

The a-weights are the first type of weights modified by learning. These weights are used for connections between S-cells and C-cells which belong to their connection areas. Features extracted by S-cells are encoded in these a-weights. Adjusting of a-weights is performed during learning of the network according to the presented training patterns.

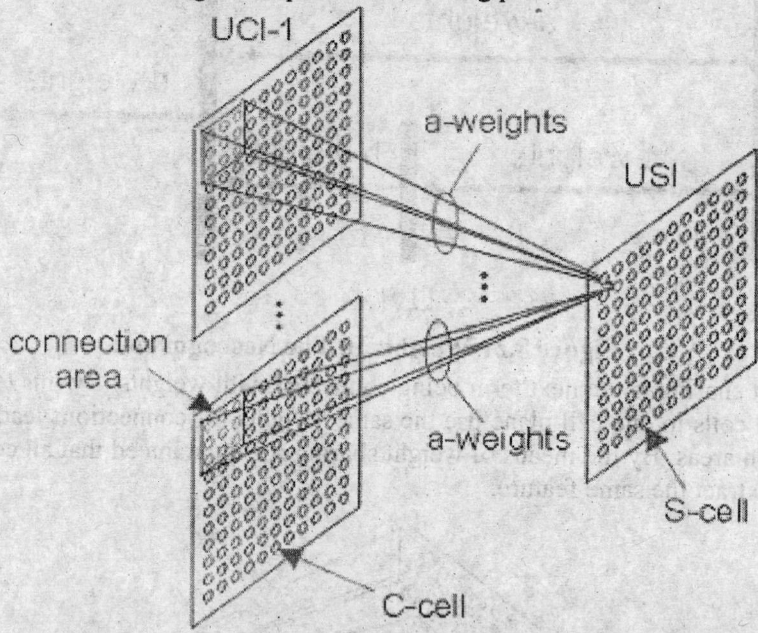

Figure 8.23 a-weights

2. b-weights

The b-weights are the second type of weights modified by learning. These weights are used for connections between S-cells and corresponding V-cells. Adjusting of b-weights is performed during learning of the network according to the presented training patterns as well.

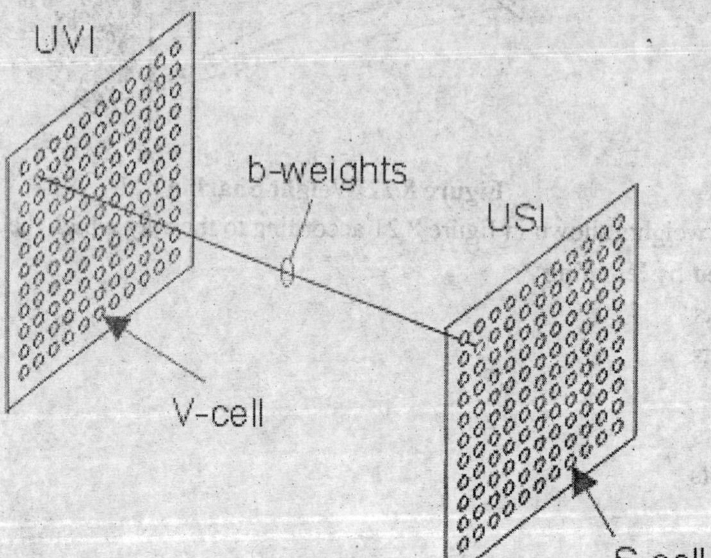

Figure 8.24 b-weights

3. c-weights

Fixed c-weights are used for connections between V-cells and C-cells which belong to their connection areas. Values of c-weights are determined at construction of the network. These weights are most often set up in such a way that they mostly reduce transfer of information from the periphery of connection area and towards to the center of area the degree of reduction decreases.

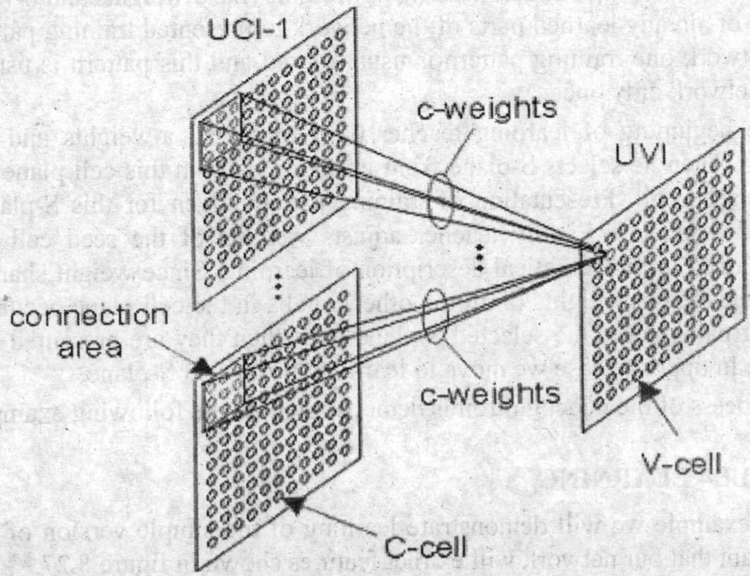

Figure 8.25 c-weights

4. d-weights

Fixed d-weights are used for connections between C-cells and S-cells which belong to their connection areas. As well as c-weights also d-weights are determined at construction of the network and again in such a way so as to reduce transfer of information from periphery of connection areas mostly.

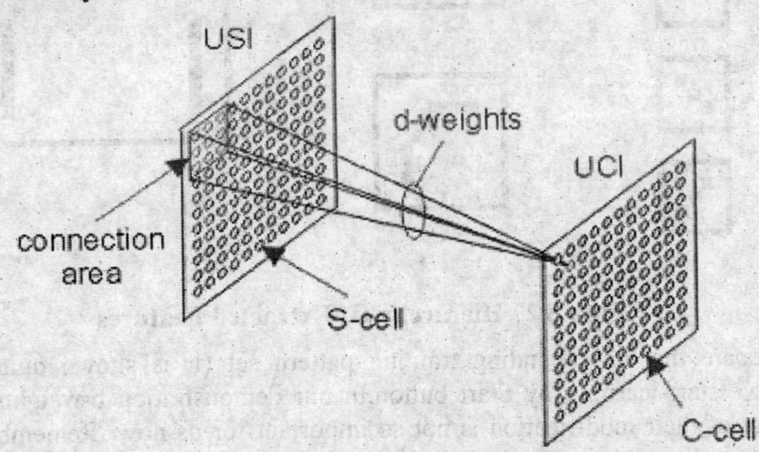

Figure 8.26 d-weights

8.8. LEARNING

Learning in this version of the network is controlled by a teacher. His task is to determine what features shall be extracted in particular stages of the network and to prepare corresponding training patterns before beginning of learning.

Learning of the neocognitron proceeds stage by stage from the lowest stage of the network and it inheres in adjusting of modifiable weights (i.e. a-weights and b-weights) according to the response of already learned parts of the network to presented training patterns. For each S-plane in the network one training pattern is usually used and this pattern is usually necessary to present to the network only once.

On the beginning of learning teacher have to set all a-weights and b-weights in the network to zero. Then he selects S-plane from layer US1 and in this cell plane he selects one of cells, so-called seed cell. Presentation of training pattern given for this S-plane into the input layer U0 is the next step. Finally teacher adjusts weights of the seed cell according to the equations mentioned in mathematical description of learning. Since weight sharing is used in the neocognitron adjusting of weights of all the other S-cells in the cell plane occurs simultaneously. If more training patterns for the selected S-plane exist then they are presented subsequently and process repeats. In opposite case we move to learning of the next S-plane.

The learning process of the neocognitron is demonstrated on the following example in detail.

8.8.1. EXAMPLE - LEARNING

In this example we will demonstrate learning of the simple version of the neocognitron network. We want that our network will extract features shown in figure 8.27.

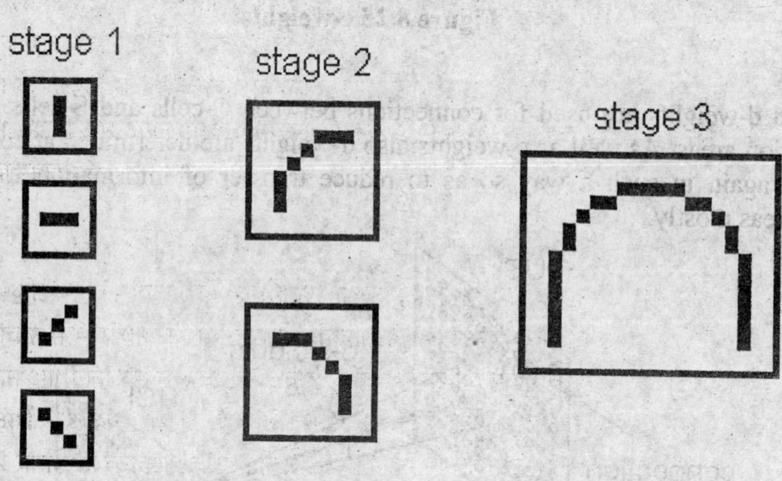

Figure 8.27 Hierarchy Of Extracted Features

We prepare the corresponding training pattern set (it is shown quite in the left in example) and we start learning by Start button.In our demonstration b-weights are not shown because the way of their modification is not so important for us now. Remember however that both a-weights and b-weights are adjusted during learning. Notice that together with seed cell selecting their connection areas and receptive field are selected as well.

8.8.2. RECALL

Recall in the neocognitron inheres in evaluation of output values of all cells stage by stage. The result of this process is a decision to which of learned categories presented pattern belongs. The process of recall begins with presentation of pattern intended for recognition to the input layer U0. Then output values of V-cells in the layer UV1 are evaluated. S-cells from the layer US1 can extract the simplest features and C-cells from layer UC1 ensure decreasing of effect of extracted features shifts. The whole process repeats analogically for all the following layers of the network. After completion of recall output values of C-cells from the highest layer of the network correspond to measures of belonging presented pattern to categories which the particular C-cells represent.

In figure 8.28 the process of recall in the neocognitron is demonstrated schematically.

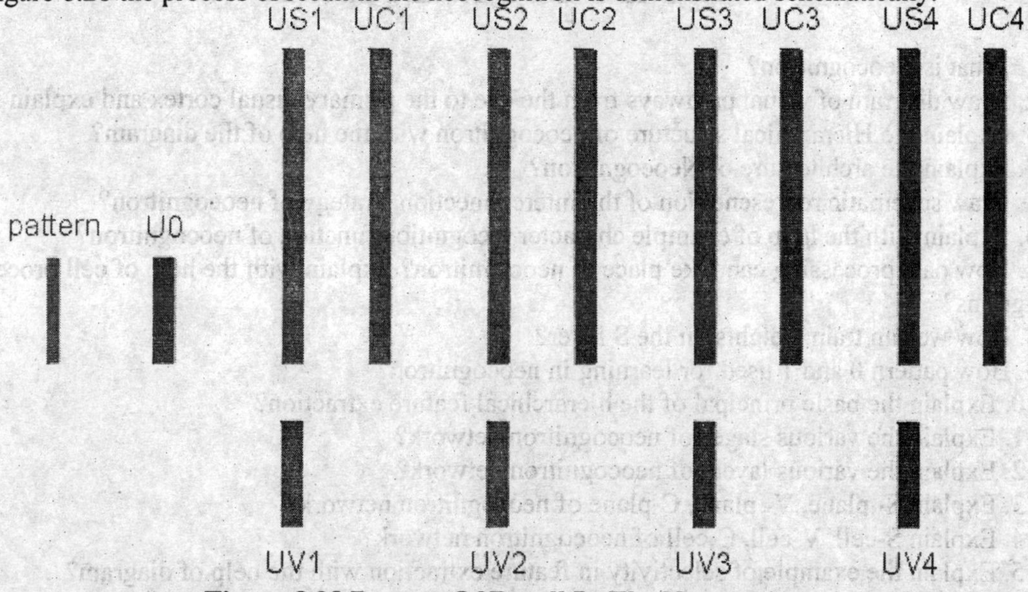

Figure 8.28 Process Of Recall In The Neocognitron

On the following example we will examine recall on the simulator of the neocognitron in detail.

8.9. EXAMPLE - SIMULATOR OF THE NEOCOGNITRON

At the end, we have prepared simulator of the neocognitron network mentioned in the first example.

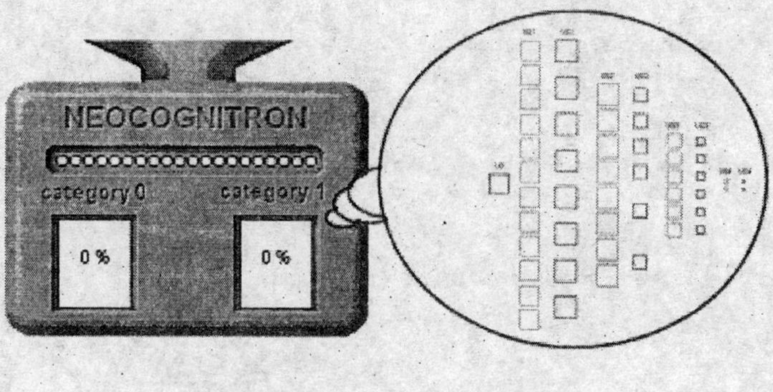

Each quadrangle in the simulator represents one certain cell plane in the network. For simplicity V-planes are not shown here because their content is not so important for us. Output values of cells in cell planes are expressed by different intensity of color. The higher the output value of cell the darker the color is. After clicking on any cell in any cell plane all its connection areas and receptive field are marked.

In control panel select one of patterns and observe state of the network after its presentation. Examine what features are extracted in particular S-planes and in detailed view how these features are encoded in a-weights.

QUESTION BANK

Q1. What is Neocognitron?
Q2. Draw diagram of visual pathways from the eye to the primary visual cortex and explain it?
Q3. Explain the Hierarchical structure of neocognitron with the help of the diagram?
Q4. Explain the architecture of Neocognitron?
Q5. Draw schematic representation of the interconnection strategy of neocognitron?
Q6. Explain with the help of example character recognition function of neocognitron?
Q7. How data processing can take place in neocognitron? Explain with the help of cell processing diagrams?
Q8. How we can train weights on the S layer?
Q9. How pattern 0 and 1 used for learning in neocognitron?
Q10. Explain the basic principal of the hierarchical feature extraction?
Q11. Explain the various stages of neocognitron network?
Q12. Explain the various layers of neocognitron network?
Q13. Explain S- plane, V- plane, C-plane of neocognitron network?
Q14. Explain S-cell, V-cell, C-cell of neocognitron network?
Q15. Explain the example of selectivity in feature extraction with the help of diagram?
Q16. Explain the example of tolerance of feature shifts with the help of diagram?
Q17. Explain the concept of weights and connection in neocognitron?
Q18. Demonstrate learning of the simple version of neocognitron network?
Q19. Explain the process of recall in the neocognitron?
Q20. Discuss the implementation of simulator of neocongnitron?

CHAPTER 9

BIDIRECTIONAL ASSOCIATIVE MEMORY

9.1 INTRODUCTION

Bidirectional Associative Memory usually referred to as **BAM** is a type of recurrent neural network. BAM was introduced by Bart Kosko in 1988. There are two types of associative memory, auto-associative and hetro-associative. BAM is hetro-associative, meaning given a pattern it can return another patten which is potentially of a different size. It is similar to the Hopfield network in that they are both forms of associative memory. However, Hopfield nets return patterns of the same size.

BAM has 2 layers: input and output and information can go in both directions - from input to output and back from output to input. This page presents some demo that can demonsrate learning of BAM. A BAM stores a set of pattern associations by summing bipolar correlation matrices (an n by m outer product matrix for each pattern to be stored). The architecture of the net consists of two layers of neurons, connected by directional weighted connection paths. The net iterates, sending signals back and forth between the two layers until all neurons reach equilibrium. Bidirectional associative memory neural nets can respond to input to either layer. Because the weights are bidirectional and the algirithm alternates between updating the activations for each layer, we shall refer to the layer as the X-layer and the Y-layer.

Three varities of BAM—binary, bipolar, and continuous—are considered here. Several other variations exist. The architecture for each is same and is illustrated in figure9.1.

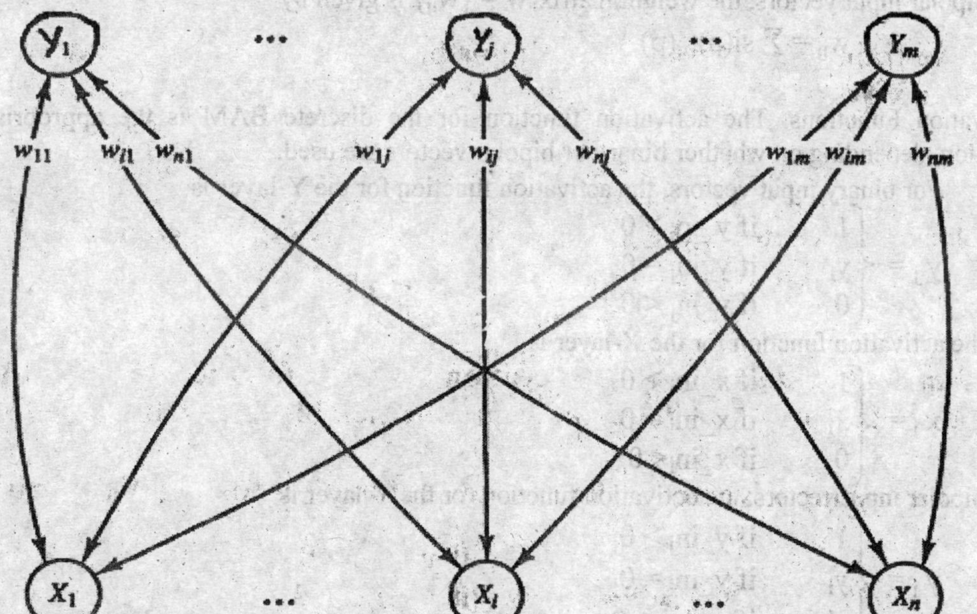

Figure 9.1 Bidirectional Associative Memory

9.2 ARCHITECTURE

The single-layer nonlinear feedback BAM network (with heteroassociative content-addressable memory) has n units in its X-layer and m units in its Y-layer. The connections between the layers are bidirectional; i.e., if the weight matrix for signals sent from the X-layer to the Y-layer is W, the weight matrix for signals sent from the Y-layer to the X-layer is W^T.

9.3 ALGORITHM

9.3.1 DISCRETE BAM

The two bivalent (binary or bipolar) forms f BAM are closely related. In each, the weights are found from the sum f the outer products of the bipolar form of the training vectors pairs. Also, the activation function is a step function, with the possibility of a nonzero threshold. It has been shown that bipolar vectors improve the performance of the net.

Setting the Weights. The weight matrix to store a set of input and target vectors s(p):t(p), p = 1,.....,P, where

$$s(p) = (s_1(p),\ldots, s_i(p),\ldots s_n(p))$$

and

$$t(p) = (t_1(p),\ldots, t_j(p),\ldots t_m(p))$$

can be determined by the Hebb rule. The formulas for the entries depend on whether the training vectors are binary or bipolar. For binary input vectors, the weight matrix W = {w_{ij}} is given by

$$w_{ij} = \sum_p (2s_i(p) - 1)(2t_j(p) - 1).$$

For bipolar input vectors, the weight matrix W = {w_{ij}} is given by

$$w_{ij} = \sum_p si(p)t_{ij}(p).$$

Activation Functions. The activation function for the discrete BAM is the appropriate step function, depending on whether binary or bipolar vectors are used.

For binary input vectors, the activation function for the Y-layer is

$$y_j = \begin{cases} 1 & \text{if } y\_in_j > 0 \\ y_i & \text{if } y\_in_j = 0 \\ 0 & \text{if } y\_in_j < 0 \end{cases}$$

and the activation function for the X-layer is

$$x_i = \begin{cases} 1 & \text{if } x\_in_i > 0 \\ x_i & \text{if } x\_in_i = 0 \\ 0 & \text{if } x\_in_i < 0 \end{cases}$$

For bipolar input vectors, the activation function for the Y-layer is

$$y_j = \begin{cases} 1 & \text{if } y\_in_j > \theta_j \\ y_i & \text{if } y\_in_j = \theta_j \\ -1 & \text{if } y\_in_j < \theta_j \end{cases}$$

and the activation function for the X-layer is

$$x_i = \begin{cases} 1 & \text{if } x\_in_i > \theta_j \\ x_i & \text{if } x\_in_i = \theta_j \\ -1 & \text{if } x\_in_i < \theta_j \end{cases}$$

Note that if the net input is exactly equal to the threshold value, the activation function "decides" to leave the activation of that unit at its previous value. For that reason, the activations of all units are initialized to zero in the algorithm that follows. The algorithm is written for the first signal to be sent from the X-layer to the Y-layer. However, if the input signal for the X-layer is the zero vector, the input signal to the Y-layer will be unchanged by the activation function, and the process will be the same as if the first piece of information had been sent from the Y-layer to the X-layer. Signals are sent only from one layer to the other at any step of the process, not simultaneously in both directions.

ALGORITHM.

Step 0. Initialize the weights to store a set of P vectors;
Initialize all activations to 0.

Step 1. For each testing input, do Steps 2-6.

Step 2a. Present input pattern x to the X-layer
(i.e., set activations of X-layer to current input pattern).

Step 2b. Present input pattern y t the Y-layer.
(Either of the input patterns may be the zero vector.)

Step 3. While activation are not converged, do Steps 4-6.

Step 4. Update activations of units in Y-layer.

Compute net inputs:

$$y\_in_j = \sum_i w_{ij} x_i.$$

Compute activations:

$$y_j = f(y\_in_j).$$

Send signal to X-layer.

Step 5 Update activations of units in X-layer.

Compute net inputs:

$$x\_in_i = \sum_j w_{ij} x_j.$$

Compute activations:

$$x_i = f(x\_in_i).$$

Send signal to Y-layer.

Step 6. Test for convergence:

If the activation vectors x and y have reached equilibrium, then stop; otherwise, continue.

9.3.2 CONTINUOUS BAM

A continuous bidirectional associative memory transforms input smoothly and continuously into output in the range [0, 1] using he logistic sigmoid function as the activation function for all units.

For binary input vectors (s(p), t(p)), p = 1, 2,….,P, the weights are determined by the aforementioned formula

$$w_{ij} \sum (2s_i(p) - 1)(2t_j(p) - 1).$$

The activation function is the logistic sigmoid

$$f(y\_in_j) = \frac{1}{1 + \exp(-y\_in_j)},$$

where a bias is included in calculating the net input to any unit

$$y\_in_j = b_j + \sum_i x_i w_{ij}$$

and corresponding formulas apply for the units n the X-layer.

A number of other forms of BAMs have been developed. In some, the activations change based on a differential equation known as Cohen-Grossberg activation dynamics [Cohen & Grossberg, 1983]. Note, however, that Kosko uses the term "activation" to refer to the activity level of a neuron before the output function (such as the logistic sigmoid function) is applied.

9.4 APPLICATIONS

EXAMPLE 9.1 A BAM NET TO ASSOCIATE LETTERS WITH SIMPLE BIPOLAR CODES

Consider the possibility of using a (discrete) BAM network (with bipolar vectors) to map to simple letters (given by 5 x 3 patterns) to the following bipolar codes:

```
.#.        .##
#.#        #..
###        #..
#.#        #..
#.#        .##
(-1, 1)    (1, 1)
```

The weight matrices are:

(to store A → -11)

$$\begin{pmatrix} 1 & -1 \\ -1 & 1 \\ 1 & -1 \\ -1 & 1 \\ 1 & -1 \\ -1 & 1 \\ -1 & 1 \\ -1 & 1 \\ -1 & 1 \\ -1 & 1 \\ 1 & -1 \\ -1 & 1 \\ -1 & 1 \\ 1 & -1 \\ -1 & 1 \end{pmatrix}$$

(C → 11)

$$\begin{pmatrix} -1 & 1 \\ 1 & 1 \\ 1 & 1 \\ 1 & 1 \\ -1 & -1 \\ -1 & -1 \\ 1 & 1 \\ -1 & -1 \\ -1 & -1 \\ 1 & 1 \\ -1 & -1 \\ -1 & -1 \\ -1 & -1 \\ 1 & 1 \\ 1 & 1 \end{pmatrix}$$

(W, to store both)

$$\begin{pmatrix} 0 & -2 \\ 0 & 2 \\ 2 & 0 \\ 0 & 2 \\ 0 & -2 \\ -2 & 0 \\ 0 & 2 \\ -2 & 0 \\ -2 & 0 \\ 0 & 2 \\ 0 & -2 \\ -2 & 0 \\ -2 & 0 \\ 2 & 0 \\ 0 & 2 \end{pmatrix}$$

To illustrate the use of a BAM, we first demonstrate that the net gives the correct Y vector when presented with the x vector for either the pattern A or the pattern C:

Input Pattern A

(-1 1 – 1 1 – 1 1 1 1 1 1 – 1 1 1 – 1 1)W = (- 14, (16) $\rightarrow$ (- 1, 1)

Input Pattern C

(- 1 1 1 1 – 1 – 1 1 – 1 – 1 1 – 1 – 1 – 1 1 1) W = (14, 16) $\rightarrow$ (1, 1).

To see the bidirectional nature of the net, observe that the Y vectors can also be used as input. For signals sent from the Y-layer to the X-layer, the weight matrix is the transpose of the matrix W, i.e.,

$$W^T = \begin{pmatrix} 0 & 0 & 2 & 0 & 0 & -2 & 0 & -2 & -2 & 0 & 0 & -2 & -2 & 2 & 0 \\ -2 & 2 & 0 & 2 & -2 & 0 & 2 & 0 & 0 & 2 & -2 & 0 & 0 & 0 & 2 \end{pmatrix}$$

For the input vector associated with pattern A, namely, (-1, 1), we have

$(-1, 1)\, W^T =$

$$(-1, 1) = \begin{pmatrix} 0 & 0 & 2 & 0 & 0 & -2 & 0 & -2 & -2 & 0 & 0 & -2 & -2 & 2 & 0 \\ -2 & 2 & 0 & 2 & -2 & 0 & 2 & 0 & 0 & 2 & -2 & 0 & 0 & 0 & 2 \end{pmatrix}$$

$= (-2\ 2\ -2\ 2\ -2\ 2\ 2\ 2\ 2\ 2\ -2\ 2\ 2\ -2\ 2)$

$\rightarrow (-1\ 1\ -1\ 1\ -1\ 1\ 1\ 1\ 1\ 1\ -1\ 1\ 1\ -1\ 1).$

This is pattern A.

Similarly, if we input the vector associated with pattern C, namely, (1, 1), we obtain

$(1, 1)\, W^T =$

$$(1, 1) \begin{pmatrix} 0 & 0 & 2 & 0 & 0 & -2 & 0 & -2 & -2 & 0 & 0 & -2 & -2 & 2 & 0 \\ -2 & 2 & 0 & 2 & -2 & 0 & 2 & 0 & 0 & 2 & -2 & 0 & 0 & 0 & 2 \end{pmatrix}$$

$= (-2\ 2\ 2\ 2\ -2\ -2\ 2\ -2\ -2\ 2\ -2\ -2\ -2\ 2\ 2)$

$\rightarrow (-1\ 1\ 1\ 1\ -1\ -1\ 1\ -1\ -1\ 1\ -1\ -1\ -1\ 1\ 1),$

which is pattern C.

The net can also be used with noisy input for the x vector, the y vector, or both, as is shown in the next example.

EXAMPLE 9.2 TESTING A BAM NET WITH NOISY INPUT

In this example, the net is given a y vector as input that is a noisy version of one of the training y vectors and no information about the corresponding x vector (i.e., the x vector is identically 0). The input vector is (0,1); the response of the net is

$(0.1)\, W^T =$

$$(0,1) = \begin{pmatrix} 0 & 0 & 2 & 0 & 0 & -2 & 0 & -2 & -2 & 0 & 0 & -2 & -2 & 2 & 0 \\ -2 & 2 & 0 & 2 & -2 & 0 & 2 & 0 & 0 & 2 & -2 & 0 & 0 & 0 & 2 \end{pmatrix}$$

$= (-2\ 2\ 0\ 2\ -2\ 0\ 2\ 0\ 0\ 2\ -2\ 0\ 0\ 0\ 2)$

$\rightarrow$ (-1 1 0 1 -1 0 1 0 0 1 -1 0 0 0 1).

Note that the units receiving 0 net input have their activations left at that value, since the initial x vector is 0. This x vector is then sent back to the Y-layer, using the weight matrix W:

$$(-1\ 1\ 0\ 1\ -1\ 0\ 1\ 0\ 0\ 1\ -1\ 0\ 0\ 0\ 1)\ 0\ -2\begin{pmatrix} 0 & 2 \\ 2 & 0 \\ 0 & 2 \\ 0 & -2 \\ -2 & 0 \\ 0 & 2 \\ -2 & 0 \\ -2 & 0 \\ 0 & 2 \\ 0 & -2 \\ -2 & 0 \\ -2 & 0 \\ 2 & 0 \\ 0 & 2 \end{pmatrix}$$

$\rightarrow$ (0 1).

This result is not too surprising, since the net had no information to give it a preference for either A or C. The net has converged (since, obviously, no further changes in the activations will take place) to a spurious stable state, i.e., the solution is no is not one of the stored pattern pairs.

If, on the other hand, the net was given both the input vector y, as before, and some information about the vector, x for example,

y = (0 1), x = (0 0 -1 0 0 1 0 1 1 0 0 1 1 -1 0).

the net would be able to reach a stable set of activations corresponding to one of the stored pattern pairs.

Note that the x vector is a noisy version of

A = (-1 1 -1 1 -1 1 1 1 1 1 -1 1 1 -1 1),

where the nonzero components are those that distinguish A from

C (-1 1 1 1 -1 -1 1 -1 -1 1 -1 -1 -1 1 1).

Now, since the algorithm specifies that if the net input to a unit is zero, the activation of that unit remains unchanged, we get

$(0, 1)W^T =$

$$(0,1) = \begin{pmatrix} 0 & 0 & 2 & 0 & 0 & -2 & 0 & -2 & -2 & 0 & 0 & -2 & -2 & 2 & 0 \\ -2 & 2 & 0 & 2 & -2 & 0 & 2 & 0 & 0 & 2 & -2 & 0 & 0 & 0 & 2 \end{pmatrix}$$

= (-2 2 0 2 -2 0 2 0 0 2 -2 0 0 0 2)

$\rightarrow$ (-1 1 -1 1 -1 1 1 1 1 1 -1 1 1 -1 1).

which is pattern A.

Since this example is fairly extreme, i.e., every component that distinguishes A from C was given an input value for A, let us try something with less information given concerning x.

For example, let y = (0 1) and x = (0 0 -1 0 0 1 0 1 0 0 0 0 0 0 0). Then

$(0, 1)W^T =$

$$(0,1) = \begin{pmatrix} 0 & 0 & 2 & 0 & 0 & -2 & 0 & -2 & -2 & 0 & 0 & -2 & -2 & 2 & 0 \\ -2 & 2 & 0 & 2 & -2 & 0 & 2 & 0 & 0 & 2 & -2 & 0 & 0 & 0 & 2 \end{pmatrix}$$

$$= (-2\ 2\ 0\ 2\ -2\ 0\ 2\ 0\ 0\ 2\ -2\ 0\ 0\ 0\ 2)$$

$$\rightarrow (-1\ 1\ -1\ 1\ -1\ 1\ 1\ 1\ 0\ 1\ -1\ 0\ 0\ 0\ 1),$$

which is not quite pattern A.

So we try iterating, sending the x vector back to the Y-layer using the weight matrix W:

$$(-1\ 1\ 0\ 1\ -1\ 0\ 1\ 0\ 0\ 1\ -1\ 0\ 0\ 0\ 1) \begin{pmatrix} 0 & -2 \\ 0 & 2 \\ 2 & 0 \\ 0 & 2 \\ 0 & -2 \\ -2 & 0 \\ 0 & 2 \\ -2 & 0 \\ -2 & 0 \\ 0 & 2 \\ 0 & -2 \\ -2 & 0 \\ -2 & 0 \\ 2 & 0 \\ 0 & 2 \end{pmatrix}$$

$$\rightarrow (-6, 10) \rightarrow (-1, 1).$$

If this pattern is fed back to the X-layer one more time, the pattern A will be produced.

9.5 HAMMING DISTANCE

The number of different bits in two binary or bipolar vectors x_1 and x_2 is called the Hamming distance between the vectors and is denoted by $H[x_1, x_2]$. The average Hamming distance between the vectors is $\underline{1}$ $H[x_1, x_2]$, where n is the number of n components is each vector. the x vectors in Examples 9.1 and 9.2, namely,

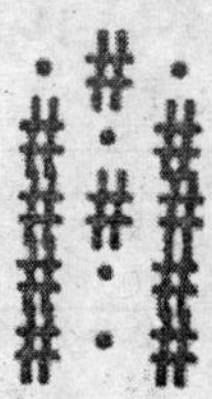

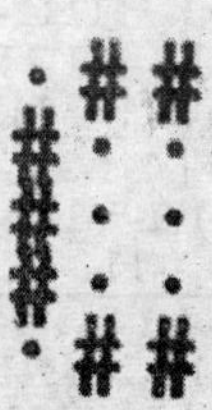

differ in the 3rd, 6th, 8th, 9th, 12th, 13th, and 14th positions. This gives an average Hamming distance between these vectors of 7/15. The average Hamming distance between the corresponding y vectors is 1/2.

Kosko (1988) has observed that "correlation encoding" (as is used in the BAM neural net) is improved to the extent that the average Hamming distance between paris of input patterns is comparable to the average Hamming distance between the corresponding pairs of output patterns. If that is the case, input patterns that are separated by a small Hamming distance are mapped to output vectors that are also so separated, while input vectors that are separated while input vectors that are separated by a large Hamming distance go to correspondingly distant (dissimilar) output patters. This is analogous to the behavior of a continuous function.

9.6 ERASING A STORED ASSOCIATION

The complement of a bipolar vector x is denoted x^e; it is the vector formed by changing all of the 1's in vector x to -1's and vice versa. Encoding (storing the pattern pair s^c:t^c stores the same information as encoding s:t; encoding s^c:t or s:t^c will erase the encoding of s:t [Kosko, 1988].

9.7 STORAGE CAPACITY

Kosko (1988) has shown that the upper limit on the no. p of pattern pairs which can be stored and successfully retrieved is min (m, n). The substantiation for this estimate is rather heuristic. The memory storage capacity of BAM is

$P \le \min(m,n)$

A more conservative heuristic capacity measure is used in a literature,

$P = \sqrt{\min(m,n)}$

9.8. RESULTS

The network has 49 neurons in first layer and five neurons in the second layer. With this configuration the network is capable of storing six alphabets. The alphabets have been represented as a pattern grid of size 7×7. From the pattern grid each alphabet is obtained in the form of a vector with entries 1 and -1. All the alphabets in the form vector **a** and its associated output as vector **b** is stored. Weight matrix is obtained by taking inner product of **a** and **b**. The network has been tested for A, I, L, M, X, and P. The network gives the correct associated output when these characters are given at the time of testing. The result has been shown in table 9.1.

CHARACTER	INPUT	OUTPUT
A	a = [-1-1111-1-1-11-1-1-11-11-1-1-1-1-111111111-1-1-1-111-1-1-1-1-111-1-1-1-1-11] b = [-1-1-1-11]	-1-1-1-11
I	a =[-111111-1-1-1-11-1-1-1-1-1-11-1-1-1-1-1-11-1-1-1-1-1-11-1-1-1-1-1-11-1-1-1-111111-1] b = [-11-1-11]	-11-1-11
L	a = [1-1-1-1-1-1-11-1-1-1-1-1-11-1-1-1-1-1-11-1-1-1-1-1-11-1-1-1-1-1-11-1-1-1-1-1-1111111] b = [-111-1-1]	-111-1-1
M	a = [1-1-1-1-1-1111-1-1-1111-11-11-111-1-11-1-111-1-1-1-1-11-1-1-1-1-111-1-1-1-1-11] b = [-111-11]	-111-11
P	a = [11111-1-11-1-1-1-11-11-1-1-1-1-111-1-1-1-11-111111-1-11-1-1-1-1-1-11-1-1-1-1-1-1] b = [1-1-1-1-1]	1-1-1-1-1
X	a = [1-1-1-1-1-11-11-1-1-11-1-1-11-11-1-1-1-1-11-1-1-1-1-11-11-1-1-11-1-1-11-11-1-1-1-1-11] b = [11-1-1-1]	11-1-1-1

9.9 . MERITS AND DEMERITS

In BAM, a distorted input pattern may also cause correct heteroassociation at the output. The logical symmetry of interconnection severely hampers the efficiency of BAM in pattern storage and recall capability. It also limits their use for knowledge representation and inference . There is limitation on number of pattern pairs, which can be stored and successfully retrieved.

QUESTION BANK

Q1. What is bidirectional associative memory?
Q2. Explain the architecture of BAM network?
Q3. Write an algorithm for discrete BAM?
Q4. Write an algorithm for continuous BAM?
Q5. Explain various application of BAM network?
Q6. What do you mean by hamming distance?
Q7. Explain the memory storage of BAM?
Q8. What are the merits and demerits of BAM?

CHAPTER 10

CASE STUDIES

CASE STUDY 1- SPEECH RECOGNITION

10.1 INTRODUCTION

Speech is a natural mode of communication for people. We learn all the relevant skills during early childhood, without instruction, and we continue to rely on speech communication throughout our lives. It comes so naturally to us that we don't realize how complex a phenomenon speech is. The human vocal tract and articulators are biological organs with nonlinear properties, whose operation is not just under conscious control but also affected by factors ranging from gender to upbringing to emotional state. As a result, vocalizations can vary widely in terms of their accent, pronunciation, articulation, roughness, nasality, pitch, volume, and speed; moreover, during transmission, our irregular speech patterns can be further distorted by background noise and echoes, as well as electrical characteristics (if telephones or other electronic equipment are used). All these sources of variability make speech recognition, even more than speech generation, a very complex problem.

What makes people so good at recognizing speech? Intriguingly, the human brain is known to be wired differently than a conventional computer; in fact it operates under a radically different computational paradigm. While conventional computers use a very fast & complex central processor with explicit program instructions and locally addressable memory, by contrast the human brain uses a massively parallel collection of slow & simple processing elements (neurons), densely connected by weights (synapses) whose strengths are modified with experience, directly supporting the integration of multiple constraints, and providing a distributed form of associative memory.

The brain's impressive superiority at a wide range of cognitive skills, including speech recognition, has motivated research into its novel computational paradigm since the 1940's, on the assumption that brainlike models may ultimately lead to brainlike performance on many complex tasks. This fascinating research area is now known as connectionism, or the study of artificial neural networks.

What is the current state of the art in speech recognition? This is a complex question, because a system's accuracy depends on the conditions under which it is evaluated: under sufficiently narrow conditions almost any system can attain human-like accuracy, but it's much harder to achieve good accuracy under general conditions. The conditions of evaluation - and hence the accuracy of any system - can vary along the following dimensions:

1. Vocabulary size and confusability. As a general rule, it is easy to discriminate among a small set of words, but error rates naturally increase as the vocabulary size grows. For example, the 10 digits "zero" to "nine" can be recognized essentially perfectly , but vocabulary sizes of 200, 5000, or 100000 may have error rates of 3%, 7%, or 45%. On the other hand, even a small vocabulary can be hard to recognize if it contains confusable words. For example, the 26 letters of the English alphabet (treated as 26 "words") are very difficult to discriminate because they contain so many confusable words (most notoriously, the E-set: "B, C, D, E, G, P, T, V, Z"); an 8% error rate is considered good for this vocabulary

2. Speaker dependence vs. independence. By definition, a speaker dependent system is intended for use by a single speaker, but a speaker independent system is intended for use by any speaker. Speaker independence is difficult to achieve because a system's parameters become tuned to the speaker(s) that it was trained on, and these parameters tend to be highly speaker-specific.

3. Isolated, discontinuous, or continuous speech. Isolated speech means single words; discontinuous speech means full sentences in which words are artificially separated by silence; and continuous speech means naturally spoken sentences. Isolated and discontinuous speech recognition is relatively easy because word boundaries are detectable and the words tend to be cleanly pronounced.

4. Task and language constraints. Even with a fixed vocabulary, performance will vary with the nature of constraints on the word sequences that are allowed during recognition. Some constraints may be task-dependent (for example, an airlinequerying application may dismiss the hypothesis "The apple is red"); other constraints may be semantic (rejecting "The apple is angry"), or syntactic (rejecting "Red is apple the"). Constraints are often represented by a grammar, which ideally filters out unreasonable sentences so that the speech recognizer evaluates only plausible sentences. Grammars are usually rated by their perplexity, a number that indicates the grammar's average branching factor (i.e., the number of words that can follow any given word). The difficulty of a task is more reliably measured by its perplexity than by its vocabulary size.

5. Read vs. spontaneous speech. Systems can be evaluated on speech that is either read from prepared scripts, or speech that is uttered spontaneously. Spontaneous speech is vastly more difficult, because it tends to be peppered with disfluencies like "uh" and "um", false starts, incomplete sentences, stuttering, coughing, and laughter; and moreover, the vocabulary is essentially unlimited, so the system must be able to deal intelligently with unknown words (e.g., detecting and flagging their presence, and adding them to the vocabulary, which may require some interaction with the user).

6. Adverse conditions. A system's performance can also be degraded by a range of adverse conditions. These include environmental noise (e.g., noise in a car or a factory); acoustical distortions (e.g, echoes, room acoustics); different microphones (e.g., close-speaking, omnidirectional, or telephone); limited frequency bandwidth (in telephone transmission); and altered speaking manner (shouting, whining, speaking quickly, etc.).

In order to evaluate and compare different systems under well-defined conditions, a number of standardized databases have been created with particular characteristics. For example, one database that has been widely used is the DARPA Resource Management database - a large vocabulary (1000 words), speaker-independent, continuous speech database, consisting of 4000 training sentences in the domain of naval resource management, read from a script and recorded under benign environmental conditions; testing is usually performed using a grammar with a perplexity of 60. Under these controlled conditions, state-of-the-art performance is about 97% word recognition accuracy (or less for simpler systems).

10.2 FUNDAMENTALS OF SPEECH RECOGNITION

Speech recognition is a multileveled pattern recognition task, in which acoustical signals are examined and structured into a hierarchy of subword units (e.g., phonemes), words, phrases, and sentences. Each level may provide additional temporal constraints, e.g., known word pronunciations or legal word sequences, which can compensate for errors or uncertainties at lower levels. This hierarchy of constraints can best be exploited by combining decisions probabilistically at all lower levels, and making discrete decisions only at the highest level.

The structure of a standard speech recognition system is illustrated in Figure. The elements are as follows:

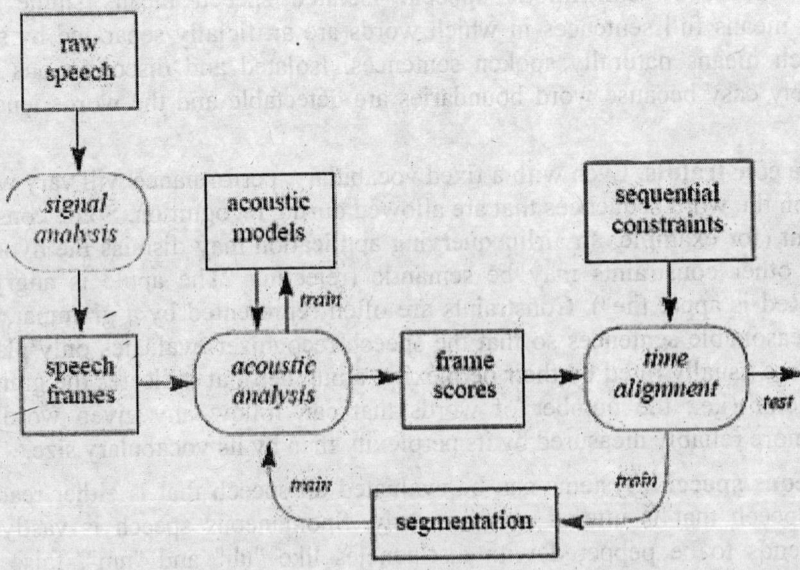

Figure10.1 Structure Of A Standard Speech Recognition System.

- **Raw speech.** Speech is typically sampled at a high frequency, e.g., 16 KHz over a microphone or 8 KHz over a telephone. This yields a sequence of amplitude values over time.
- **Signal analysis.** Raw speech should be initially transformed and compressed, in order to simplify subsequent processing. Many signal analysis techniques are available which can extract useful features and compress the data by a factor of ten without losing any important information. Among the most popular:
  - Fourier analysis (FFT) yields discrete frequencies over time, which can be interpreted visually. Frequencies are often distributed using a Mel scale, which is linear in the low range but logarithmic in the high range, corresponding to physiological characteristics of the human ear.
  - Perceptual Linear Prediction (PLP) is also physiologically motivated, but yields coefficients that cannot be interpreted visually.
  - Linear Predictive Coding (LPC) yields coefficients of a linear equation that approximate the recent history of the raw speech values.

- Cepstral analysis calculates the inverse Fourier transform of the logarithm of the power spectrum of the signal.

In practice, it makes little difference which technique is used1. Afterwards, procedures such as Linear Discriminant Analysis (LDA) may optionally be applied to further reduce the dimensionality of any representation, and to decorrelate the coefficients.

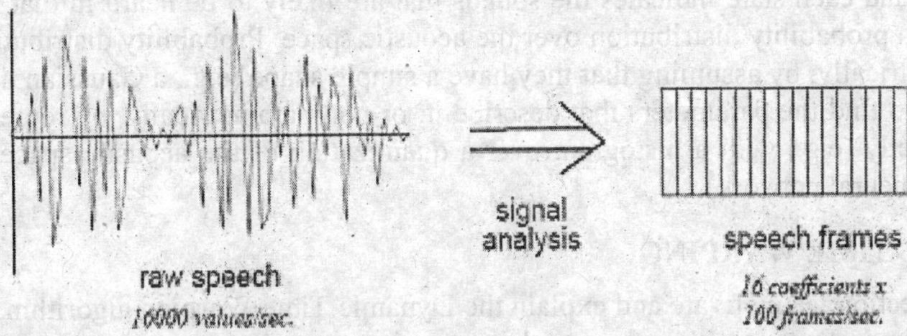

- **Speech frames.** The result of signal analysis is a sequence of speech frames, typically at 10 msec intervals, with about 16 coefficients per frame. These frames may be augmented by their own first and/or second derivatives, providing explicit information about speech dynamics; this typically leads to improved performance. The speech frames are used for acoustic analysis.
- **Acoustic models.** In order to analyze the speech frames for their acoustic content, we need a set of acoustic models. There are many kinds of acoustic models, varying in their representation, granularity, context dependence, and other properties.

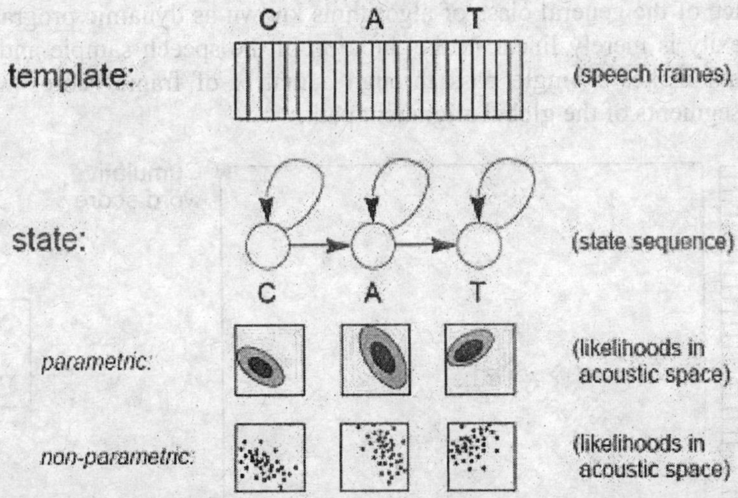

Figure 10.2 Acoustic Models: Template And State Representations For The Word "Cat".

Figure shows two popular representations for acoustic models. The simplest is a template, which is just a stored sample of the unit of speech to be modeled, e.g., a recording of a word. An unknown word can be recognized by simply comparing it against all known templates, and finding the closest match. Templates have two major drawbacks: (1) they cannot model acoustic variabilities, except in a coarse way by assigning multiple templates to each word; and (2) in practice they are limited to whole-word models, because it's hard to record or segment a sample shorter than a word - so templates are useful only in small systems which can afford the luxury of using whole-word models. A more flexible representation, used in larger systems, is based on trained acoustic models, or states. In this approach, every word is modeled by a sequence of trainable states, and each state indicates the sounds that are likely to be heard in that segment of the word, using a probability distribution over the acoustic space. Probability distributions can be modeled parametrically, by assuming that they have a simple shape (e.g., a Gaussian distribution) and then trying to find the parameters that describe it; or non-parametrically, by representing the distribution directly (e.g., with a histogram over a quantization of the acoustic space, or, as we shall see, with a neural network).

10.3 DYNAMIC TIME WARPING

In this section we motivate and explain the Dynamic Time Warping algorithm, one of the oldest and most important algorithms in speech recognition.

The simplest way to recognize an isolated word sample is to compare it against a number of stored word templates and determine which is the "best match". This goal is complicated by a number of factors. First, different samples of a given word will have somewhat different durations. This problem can be eliminated by simply normalizing the templates and the unknown speech so that they all have an equal duration. However, another problem is that the rate of speech may not be constant throughout the word; in other words, the optimal alignment between a template and the speech sample may be nonlinear. Dynamic Time Warping (DTW) is an efficient method for finding this optimal nonlinear alignment.

DTW is an instance of the general class of algorithms known as dynamic programming. Its time and space complexity is merely linear in the duration of the speech sample and the vocabulary size. The algorithm makes a single pass through a matrix of frame scores while computing locallyoptimized segments of the global alignment path.

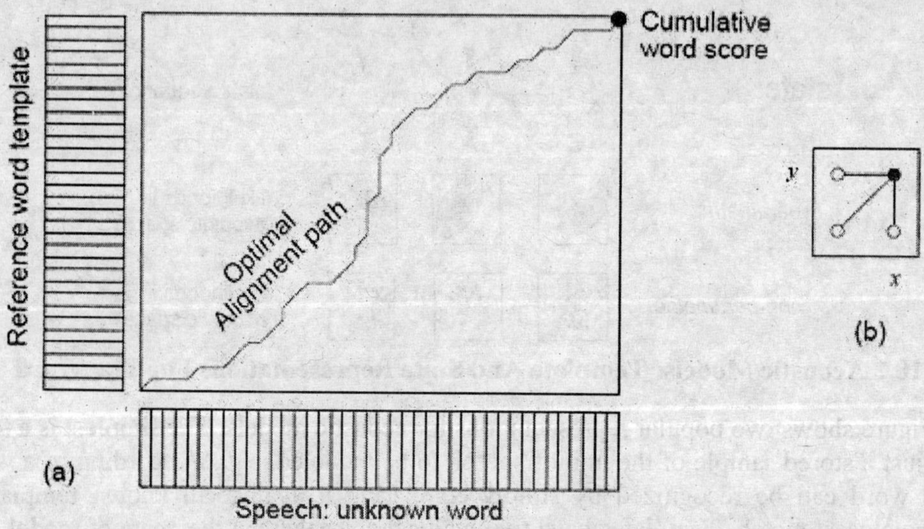

Figure 10.3 Dynamic Time Warping (Speech Recognition)

If D(x,y) is the Euclidean distance between frame x of the speech sample and frame y of the reference template, and if C(x,y) is the cumulative score along an optimal alignment path that leads to (x,y), then

$$C(x, y) = MIN(C(x-1,y), C(x-1,y-1), C(x, y-1)) + D(x, y)$$

The resulting alignment path may be visualized as a low valley of Euclidean distance scores, meandering through the hilly landscape of the matrix, beginning at (0, 0) and ending at the final point (X, Y). By keeping track of backpointers, the full alignment path can be recovered by tracing backwards from (X, Y). An optimal alignment path is computed for each reference word template, and the one with the lowest cumulative score is considered to be the best match for the unknown speech sample.

There are many variations on the DTW algorithm. For example, it is common to vary the local path constraints, e.g., by introducing transitions with slope 1/2 or 2, or weighting the transitions in various ways, or applying other kinds of slope constraints (Sakoe and Chiba 1978). While the reference word models are usually templates, they may be state-based models (as shown previously in Figure). When using states, vertical transitions are often disallowed (since there are fewer states than frames), and often the goal is to maximize the cumulative score, rather than to minimize it.

A particularly important variation of DTW is an extension from isolated to continuous speech. This extension is called the One Stage DTW algorithm (Ney 1984). Here the goal is to find the optimal alignment between the speech sample and the best sequence of reference words. The complexity of the extended algorithm is still linear in the length of the sample and the vocabulary size. The only modification to the basic DTW algorithm is that at the beginning of each reference word model (i.e., its first frame or state), the diagonal path is allowed to point back to the end of all reference word models in the preceding frame. Local backpointers must specify the reference word model of the preceding point, so that the optimal word sequence can be recovered by tracing backwards from the final point of the word W with the best final score. Grammars can be imposed on continuous speech recognition by restricting the allowed transitions at word boundaries.

10.4 NEURAL NETWORK APPROACHES

Because speech recognition is basically a pattern recognition problem, and because neural networks are good at pattern recognition, many early researchers naturally tried applying neural networks to speech recognition. The earliest attempts involved highly simplified tasks, e.g., classifying speech segments as voiced/unvoiced, or nasal/fricative/plosive. Success in these experiments encouraged researchers to move on to phoneme classification; this task became a proving ground for neural networks as they quickly achieved world-class results.

There are two basic approaches to speech classification using neural networks: static and dynamic, as illustrated in Figure. In static classification, the neural network sees all of the input speech at once, and makes a single decision. By contrast, in dynamic classification, the neural network sees only a small window of the speech, and this window slides over the input speech while the network makes a series of local decisions, which have to be integrated into a global decision at a later time. Static classification works well for phoneme recognition, but it scales poorly to the level of words or sentences; dynamic classification scales better.

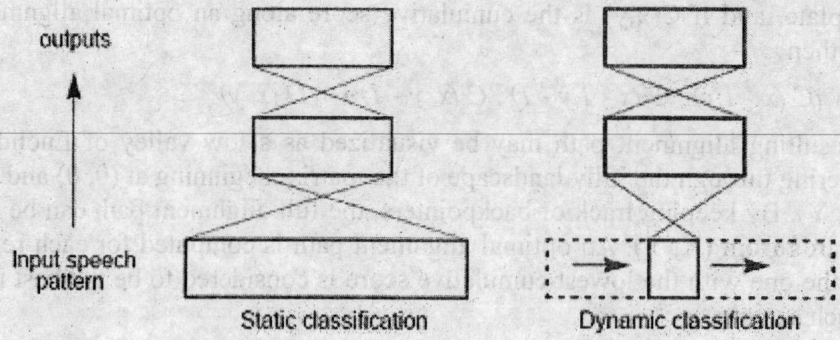

Figure 10.4 Static And Dynamic Approaches To Classification.

Either approach may make use of recurrent connections, although recurrence is more often found in the dynamic approach.

10.4.1 PHONEME CLASSIFICATION

Phoneme classification can be performed with high accuracy by using either static or dynamic approaches. Here we review some typical experiments using each approach.

10.4.2 STATIC APPROACHES

A simple but elegant experiment was performed by Huang & Lippmann (1988), demonstrating that neural networks can form complex decision surfaces from speech data. They applied a multilayer perceptron with only 2 inputs, 50 hidden units, and 10 outputs, to Peterson & Barney's collection of vowels produced by men, women, & children, using the first two formants of the vowels as the input speech representation. After 50,000 iterations of training, the network produced the decision regions shown in Figure below. These decision regions are nearly optimal, resembling the decision regions that would be drawn by hand, and they yield classification accuracy comparable to that of more L

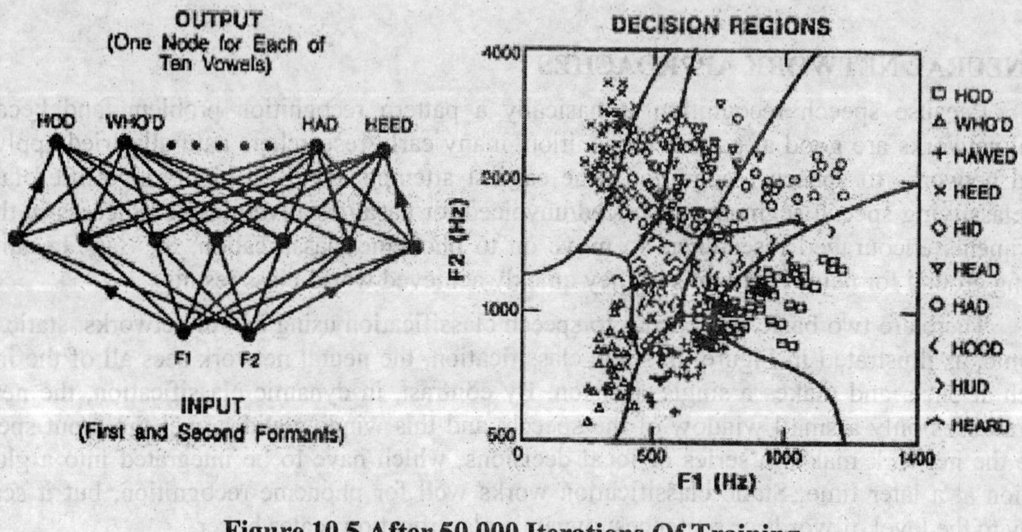

Figure 10.5 After 50,000 Iterations Of Training

Decision regions formed by a 2-layer perceptron using backpropagation training and vowel formant data. (From Huang & Lippmann, 1988.)

In a more complex experiment, Elman and Zipser (1987) trained a network to classify the vowels /a,i,u/ and the consonants /b,d,g/ as they occur in the utterances ba,bi,bu; da,di,du; and ga,gi,gu. Their network input consisted of 16 spectral coefficients over 20 frames (covering an entire 64 msec utterance, centered by hand over the consonant's voicing onset); this was fed into a hidden layer with between 2 and 6 units, leading to 3 outputs for either vowel or consonant classification. This network achieved error rates of roughly 0.5% for vowels and 5.0% for consonants. An analysis of the hidden units showed that they tend to be feature detectors, discriminating between important classes of sounds, such as consonants versus vowels.

Among the most difficult of classification tasks is the so-called E-set, i.e., discriminating between the rhyming English letters "B, C, D, E, G, P, T, V, Z". Burr (1988) applied a static network to this task, with very good results. His network used an input window of 20 spectral frames, automatically extracted from the whole utterance using energy information. These inputs led directly to 9 outputs representing the E-set letters. The network was trained and tested using 180 tokens from a single speaker. When the early portion of the utterance was oversampled, effectively highlighting the disambiguating features, recognition accuracy was nearly perfect.

10.4.3 DYNAMIC APPROACHES

In a seminal paper, Waibel et al (1987=1989) demonstrated excellent results for phonemean classification using a Time Delay Neural Network (TDNN), shown in Figure.

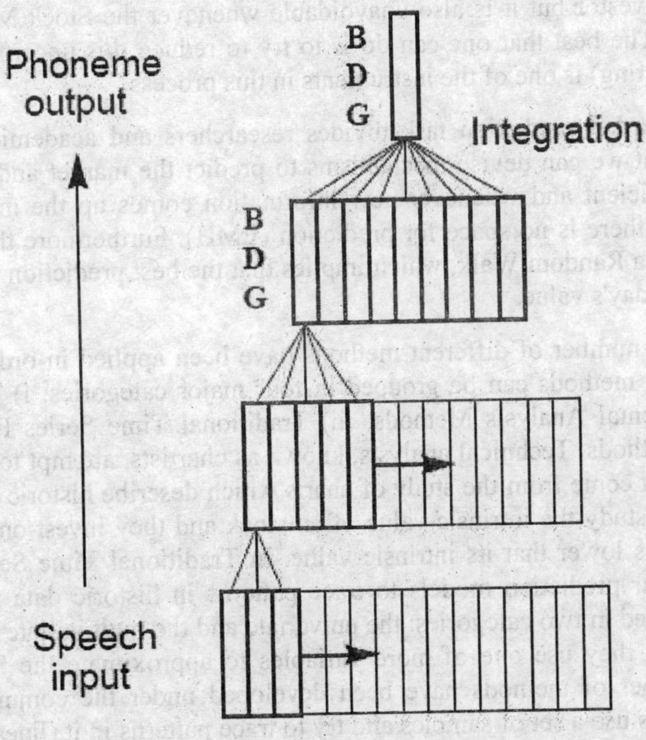

Figure 10.6 Time Delay Neural Network

This architecture has only 3 and 5 delays in the input and hidden layer, respectively, and the final output is computed by integrating over 9 frames of phoneme activations in the second hidden layer. The TDNN's design is attractive for several reasons: its compact structure economizes on weights and forces the network to develop general feature detectors; its hierarchy of delays optimizes these feature detectors by increasing their scope at each layer; and its temporal integration at the output layer makes the network shift invariant (i.e., insensitive to the exact positioning of the speech). The TDNN was trained and tested on 2000 samples of / b,d,g/ phonemes manually excised from a database of 5260 Japanese words. The TDNN achieved an error rate of 1.5%, compared to 6.5% achieved by a simple HMM-based recognizer.

CASE STUDY 2 - STOCK MARKET PREDICTION

10.5 INTRODUCTION

It is nowadays a common notion that vast amounts of capital are traded through the Stock Markets all around the world. National economies are strongly linked and heavily influenced of the performance of their Stock Markets. Moreover, recently the Markets have become a more accessible investment tool, not only for strategic investors but for common people as well. Consequently they are not only related to macroeconomic parameters, but they influence everyday life in a more direct way. Therefore they constitute a mechanism which has important and direct social impacts. The characteristic that all Stock Markets have in common is the uncertainty, which is related with their short and long-term future state. This feature is undesirable for the investor but it is also unavoidable whenever the Stock Market is selected as the investment tool. The best that one can do is to try to reduce this uncertainty. Stock Market Prediction (or Forecasting) is one of the instruments in this process.

The Stock Market prediction task divides researchers and academics into two groups those who believe that we can devise mechanisms to predict the market and those who believe that the market is efficient and whenever new information comes up the market absorbs it by correcting itself, thus there is no space for prediction (EMH). Furthermore they believe that the Stock Market follows a Random Walk, which implies that the best prediction you can have about tomorrow's value is today's value.

In literature a number of different methods have been applied in order to predict Stock Market returns. These methods can be grouped in four major categories: i) Technical Analysis Methods, ii) Fundamental Analysis Methods, iii) Traditional Time Series Forecasting and iv) Machine Learning Methods. Technical analysts, known as chartists, attempt to predict the market by tracing patterns that come from the study of charts which describe historic data of the market. Fundamental analysts study the intrinsic value of an stock and they invest on it if they estimate that its current value is lower that its intrinsic value. In Traditional Time Series forecasting an attempt to create linear prediction models to trace patterns in historic data takes place. These linear models are divided in two categories: the univariate and the multivariate regression models, depending on whether they use one of more variables to approximate the Stock Market time series. Finally a number of methods have been developed under the common label Machine Learning these methods use a set of samples and try to trace patterns in it (linear or non-linear) in order to approximate the underlying function that generated the data.

10.6 STOCK MARKETS AND PREDICTION

Investment Theories: An investment theory suggests what parameters one should take into account before placing his (or her) capital on the market. Traditionally the investment community accepts two major theories: the Firm Foundation and the Castles in the Air. Reference to these theories allows us to understand how the market is shaped, or in other words how the investors think and react. It is this sequence of 'thought and reaction' by the investors that defines the capital allocation and thus the level of the market.

There is no doubt that the majority of the people related to stock markets is trying to achieve profit. Profit comes by investing in stocks that have a good future (short or long term future). Thus what they are trying to accomplish one way or the other is to predict 16 the future of the market. But what determines this future? The way that people invest their money is the answer; and people invest money based on the information they hold. Therefore we have the following schema:

INFORMATION → INVESTOR → MARKET LEVEL

The factors that are under discussion on this schema are: the content of the 'Information' component and the way that the 'Investor' reacts when having this info.

On the other hand, according to the Castles in the Air theory the investors are triggered by information that is related to other investors' behavior. So for this theory the only concern that the investor should have is to buy today with the price of 20 and sell tomorrow with the price of 30, no matter what the intrinsic value of the firm he (or she) invests on is.

Prediction Methods: The prediction of the market is without doubt an interesting task. In the literature there are a number of methods applied to accomplish this task. These methods use various approaches, ranging from highly informal ways (e.g. the study of a chart with the fluctuation of the market) to more formal ways (e.g. linear or non-linear regressions). We have categorized these techniques as follows:

- Technical Analysis Methods
- Fundamental Analysis Methods
- Traditional Time Series Prediction Methods
- Machine Learning Methods

The criterion to this categorization is the type of tools and the type of data that each method is using in order to predict the market. What is common to these techniques is that they are used to predict and thus benefit from the market's future behavior.

Technical Analysis: "Technical analysis is the method of predicting the appropriate time to buy or sell a stock used by those believing in the castles-in-the-air view of stock pricing". The idea behind technical analysis is that share prices move in trends dictated by the constantly changing attributes of investors in response to different forces. Using technical data such as price, volume, highest and lowest prices per trading period the technical analyst uses charts to predict future stock movements. Price charts are used to detect trends, these trends are assumed to be based on supply and demand issues which often have cyclical or noticeable patterns. From the study of these charts trading rules are extracted and used in the market environment. The technical analysts are known and as 'chartists'. Most chartists believe that the market is only 10 percent logical and 90 percent psychological. The chartist's belief is that a careful study of what the other investors are doing will shed light on what the crowed is likely to do in the future.

This is a very popular approach used to predict the market, which has been heavily criticized. The major point of criticism is that the extraction of trading rules from the study of charts is highly subjective therefore different analysts might extract different trading rules by studying the same charts. Although it is possible to use this methodology to predict the market on daily basis we will not follow this approach on this study due to its subjective character.

Fundamental Analysis: "Fundamental analysis is the technique of applying the tenets of the firm foundation theory to the selection of individual stocks". The analysts that use this method of prediction use fundamental data in order to have a clear picture of the firm (industry or market) they will choose to invest on. They are aiming to compute the 'real' value of the asset that they will invest in and they determine this value by studying variables such as the growth, the dividend payout, the interest rates, the risk of investment, the sales level, the tax rates an so on. Their objective is to calculate the intrinsic value of an asset (e.g. of a stock). Since they do so they apply a simple trading rule. If the intrinsic 21 value of the asset is higher than the value it holds in the market, invest in it. If not, consider it a bad investment and avoid it. The fundamental analysts believe that the market is defined 90 percent by logical and 10 percent by physiological factors. This type of analysis is not possible to fit in the objectives of our study. The reason for this is that the data it uses in order to determine the intrinsic value of an asset does not change on daily basis. Therefore fundamental analysis is helpful for predicting the market only in a long-term basis.

Traditional Time Series Prediction: The Traditional Time Series Prediction analyzes historic data and attempts to approximate future values of a time series as a linear combination of these historic data. In econometrics there are two basic types of time series forecasting: univariate (simple regression) and multivariate (multivariate regression). These types of regression models are the most common tools used in econometrics to predict time series. The way they are applied in practice is that firstly a set of factors that influence (or more specific is assumed that influence) the series under prediction is formed. These factors are the explanatory variables xi of the prediction model.

Then a mapping between their values xit and the values of the time series yt (y is the to-be explained variable) is done, so that pairs {xit , yt} are formed. These pairs are used to define the importance of each explanatory variable in the formulation of the to-be explained variable. In other words the linear combination of xi that approximates in an optimum way y is defined. Univariate models are based on one explanatory variable (I=1) while multivariate models use more than one variable (I>1). Regression models have been used to predict stock market time series.

Machine Learning Methods: Several methods for inductive learning have been developed under the common label "Machine Learning". All these methods use a set of samples to generate an approximation of the underling function that generated the data. The aim is to draw conclusions from these samples in such way that when unseen data are presented to a model it is possible to infer the to-be explained variable from these data. The methods we discuss here are: The Nearest Neighbor and the Neural Networks Techniques.

10.7 PREDICTION USING NEURAL NETWORKS

The experiment consisted of three phases. In the first phase a genetic algorithm (GA) searched the space of NNs with different structures and resulted a generation with the fittest of all networks searched based on a metric which was either: TheilA or TheilB or TheilC or MAE. The GA search was repeated three times for each metric. Then the best three networks were selected from each repetition of the GA search and for each one of the metrics.

The output of the first phase was a set of thirtysix network structures. In the second phase for each one of the thirty-six resulting network structures we applied the following procedure. We trained (on Training1 set) and validated (on Validation1 set) the network. Then we used the indicated number of epochs from the validation procedure and based on it we retrained the network on the Training1 plus the Validation1 set. Finally we tested the performance of the network on unseen data (Validation2 set).

This procedure was repeated 50 times for each network structure for random initializations of its weights. From the nine networks for each performance statistic, we selected the most stable in terms of standard deviation of their performance. Thus the output of the second phase was a set of four network structures. During the third phase for each one of these four networks we applied the following procedure 50 times. We trained each network on the first half of the Training Set and we used the remaining half for validation. Then, using the indicated epochs by the validation procedure, we retrained the network on the complete Training Set. Finally we tested the network on the Test Set calculating all four metrics.The performance for each network on each metric was measured again in terms of standard deviation and mean of its performance over 50 times that it was trained, validated and tested.

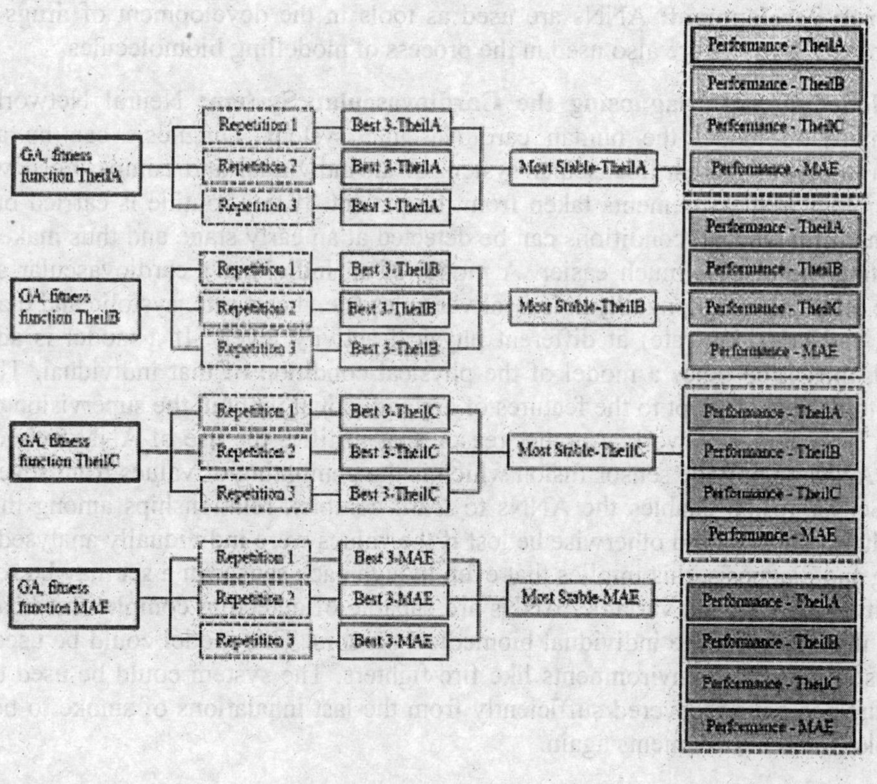

NEURAL NETWORKS IN MEDICINE

10.8 INTRODUCTION

Medicine has always benefited from the forefront of technology. Technology advances like computers, lasers, ultrasonic imaging, etc. have boosted medicine to extraordinary levels of achievement. Artificial Neural Networks (ANN) is currently the next promising area of interest. It is believed that neural networks will have extensive application to biomedical problems in the next few years. Already, it has been successfully applied to various areas of medicine, such as diagnostic systems, biochemical analysis, image analysis, and drug development.

Diagnostic systems: ANNs are extensively used in diagnostic systems. They are normally used to detect cancer and heart problems. The benefits of using ANNs is that they are not affected by factors such as fatigue, working conditions and emotional state.

Biochemical Analysis: ANNs are used in a wide variety of analytical chemistry applications. In medicine, ANNs have been used to analyse blood and urine samples, track glucose levels in diabetics, determine ion levels in body fluids, and detect pathological conditions such as tuberculosis.

Image analysis: ANNs are used in the analysis of medical images from a variety of imaging modalities. Applications in this area include tumour detection in ultra-sonograms, classification of chest x-rays, tissue and vessel classification in magnetic resonance images (MRI), determination of skeletal age from x-ray images, and determination of brain maturation.

Drug development: ANNs are used as tools in the development of drugs for treating cancer and AIDS. ANNs are also used in the process of modelling biomolecules.

Modeling and Diagnosing the Cardiovascular System: Neural Networks are used experimentally to model the human cardiovascular system. Diagnosis can be achieved by building a model of the cardiovascular system of an individual and comparing it with the real time physiological measurements taken from the patient. If this routine is carried out regularly, potential harmful medical conditions can be detected at an early stage and thus make the process of combating the disease much easier. A model of an individual's cardiovascular system must mimic the relationship among physiological variables (i.e., heart rate, systolic and diastolic blood pressures, and breathing rate) at different physical activity levels. If a model is adapted to an individual, then it becomes a model of the physical condition of that individual. The simulator will have to be able to adapt to the features of any individual without the supervision of an expert. This calls for a neural network. Another reason that justifies the use of ANN technology, is the ability of ANNs to provide sensor fusion which is the combining of values from several different sensors. Sensor fusion enables the ANNs to learn complex relationships among the individual sensor values, which would otherwise be lost if the values were individually analysed. In medical modelling and diagnosis, this implies that even though each sensor in a set may be sensitive only to a specific physiological variable, ANNs are capable of detecting complex medical conditions by fusing the data from the individual biomedical sensors. This model could be used to monitor employees in hazardous environments like fire-fighters. The system could be used to determine whether firemen have recovered sufficiently from the last inhalations of smoke to be allowed to enter smoke-filled environments again.

The advantages that such a system can offer are obvious. People can be checked for heart diseases quickly and painlessly and thus detecting any disease at an early stage. Of course, the system doesn't eliminate the need for doctors since a human expert is more reliable.

Electronic noses: ANNs are used experimentally to implement electronic noses. Electronic noses have several potential applications in telemedicine. Telemedicine is the practice of medicine over long distances via a communication link. The electronic nose would identify odours in the remote surgical environment. These identified odours would then be electronically transmitted to another site where an odour generation system would recreate them. Because the sense of smell can be an important sense to the surgeon, telesmell would enhance telepresent surgery.

Pattern Recognition of Pathology Images: Pathology is an imaging technique in medicine which deals with the nature of disease (structural and functional changes in tissue). Its need of colour and high resolution makes the use of digital image technology very difficult to implement.

Pattern recognition is an idea of classifying input data into identifiable classes by use of significant feature attributes of the data (sample), where the feature attributes are extracted from a background of irrelevant detail.

Neural Networks are used in pattern recognition because of their ability to learn and to store knowledge. Because of their 'parallel' nature can achieve, ANNs can achieve very high computation rates which is vital in application like telemedicine.

Instant physician: An application developed in the mid-1980s called the "instant physician" trained an autoassociative memory neural network to store a large number of medical records, each of which includes information on symptoms, diagnosis, and treatment for a particular case. After training, the net can be presented with input consisting of a set of symptoms; it will then find the full stored pattern that represents the "best" diagnosis and treatment.

Conclusion: ANNs have a lot to offer to modern medicine. At the moment they are mainly used for pattern recognition using images but experiments are being done in using ANNs to model parts of the human body. The high computation rates of ANNs are vital to telemedicine which is a 'hot' research area at the moment. Neural networks will never replace human experts but they can help in screening and can be used by experts to double-check their diagnosis.

GLOSSARY

Activation: A node's level of activity; the result of applying the activation function to the net input to the node. Typically this is also the value the node transmits.

Activation function: A function that transforms the net input to a neuron into its activation. Also known as a transfer, or output, function.

Adaline (Adaptive Linear Neuron): Developed by Bernard Widrow, an Adaline's output is +1 if the weighted sum of its inputs is greater than a threshold, -1 otherwise. The weights are calculated by the delta rule, which is also known as the Widrow Hoff rule [Widrow & Hoff, 1960] .

Adaptive filter Network that contains delays and whose weights are adjusted after each new input vector is presented. The network adapts to changes in the input signal properties if such occur. This kind of filter is used in long distance telephone lines to cancel echoes.

Adaptive learning rate Learning rate that is adjusted according to an algorithm during training to minimize training time.

Adaptive resonance theory (ART): Adaptive resonance theory is a quantitative explanation of learning and memory developed by Gail Carpenter, Stephen Grossberg and others. ART1 and ART2 are neural net architectures based on adaptive resonance theory. Each of these neural nets self-organizes the input data into categories with the variation allowed within a category depending on a user selected vigilance parameter. ART1 is used for binary input, ART2 for continuous input [Carpenter & Grossberg, 1987a, 1987b].

Algorithm: A computational procedure; a neural net training algorithm is a step by step procedure for setting the weights of the net. Training algorithms are also known as learning rules.

Architecture: Arrangement of nodes and pattern of connection links between them in a neural network.

Associative memory: A neural net in which stored information (patterns, or pattern pairs) can be accessed by presenting an input pattern that is similar to a stored pattern. The input pattern may be an inexact or incomplete version of a stored pattern.

Autoassociative memory: An associative memory in which the desired response is the stored pattern.

Axon: Long fiber over which a biological neuron transmits its output signal to other neurons.

Backpropagation: A learning algorithm for multilayer neural nets based on minimizing the mean, or total, squared error.

Backpropagation learning rule Learning rule in which weights and biases are adjusted by error-derivative (delta) vectors backpropagated through the network. Backpropagation is commonly applied to feedforward multilayer networks. Sometimes this rule is called the *generalized delta rule*.

Bias(j): the weight on the connection between node j and a mythical unitwhose output is always 1; i.e. a term which is included in the net input for node j along with the weighted inputs from all nodes connected to node j.

Bidirectional associative memory (BAM): A recurrent heteroassociative neural net developed by Bart Kosko .

Binary: 0 or 1

Binary sigmoid: Continuous, differentiable S-shaped activation function whose values range between 0 and 1. See sigmoid.

Bivalent: Either binary, bipolar, or any other pair of values.

Boltzmann machine (without learning): A class of natural networks used for solving constrained optimization problems. In a typical Boltzmann machine, the weight are fixed to represent the constrains of the problem and the function to be optimized. The net seeks the solution by changing the activations (either 1 or 0) of the units based on a probability distribution and the effect that the change would have on the energy function or consensus function for the net [Aarts & Korst, 1989]. See also simulated annealing.

Boltzmann machine (with learning): A net that adjusts its weight so that the equilibrium configuration of the net will solve a given problem, such as an encoder problem [Ackley , Hinton, & Sejnowski, 1985].

Bayesian framework Assumes that the weights and biases of the network are random variables with specified distributions.

Clasification: Problem in which patterns are to be assigned to one of several classes. In this text the term "classification" is used only for supervised learning problems in which examples of the desired group assignments are known.

Cluster unit: A unit in a competitive layer of a neural net; an output unit selforganizing net such as ART or SOM or a hidden unit in a counter propagation net.

Clustering: Grouping of similar patterns together. In this text term "clusteing" is used only for unsupervised learning problems in which the desired grouping are not known in advance.

Competitive learning: Unsupervised learning in which a competitive neural net (or subnet) adjusts its weights after the winning node has been chosen. See competitive neural net.

Competitive neural net: A neural net (or subnet) in which a group of neurons complete for the right to become active (have a non-zero activation). In the most extreme (and most common) example, the activation of the node with the largest net input is set equal to 1 and the activations of all other nodes are set equal to 0; this is often called "winner-take-all". MAXNET is an example of a competitive neural net which can be used as a subnet in the Hamming and other neural nets [Lippmann, 1987].

Competitive transfer function Accepts a net input vector for a layer and returns neuron outputs of 0 for all neurons except for the winner, the neuron associated with the most positive element of the net input **n**.

Concurrent input vectors Name given to a matrix of input vectors that are to be presented to a network simultaneously. All the vectors in the matrix are used in making just one set of changes in the weights and biases.

Connection One-way link between neurons in a network.

Connection strength Strength of a link between two neurons in a network. The strength, often called weight, determines the effect that one neuron has on another.

Convergence: Recurrent nets converge if the configuration (pattern of activations of the units) eventually stops changing; iterative training processes converge if the weight updates reach equilibrium (stop changing).

Counterpropagation: A neural network developed by Report Hecht-Nielson based on a two-stage training process. During the first phase, clusters are formed from the input patterns; during the second phase weight from the clusters to the output units are adjusted to produce the desired response [Hecht-Nielsen, 1987a, 1987b].

Cycle Single presentation of an input vector, calculation of output, and new weights and biases.

Decision boundary: Boundary between regions where the input vector will produce a positive response and regions where the response will be negative.

Delta rule: Learning rule based on minimization of squared error for each training pattern; used for single layer perceptron. Also called Least Mean Square (LMS) or Widrow-Hoff learning.

Dendrites: The portion of a biological neuron that receives incoming signals from other neurons.

Echo cancellation: An early application of ADALINES to be area of telephone communication [Widrow & Stearns, 1985].

Fast learning: Learning mode for ART in which it is assumed that all weight updates reach equilibrium on each learning trial.

Fault tolerance: A neural net is fault tolerant oif removing some nodes from the net makes little difference in the computed output. Also, neural nets are in general tolerant of noice in the input patterns.

Feedforward: A neural net in which the signals pass from the input units to the output units (possibly through intermediate layers of hidden units) without any connections back to previouse layers. In contrast, recurrent nets have feedback connections.

Fixed weight nets: Neural nets in which the weights do not change. Examples include Hopfield nets (discrete and continuous), Boltzmann machine without learning, and M_{AXNET}.

Function approximation Task performed by a network trained to respond to inputs with an approximation of a desired function.

Gain: See weight ; also called strength or synapse.

Generalization: The ability of a neural net to produce reasonable responses to input patterns that are similar, but not identical, to training patterns. A balance between memorization and generalization is usually desired.

Generalized delta rule: The delta rule (with arbitrary differentiable activation funetions) for multilayer neural nets. See backpropagation.

Gradient descent Process of making changes to weights and biases, where the changes are proportional to the derivatives of network error with respect to those weights and biases. This is done to minimize network error.

Grossberg learning: Learning rule for the output units in counterpropagation nets. This is a special case of (Grossberg) outstar learning.

Handwritten character recognition: One example of pattern recognition problems to which many types of neural networks are being applied.

Heeb net: A simple net trained using the Hebb rule. When used for pattern association problems (the most typical use of the Hebb rule) the nets are usually known as autoassiciative or heterassociative nets.

Hebb rule: A learning algorithm based on the premise that the strength of the connection between two neurons should be increased if both neurons are behaving in the same manner (both have positive activations or both have negative activations). Also known as correlation encoding.

Hidden units: Units that are neither input units nor output units.

Input units: Units that receive signals from outside the neural net; typically they transmit the input signal to all neurons to which they are connected, without modification. Their activation function is the identity function.

Kohonen learning rule: Weight update rule in which the new weight is a convex combination of the old weight and the current input pattern. The coefficient that multiplies the input pattern, the learning rate, is gradually reduced during the learning process.

Kohonen self-organizing map: A clustering neural net, with topological structure among cluster units.

Layer: Pattern of weighted connections between two slabs of neurons; in neural net literature the term layer is also used frequently for a group of neurons that function in the same way (a slab).

Learning algorithms: Procedures for modifying the weights on the connection links in a neural net (also known as training algorithm, learning rules).

Learning rate: A parameter that controls the amount by which weights are changed during training. In some nets the learning rate may be constant (as in standard backpropagation); in others it is reduced as training progresssto achieve stability)(for example, in Kohonen learning).

Learning vector quantization (LVQ): A neural net for pattern classification; trained using one of several variations on Kohonen learning. The input space is divided into regions that are represented by one or more output units (each of which represents an output class). The weight vector for an output unit is also known as a codebook vector [Kohenen, 1989a].

Linear separability: Training patterns belonging to one output class can be separated from training patterns belonging to another class by a straight line, plane, or hyperplane. Linearly separable patterns can be learned by a single layer neural net.

Linear threshold units: Neurons that form a linear combination of their weighted input signals (their net input) and send an output signal (equal to 1) if the net input is greater than the threshold (otherwise the output is 0); see Perceptron.

Logic functions: Functions with bivalent inputs (true or false, 1 or 0, 1 or 1) and a single bivalent output. There are 16 different logic functions with two inputs.

Long term memory: The weight in a neural network represent the long term memory of the information the net has learned.

McCulloch-Pitts neuron: Generally regarded as the first artificial neuron; a McCulloch-Pitts has fixed weights, a threshold activation function, and a fixed discrete (non-zero) time step for the transmission of a signal from one neuron to the next. Neurons, and networks of neurons, can be constructed to represent any problem that can be modeled by logic functions with unit time steps [McCulloch & Pitts, 1943]. A neuron that uses a threshold activation function (but does not satisfy the other requirements of the original model) is sometimes also called a McCulloch-Pitts neuron [Takefuji, 1992].

Madaline: Multi-Adaline; a neural net composed of many Adaline using [Widrow & Lehr, 1990].

Mean squared error: Sometimes used in place of 'squared error' or 'total squared error' in the derivation of delta rule and backpropagation training algorithms or in stopping conditions. Mean squared error may be the squared error divided by the number of output components, or the total squared error divided by the number of training patterns.

Multilayer perceptron: A neural net composed of three or more slabs (and therefore two or more layers of weighted connection paths); such nets are capable of solving more difficult problems than are single layer nets. They are often trained by backpropagation.

Neocognitron: Multi-stage pattern recognizer and feature extractor developed by Kunihiko Fukushima to recognize patterns (the alphabet or digits) even when the input image is distorted or shifted [Fukushima, Miyaka, & Ito, 1983].

Net input: The sum of the input signals that a neuron receives, each multiplied by the weight on the connection link, possibly along with a bias term.

Neural Networks: Information processing systems, inspired by biological neural systems but not limited to modeling such systems. Neural networks consist of many simple processing elements joined by weighted connection paths. A neural net produces an output signal in response to an input pattern; the output is determined by the values of the weights.

Neural nets: Neural networks, also known as artificial neural nets (ANNs), connectionist models, parallel distributed processing models, massively parallel models, artificial information processing models.

Neurocomputing: The use of neural networks emphasizing their computational power, rather than their ability to model biological neural systems.

Neuron: See processing element; also called node or unit.

Node: See processing element; also called neuron or unit.

Noise: Small changes to the components of a training or testing input vector. Noise may be introduced into training patterns to create additional patterns or to improve the ability of the net to generalize. Noise may also be present as a result of inaccuracies in measurements, etc. Neural nets are relatively robust to noisy testing patterns; this is often called generalization.

Output: The value a node transmits.

Output unit: A unit whose activation can be observed and interpreted as giving the response of the net.

Outstar: A neural network structure developed by Stephen Grossberg in which an output unit receives both signals from other units and a training input. differential equation control both the change in the activation of the unit, and the change in the weights [Grossberg, 1969]. See also discussion in [Caudill, 1989].

Pattern: Information processed by a neural network; a pattern is represented by a vector with discrete of continuous valued components.

Pattern assoiciator: Neural net consisting of a set of input units connected to a set of output units by a single layer of adjustable weights, trained by the Hebb or delta learning rules. [McClelland & Rumelhart, 1988].

Pattern association: Problems in which the desired mapping is from an input pattern to an output pattern (which may be the same, or similar to the input pattern).

Pattern classification: Problems in which the desired mapping is from an input pattern to one (or more) of several classes to which the pattern does or does not belong. In this text, the term classification is reserved for problems in which the correct class memberships are known for the training patterns. In general pattern classification is also used for problems where similar patterns are groupings are then defined to be the classes.
Pattern classifier: A neural net to determine whether an input pattern is or is not a member of a particular class. Training data consist of input patterns and the class to which each belongs, but does not require a description of each class; the net forms exemplar vectors for each class as it learns the training patterns.

Perceptrons: Neural nets studied by Rosenblatt, Block, Minsky and Papert, and others; the term is often used to refer to a single layer pattern classification network with linear thereshold units [Rosenblatt, 19962; Minsky & Papert,, 1988].

Perceptron learning rule: Iterative training rule, guaranteed to find weights that will correctly classify all training pattern, if such weight exist, i.e. if the patterns are linearly separable.

Processing element (PE): The computational unit in a neural network. Each processing element receives input signals from one or more other PEs, typically multiplied by the weight on the connection between the sending PE and the receiving PE. This weighted sum the inputs is transformed into the PEs activation by the activation function. The PEs output signal (its activation) is then sent on to other PEs or used as output from the net. Processing elements are also called (artificial) neurons, nodes, or units.

Recurrent net: A neural net with feedback connections, such as a BAM, Hopfield net, Boltzmann machine, or recurrent backpropagation net. In contrast, the signal in a feedforward neural net passes from the input units (through any hidden units) to the output units.

Resonance: The learning phase in ART, after an acceptable cluster unit has been selected; top-down and bottom-up signals 'resonate' as the weight changes occur.

Self-organization: The process by which a neural net clusters input patterns into groups of similar patterns.

Self-organizing map (SOM): See Kohonen's self-organizing map.

Short term memory: The activations of the neurons in a neural net are sometimes considered model the short term memory of a biological system.

Sigmoid function: An S-shaped curve; several common sigmoid functions are:

binary (logistic): $f(x) = \dfrac{1}{1 + \text{expt}(-x)}$;

arctan (range from -1 to 1); $h(x) = \dfrac{2}{\pi} \arctan(x)$;

bipolar: $g(x) = \dfrac{2}{1 + \exp(-x)} - 1 = \dfrac{1 - \exp(-x)}{1 + \exp(-x)}$;

tanh: $\tanh(x) = \dfrac{\exp(x) - \exp(-x)}{\exp(x) + \exp(-x)} = \dfrac{1 - \exp(-2x)}{1 + \exp(-2x)}$

Signals: Information received by the input units of a neural net, transmitted within the net, or produced by the output units.

Single-layer perceptron: One of many neural nets developed by Rosenblatt in the 1950's, used in pattern classification, trained with supervision [Rosenblatt, 1958, 1959, 1962].

Single-layer neural net: A neural net with no hidden units; or equivalently, a neural net with only one layer of weighted connections.

Square error: Sum of all output components of the square of the difference between the target and the computed output, for a particular training pattern. This quantity (or sometimes, for convenience, one half of this sum) is used in deriving the delta rule and backporpagation training algorithms. See also 'mean squared error' and 'total squared error'.

Supervised training: Process of adjusting the weights in a neural net using a learning algorithm; the desired output for each of a set of training input vectors is presented to the net. Many iterations through the training data may be required.

Synapse: See weight; also called gain or strength. In a biological neural system, the synapse is the connection between different neurons, where their membranes almost touch and signals are transmitted from one to the other by chemical neurotransmitters.

Tapped delay line Sequential set of delays with outputs available at each delay output.

Target vector Desired output vector for a given input vector.

Threshold: A value used in some activation functions to determine the unit's output. Mathematically the effect of changing the threshold is to shift the graph of the activation function to the right or left; the same effect can be accomplished by including a bias.

Threshold function: See step function.

Tolerance: User supplied parameter used in stopping conditions (as in "total squared error less than specified tolerance"), or in evaluating performance (as in "the response of the net is considered correct if the output signal is within a specified tolerance of the target values").

Topology functions Ways to arrange the neurons in a grid, box, hexagonal, or random topology.

Top-down weights: Weights from the cluster (F2 layer) units to the input (F1 layer) units in an ART net.

Total squared error: Used in stopping conditions for backpropagation training. The square of the error is summed over all output components and over all training patterns. See also, Squared Error and Mean Squared Error.

Transfer function Function that maps a neuron's (or layer's) net output **n** to its actual output.

Traveling salesman problem: A classic constrained optimization problem in which a salesman is required to visit each of a group of cities exactly once, before returning to the starting city. It is desired to find the tour with the shortest length.

Unit: See processing element; also called neuron or node.

Unsupervised learning: A means of modifying the weights of a neural net without specifying the desired output for any input patterns. Used in self-organizing neural nets for clustering data, extracting principal components, or curve fitting.

Vector: An ordered set of numbers, an n-tuple. An input pattern is an example of a vector.

Vector quantization: The task of forming clusters of input vectors in order to compress the amount of data without losing important information.

Weight: A value associated with a connection path between two processing elements in a neural network. It is used to modify the strength of a transmitted signal in many networks. The weights contain fundamental information concerning the problem being solved by the net. In many nets the weights are modified during training using a learning algorithm. The terms strength, synapse, and gain are also used for this value.

Weight function Weight functions apply weights to an input to get weighted inputs, as specified by a particular function.

Weight matrix Matrix containing connection strengths from a layer's inputs to its neurons. The element wi,j of a weight matrix W refers to the connection strength from input j to neuron i.

Weighted input vector
Result of applying a weight to a layer's input, whether it is a network input or the output of another layer.

Widrow-Hoff learning rule: See the delta rule; also called Least Mean Squares (LMS).

Winner-Take-All: The most extreme form of competition in a neural net, in which only the winning unit (typically the unit with the largest input signal, or the unit whose weight vector is closet to the input pattern) remain active.